BLUETOOTH® APPLICATION PROGRAMMING WITH THE JAVA™ APIs

The Morgan Kaufmann Series in Networking

Series Editor: **David Clark, M.I.T.**

*For further information on these books and for a list of forthcoming titles,
please visit our website at http://www.mkp.com*

BLUETOOTH® APPLICATION PROGRAMMING WITH THE JAVA™ APIs

C BALA KUMAR

PAUL J. KLINE

TIMOTHY J. THOMPSON

MOTOROLA SEMICONDUCTOR PRODUCTS SECTOR

MORGAN KAUFMANN PUBLISHERS

AN IMPRINT OF ELSEVIER SCIENCE

AMSTERDAM   BOSTON   LONDON   NEW YORK
OXFORD   PARIS   SAN DIEGO   SAN FRANCISCO
SINGAPORE   SYDNEY   TOKYO

Acquisitions Editor:	Rick Adams
Associate Editor:	Karyn P. Johnson
Publishing Services Manager:	Simon G. Crump
Project Manager:	Mamata N. Reddy
Designer:	Eric DeCicco
Production Services:	Graphic World Publishing Services
Composition:	Expo
Illustration:	Dartmouth Publishing
Printer:	The Maple-Vail Book Manufacturing Group
Cover Printer:	Phoenix Color

Permissions may be sought directly from Elsevier's Science & Technology Rights Department in Oxford, UK. Telephone: (+44) 1865 843830; FAX: (+44) 1865 853333; E-mail: *permissions@elsevier.com.uk*. You may also complete your request online via the Elsevier homepage (*www.elsevier.com*), by selecting "Customer Support" and then "Obtaining Permissions."

Morgan Kaufmann Publishers
An imprint of Elsevier Inc.
500 Sansome Street, Suite 400
San Francisco, CA 94111
www.mkp.com

Library of Congress Control Number: 2003107476
International Standard Book Number: 1-55860-934-2

This book is printed on acid-free paper.

To my wife, Sundari, and sons, Sailesh and Shiva
—Bala

To my wife, Dianne
—Paul

To my wife, Karmen
—Tim

Contents

List of Tables

List of Figures

Preface

Bluetooth® wireless technology is a short-range radio standard that provides new opportunities for wireless devices. This radio standard was designed originally as a way of eliminating the cables currently attached to nearly all consumer electronic devices. However, the goals for Bluetooth wireless technology grew as its designers recognized that it enables a new kind of wireless network between electronic devices.

Recent developments in the Java™ programming language make it possible for Java developers to write applications for wireless devices such as cell phones and personal digital assistants. In 2000, the Java programming community recognized the importance of creating a standard extension to the Java programming language for use with Bluetooth devices. A standard application programming interface (API) for Bluetooth was needed because each Bluetooth software protocol stack had its own API for application programmers. These proprietary APIs meant that a Bluetooth application had to be ported to different Bluetooth stacks to run on different devices. Apart from the work involved in writing the code, interoperability testing on the various devices cost time and money for the involved companies. A standard API would help alleviate all these problems.

A team of experts from across the industry was assembled for this effort under Java Specification Request 82 (JSR-82). The result was a specification for Java APIs for Bluetooth wireless technology (JABWT). The specification was the result of collaboration of many companies and individuals in the industry. Some helped define the specification by participating in the JSR-82 expert group, and many others contributed by providing valuable comments.

This book introduces and explains to the community of Java programmers the new standard extensions of the Java programming language for Bluetooth wireless technology.

Specification documents provide you with the API to which you are programming. But a book like this one explains why an API is needed and how to use it. In addition, because we were members of the Motorola team leading the JSR-82 standardization effort, we believe we can explain the rationale for various features of JABWT.

The objectives of this book are to

- Give an overview of Java 2 Platform, Micro Edition (J2ME™) and Bluetooth wireless technology
- Outline the JABWT architecture
- Explain the API in detail
- Provide example applications
- Present the issues related to implementing JABWT on a device

Intended Audience

The book is intended for software developers, academics, and other professionals who want to develop Java software for Bluetooth devices. The book also is aimed at device manufacturers who want to build devices with Java technology and Bluetooth wireless technology. To gain the most out of this book, you will find it helpful to have a working knowledge of J2ME and familiarity with Bluetooth wireless technology. The book cites several references that provide additional information on these subjects. We believe that a J2ME programmer will need no additional reading beyond this book to write JABWT applications.

How This Book Is Organized

Different readers of this book will be seeking different information. We have identified three sets of people:

1. Those looking for an overview to make decisions on projects
2. Those who will be leading projects or managing projects in this area
3. Programmers who need detailed information on how to program using JABWT

Apart from the introductory chapters, the chapters are organized into three main sections to accommodate the three sets of people identified above. The three divisions are

1. Overview: The executive introduction
2. API capabilities: The explanation for the project manager
3. Programming with the API: The programmer's guide

Readers can choose the sections that suit their needs in each chapter. Chapters 1 through 3 are overview chapters. Chapters 4 through 8 detail the various sections of the API. Chapter 9 provides examples of JABWT applications. Chapter 10 explains how device manufacturers can implement JABWT on a new device. Throughout the book many code examples are given to explain the API. The complete code for the examples can be found either in the chapters or in Appendix A. The complete JSR-82 API is in Appendixes B and C.

There is a website for this book where you can access the complete code examples found in the book. In addition, you can find the latest news about JABWT, book errata, and other useful links. To access the website, go to www.mkp.com and use the search option with the title of this book.

The topics in this book are organized as follows:

Chapter 1, Introduction, presents an overview of Bluetooth wireless technology and J2ME. It also provides a context for the JABWT specification.

Chapter 2, An Overview of JABWT, defines the goals, characteristics, and scope of JABWT.

Chapter 3, High-Level Architecture, presents the high-level architecture of JABWT.

Chapter 4, RFCOMM, discusses the APIs for Bluetooth serial port communications using RFCOMM.

Chapter 5, OBEX, introduces the architecture and the APIs for making OBEX connections.

Chapter 6, Device Discovery, discusses the APIs for Bluetooth device discovery.

Chapter 7, Service Discovery, describes the APIs for service discovery and service registration.

Chapter 8, L2CAP, presents the API for Bluetooth communications using the logical link control and adaptation protocol.

Chapter 9, Example Applications, illustrates the use of JABWT through two sample applications.

Chapter 10, Implementing JABWT on a Device, describes the basic porting process and highlights the major issues.

Chapter 11, Closing Remarks, provides a summary of the topics discussed in the book and discusses future trends.

Appendix A contains code for the examples from Chapters 7 and 8.

Appendix B contains the Bluetooth API from the package javax.bluetooth.

Appendix C contains the OBEX API from the package javax.obex.

Acknowledgments

A large number of people were involved with the original development of the Java APIs for Bluetooth wireless technology. As the three of us set out to write a book explaining those Bluetooth APIs, we were pleased to discover that we would again receive contributions and assistance from a large number of dedicated and talented individuals.

The authors thank Glade Diviney, Peter Kembro, and Ashwin Kamal Whitchurch for reviewing the entire book in draft form and making valuable comments and suggestions. Thanks also to R. Thiagarajan, N. Murugan, and Franck Thibaut, who commented on various chapters. Ramesh Errabolu, Ranjani Vaidyanathan, and Ravi Viswanathan from the Motorola JSR-82 team also reviewed and commented on several of the chapters. Of course, the authors are totally responsible for any errors that remain.

When this book was in the proposal stage, we received excellent advice and suggestions from Alok Goyal, Teck Yang Lee, Girish Managoli, Brent Miller, Venugopal Mruthyunjaya, N. Ramachandran, Rajeev Shorey, and Mark VandenBrink.

The Java APIs for Bluetooth wireless technology were developed by a team of industry experts, the JSR-82 expert group, and the team at Motorola that drafted the specification, wrote the reference implementation, and developed the conformance tests. The authors believe that the efforts and contributions of all these individuals produced an API that will have important benefits to the Java community. The authors would like to thank the members of the JSR-82 expert group for all their work on the API: Jouni Ahokas, Patrick Connolly, Glade Diviney, Masahiro Kuroda, Teck Yang Lee, Paul Mackay, Brent Miller, Jim Panian, Farooq Anjum, Charatpong Chotigavanich, Peter Dawson, Peter Duchemin, Jean-Philippe Galvan, Daryl Hlasny, Knud Steven Knudsen, Andrew Leszczynski, Martin Mellody, Anthony Scian, and Brad Threatt.

We greatly appreciate all of the contributions of the other members of the JSR-82 team at Motorola: Lawrence Chan, Judy Ho, Will Holcomb, Judy Lin, Mitra Mechanic, and Allen Peloquin. Jim Erwin, Jim Lynch, Aler Krishnan, Ed Wiencek, and Mark Patrick provided a great deal of assistance to the JSR-82 team. Special thanks go to Anne-Marie Larkin, vice president and director, Wireless Software, Applications and Services for her encouragement and her support of this project.

The authors would like to thank Rococo Software for providing us with their Impronto simulator for use as a second JABWT implementation to check the code examples.

The authors are very grateful to Rick Adams, Karyn Johnson, and Mamata Reddy of Morgan Kaufmann for giving us this opportunity and for all their hard work in producing the finished book.

Bala thanks Sundari, Sailesh, and Shiva for their understanding and support through long nights and weekends working on this project. Bala also thanks his mother, Suseela, and sister, Surya, for all their patient nurturing and Mr. B. Kanakasabai for being his lifelong friend and mentor.

Paul thanks his wife, Dianne, for her support and encouragement.

Tim thanks his wife, Karmen, for her encouragement, patience, and support.

C Bala Kumar

Paul Kline

Tim Thompson

1 Introduction

This chapter begins with an introduction to wireless connectivity and Bluetooth® wireless technology. It then gives:

- An overview of the Bluetooth protocol stack
- An overview of the Java™ 2 Platform, Micro Edition
- A description of the need for Java technology in Bluetooth devices

1.1 Wireless Connectivity

The rapid emergence of the Internet has changed the landscape of modern computing. We are in the information age. The term "information age" came about because of the exchange of massive amounts of data between computing devices using wired and wireless forms of communication. We are rapidly moving toward a world in which communications and computing are ubiquitous.

The convergence of computing and communications began in the early 1960s with the development of modems and the private branch exchange (PBX). The modem allowed computers to communicate with each other over telephone lines, and the PBX allowed computers to control the telephone exchange. The result was computer networks. Today, high-speed networks connect servers, personal computers, and other personal computing devices. High-end routers manage the networks. The distinction between voice and data networks has blurred, and the same network tends to carry both types of traffic. The desire and need to communicate with distant computers led to the creation of the Internet. The days of consumers' buying a personal computer for stand-alone applications have disappeared. These days the primary motive for buying a personal computer is to use it as a communication tool, so that one can have Internet access to e-mail and the World Wide Web.

Increased dependence on the Internet and the need to stay connected from anywhere at all times have led to advances in mobile computing and communications. We have been communicating without wires for some time with satellites, cordless phones, cellular phones, and remote-control devices. However, in recent years the wireless communications industry has seen explosive growth. Long-range wireless communication invariably uses radio frequency (RF). Typically long-range communications use the licensed parts of the RF spectrum, and user fees apply. Short-range communications can use either RF or infrared and typically use unlicensed (i.e., free) parts of the frequency spectrum.

There are many short-range wireless standards, but the three main ones are Infrared from the Infrared Data Association® (IrDA®), Bluetooth wireless technology, and wireless local area network (WLAN). WLAN is also known as IEEE 802.11, and it comes in three main variants, 802.11b and 802.11g, which operate at 2.4 gigahertz (GHz), and 802.11a, which operates at 5 GHz. The IrDA created a wireless communications system that makes use of infrared light. Whereas RF communication can penetrate many objects, IrDA is limited to line of sight. Both 802.11b and Bluetooth wireless technologies communicate in the 2.4-GHz RF band but are aimed at different market segments. The 802.11b technology has a longer range but consumes substantially more power than Bluetooth wireless technology. The 802.11 variant is primarily for data. The only protocol for supporting voice is Voice over Internet Protocol (VoIP). Table 1.1 provides a comparison of these three technologies.

Wireless communications allow computing and communication devices to be used almost anywhere and to be used in new, progressive ways. The increase in wireless mobile Internet devices is proof that wireless connectivity is pervasive. Powerful software programming environments will help fuel this mobile computing explosion by enabling the development of compelling applications. The Java platform provides a powerful programming environment that has great promise for wireless devices. Many mobile devices now come with support for Java 2, Micro Edition (J2ME™) programs. This book explains how to program Bluetooth applications with the Java programming language.

Table 1.1 Comparison of Wireless Communication Technologies

Feature and Function	IrDA	Wireless LAN	Bluetooth Communication
Connection type	Infrared, narrow beam, line of sight	Spread spectrum, spherical	Spread spectrum, spherical
Spectrum	Optical 850–900 nm	RF 2.4 GHz (5 GHz for 802.11a)	RF 2.4 GHz
Transmission power	40-500 mW/Sr	100 mW	10–100 mW
Maximum data rate	9600 bps–16 Mbps (very rare)	11 Mbps (54 Mbps for 802.11a, 802.11g)	1 Mbps
Range	1 m	100 m	10–100 m
Supported devices	2	Connects through an access point	8 (active), 200 (passive)
Voice channels	No support	VoIP	3
Addressing	32-bit physical ID	48-bit MAC	48-bit MAC

1.2 What Is Bluetooth Wireless Technology?

Bluetooth wireless technology is an open specification for a low-cost, low-power, short-range radio technology for ad hoc wireless communication of voice and data anywhere in the world. Let's examine each of these attributes:

- An open specification means that the specification is publicly available and royalty free.
- Short-range radio technology means devices can communicate over the air using radio waves at a distance of 10 meters (m). With higher transmission power the range increases to approximately 100 m.
- Because communication is within a short range, the radios are low power and are suited for portable, battery-operated devices.
- Bluetooth wireless technology supports both voice and data, allowing devices to communicate either type of content.

- Bluetooth wireless technology works anywhere in the world because it operates at 2.4 GHz in the globally available, license-free, industrial, scientific, and medical (ISM) band.

The ISM frequency band is available for general use by ISM applications, hence several other devices (e.g., WLAN, cordless phones, microwave ovens) operate in this band. Bluetooth wireless technology is designed to be very robust in the face of interference from other devices.

1.2.1   History of Bluetooth Wireless Technology

The origins of Bluetooth communications started in 1994, when Ericsson began a study to find alternatives to connecting mobile phones to its accessories. The engineers looked at a low-power and low-cost radio interface to eliminate cables between the devices. But the engineers also realized that for the technology to be successful it has to be an open standard and not a proprietary one. In early 1998, Ericsson joined Intel, International Business Machines (IBM), Nokia, and Toshiba and formed the Bluetooth Special Interest Group (SIG) to focus on developing an open specification for Bluetooth wireless technology. The original companies, known as promoter companies, publicly announced the global Bluetooth SIG in May 1998 and invited other companies to join the Bluetooth SIG as Bluetooth adopters in return for a commitment to support the Bluetooth specification. In July 1999, the Bluetooth SIG published version 1.0 of the Bluetooth specification. In December 1999, four new promoter companies—3Com, Agere, Microsoft, and Motorola—joined the Bluetooth SIG.

Since then, the awareness of Bluetooth wireless technology has increased, and many other companies have joined the Bluetooth SIG as adopters, which gives them a royalty-free license to produce Bluetooth-enabled products. Adopter companies also have early access to specifications and the ability to comment on them. Interest in the Bluetooth SIG has grown, and there are currently more than 2000 member companies. These companies represent academia and a variety of industries.

Why is this technology called Bluetooth wireless technology? It was named after a Danish Viking king, Harald Blåtand, who ruled circa A.D. 940–981. *Blåtand* loosely translates to "blue tooth." During his

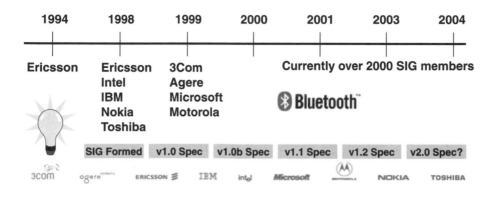

Figure 1.1 Bluetooth SIG timeline.

reign, King Harald Blåtand is supposed to have united and controlled Denmark and Norway. Because this new radio technology was expected to unify the telecommunication and computing industries, it seemed fitting to name it after King Harald. A part-time historian on the team proposed *Bluetooth* as the internal code name. Because the Bluetooth SIG marketing team could not come up with a better name that was not already trademarked, the name stuck.

1.2.2 Bluetooth Vision

Bluetooth wireless technology was originally developed as a cable replacement technology for connecting devices such as mobile phone handsets, headsets, and portable computers with each other (Figure 1.2). However, wireless connectivity between fixed and mobile devices enables many other usage scenarios other than cable replacement. By enabling wireless links and communication between devices, a short-range wireless network was created that gave rise to the notion of a personal area network (PAN). Designed as an inexpensive wireless networking system for all classes of portable devices, Bluetooth devices have the capability to form ad hoc networks. These networks should enable easy and convenient connections to printers, Internet access points, and personal devices at work and at home.

There are so many usage scenarios for Bluetooth wireless technology that the technology will likely be put to wide use. Let's look at a couple of the usage models.

The three-in-one phone usage model allows a mobile telephone to be used as a cellular phone in the normal manner, as a cordless phone that connects to a voice access point (e.g., cordless base station), and as an intercom or "walkie-talkie" for direct communication with another device. The cordless telephony and the intercom features use Bluetooth wireless technology.

The second use case is wireless telematics. Assume that a user who is talking on a cell phone approaches his or her automobile but wants to continue the phone conversation in the hands-free mode. Using Bluetooth communication the user can continue the phone conversa-

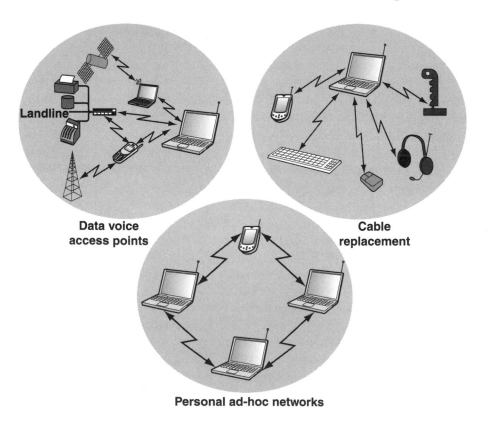

Data voice access points

Cable replacement

Personal ad-hoc networks

Figure 1.2   Bluetooth use cases.

tion using the microphone and speakers equipped in the dashboard of the automobile.

Another use case is the instant post card, whereby a user (on vacation, for example) with a digital camera transmits a photo via a data access point that could be a mobile phone or a local area network (LAN) access point. Similar use cases include automatic synchronization, business card exchange, hotel and airline check-in, electronic ticketing, and wireless games.

1.2.3 Bluetooth Specification

The Bluetooth specification is the result of cooperation by many companies under the Bluetooth SIG umbrella. The specification defines the over-the-air behavior to ensure compatibility of Bluetooth devices from different vendors. It defines the complete system from the radio up to the application level, including the software stack. The specification is very lengthy because of the breadth of topics it covers. At the highest level, the specification (version 1.1) is split into two volumes (in version 1.2 they are split into several subvolumes). Volume 1 [1] is the core specification and describes the protocol stack and related items such as testing and qualification. The Bluetooth protocol stack is defined as a series of layers somewhat analogous to the familiar Open Systems Interconnect (OSI) [2] standard reference for communication protocol stacks. Each layer of the protocol stack represents a different protocol and is separately described in the core specification.

The Bluetooth profiles are described in volume 2 of the Bluetooth version 1.1 specification [3]. Bluetooth profiles, essentially usage models, describe how applications are to use the Bluetooth stack. A Bluetooth profile is a set of capabilities of the protocol layers that represent a default solution for a usage model. Bluetooth profiles are the basis of Bluetooth protocol stack qualification, and any new implementations of a Bluetooth profile have to go through the qualification process described herein. The specification and profiles continue to evolve as new areas are identified in which Bluetooth wireless technology can be used. Bluetooth protocols and profiles are discussed in detail in the next section. For a detailed description of Bluetooth wireless technology, see books by Miller [4] and Bray [5] and their colleagues.

1.3 Overview of the Bluetooth Stack Architecture

This section provides a brief overview of the Bluetooth protocol stack. The Bluetooth protocol stack can be broadly divided into two components: the Bluetooth host and the Bluetooth controller (or Bluetooth radio module). The Host Controller Interface (HCI) provides a standardized interface between the Bluetooth host and the Bluetooth controller. Figure 1.3 illustrates the Bluetooth host and Bluetooth device classification.

The Bluetooth host is also known as the upper-layer stack and usually is implemented in software. It is generally integrated with the system software or host operating system. Bluetooth profiles are built on top of the protocols. They are generally in software and run on the host device hardware. For example, a laptop computer or a phone would be the host device. The Bluetooth host would be integrated with the operating system on the laptop or the phone.

The Bluetooth radio module or controller usually is a hardware module like a PC card (see Figure 1.3) that plugs into a target device. More and more devices have the Bluetooth controller built into the device. The upper stack interfaces to the Bluetooth radio module via the HCI. The Bluetooth radio module usually interfaces with the host

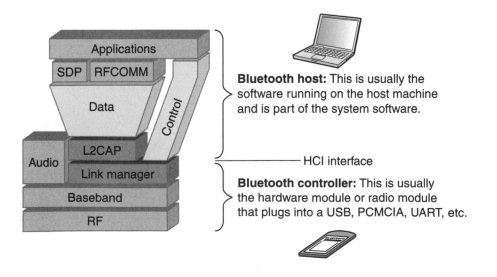

Figure 1.3 Bluetooth host and device classification.

system via one of the standard input/output (I/O) mechanisms, such as peripheral component microchannel interconnect architecture (PCMCIA), universal asynchronous receiver-transmitter (UART), and universal serial bus (USB). Although the Bluetooth host and the Bluetooth controller classifications apply to most devices, the two are integrated in some devices, headsets, for example, and HCI is not used. The various blocks in Figure 1.3 are part of the Bluetooth protocol stack, which is discussed next.

1.3.1 Bluetooth Protocols

Figure 1.4 shows a block diagram of the Bluetooth protocol stack. Several protocols are defined in the Bluetooth specification, but Figure 1.4 shows the common ones. The shaded boxes represent the protocols addressed by Java APIs for Bluetooth wireless technology (JABWT, where API stands for application programming interface). The protocol stack is composed of protocols specific to Bluetooth wireless technology, such as

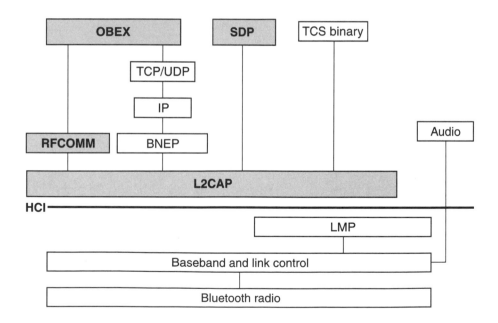

Figure 1.4 Bluetooth protocol stack.

the Service Discovery Protocol (SDP) and other adopted protocols, such as the Object Exchange protocol (OBEX™).

- The Bluetooth radio (layer) is the lowest defined layer of the Bluetooth specification. It defines the requirements of the Bluetooth transceiver device operating in the 2.4-GHz ISM band.

- The baseband and link control layer enables the physical RF link between Bluetooth units making a connection. The baseband handles channel processing and timing, and the link control handles the channel access control. There are two different kinds of physical links: synchronous connection oriented (SCO) and asynchronous connectionless (ACL). An ACL link carries data packets, whereas an SCO link supports real-time audio traffic.

- Audio is really not a layer of the protocol stack, but it is shown here because it is uniquely treated in Bluetooth communication. Audio data is typically routed directly to and from the baseband layer over an SCO link. Of course, if a data channel is used (e.g., in VoIP applications), audio data will be transmitted over an ACL link.

- The Link Manager Protocol (LMP) is responsible for link setup and link configuration between Bluetooth devices, managing and negotiating the baseband packet sizes. The LMP manages the security aspects, such as authentication and encryption, by generating, exchanging, and checking link and encryption keys.

- The HCI provides a command interface to the radio, baseband controller, and link manager. It is a single standard interface for accessing the Bluetooth baseband capabilities, the hardware status, and control registers.

- Logical Link Control and Adaptation Protocol (L2CAP) shields the upper-layer protocols from the details of the lower-layer protocols. It multiplexes between the various logical connections made by the upper layers.

- SDP provides a means for applications to query services and characteristics of services. Unlike in an LAN connection, in which one connects to a network and then finds devices, in a Bluetooth environment one finds the devices before one finds the service. In addition, the set of services available changes in an environment when devices are in motion. Hence SDP is quite different from service discovery in traditional network-based environments. SDP is built on top of L2CAP.

- Serial ports are one of the most common communications interfaces used in computing and communication devices. The RFCOMM protocol provides emulation of serial ports over L2CAP. RFCOMM provides transport capabilities for upper-level services that use a serial interface as a transport mechanism. RFCOMM provides multiple concurrent connections to one device and provides connections to multiple devices.

- Bluetooth-enabled devices will have the ability to form networks and exchange information. For these devices to interoperate and exchange information, a common packet format must be defined to encapsulate layer 3 network protocols. The Bluetooth Network Encapsulation Protocol (BNEP) [6] encapsulates packets from various networking protocols, and the packets are transported directly over L2CAP. BNEP is an optional protocol developed after Bluetooth specification version 1.1 but based on the 1.1 version of the specification.

- Telephony Control Protocol Specification, Binary (TCS binary) defines the call control signaling for establishment of voice and data calls between Bluetooth devices. It is built on L2CAP.

- Adopted protocols such as OBEX and the Internet Protocol (IP), are built on one of the protocols discussed earlier (e.g., OBEX is built on RFCOMM, and IP is built on BNEP).

- The Bluetooth SIG also is defining newer protocols built on one of the protocols discussed earlier, but mainly they are built on top of L2CAP. Hardcopy Control Channel [7], Hardcopy Notification Channel [7], Audio/Video Control Transport Protocol [8], and Audio/Video Distribution Transport Protocol [9] are examples of some newer protocols.

1.3.2 Bluetooth Profiles

In addition to the protocols, Bluetooth profiles have been defined by the Bluetooth SIG [3]. A Bluetooth profile defines standard ways of using selected protocols and protocol features that enable a particular usage model. In other words, it defines how different parts of the Bluetooth specification can be used for a particular use case. A profile can be described as a vertical slice through the protocol stack. It defines options in each protocol that are needed for the profile. The dependency of the profiles on protocol layers and features varies. Two profiles may use a different set of protocol layers and a different set of features within the same protocol layer.

A Bluetooth device can support one or more profiles. The four "basic" profiles are the Generic Access Profile (GAP), the Serial Port Profile (SPP), the Service Discovery Application Profile (SDAP), and the Generic Object Exchange Profile (GOEP).

- The GAP is the basis of all other profiles. Strictly speaking, all profiles are based on the GAP. GAP defines the generic procedures related to establishing connections between two devices, including the discovery of Bluetooth devices, link management and configuration, and procedures related to use of different security levels.

- The SDAP describes the fundamental operations necessary for service discovery. This profile defines the protocols and procedures to be used by applications to locate services in other Bluetooth-enabled devices.

- The SPP defines the requirements for Bluetooth devices necessary for setting up emulated serial cable connections using RFCOMM between two peer devices. SPP directly maps to the RFCOMM protocol and enables legacy applications using Bluetooth wireless technology as a cable replacement.

- The GOEP is an abstract profile on which concrete usage case profiles can be built. These are profiles using OBEX. The profile defines all elements necessary for support of the OBEX usage models (e.g., file transfer, synchronization, or object push).

Figure 1.5 shows the relationships among the various Bluetooth profiles. The Bluetooth profiles are hierarchical. For example, the File Transfer Profile is built on top of GOEP, which depends on SPP, which is built upon GAP. Bluetooth profiles also can be classified on the basis of the functional or services point of view. From a programming perspective, however, it is the profile hierarchy that is applicable. The basic profiles—GAP, SDAP, SPP, and GOEP—also are known as *transport profiles*, upon which other profiles, known as *application profiles*, can be built.

Many profiles are based on the basic profiles. More details on these profiles can be obtained from www.bluetooth.com. Figure 1.5 will

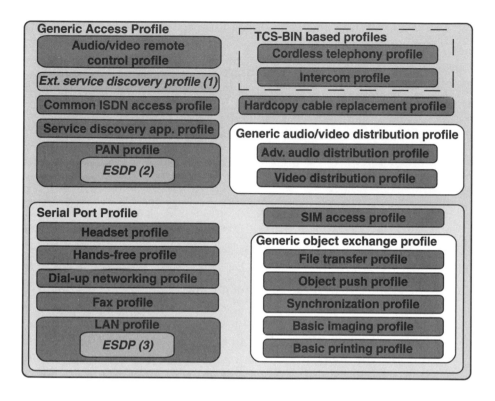

Figure 1.5   Bluetooth profile hierarchy.

probably be obsolete soon because more profiles are being continuously developed. Refer to the Bluetooth website for specifications on the latest available profiles.

1.3.3   Bluetooth Qualification

Bluetooth qualification is the certification process required for any product using Bluetooth wireless technology. The qualification process ensures that products comply with the Bluetooth specification. Only qualified products are entitled to use the free license to the patents required to implement Bluetooth wireless technology, the Bluetooth brand, and the Bluetooth logo. Essentially, there are three levels of Bluetooth qualification testing:

- Core specification conformance
- Interoperability testing to ensure that devices work with one another at the profile level
- Bluetooth branding conformance

More details on the qualification process can be obtained from the Bluetooth Qualification Program Website [10].

1.4 What is J2ME?

This section gives a brief overview of J2ME. For details about J2ME, refer to books by Topley [11] and Riggs and colleagues [12].

J2ME is the Java platform for consumer and embedded devices such as mobile phones, pagers, personal organizers, television set-top boxes, automobile entertainment and navigation systems, Internet televisions, and Internet-enabled phones. J2ME is one of the three platform editions. The other two platform editions are Java 2 Platform, Enterprise Edition (J2EE™) for servers and enterprise computers and Java 2 Platform, Standard Edition (J2SE™) for desktop computers. A related technology is Java Card™ technology. The Java Card specifications enable Java technology to run on smart cards and other devices with more limited memory than a low-end mobile phone. These groupings are needed to tailor the Java technology to different areas of today's vast computing industry. Figure 1.6 illustrates the Java 2 platform editions and their target markets.

The J2ME platform brings the power and benefits of Java technology (code portability, object-oriented programming, and a rapid development cycle) to consumer and embedded devices. The main goal of J2ME is to enable devices to dynamically download applications that leverage the native capabilities of each device. Consumer and embedded space covers a range of devices from pagers to television set-top boxes that vary widely in memory, processing power, and I/O capabilities. To address this diversity, the J2ME architecture defines configurations, profiles, and optional packages to allow for modularity and customizability. Figure 1.7 shows the high-level relations between the layers of the J2ME architecture. The layers are explained further in the next section.

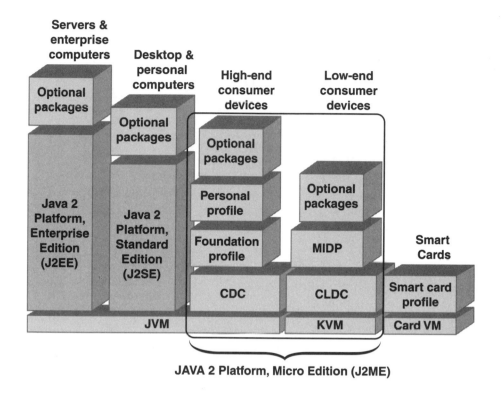

Figure 1.6 Java 2 Platforms.

1.4.1 Configurations

A Java virtual machine interprets the Java byte codes generated when Java programs are compiled. A Java program can be run on any device that has a suitable virtual machine and a suitable set of Java class libraries.

Configurations are composed of a Java virtual machine and a minimal set of class libraries. The Java virtual machine usually runs on top of a host operating system that is part of the target device's system software. The configuration defines the minimum functionality for a particular category or grouping of devices. It defines the minimum capabilities and requirements for a Java virtual machine and class libraries available on all devices of the same category or grouping. Currently, there are two J2ME configurations: the Connected, Limited Device

Configuration (CLDC) [13] and the Connected Device Configuration (CDC) [14].

Connected, Limited Device Configuration

The CDLC focuses on low-end consumer devices and is the smaller of the two configurations. Typical CLDC devices, such as personal organizers, mobile phones, and pagers, have slow processors and limited memory, operate on batteries, and have only intermittent network connections. A CLDC implementation generally includes a kilobyte virtual machine (KVM). It gets its name because of its small memory footprint (on the order of kilobytes). The KVM is specially designed for memory-constrained devices.

Connected Device Configuration

The CDC focuses on high-end consumer devices that have more memory, faster processors, and greater network bandwidth. Typical examples of CDC devices are television set-top boxes and high-end communicators. CDC includes a virtual machine that conforms fully to the Java Virtual Machine Specification [15]. CDC also includes a much larger subset of the J2SE platform than does CLDC.

1.4.2 Profiles

Configurations do not usually provide a complete solution. Profiles add the functionality and the APIs required to complete a fully functional

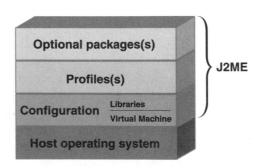

Figure 1.7   Components of J2ME architecture.

runtime environment for a class of devices. Configurations must be combined with profiles that define the higher-level APIs for providing the capabilities for a specific market or industry. It is possible for a single device to support several profiles. Examples of profiles are Mobile Information Device Profile (MIDP), Foundation Profile (FP), and Personal Profile (PP). A clarification: the Bluetooth profiles defined previously are not to be confused with the J2ME profiles discussed here. The two profiles are not related. *Bluetooth profile* refers to a set of functionality of the Bluetooth protocols for a particular usage case. J2ME profiles are a set of APIs that extend the functionality of a J2ME configuration.

Mobile Information Device Profile

The first profile that was created was MIDP [16]. This profile is designed for mobile phones, pagers, and entry-level personal organizers. MIDP combined with CLDC offers core application functionality, such as a user interface, network capability, and persistent storage. MIDP provides a complete Java runtime environment for mobile information devices. MIDP applications are called *MIDlets*. `MIDlet` is a class defined in MIDP and is the superclass for all MIDP applications.

Foundation Profile

The FP [17] is the lowest-level profile for CDC. Other profiles can be added on top as needed to provide application functionality. The FP is meant for embedded devices without a user interface but with network capability.

Personal Profile

The PP [18] is for devices such as high-end personal organizers, communicators, and game consoles that require a user interface and Internet applet support. PP replaces the PersonalJava™ technology and provides PersonalJava applications a clear migration path to the J2ME platform.

In addition there is a Personal Basis Profile (PBP) [19], which is a subset of PP aimed at devices that requires only a basic level of graphical presentation (for example, television set-top boxes).

1.4.3 Optional Packages

Many J2ME devices include additional technologies such as Bluetooth wireless technology, multimedia, wireless messaging, and database connectivity. Optional packages were created to fully leverage these technologies through standard Java APIs. Device manufacturers can include these optional packages as needed to fully utilize the features of each device.

In addition to the configurations, profiles, and optional packages, device manufacturers are able to define additional Java classes to take advantage of features specific to the device. These classes are called *licensee open classes* (LOCs). An LOC defines classes available to all developers. *Licensee closed classes* (LCCs) define classes available only to the device manufacturer. Programs using these classes may not be portable across devices having the same configuration and profiles.

1.5 Why Java Technology for Bluetooth Devices?

How an end user uses Bluetooth wireless technology varies from person to person. Two people with the same model of a Bluetooth-enabled phone might want to use it for different purposes. One person might want to be able to download video games to the phone and use the phone as a television remote control. The other person might want to use the same model phone to unlock car doors, operate kitchen appliances, and open and close garage doors. One way for both people to achieve their goals is to make it possible to download Bluetooth applications onto personal organizers and mobile phones to customize those handheld devices. To make downloading applications a reality, one needs a standard API that lets programmers write Bluetooth applications that work across many hardware platforms. To define this standard API, the Java language is the ideal choice. A Java API enables applications to run on different types of hardware, operating systems, and classes of device. In addition to portability, the Java language provides several other benefits:

- Rapid development of applications because of the better abstractions and high-level programming constructs provided by an object-oriented programming language.

- Ability to dynamically expand a program's functionality during execution by loading classes at runtime.

- Class file verification and security features that provide protection against malicious applications. These safeguards are required to customize devices by downloading applications.

- Standards with better user interfaces and that support sophisticated user interaction.

- Large developer community. The number of people who program in the Java language is continuously growing. The developer talent needed for programming in the Java language already exists, and there is no need to grow a developer community.

For these reasons, the decision was made to develop a standard API for Bluetooth wireless technology using the Java programming language. This standardization effort resulted in the Java APIs for Bluetooth Wireless Technology, or JABWT. As you will see later in this book, this standardization effort complements existing technologies rather than replacing them. JABWT is built on top of the already established and widely used Bluetooth protocol stack.

1.5.1　Java Community Process and JSR-82

Standard APIs in the Java programming language are defined though the Java Community Process^{SM} (JCP). The JCP coordinates the evolution of the Java programming language. Each new API is developed as a Java Specification Request (JSR). All J2ME configurations, profiles, and optional packages are defined as JSRs. The process for defining a standard Java API is as follows:

1. The potential specification lead submits a new JSR.

2. The JCP executive committee reviews and votes on the JSR.

3. After JSR approval, the specification lead forms an expert group.

4. The expert group defines the specification.

5. JCP members review the specification during the community review period.

6. The specification is open for public review.

7. The specification lead submits the specification as the proposed final draft.

8. The executive committee votes on the specification to accept or deny the API.

9. If the vote passes, the final release of the specification is announced.

The above process was followed in standardizing the JABWT under JSR-82 [20]. The expert group that defined JABWT consisted of 18 companies and three individuals. The companies were Extended Systems, IBM, Mitsubishi Electric, Motorola, Newbury Networks, Nokia, Parthus Technologies, Research in Motion, Rococo Software, Sharp Laboratories of America, Sony Ericsson Mobile Communications, Smart Fusion, Smart Network Devices, Sun Microsystems, Symbian, Telecordia, Vaultus, and Zucotto. The API was defined as an optional package for J2ME devices based on CLDC.

1.5.2   What about J2SE and PersonalJava?

Because Bluetooth wireless technology can be found in J2SE and PersonalJava devices, you may ask why this standardization effort focused on J2ME devices. The expert group believed that the initial set of devices that would use Java language capabilities over the Bluetooth protocols would be in the J2ME device space. But, as the next chapters show, the API was defined in such a way as to rely heavily on one set of CLDC APIs known as the *Generic Connection Framework* (GCF).

That thinking paid off. An effort was undertaken to include the GCF in J2SE under JSR-197 (Generic Connection Framework Optional Package) [21]. The main goal of JSR-197 is to make the GCF into an optional package that allows applications that rely on the GCF in J2ME to migrate to J2SE. JSR-197 will bring the benefits of JABWT to J2SE.

1.5.3   Jini, JXTA, and Bluetooth Networks

As Bluetooth wireless technology becomes part of the Java programming language, many Java developers are confused about how JABWT will fit in with other Java technologies, such as the Jini architecture [22] and the JXTA (for Juxtapose) research project [23]. Jini is an architecture developed by Sun Microsystems to allow developers to create adaptive network services. Jini works by moving Java objects and data over a network to allow the network to change as the environment of the network changes. JXTA also was developed originally by Sun

Microsystems, but Sun turned it into an open source research project. The goal of the JXTA project is to develop a high-level virtual peer-to-peer network. The JXTA project has defined a communication protocol to enable peer-to-peer networking. The project is currently working on revising communication protocols and identifying applications and services that use the protocols.

Although these three technologies share many basic concepts, Bluetooth wireless technology is not a competitor of Jini and JXTA. Nor does using Bluetooth wireless technology eliminate the ability or need to use Jini and JXTA. These three technologies are similar because they all provide a way to dynamically identify peers and a peer's capabilities. Bluetooth wireless technology differs from Jini and JXTA because Bluetooth wireless technologies defines a set of communication protocols that allow two devices to communicate with each other, in particular, a wireless communication protocol. Whereas Jini and JXTA operate only at a higher level, the Bluetooth specification defines all the components from the application layer down to the physical communication layer. Jini and JXTA can seamlessly span different communications networks. For example, a Jini application could use a Bluetooth protocol to talk to an access point, which converts the requests to Telephony Control Protocol/Internet Protocol (TCP/IP) packets to talk to the Jini service. The Bluetooth specification addresses only how Bluetooth devices communicate, not how to transform requests over any communication medium.

It is likely that Jini and JXTA implementations in the future will use Bluetooth communications and be available over TCP/IP. The Jini and

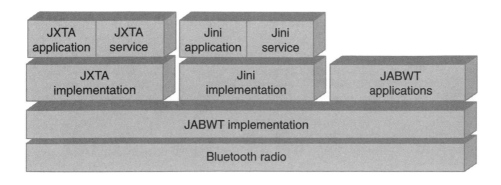

Figure 1.8 Jini and JXTA on a Bluetooth device with JABWT.

JXTA implementations themselves will be Bluetooth services. Figure 1.8 shows that from a JABWT implementation perspective, JXTA and Jini are simply other Bluetooth applications. In this way, Jini and JXTA provide added capabilities to a JABWT implementation.

1.6 Summary

The JABWT specification provides a standard set of APIs for developing Bluetooth applications. Tha Java APIs defined by JABWT are considered optional packages for J2ME. Applications written with JABWT are potentially portable to a wide range of devices with a wide range of Bluetooth radio modules and Bluetooth protocol stacks.

This chapter gives an overview of Bluetooth wireless technology and J2ME. These are two very large topics. To learn more about Bluetooth wireless technology, refer to the Bluetooth specifications [1, 3] or books on the subject [4, 5]. The following websites are a good place to start:

www.bluetooth.com

www.palowireless.com

To learn more about J2ME, see the books by Topley [11] and by Riggs and associates [12]. Helpful websites for J2ME and JABWT are

java.sun.com

www.jcp.org

www.jcp.org/jsr/detail/82.jsp

There are several articles [24], white papers, and tutorials on these subjects on the Web. There are several newsgroups on Bluetooth wireless technology, but the following two are devoted to JABWT:

groups.yahoo.com/group/jabwt

groups.yahoo.com/group/jsr82

This chapter notes the need for Java technology on Bluetooth devices and explains the process of defining JABWT.

2 CHAPTER An Overview of JABWT

This chapter describes

- The goals of the JABWT specification
- The characteristics of the JABWT specification
- The scope of the JABWT specification

Some sections in the chapter may not seem relevant for those primarily interested in programming with JABWT. But the overview of JABWT is presented to lead to a better understanding of the capabilities and the reasoning behind these APIs.

2.1 Goals

The Bluetooth specification defines the over-the-air behavior for ensuring compatibility of Bluetooth devices from different vendors. The Bluetooth specification does not standardize a software API to Bluetooth stacks for use by Bluetooth applications. JABWT helps solve this problem by defining the first standard API for Bluetooth application developers. The overall goal of the JABWT standardization effort discussed in this book is to define a standard set of APIs that will enable an open, third-party application development environment for Bluetooth wireless technology.

The goals were to minimize the number of classes (the total number of classes in JABWT is 21); keep the API simple and easy to learn and program; and keep it powerful. The meaningful high-level abstractions help in third-party application development. This API brings together the benefits of two different technologies: Bluetooth wireless technology and Java technology. Having this standard API in the Java language brings in all the benefits of Java technology, some of which are discussed in Chapter 1. The abstractions and ease of programming of the Java language facilitate easy development of complex programs. The goal of JABWT is to present access to Bluetooth wireless technology in the easy but powerful form of the Java language.

2.1.1 Target Devices

JABWT is aimed mainly at devices that are limited in processing power and memory and are primarily battery operated. These devices can be manufactured in large quantities. Low cost and low power consumption are primary goals of the manufacturers. JABWT takes these factors into consideration. Figure 2.1 shows the types of devices that might use JABWT. Some of the devices shown, such as the car, laptop, and LAN access point, are not J2ME devices. These devices are likely to operate with J2SE, CDC, or PersonalJava. Some manufacturers of these products, however, are already incorporating JABWT in their designs. In addition, work completed under JSR-197 will make integrating JABWT into these products easier. JSR-197 [21] is intended to create an optional package out of GCF alone, allowing applications that rely on the GCF to migrate to J2SE. JSR-197 also is intended to use GCF APIs as defined by the J2ME Foundation profile along with improvements proposed in CLDC 1.1 (JSR-139) [25].

2.1.2 Keeping Up with the Bluetooth Profiles

One initial idea was to define an API based on the Bluetooth profiles. But the JSR-82 expert group realized that the number of Bluetooth profiles is constantly growing and that it would not be possible to keep up with the new profiles in the JABWT specification. Instead the JSR-82 expert group decided to provide support for only basic protocols and profiles rather than introducing new API elements for each Bluetooth profile. The intent of the JABWT design is to enable new Bluetooth profiles to be built on top of this API with the Java programming language. Bluetooth profiles are being built on top of OBEX, RFCOMM, and L2CAP. For this reason, all three of these communication protocols are incorporated in JABWT. Writing future Bluetooth profiles in the Java programming language enables portability across all operating systems and Bluetooth protocol stacks.

   In addition to APIs for accessing the protocols, there are APIs for some Bluetooth profiles. JABWT addresses the following: GAP, SDAP,

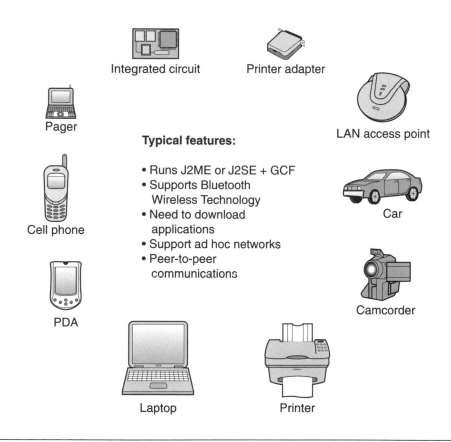

Figure 2.1 Target devices for JABWT

SPP, and GOEP. Detailed information on Bluetooth profiles and relations to protocols such as OBEX, RFCOMM, and L2CAP are given in the Bluetooth Core specification [1] and the Bluetooth Profile specification [3].

JABWT is based on Bluetooth specification version 1.1. However, nothing in the JABWT specification is intended to preclude operating with version 1.0–compliant stacks or hardware. In addition, if future versions are backward compatible with version 1.1, implementations of the JABWT specification also should operate on those versions of stacks or hardware.

2.1.3   JABWT Use Cases

Any technology does better when more applications are created for it. Standardized APIs foster an environment to create a variety of applications. In addition, standard APIs make it possible for certain types of applications and markets that otherwise would not be possible. The portability of Java applications and standardization of JABWT facilitate the use cases discussed herein.

Peer-to-Peer Networking

Peer-to-peer networking can be defined and interpreted in many ways. For the purpose of this discussion, a peer-to-peer network is defined as a network between two or more devices whereby each device can be both a server and a client. JABWT supports peer-to-peer networking with Bluetooth wireless technology. An example of a peer-to-peer network application is a game played between two or more devices connected through Bluetooth communication.

The devices involved can belong to entirely different device classes, such as a phone and a personal digital assistant (PDA) using different hardware and operating systems. If these devices are JABWT enabled, the software games can be written once in the Java programming language and run on all of the devices. In addition, the device independence of these JABWT applications makes it possible to share and download these games onto different devices.

Kiosk

It is impractical for a kiosk that sells software to store different executables for the various Bluetooth devices that have been manufactured. With JABWT, an application can be written once, purchased, and executed on all Bluetooth devices that have implemented this API. This capability enables establishments such as airports, train stations, and malls to have custom applications that work best in their environment. Bluetooth devices with JABWT implemented can download these custom applications from kiosks.

Buying Soda and Bluetooth Applications through Vending Machines

Another example of the benefit of this API is a scenario in which people purchase or download Bluetooth applications to their Bluetooth devices while using the same device to purchase a soda from a vending machine. The API allows applications to be written once and run on many different Bluetooth platforms. The vending machine stores these applications and transfers them via Bluetooth transports. A game manufacturer might buy advertising space on vending machines to house a sample game. Customers purchasing soda could be given the option of downloading a free sample game, which can be upgraded later when the game is purchased.

2.2 API Characteristics and Hardware Requirements

This section describes the characteristics of JABWT and the hardware requirements followed in defining JABWT. There were two categories of hardware requirements:

- The requirements of the J2ME device
- The requirements of the Bluetooth subsystem in the device

2.2.1 JABWT Specification Characteristics

This API design was challenging because both Java technology and Bluetooth wireless technology appear in a variety of devices. It was difficult to try to cover all the devices with one API. The initial goal of the JABWT specification was to define an API that could be used by all devices that support J2ME. As stated earlier, the expert group believed that J2ME devices would be the first to implement JABWT. Hence the API was built with standard J2ME APIs and the GCF defined in CLDC. Thus JABWT can be ported to any Java platform that supports the GCF. The first two characteristics below resulted from this thinking. JSR-197 adds the GCF into J2SE platforms and will help JABWT and other J2ME APIs to be usable on other Java 2 platforms.

The characteristics of the JABWT specification are as follows:

1. Requirement for only CLDC libraries.
2. Scalability—ability to run on any Java 2 platform that supplies the GCF.
3. OBEX API definition independent of Bluetooth protocols. By contrast, applications written with the Bluetooth API are expected to run only on platforms that incorporate Bluetooth wireless

technology. While defining the API for OBEX, the expert group recognized that OBEX could be used over a number of different transports (e.g., IrDA, USB, TCP). Therefore, the OBEX API is defined to be transport independent. The OBEX API is in a separate `javax.obex` package.

4. Use of the OBEX API without the Bluetooth API. An IrDA device could implement the `javax.obex` package and not implement the `javax.bluetooth` package, which contains the Bluetooth API.

5. Prevents applications from interfering with each other. The concept of the Bluetooth Control Center (BCC), discussed in Chapter 3, was introduced for this reason. The intent of the BCC is to allow multiple Bluetooth applications to run simultaneously and be able to access Bluetooth resources.

6. Ability of applications to be both client and server to enable peer-to-peer networking. This is one of the vital use cases for Bluetooth wireless technology. One aspect of being a server is the ability to register services for clients to discover. Although the Bluetooth specification thoroughly addresses the client side of service discovery, the mechanisms used by server applications to register their services with a service discovery server are not standardized. The JSR-82 expert group saw the need for defining service registration in detail to standardize the registration process for the application programmer.

7. Allowance for the possibility of building Bluetooth profiles on top of the RFCOMM, L2CAP, and OBEX APIs. The expert group realized that keeping up with the growing number of Bluetooth profiles would be difficult (see Section 2.1.2).

2.2.2 J2ME Device Requirements

JABWT is not intended to be a complete solution by itself. It is an optional API based on GCF and extends a Java 2 platform to add support for accessing Bluetooth wireless technology. As mentioned earlier, the initial target devices are CLDC based. General J2ME device requirements on which the API is designed to operate are listed below. More detailed hardware requirements for various J2ME configurations and profiles can be obtained from the respective specifications, which are available at www.jcp.org.

- 512K minimum total memory available for Java 2 platform (ROM/Flash and RAM). Application memory requirements are additional.

- Bluetooth communication hardware, with necessary Bluetooth stack and radio. More detailed requirements are given in Section 2.2.3.

- Compliant implementation of the J2ME CLDC [13, 25] or a superset of CLDC APIs, such as the J2ME CDC [14] or any flavor of Java 2 platform with JSR-197 APIs.

Chapter 10 discusses detailed device requirements and issues related to implementing JABWT.

2.2.3 Bluetooth System Requirements

The Bluetooth part of the JABWT implementation is not designed to access the Bluetooth hardware directly. It accesses the Bluetooth hardware through an underlying Bluetooth stack. The Bluetooth stack can be implemented in many ways, such as making it part of the JABWT implementation or writing it completely in the Java language. Typically, JABWT is to be implemented on top of a native (written in C or C++) Bluetooth stack, thus allowing native Bluetooth applications and Java Bluetooth applications to run on a system. The requirements of the underlying Bluetooth system on which this API is built are as follows:

- The underlying system is qualified in accordance with the Bluetooth Qualification Program for at least the GAP, SDAP, and SPP.

- The following layers are supported as defined in Bluetooth specification version 1.1, and the JABWT has access to them.
  SDP
  RFCOMM
  L2CAP

- The BCC is provided by either the Bluetooth stack or system software. The BCC is a "control panel"–like application that allows a user or an original equipment manufacturer (OEM) to define specific values for certain configuration parameters in a stack. The details of the BCC are discussed in Chapter 3.

Unlike the Bluetooth part of the API, the OBEX API can either be implemented completely in the Java programming language within the JABWT implementation or use the OBEX implementation in the underlying Bluetooth stack. If OBEX is being implemented on another transport, the OBEX API can use the OBEX implementation over that transport system. More of the implementation details are discussed in Section 10.3.3.

2.3 Scope

The Bluetooth specification covers many layers and profiles, and it is not possible to include all of them in this API. Rather than try to address all of them, the JABWT expert group agreed to prioritize the API functions on the basis of size requirements and the breadth of usage of the API. Moreover, under the JCP rules, when JABWT is implemented, all portions of the API must be implemented (i.e., if the `javax.bluetooth` package is implemented, then RFCOMM, SDP, and L2CAP must be implemented; if `javax.obex` is implemented, then OBEX must be implemented). The Bluetooth specification is different because it is flexible about the parts of the Bluetooth specification a device manufacturer chooses to implement. The expert group addressed areas considered essential to achieving broad usage and areas expected to use the benefit of the Java language the most. As stated earlier, these APIs are aimed at small, resource-constraint devices and at devices of different classes. The Headset Profile [3] or the Dial-Up Networking Profile [3] defined in the Bluetooth specification will likely be developed by a device manufacturer as an application native to the system software. For the first version of JABWT, support for voice channels and telephony control–related areas were not included in JABWT. The basic Bluetooth profiles and fundamental protocol layers required to help build future profiles were included. In addition, service registration was defined in detail.

Figure 2.2 shows that JABWT applications have access to some but not all of the functionality of the Bluetooth protocol stack. The bottom of Figure 2.2 reproduces Figure 1.4 from Chapter 1, which shows the layers in a Bluetooth stack. In Figure 2.2, interface points have been added to represent the capabilities or functions of protocols that could potentially be used by applications. In Figure 2.2 dashed arrows connect the JABWT application at the top of the figure with interface points on the protocols in the Bluetooth protocol stack. An arrow connecting to an interface point indicates that JABWT applications have access to the functionality represented by that interface point. As shown in Figure 2.2, JABWT provides access to capabilities of the following Bluetooth protocols:

- L2CAP
- RFCOMM
- SDP
- OBEX
- LMP

JABWT does not provide APIs for the following Bluetooth protocols.

- Audio (voice) transmissions over voice channels
- TCS Binary
- BNEP

Even when it does provide access to a Bluetooth protocol layer, JABWT might not provide access to all of the functions provided by that layer. For example, JABWT applications have access to connection-oriented L2CAP channels but do not have access to connectionless L2CAP channels. This possibility is indicated in Figure 2.2 by an interface point that has nothing connected to it.

Figure 2.2 shows that in addition to providing access to the functionality of Bluetooth *protocols*, JABWT provides access to the functionality specified by the Bluetooth *profiles*. The star shapes in Figure 2.2 represent Bluetooth profiles. JABWT applications have access to selected functionality from the following Bluetooth profiles:

- GAP
- SDAP
- SPP
- GOEP

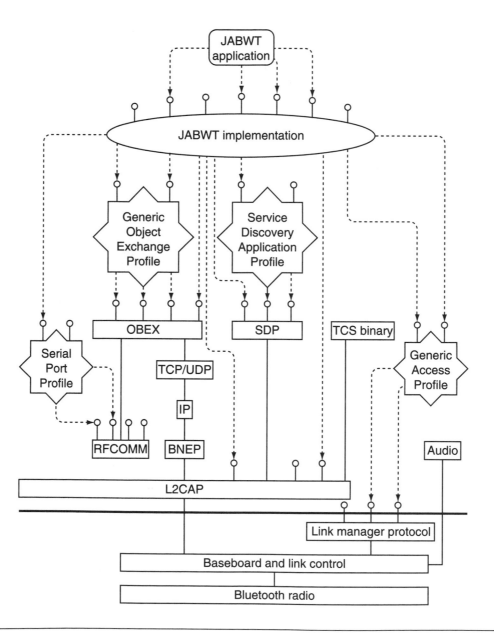

Figure 2.2   JABWT provides access to selected functionality of the Bluetooth stack.

In functional terms, JABWT provides the following Bluetooth capabilities:

- Registering services
- Discovering devices and services
- Establishing RFCOMM, L2CAP, and OBEX connections
- Conducting the above three activities in a secure manner

The following capabilities were considered to be outside the scope of JABWT. However, there is no incompatibility between JABWT and these functions, so JABWT applications may have access to these functions on some devices:

- Layer management: Many aspects of layer management are system specific and are difficult to standardize, such as power modes and park mode.
- Downloading and storing applications: These features are implementation specific and therefore are not defined in JABWT. Over-the-air provisioning is being addressed in other JSRs (JSR-37 [16] and JSR-118 [26]).
- Asynchronous start of applications: Methods by which an application can be started asynchronously because of external requests are permitted but are not specified in detail. For example, a service does not have to be running after it has registered itself but could be started when a client connects to that service.

2.4 Summary

This chapter discusses the goals, capabilities, characteristics, and scope of JABWT. Although the Bluetooth specification defines a standard for over-the-air communication, JABWT standardizes software APIs for use by Bluetooth applications. One of the design goals for this API was to make it possible to write Bluetooth profiles in the Java programming language using JABWT. For this reason, JABWT provides support for the most basic Bluetooth protocols and the most basic Bluetooth profiles.

The following are some of the key characteristics of JABWT:

- It uses the CLDC generic connection framework.
- It requires a BCC for system control.

- It provides a definition for service registration.
- It defines an OBEX API that is transport independent.

JABWT defines two separate Java packages, `javax.bluetooth` and `javax.obex`. Under JCP licensing rules, these JABWT packages must be implemented exactly as defined without addition or removal of public classes, interfaces, or methods. The underlying Bluetooth system needs to be qualified for GAP, SDAP, and SPP. In addition, the underlying Bluetooth system must provide access to SDP, RFCOMM, and L2CAP. Section 2.3 discusses the scope of the JABWT specification. The three main areas that JABWT does not currently support are audio over SCO links, TCS-BIN, and BNEP.

JABWT is aimed mainly at J2ME devices. In conjunction with JSR-197, however, which adds optional support for the GCF to J2SE, JABWT also is well suited for J2SE devices.

3 High-Level Architecture

This chapter discusses the high-level architecture of JABWT. The chapter introduces the following:

- Architecture of the JABWT specification
- The Bluetooth Control Center
- A sample JABWT application

3.1 Architecture of JABWT

The functionality provided by JABWT falls into three major categories:

1. Discovery
2. Communication
3. Device management

Discovery includes device discovery, service discovery, and service registration. Communication includes establishing connections between devices and using those connections for Bluetooth communication between applications. These connections can be made over several different protocols, namely RFCOMM, L2CAP, and OBEX. Device management allows for managing and controlling these connections. It deals with managing local and remote device states and properties. It also facilitates the security aspects of connections. JABWT is organized into these three functional categories.

3.1.1 CLDC, MIDP, and JABWT

JABWT depends only on the CLDC and uses the GCF. But CLDC does not necessarily make a complete solution. It is usually coupled with a

J2ME profile such as the MIDP [16, 26]. MIDP devices are expected to be the first class of devices to incorporate JABWT.

Figure 3.1 is an example of how the APIs defined in JABWT fit in a CLDC + MIDP architecture. Although shown here on an MIDP device, JABWT does not depend on MIDP APIs. The lowest-level block in the figure is the system software or host operating system. The host operating system contains the host part of the Bluetooth protocol stack and other libraries used internally and by native applications of the system. Native Bluetooth applications interface with the operating system directly, as shown in Figure 3.1. The CLDC/KVM implementation sits on top of the host system software. This block provides the underlying Java execution environment on which the higher-level Java APIs can be built. The figure shows two such APIs that can be built on top of CLDC:

- JABWT, the set of APIs specified by JSR-82
- MIDP, the set of APIs defined by JSR-37 and JSR-118

As shown in Figure 3.1, an application written for an MIDP + JABWT device can access MIDP, JABWT, and CLDC layers directly.

These diagrams describe the architecture of the JABWT reference implementation developed by us and our team at Motorola. Other JABWT implementations may involve different components or have their components layered in a different way from that shown.

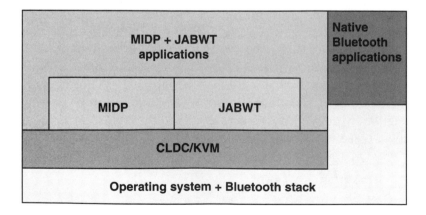

Figure 3.1   CLDC + MIDP + Bluetooth architecture diagram.

3.1.2 Java Packages

As stated in Chapter 2, JABWT essentially defines two separate APIs. Hence two Java packages are defined. The packages are as follows:

1. `javax.bluetooth`
2. `javax.obex`

The OBEX API is defined independently of the Bluetooth transport layer and is packaged separately. Each of the two Java packages represents a separate optional package, the implication being that a CLDC implementation can include neither of them, one of them, or both of them. The `javax.bluetooth` package contains the Bluetooth API, and the `javax.obex` package contains the APIs for OBEX.

Figure 3.2 shows the package structure. The `javax.obex` and `javax.bluetooth` packages depend on the `javax.microedition.io` package, which contains the GCF.

3.1.3 Client and Server Model

An overview of the Bluetooth client and server model is given in this section. Additional details are provided in later chapters.

A Bluetooth service is an application that acts as a server and provides assistance to client devices via Bluetooth communication. This assistance typically takes the form of a capability or a function unavailable locally on the client device. A printing service is one example of a Bluetooth server application. Three Bluetooth profiles are devoted to

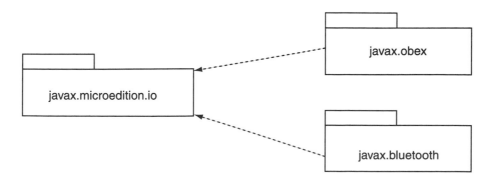

Figure 3.2 Package structure.

printing [7, 27, 28]. Additional examples of Bluetooth server applications can be found in the Bluetooth profiles specification [3]: LAN access servers, file and object servers, synchronization services, and so on. JABWT developers can create Bluetooth server applications to implement one of the Bluetooth profiles or to implement their own custom service. These services are made available to remote clients by the definition of a service record that describes the service and the addition of that service record to the service discovery database (SDDB) of the local device.

Figure 3.3 illustrates the Bluetooth components involved in service registration and service discovery. The SDP is a Bluetooth protocol for discovering the services provided by a Bluetooth device. A server application adds a service record to the SDDB. The Bluetooth stack provides an SDP server, which maintains this database of service records. Service discovery clients use SDP to query the SDP server for any service records of interest [1]. A service record provides sufficient information to allow an SDP client to connect to the Bluetooth service on the server device.

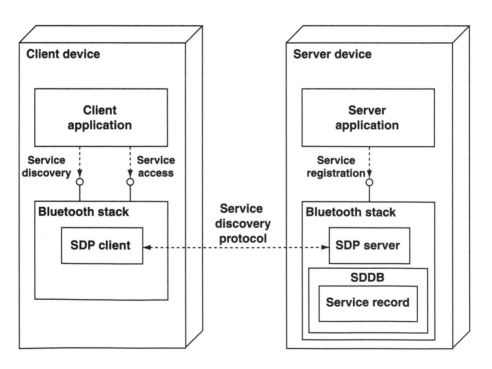

Figure 3.3   Bluetooth components involved in service discovery.

After registering a service record in the SDDB, the server application waits for a client application to initiate contact with the server to access the service. The client application and the server application then establish a Bluetooth connection to conduct their business.

Although the Bluetooth specification was used as a guide for defining the capabilities that should be offered in JABWT, defining the capabilities of the server applications was more difficult, because the Bluetooth specifications do not specify:

- How or when server applications register service records in the SDDB

- What internal format or database mechanism is used by the SDDB

- How server applications interact with the Bluetooth stack to form connections with remote clients

These aspects of server applications are outside the scope of the Bluetooth specification and are likely to vary from one Bluetooth stack implementation to another. They do not require standardization to ensure interoperability of Bluetooth devices from different manufacturers. However, the JABWT specification for service registration allows server applications to take full advantage of Bluetooth communications. Standardization of server registration is an additional benefit JABWT bring to the programming community.

JABWT defines the following division of responsibilities among the server application, the client application, and the Bluetooth stack.

Typical responsibilities of a Bluetooth server application are to:

- Create a service record describing the service offered by the application

- Add a service record to the server's SDDB to make potential clients aware of this service

- Register the Bluetooth security measures associated with this service that should be enforced for connections with clients

- Accept connections from clients that request the service offered by the application

- Update the service record in the server's SDDB if characteristics of the service change

- Remove or disable the service record in the server's SDDB when the service is no longer available

Typical responsibilities of a Bluetooth client application are to

- Use SDP to query a remote SDDB for desired services
- Register the Bluetooth security measures associated with this service that should be enforced for connections with servers
- Initiate connections to servers offering desired services

The Bluetooth stack is assumed to provide the following capabilities for Bluetooth server applications:

- A repository for service records that allows servers to add, update, and remove their own service records
- Connections with remote client applications

The Bluetooth stack is assumed to provide the following capabilities for service discovery clients:

- Search and retrieval of service records stored in the server's SDDB (i.e., acting as an SDP server)
- Connections to server applications

Peer-to-Peer Applications

Although it is important to understand the distinction between a Bluetooth client application and a Bluetooth server application, it is possible for the same Bluetooth application to play both the client role and the server role. It is one of the stated goals of JABWT to support peer-to-peer applications in which the peer-to-peer application is capable of being both server and client. For example, it is not likely that a two-person Bluetooth game would be sold in client and server versions. Instead, the game software would do both of the following:

- Initiate attempts to connect to nearby devices that have the same game (client)
- Accept connections requested by nearby devices with the same game (server)

Whereas JABWT tends to describe the client and server techniques separately, these techniques are not incompatible, and applications can use them both. Service discovery and service registration are discussed in more detail in Chapter 7.

3.1.4 Device Properties

Various Bluetooth products need to be configured differently depending on the product and the market. A set of device properties facilitates such variations and differentiations. JABWT defines system properties that may be retrieved by a call to `LocalDevice.getProperty()`. These properties do either of the following:

- Provide additional information about the Bluetooth system, that is, the capabilities of the device or the underlying Bluetooth protocol stack.

- Define restrictions placed on an application by an implementation. The device manufacturer may want to restrict certain capabilities for various reasons.

An example of these device properties is `bluetooth.connected.devices.max`, which indicates the maximum number of Bluetooth devices that can connect to this device. Device properties are discussed in Chapter 6.

3.2 Bluetooth Control Center

The BCC is part of the JABWT specification, but it does not have any Java APIs that provide direct access to it. In other words, the BCC is a concept defined by the JABWT specification, which is part of a JABWT implementation. The need for the BCC arises from the desire to prevent one application from adversely affecting another application. The BCC is the central authority for local Bluetooth device settings. The details of the BCC are left to the implementation. It may be an interactive application with a user interface or an application that provides no user interaction. The BCC may be a native application, an application with a separate private Java API, or simply a group of settings specified by the manufacturer.

The BCC performs three specific tasks:

1. Resolving conflicting requests between applications
2. Enabling modifications to the properties of the local Bluetooth device
3. Handling security operations that may require user interaction

Each of these tasks is discussed individually in the next sections.

As Figure 3.4 shows, the BCC is not directly accessible with JABWT applications. Instead, the JABWT implementation issues requests

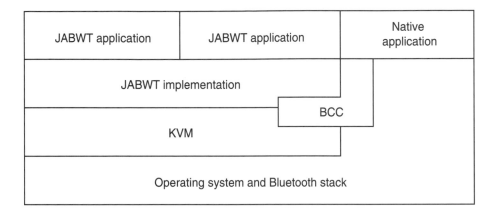

Figure 3.4   How the BCC fits into a JABWT implementation.

through the BCC to the Bluetooth stack. The BCC also can be used by native applications. The BCC can prevent conflicting requests between the JABWT applications and the native applications.

How does a user modify the values of the BCC? This procedure also is up to an implementation of the BCC. It is expected that most implementations will use a native application to manipulate the settings in the BCC.

3.2.1   Conflict Resolution

The JABWT specification allows a great deal of flexibility within a JABWT implementation. This feature was included for two reasons. First, the flexibility resulted from the desire to allow the JABWT implementation to be ported to a large number of Bluetooth stacks and radios. Second, JABWT implementations are able to differentiate themselves on the basis of the policies the implementation enforces.

Because multiple applications are able to run and access the local Bluetooth device at the same time, conflicting requests can be made to the Bluetooth device. As far as JABWT is concerned, two types of requests can conflict with another application using the same Bluetooth device. First, two applications may request different security settings on a link (Bluetooth security is described in Section 4.1). Second, two applications may request to set the device into two different discoverable modes (discoverable modes are described in Chapter 6). The BCC is responsible for resolving these conflicting requests.

3.2.2 Modifying Device Properties

Although JABWT allows an application to retrieve certain properties of the local device, no methods within JABWT allow direct modification of a device's properties. In particular, setting of the friendly name, the class of device record, the list of pre-known devices, the list of trusted devices, the minimum security requirements, and support for the different connectable/discoverable modes are handled by the BCC. (Each of these concepts is described later in this book.) The friendly name is a user-friendly name given to a Bluetooth device. The name does not uniquely identify a Bluetooth device but provides a name of a device that can be displayed to a user instead of a device's Bluetooth address. For example, a user named Bob may assign his PDA the friendly name "Bob's PDA."

3.2.3 User Interaction

Certain operations within Bluetooth security may require input from the user of a device outside the scope of the application. The BCC is responsible for retrieving this information from the user and injecting the information into the Bluetooth security process. What type of information can the BCC retrieve from the user? It can range from a PIN to simply responding to a permission request.

3.2.4 BCC on Devices with No User Interface

Because JABWT is based on CLDC, there is no guarantee that a user interface (UI) is available on the device. In this situation, the OEM or device manufacturer is expected to set the BCC setting in the device. Actions that require user interaction are more complicated. A BCC on a non–graphical user interface (GUI) device might not support these types of actions or can specify the responses to these actions when the device is manufactured.

3.3 Simple JABWT Application

Before describing the details of the classes and methods defined in JABWT, the traditional "Hello, World" application is shown. This example shows how code is presented in the remainder of the book. Because Bluetooth technology is a wireless radio technology, developing applications requires hardware or a simulator. To enable readers to try out the code in this book, the following section also describes how to set up a development environment that makes it possible to build and test JABWT code in a simulated environment.

Development Tools

Developing and testing J2ME applications, especially testing on a device, can be a complicated process. Device testing is complicated due to a general lack of debug tools and the effort it takes to download and install an application. Therefore device simulators have been developed to allow developers to create and debug applications on a desktop computer before testing them on a device. A common tool for J2ME development is the J2ME Wireless Toolkit available at java.sun.com/j2me. The Wireless Toolkit provides software emulation of devices that support the CLDC and MIDP specifications. Many device manufacturers provide tools that allow specific device emulation. The Wireless Toolkit is not a full integrated development environment (IDE), but it provides a simple interface to the tools a J2ME developer needs.

Although the J2ME Wireless Toolkit provides support for J2ME emulation, a separate tool is needed for Bluetooth networking simulation. The Impronto™ Simulator developed by Rococo Software and available at www.rococosoft.com is an example of a Bluetooth network simulation package. These tools can easily be combined so that initial application testing can be done quickly. It is important to note that nothing replaces device testing. Different devices have subtle differences that can dramatically affect the user experience. Therefore, final testing should always be done on a device.

All the examples in this book have been tested with the Motorola JABWT reference implementation and the J2ME Wireless Toolkit with the Impronto Simulator. The process of setting up and running the J2ME Wireless Toolkit and the Impronto Simulator is simple. Complete the following steps to correctly set up the J2ME Wireless Toolkit and the Impronto Simulator for Windows 2000. (These steps apply to the J2ME Wireless Toolkit 1.0.4 and Impronto Simulator 1.1. The steps may need to be modified if a different version of these tools is used or if the tools will be running on Linux.)

1. Download and install the J2ME Wireless Toolkit from java.sun.com.

2. Download and install the Impronto Simulator from www.rococosoft.com.

3. Let %ROCOCO% be the directory in which the Impronto Simulator is installed and %WTK% be the directory in which the J2ME Wireless Toolkit is installed. Copy %ROCOCO%\ ImprontoSimulator\lib\isim_midp.jar to %WTK%\apps\lib.

4. Start the Impronto Simulator and the KToolBar application (part of the J2ME Wireless Toolkit).

5. Start coding, building, and testing your JABWT applications.

Consult the documentation for these tools for directions on how to use and modify the tools.

Throughout the remainder of this book, screen shots of example applications are provided. These screen shots are based on the J2ME Wireless Toolkit and Rococo Impronto Simulator. Although these screen shots may look like they come from an actual Motorola wireless phone, they are just emulations. The phone whose image is used in the screen shots does not support JABWT.

Sample Application

Before introducing the details of JABWT, let's take a look at how simple it is to get up and running with JABWT. A simple "Hello, World" application follows. The `HelloClient` MIDlet locates a `HelloServer` MIDlet and sends the text "Hello, World" to the server to be displayed by the `HelloServer` on its screen. Before showing the JABWT code, the `BluetoothMIDlet` class is introduced. `HelloClient` and `HelloServer` use this class as a building block. `BluetoothMIDlet` starts a processing thread and destroys the MIDlet when a `Command` is selected.

```
package com.jabwt.book;

import java.lang.*;
import java.io.*;
import javax.microedition.io.*;
import javax.microedition.lcdui.*;
import javax.microedition.midlet.*;
import javax.bluetooth.*;

public class BluetoothMIDlet extends MIDlet implements
    Runnable, CommandListener {

    public BluetoothMIDlet() {}
```

```java
/**
 * Starts a background thread when the MIDlet is
 * started.
 */
public void startApp()
  throws MIDletStateChangeException {
    new Thread(this).start();
}

public void pauseApp() {}

public void destroyApp(boolean unconditional) {}

public void run() {}

/**
 * Destroys the MIDlet when a Command occurs.
 */
public void commandAction(Command c, Displayable d) {
    notifyDestroyed();
}
}
```

The next step is to write the `HelloServer` code. The `run()` method of `HelloServer` does all the work. It makes the server device discoverable so that the client can find the server. Next, the `run()` method waits for a client to connect and reads all the data sent from the client. The `run()` method displays the data sent from the client on the screen.

```java
package com.jabwt.book;

import java.lang.*;
import java.io.*;
import javax.microedition.lcdui.*;
import javax.microedition.io.*;
import javax.bluetooth.*;

public class HelloServer extends BluetoothMIDlet {
    /**
     * Creates a server object. Accepts a single
     * connection from a client and prints the data
     * sent from the client to the screen.
     */
```

```java
public void run() {
    // Create a Form and add the Exit command to the Form
    Form f = new Form("Server");
    f.addCommand(new Command("Exit", Command.EXIT, 1));
    f.setCommandListener(this);
    Display.getDisplay(this).setCurrent(f);

    try {
        // Make the local device discoverable for the
        // client to locate
        LocalDevice local = LocalDevice.getLocalDevice();
        if (!local.setDiscoverable(DiscoveryAgent.GIAC)) {
            f.append("Failed to change to the " +
                "discoverable mode");
            return;
        }

        // Create a server connection object to accept
        // a connection from a client
        StreamConnectionNotifier notifier =
            (StreamConnectionNotifier)
                Connector.open("btspp://localhost:" +
                    "86b4d249fb8844d6a756ec265dd1f6a3");

        // Accept a connection from the client
        StreamConnection conn = notifier.acceptAndOpen();
        // Open the input to read data from
        InputStream in = conn.openInputStream();
        ByteArrayOutputStream out = new
            ByteArrayOutputStream();

        // Read the data sent from the client until
        // the end of stream
        int data;
        while ((data = in.read()) != -1) {
            out.write(data);
        }

        // Add the text sent from the client to the Form
        f.append(out.toString());

        // Close all open resources
        in.close();
```

```
        conn.close();
        notifier.close();
    } catch (BluetoothStateException e) {
        f.append("BluetoothStateException: ");
        f.append(e.getMessage());
    } catch (IOException e) {
        f.append("IOException: ");
        f.append(e.getMessage());
    }
  }
}
```

After the `HelloServer` MIDlet is created, the `HelloClient` MIDlet
must be written to send the "Hello, World" message to the server. All
the work for the `HelloClient` MIDlet occurs in the `run()` method.
The `run()` method uses the `selectServices()` method to discover
the `HelloServer`. After discovering the server, the `HelloClient` connects to the server and sends the text. Figure 3.5 shows a successful run
of the `HelloClient` and `HelloServer` MIDlets.

```
package com.jabwt.book;

import java.lang.*;
import java.io.*;
import javax.microedition.io.*;
import javax.microedition.lcdui.*;
import javax.bluetooth.*;

public class HelloClient extends BluetoothMIDlet {
    /**
     * Connects to the server and sends 'Hello, World'
     * to the server.
     */
    public void run() {
      // Creates the Form and adds the Exit Command to it
      Form f = new Form("Client");
      f.addCommand(new Command("Exit", Command.EXIT, 1));
      f.setCommandListener(this);
      Display.getDisplay(this).setCurrent(f);

      try {
```

A   B

Figure 3.5 A run using the Impronto Simulator. **(A)** `HelloServer`; **(B)** `HelloClient` (emulation only)

```
// Retrieve the connection string to connect to
// the server
LocalDevice local =
  LocalDevice.getLocalDevice();
DiscoveryAgent agent = local.getDiscoveryAgent();

String connString = agent.selectService(
  new UUID("86b4d249fb8844d6a756ec265dd1f6a3", false),
  ServiceRecord.NOAUTHENTICATE_NOENCRYPT, false);

if (connString != null) {
  try {
    // Connect to the server and send 'Hello, World'
    StreamConnection conn = (StreamConnection)
```

```
        Connector.open(connString);

      OutputStream out = conn.openOutputStream();
      out.write("Hello, World".getBytes());
      out.close();
      conn.close();

      f.append("Message sent correctly");
    } catch (IOException e) {
      f.append("IOException: ");
      f.append(e.getMessage());
    }
  } else {
     // Unable to locate a service so just print an error
     // message on the screen
    f.append("Unable to locate service");
  }
} catch (BluetoothStateException e) {
   f.append("BluetoothStateException: ");
   f.append(e.getMessage());
  }
 }
}
```

3.4 Summary

This chapter presents the high-level architecture of JABWT to set the
stage for the detailed API discussions in the coming chapters. Because
JABWT is expected to be implemented first on CLDC/MIDP devices,
Section 3.1.1 describes how JABWT can fit into a CLDC/MIDP device. A
client-server model is basic to the operation of Bluetooth wireless technology, and that client-server model is reflected in JABWT. JABWT goes
a step further than the Bluetooth specification in standardizing service
registration. To allow for variations in Bluetooth product configuration,
JABWT define configurable system properties.

   JABWT introduces the concept of a BCC to allow for system
control and monitoring. Some form of BCC must be part of all JABWT
implementations. However, the details of the BCC are left to the JABWT
implementation. The three main tasks the BCC performs are conflict
resolution, modification of system properties, and user interaction.

   Section 3.3 presents a simple "Hello, World" JABWT application to
introduce the APIs discussed in the following chapters.

4 RFCOMM

CHAPTER

This chapter covers the following topics:

- What is the SPP?
- Why use RFCOMM?
- How do you establish an RFCOMM connection?
- How do you create a new RFCOMM service?
- Communicating over RFCOMM
- Bluetooth security in RFCOMM
- Specifying the master and slave device

4.1 Overview

The SPP is the Bluetooth profile that realizes an RFCOMM connection between two devices. The SPP is defined as a building block profile. This means that other Bluetooth profiles are built on the SPP. Figure 4.1 shows some of the Bluetooth profiles built on the SPP. In basic terms, the SPP profile defines how two Bluetooth devices establish two-way, reliable communication with the RFCOMM protocol.

The RFCOMM protocol is an emulation of an RS-232 serial port connection between two devices over a wireless link. Within JABWT, communicating with a remote device using RFCOMM is similar to communicating over a socket connection. In other words, data is sent between devices via streams. In most situations, RFCOMM should be the protocol to use within a JABWT application. This is because serial communications are widely used and the API is simple to use.

Before continuing, it is important to understand some of the terminology used within Bluetooth networking. Even though Bluetooth networking is a wireless technology, only a single "physical" link exists

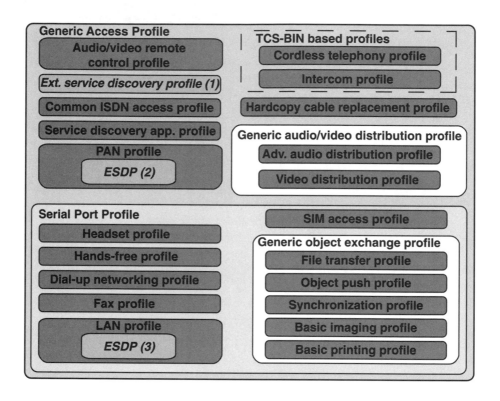

Figure 4.1   Bluetooth profiles defined by the Bluetooth SIG [3].

between any two Bluetooth devices. Although there may be only a single link, there may be multiple connections between the two devices over this link (Figure 4.2). The situation is similar to the wired networking world. Although there is only a single Ethernet cable between two devices, there may be multiple connections between the two devices.

Bluetooth wireless technology provides different levels of security over a Bluetooth link. There are four types of Bluetooth security: pairing, authentication, encryption, and authorization. Pairing is the first step in the process of Bluetooth security. When two devices come into contact with one another for the first time and want to use security, the devices must establish a shared secret used for authentication and encryption. Pairing requires the user of each device to input a common code or PIN into each device. The PIN is then used to do an

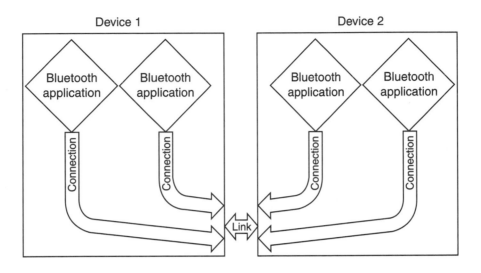

Figure 4.2 Multiple Bluetooth connections can exist over a single Bluetooth link.

initial authentication of both devices. After the initial pairing, a shared secret is established and is stored within the Bluetooth device to allow authentication of both devices in the future without the need for the pairing process. Figure 4.3 shows how two devices can retrieve the PIN to complete the pairing process. The pairing process is transparent to the application. It is the responsibility of the BCC to retrieve the PIN from the user or determine what the PIN should be.

Bluetooth authentication verifies the identity of one device to another device using a challenge and response scheme. Bluetooth authentication does not authenticate users but authenticates devices. When device A wants to authenticate device B, device A sends a challenge to device B (Figure 4.4). When it receives this challenge, device B applies the shared secret to the challenge and sends the result to device A. Device A then combines the challenge that was sent with its shared secret and compares the result with the result sent from device B. Although it authenticates device B to device A, this process does not authenticate device A to device B. The same process must be used to authenticate device A to device B. To perform authentication, device A and device B must complete the pairing process so that the shared secret can be established.

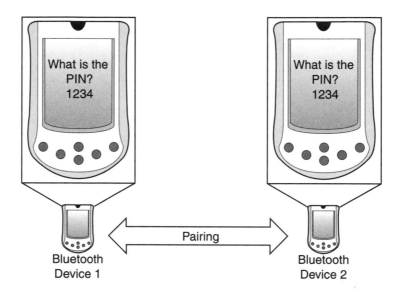

Figure 4.3   For two devices to complete the pairing process, a common PIN must be entered.

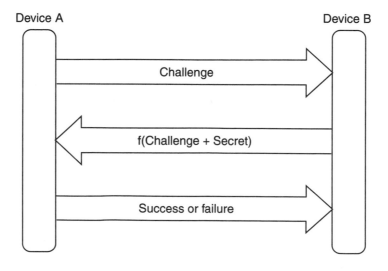

Figure 4.4   Device A attempts to authenticate device B.

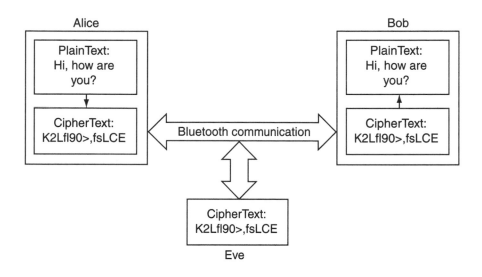

Figure 4.5 Example of encryption.

Once the authentication process has been completed, encryption can be turned on. Figure 4.5 shows an example of what it means for a link to be encrypted. Encryption is used to prevent an eavesdropper, Eve, from intercepting communication between two entities, Alice and Bob. When one device wants to turn on encryption, it must ask the other Bluetooth device to do so also. If the other device accepts the request, all packets between the devices are encrypted. If the other device rejects the request, the connection is closed. Unlike the mechanism of authentication, it is not possible for communications sent from device A to device B to be encrypted while communications sent from device B to device A are unencrypted.

Another option within Bluetooth security is authorization. Authorization is the process of determining whether a connection request from a specific Bluetooth device should be granted. Authorization is completed on a connection-by-connection basis. The Bluetooth specification has also defined the concept of a trusted device. What is a trusted device? A trusted device is a device that is automatically granted authorization when authorization is requested. In other words, a trusted device is authorized to connect to any service on the local device. When a trusted device connects to a service that requires authorization, the request is automatically accepted without the BCC asking the user if the device is authorized to use the service. The BCC is in charge of maintaining the list of trusted devices. When an authorization request is received by the BCC for a nontrusted device, the BCC requests the user to grant or deny the connection.

Each level of security builds on the previous level. Authentication requires pairing. Encryption and authorization require authentication. JABWT enforces these requirements. If encryption is requested on a link and the link has not been authenticated, the JABWT implementation authenticates the remote device before encrypting the link.

4.2 API Capabilities

No new methods or classes were defined for RFCOMM communication; instead, existing classes and interfaces from the GCF were used. As with all J2ME communication, using RFCOMM starts with the GCF. A well-defined connection string is passed to `Connector.open()` to establish the connection. For client connections, a `StreamConnection` object is returned from `Connector.open()`. `Connector.open()` returns a `StreamConnectionNotifier` object if a server connection string is used. Once a connection has been established between a client and a server, the client and server communicate via `InputStreams` and `OutputStreams`.

JABWT allows security to be modified by an application at two different times. Security can be modified when a connection is first established and after the connection is established. To set security when a connection is established, three parameters can be added to the connection string passed to `Connector.open()`. (Section 6.3.3 describes how to change security on a connection after the connection is established.) The BCC is responsible for verifying that these parameters are acceptable and resolving conflicting security requests. In other words, all security requests on a link must go through the BCC.

Resolving conflicting security requests is a complicated problem because changing security in an unexpected way can cause serious problems for an application. For example, a banking application may allow a user to pay for groceries over a Bluetooth link. The application transmits the user's bank account number over an encrypted Bluetooth link. If the link is not encrypted, someone listening on the Bluetooth link could steal the user's bank account number.

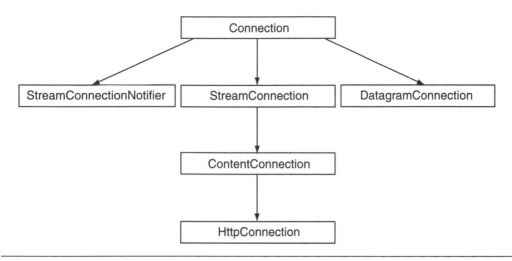

Figure 4.6 GCF defined by CLDC.

Although JABWT does not specify how conflicting security requests should be handled, it is expected that most implementations prevent one application from decreasing the security on a link as long as another application believes the link has a certain security level. This expectation is based on the fact that an implementation that does not enforce this policy would leave an application with no expectations of security at any time. This expectation leads to three possible implementations. First, the BCC enforces the same level of security on all applications. If an application requests a different level of security, the application's request fails. Second, the first application to request security on a link receives its requested level of security. If a second application comes along and requests a higher level of security, the second application's request fails. The third approach is the most complicated. As in the second approach, the first application receives the level of security it requests on a link. If the second application requests a higher level of security, the JABWT implementation attempts to increase the level of security on the link. If the request succeeds, the second application receives its connection. If the second application requests a lower level of security, the second application receives a connection with the first connection's higher level of security.

Within every Bluetooth link between two devices, one of the devices is considered the master and the other the slave of the connec-

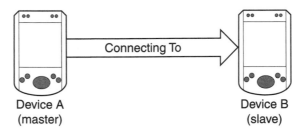

Figure 4.7   Master connects to slave.

tion. The master device drives the frequency-hopping sequence used by both devices during the wireless connection. (The frequency hopping is done for security reasons and to minimize interference with other wireless devices.) For most applications, the master and slave configuration is not important, but if a developer is implementing a Bluetooth profile, the developer may need to consider which device is the master and which is the slave. Another reason a developer would like to configure a device to be master is to enable the device to form a *piconet*. A piconet is a network of up to seven Bluetooth devices. Being the master allows a device to establish additional connections to other devices in the area. The device that initiates a connection starts out as the master of the connection. The device with the service being connected to is initially the slave (Figure 4.7).

4.3 Programming with the API

All RFCOMM communication begins with `Connector.open()` and a valid connection string. All connection strings passed to `Connector.open()` are of the form

{scheme}:{target}{params}

To use RFCOMM, the {scheme} used for both client and server connection strings is `btspp`. The {target} and {params} are different depending on whether the connection is a client or a server.

In addition to the {scheme} being the same for client and server connections, there are similar {params} for both types of connections. Table 4.1 lists all the valid {params} that may be used in an RFCOMM, L2CAP, and OBEX over RFCOMM connection string along with the

Table 4.1   Valid Parameters for RFCOMM Connection Strings

Name	Description	Valid Values	Client or Server
master	Specifies whether this device must be the master of the connection	true, false	Both
authenticate	Specifies whether the remote device must be authenticated before establishing a connection	true, false	Both
encrypt	Specifies whether the link must be encrypted	true, false	Both
authorize	Specifies whether all connections to this device must receive authorization to use the service	true, false	Server
name	Specifies the ServiceName attribute in the service record (service records are explained further in Chapter 7)	Any valid string	Server

valid values for each of the {params}. All other values would cause an `IllegalArgumentException` to be thrown by `Connector.open()`. Each of these {params} is optional and therefore does not have to be included in the connection string.

The parameters that set the security requirements of RFCOMM, L2CAP, and OBEX over RFCOMM are "authenticate," "encrypt," and "authorize." These parameters have the value "true" or "false." The security parameters do not have to be set. If the parameter is not included in the string, the implementation interprets the parameter as false unless another parameter requires this parameter to be true. For example, if "encrypt" is set to "true" and "authenticate" is not part of the connection string, the link is authenticated even though it was not set to "true" in the connection string, because encryption requires authentication.

Certain combinations of parameters are not valid. "Authenticate" cannot be set to "false" if "encrypt" or "authorize" is set to "true." If an invalid combination of parameters is passed to `Connector.open()`, a `BluetoothConnectionException` is thrown. If the authentication, encryption, or authorization request fails during the establishment of the connection, a `BluetoothConnectionException` also is thrown.

To enable implementing profiles over a JABWT implementation, JABWT provides a way for a service to request that the local device be the master of the connection. When the service makes the request to

`Connector.open()` to retrieve the service's notifier object, the connection string to produce the notifier object takes another parameter. The "master" parameter has two valid values: "true" and "false." If the "master" parameter is set to "true," then to use the service, the device initiating the connection must give up the master role. If the "master" parameter is "false," the device does not care whether it is the master or the slave. There is no API to force a device to be the slave. The "master" parameter is valid for client and server connection strings. Not all devices support changing the master of a connection. If the device does not support changing the master of a connection, then a `BluetoothConnectionException` is thrown. (For more information on connection strings, see Chapter 8 for L2CAP and Chapter 5 for OBEX.)

The "name" parameter is a server-specific parameter. The "name" parameter specifies the ServiceName attribute in the service record. The "name" parameter can have a value of any valid string.

4.3.1   Establishing a Server Connection

For establishment of a server connection, a valid server connection string must be passed to `Connector.open()`. The {scheme} to use is `btspp`. The {target} for server connections is the keyword //localhost followed by a colon and the universally unique identifier (UUID) for the service to add to the service record. Not only is a `StreamConnectionNotifier` created by `Connector.open()`, but also a basic service record is created. It is not registered into the service record database until `acceptAndOpen()` is called on the `StreamConnectionNotifier` object returned by `Connector.open()`. (See Chapter 7 for more information on service registration.)

Here are some examples of valid server connection strings and their meaning:

"btspp://localhost:102030405060708090A1B1C1D1E100;name=Print_Server; master=false" establishes a server connection with the UUID 0x102030405060708090A1B1C1D1E100 in the service record. The connection string also specifies that the ServiceName attribute is "Print_Server" and that the server can be either the master or the slave of the connection.

"btspp://localhost:1231242432434AAAABB;authenticate=true;authorize=true;name=Echo" establishes a server connection with the

0x1231242432434AAAABB UUID in the service record and the ServiceName attribute set to "Echo." All communication to the server must be authenticated and authorized.

"btspp://localhost:AB9324854381231231231ADEFE;encrypt=true;au thorize=true;master=true" creates a server connection object with a service record that has the UUID 0xAB9324854381231231231ADEFE in its service record. The server connection must be the master of the link. As far as security is concerned, the link must be authenticated, encrypted, and authorized. (Authentication is implied by setting the encrypt or authorize parameters to true.)

After `Connector.open()` returns a `StreamConnectionNotifier` object, we are ready to attempt to establish a connection. The `acceptAndOpen()` method should be called after `Connector.open()`. This method blocks until a client connects to the server. The `acceptAndOpen()` method returns a `StreamConnection` object. With the `StreamConnection` object, the application can read and write to the client application.

To show how to create a simple RFCOMM application, we will develop an echo application. The `EchoServer` MIDlet accepts connections from the `EchoClient` MIDlet, described later in this chapter. The `EchoServer` then reads messages sent from the client and sends the same message in reply. The `BluetoothMIDlet` class from earlier is reused. The thread started by the `BluetoothMIDlet` accepts connections from clients. The `run()` method of this thread creates a `Form` and sets it to the current display. An "Exit" `Command` is added to the `Form` to destroy the MIDlet. Recall that the `BluetoothMIDlet` processes all `Command` events by destroying the MIDlet, which is exactly what we need it to do here.

```
package com.jabwt.book;

import java.lang.*;
import java.io.*;
import javax.microedition.lcdui.*;
import javax.microedition.io.*;
import javax.bluetooth.*;

public class EchoServer extends BluetoothMIDlet {
    /**
     * Accepts connections from RFCOMM clients and
     * echoes back what is received from the client.
```

```
 * This method also displays the messages from a
 * client on a Form. It also displays on the Form the
 * connection string to use to connect to this service.
 */
public void run() {
    // Create the output Form and set it to be the
    // current Displayable
    Form msgForm = new Form("Echo Server");
    msgForm.addCommand(new Command("Exit",
      Command.EXIT, 1));
    msgForm.setCommandListener(this);
    Display.getDisplay(this).setCurrent(msgForm);
  }
}
```

Next, a `StreamConnectionNotifier` object must be created to accept connections from the client. After the notifier object is created, the `displayConnectionString()` method is called. This method determines the connection string that a client should use to connect to this server. This connection string is appended to the `Form`. The connection string is used by the client to eliminate the need to do device and service discovery. The changes needed to append the connection string to the `Form` are shown below. Throughout the book a gray box is used to identify additions or changes to code shown previously. Some of the code shown previously will be repeated to provide context, but this repeated code will appear outside the gray box.

```
public class EchoServer extends BluetoothMIDlet{

    ...

    /**
     * Adds the connection string to use to connect to
     * this service to the screen.
     *
     * @param f the Form to add the connection string to
     * @param notifier the notifier object to retrieve
     * the connection
     * string from
     */
    private void displayConnectionString(Form f,
      StreamConnectionNotifier notifier) {
```

```
    try {
        // Retrieve the connection string to use to
        // connect to this server
        LocalDevice device = LocalDevice.getLocalDevice();
        ServiceRecord record = device.getRecord(notifier);
        String connString = record.getConnectionURL(
          ServiceRecord.NOAUTHENTICATE_NOENCRYPT, false);
        int index = connString.indexOf(';');
        connString = connString.substring(0, index);

        // Display the connection string on the Form
        f.append("Connection String:\n");
        f.append(connString);
        f.append("\n");
    } catch (BluetoothStateException e) {
        f.append("BluetoothStateException: " +
          e.getMessage());
    }
}
```

```
...
```

```
public void run() {

  // Create the output Form and set it to be the
  // current Displayable
  Form msgForm = new Form("Echo Server");
  msgForm.addCommand(new Command("Exit", Command.EXIT, 1));
  msgForm.setCommandListener(this);

  Display.getDisplay(this).setCurrent(msgForm);
```

```
    try {
        // Create the notifier object
        StreamConnectionNotifier notifier =
          (StreamConnectionNotifier)
          Connector.open(
          "btspp://localhost:123456789ABCDE;name=Echo Server");
        //Display the connection string on the Form
        displayConnectionString(msgForm, notifier);
    } catch (IOException e) {
        msgForm.append("IOException: " + e.getMessage());
    }
```

```
  }
}
```

The final part of the `EchoServer` MIDlet is the most important. After the connection string is displayed on the `Form`, the `run()` method enters a forever loop that accepts connections from a client via a call to `acceptAndOpen()`. The input and output streams are opened once the connection has been established. The `run()` method then reads data from the `InputStream`. After the data is read, the `run()` method appends the data to the `Form` and sends the data in reply. The `run()` method continues to read data until the client closes the input stream.

```
public class EchoServer extends BluetoothMIDlet {

    ...

  public void run() {

    // Create the output Form and set it to be the
    // current Displayable
    Form msgForm = new Form("Echo Server");
    msgForm.addCommand(new Command("Exit",
      Command.EXIT, 1));
    msgForm.setCommandListener(this);

    Display.getDisplay(this).setCurrent(msgForm);

    try {
      //Create the notifier object
      StreamConnectionNotifier notifier =
        (StreamConnectionNotifier)
          Connector.open(
            "btspp://localhost:123456789ABCDE"
              + "name=Echo Server");

      // Display the connection string on the Form
      displayConnectionString(msgForm, notifier);

      // Continue accepting connections until the MIDlet
      // is destroyed
      for (;;) {
        StreamConnection conn = notifier.acceptAndOpen();

        OutputStream output = conn.openOutputStream();
        InputStream input = conn.openInputStream();

        // Continue reading the input stream until the
        // stream is closed. Display the data on the
        // screen and write it to the output stream.
```

```
      byte[] data = new byte[10];
      int length = 0;
      while ((length = input.read(data)) != -1) {
        msgForm.append(new String(data, 0, length));

        output.write(data, 0, length);
      }

      // Close the streams and the connection
      output.close();
      input.close();
      conn.close();
    }
  } catch (IOException e) {
    msgForm.append("IOException: " + e.getMessage());
  }
}
}
```

4.3.2 Establishing a Client Connection

To establish a client connection, the `btspp` {scheme} is used with the {target} starting with two slashes followed by the Bluetooth address of the device to connect to and the server channel identifier of the service to connect to. The client connection string takes "master," "authenticate," and "encrypt" as {params}. When this connection string is passed to `Connector.open()`, the JABWT implementation attempts to establish a connection to the desired service. If the connection is established, `Connector.open()` returns a `StreamConnection` object, which allows the application to read and write to the server. Unlike the server's connection, the client's connection to the server has been established once `Connector.open()` returns.

What is the server channel identifier, and how does a service get one? The server channel identifier is similar to a TCP/IP port number. It uniquely identifies a service on a device. The server channel identifier is a number between 0 and 31. The server channel identifier is assigned by the JABWT implementation for a service. The server channel identifier is set in the service record's ProtocolDescriptorList attribute. This allows the `ServiceRecord`'s `getConnectionURL()` method to generate the connection string to use to connect to the service. Because a device is not aware of the devices and services in an area, it is expected that most JABWT applications will use the `getConnectionURL()` method.

Now for some examples of client connection strings:

"btspp://008003DD8901:1;authenticate=true" creates an RFCOMM connection to the device with a Bluetooth address of 008003DD8901. It connects to the service identified by the server channel identifier 1. The connection string also causes the remote device to be authenticated.

"btspp://008012973FAE:5;master=true;encrypt=true" establishes an RFCOMM connection to the Bluetooth device with the address of 008012973FAE. The connection string connects to server channel 5. The connection string requires the local device to be the master of the connection and the link to be authenticated and encrypted.

After the connection is established and a `StreamConnection` object is obtained with `Connector.open()`, the input and output streams should be used to send and receive data. The streams are available via the `openInputStream()`, `openDataInputStream()`, `openOutputStream()`, and `openDataOutputStream()` methods. To end the connection, the `close()` method must be called on the `StreamConnection` object and any open input or output streams.

The `EchoClient` MIDlet shows how to establish an RFCOMM connection to a server and how to communicate with the server. The `EchoClient` allows a user to send messages to the `EchoServer` MIDlet, which echoes back what is sent. The `EchoClient` then reads the reply and appends the reply to a `Form` so that the user can see what was sent.

To eliminate the need to do device and service discovery, the Bluetooth address and server channel are retrieved from the user via a `Form`. The user enters the Bluetooth address and server channel from the connection string displayed on the `EchoServer` screen when the `EchoServer` starts. Figure 4.8 shows the `EchoServer` and how it displays the connection string to use to connect to this server. In this example, the Bluetooth address to connect to is 0080375a0032, and the server channel is 1. When the `EchoClient` starts, a `Form` is displayed that asks the user to enter the Bluetooth address and server channel for the echo server. After the user enters the information for the server, the user can select the "Connect" `Command`.

```
package com.jabwt.book;

import java.lang.*;
import java.io.*;
```

Figure 4.8   EchoServer MIDlet when it starts (emulation only).

```
import javax.bluetooth.*;
import javax.microedition.io.*;
import javax.microedition.lcdui.*;
import javax.microedition.midlet.*;

public class EchoClient extends BluetoothMIDlet {
    /**
     * The Form that interacts with the user. Used to
     * retrieve the connection information and the
     * text to send.
     */
    private Form connForm;

    /**
     * The Command used to Connect to the server.
     */
```

```java
    private Command connectCommand;

    /**
     * Called when the MIDlet is made active. This
     * method displays
     * a Form that retrieves the Bluetooth address and
     * the channel ID
     * of the Echo Server.
     */
    public void startApp() throws
      MIDletStateChangeException {

        // Create the Form. Add the Connect and Exit
        // Commands to the Form.
        connForm = new Form("Echo Client");
        connectCommand = new Command("Connect",
          Command.OK, 1);
        connForm.addCommand(connectCommand);
        connForm.addCommand(new Command("Exit",
          Command.EXIT, 1));
        connForm.setCommandListener(this);

        // Add the TextFields to retrieve the
        // Bluetooth address and channel
        // ID of the Echo Server
        TextField address = new TextField("Address",
          null, 12, TextField.ANY);
        connForm.append(address);

        TextField channel = new TextField("Channel",
          null, 2,
        TextField.NUMERIC);
        connForm.append(channel);
        Display.getDisplay(this).setCurrent(connForm);
    }
}
```

Now that the Bluetooth address and server channel have been retrieved, a connection must be made to the EchoServer. To make a connection, a new thread is created and started if the "Connect" Command is selected. This requires the EchoClient to implement the Runnable interface and define a run() method. The run() method creates the connection string and then attempts to establish a connection. The run() method also removes the two TextFields that retrieved the Bluetooth address and server channel ID. If a connection can be established, the "Connect" Command is replaced with the "Send" Command, and a TextField is added to the Form to request a message to send.

```
public class EchoClient extends BluetoothMIDlet {
    // The InputStream to receive data from the server.
    private InputStream input;
    // The OutputStream to send data to the server.
    private OutputStream output;
    // The connection to the server
    private StreamConnection conn;

    ...

    public void commandAction(Command c, Displayable d) {
        if (c.getCommandType() == Command.OK) {
            // The Connect Command was selected so start a
            // thread to
            // establish the connection to the server
            new Thread(this).start();
        } else {
            notifyDestroyed();
        }
    }

    /**
     * Create the connection string from the information
     * entered by the user.
     * @return the connection string
     */
    private String getConnectionString() {
        // Retrieve the TextFields from the Form
        TextField address = (TextField)connForm.get(0);
        TextField channel = (TextField)connForm.get(1);

        // Create the connection string
        StringBuffer temp = new StringBuffer("btspp://");
        temp.append(address.getString());
        temp.append(":");
        temp.append(channel.getString());

        // Remove the TextFields from the Form
        connForm.delete(0);
        connForm.delete(0);

        return temp.toString();
```

```
        }
        /**
         * Establishes a connection to the server.
         *
         * @param connString the connection string to connect
         * to the server
         * @return true if the connection was established;
         * false if the
         * connection failed
         */
        private boolean connectToServer(String connString) {
         try {

            // Establish a connection to the server
            conn = (StreamConnection)
              Connector.open(connString);

            // Retrieve the input and output streams to
            // communicate with
            input = conn.openInputStream();
            output = conn.openOutputStream();

            return true;
          } catch (IOException e) {
            connForm.append("Connect failed (IOException: ");
            connForm.append(e.getMessage());
            connForm.append(")\n");

            return false;
          }
        }
        /**
         * Retrieves the Bluetooth address and channel ID
         * from the Form.
         * This method then establishes a connection
         * to the server.
         */
        public void run() {

          String connString = getConnectionString();
          connForm.append("Connecting to Server\n");

          if (connectToServer(connString)) {
            connForm.append("Done");
```

```
          // Remove the Connect Command and add the Send
          // Command to this Form
          connForm.removeCommand(connectCommand);
          Command sendCommand = new Command("Send",
            Command.SCREEN, 1);
          connForm.addCommand(sendCommand);

          // Add a TextField to the Form to retrieve the
          // text to send to
          // the server from the user
          connForm.append(new TextField("Text to send", null, 20,
            TextField.ANY));
      }
  }
}
```

Most of the previous code handles user interaction. The only code that uses JABWT is the connectToServer() method. The connectToServer() method establishes the connection and retrieves the input and output streams. The getConnectionString() method makes the connectToServer() method work because it specifies the btspp connection scheme, which specifies that the SPP and RFCOMM should be used to connect to the server.

The next step is to add code that sends a message to the server and reads the reply. To minimize the amount of work done within the MIDP CommandListener event handler, all of the communication with the server is done in a separate thread. To perform the processing in a separate thread, a new class must be created that implements the Runnable interface. The Message class does this. The Message class takes in its constructor the message, the input stream, and the output stream. When it starts, the thread of the Message class writes the message to the OutputStream. It then reads the reply from the server and displays it on the Form the user is currently viewing.

```
public class EchoClient extends BluetoothMIDlet {
    ...

    /**
     * Sends a message and reads the echo in reply.
     * Displays the reply
     * on the string and adds the TextField to the end of
     * the Form.
```

```
  */
class Message implements Runnable {

 // The message to send to the server.
 private String theMessage;
 // The InputStream to read the reply from.
 private InputStream input;
 // The OutputStream to send the message to.
 private OutputStream output;

 /**
  * Creates a new Message to send to the server.
  *
  * @param msg the message to send
  * @param in the InputStream to read the reply from
  * @param out the OutputStream to write the message to
  */
 public Message(String msg, InputStream in,
   OutputStream out) {
   theMessage = msg;
   input = in;
   output = out;
 }

 /**
  * Sends the message to the server and reads the echo
  * in reply. This method adds the echo to the Form and
  * then adds a new TextField to the end of the Form.
  */
 public void run() {

   try {
     // Send the message to the server.
     byte[] data = theMessage.getBytes();
     output.write(data);

     // Read the reply and keep it in a StringBuffer until
     // the full reply is received.
     int fullLength = data.length;
     int length = input.read(data);
     fullLength -= length;

     StringBuffer buf = new StringBuffer(new
       String(data, 0, length));
     while (fullLength > 0) {
```

```
            length = input.read(data);
            fullLength -= length;
            buf = buf.append(new String(data, 0, length));
        }

        // Display the reply on the Form and remove the
        // final new line sent from the server
        connForm.append("\n");
        String displayString = buf.toString();
        displayString = displayString.substring(0,
            displayString.length() - 1);

        connForm.append(displayString);

    } catch (IOException e) {
        connForm.append("\nFailed to send message: " +
          e.getMessage());
    }

    connForm.append(new TextField("Text to send",
      null, 20, TextField.ANY));
    }
  }
}
```

The final step is to use the `Message` class within the `EchoClient` MIDlet. This requires modifying the `commandAction()` method. The if statement is changed to a `switch` statement to determine whether the "Send," "Exit," or "Connect" `Command` was selected. If the "Send" `Command` was selected, the `commandAction()` method determines whether the last element in the `Form` is a `TextField`. This check is done to prevent two messages from being sent at the same time. The `TextField` is not the last `Item` if a message is currently being sent. If no message is being sent, then the `Text-Field` is the last `Item`. After this check is made, the `commandAction()` method creates a new `Message` object and starts the `Message` object in a thread. This thread sends the message and receives the reply.

```
public class EchoClient extends BluetoothMIDlet {

  ...

  public void commandAction(Command c, Displayable d) {
    switch (c.getCommandType()) {
```

```
case Command.OK:
  // The Connect Command was selected so start a
  // thread to
  // establish the connection to the server
  new Thread(this).start();
  break;

case Command.SCREEN:
  // The Send Command was selected so send the
  // message to the server
  int index = connForm.size() - 1;

  // If the last Item is a TextField, then no
  // message is
  // currently being sent so send a Message.
  Item item = connForm.get(index);
  if (item instanceof TextField) {
    TextField field = (TextField)item;
    connForm.delete(index);
    // Start a thread to send the message to the server
    // and process the reply
    new Thread(new Message(field.getString() +
      "\n", input, output)).start();
  }

  break;

case Command.EXIT:
  // The Exit Command was selected so destroy the
  // MIDlet
  try {
    input.close();
    output.close();
    conn.close();
  } catch (Exception e) {
  }
  notifyDestroyed();
  break;
    }
  }

  ...
}
```

Figure 4.9 EchoClient (A) and EchoServer (B) communicating over RFCOMM (emulation only).

This completes the echo client/server application. Figure 4.9 shows the `EchoClient` and `EchoServer` running. Now the `EchoClient` is able to send messages to the server while the `EchoServer` is able to echo back any message sent from the client. Most of the code for both applications is not specific to JABWT but is MIDP code that provides for interaction between the application and the user. This is likely the case for most applications that use JABWT.

4.4 Summary

RFCOMM will likely be the most used Bluetooth protocol within JABWT because RFCOMM provides serial two-way communication and reuses familiar APIs from J2ME. The SPP is the Bluetooth profile realization of

RFCOMM. Many Bluetooth profiles are built on the SPP to take advantage of existing serial port applications and protocols developed for wired communication.

Important concepts introduced in this chapter are links and connections. Two Bluetooth devices may have only a single Bluetooth link between them, but this link allows multiple Bluetooth connections. Although links are device by device, connections are at the JABWT application layer. In addition to the terms *links* and *connection*, the concepts of master and slave devices are introduced. The master device drives the frequency-hopping sequence used to communicate between two devices. Different Bluetooth profiles require one device to be the master and another device the slave. Being the master allows a device to accept and establish connections to other devices. By establishing these additional connections, the master device is able to set up a piconet.

The basic concepts of Bluetooth security are covered. Bluetooth provides four types of security on a link basis. Pairing is the initial process of identifying two devices to each other by exchanging a PIN outside of Bluetooth communication. Pairing sets up a shared secret between the devices so that pairing does not need to be completed every time. After pairing is completed, authentication can occur. Authentication is the process of verifying the identity of another device. After authentication has occurred, encryption and/or authorization can occur. Encryption is the process of encoding and decoding a message so that an eavesdropper cannot listen in on the conversation. Finally, authorization is the process of determining whether another device has permission to use a specific service.

Because RFCOMM provides reliable two-way communication, the `StreamConnection` and `StreamConnectionNotifier` interfaces from the GCF are reused. All RFCOMM connections start with a call to `Connector.open()` with a valid RFCOMM connection string. The connection string can include parameters for master/slave and Bluetooth security. If a client connection string is used in `Connector.open()`, a `StreamConnection` object is returned when the connection is established to the server. An RFCOMM server is created by calling `Connector.open()` with a server connection string, and a `StreamConnectionNotifier` object is returned. With the `StreamConnectionNotifier` object, the server can accept connections from RFCOMM clients by calling `acceptAndOpen()`. After the connection has been established, input and output streams can be retrieved to read and write data.

5 OBEX

This chapter covers the following topics:

- What is OBEX?
- When should OBEX be used?
- How does the OBEX API fit into the JABWT specification?
- How does OBEX work?
- Establishing an OBEX connection
- Setting and retrieving OBEX headers
- Initiating and responding to OBEX requests
- Using OBEX authentication

5.1 Overview

The IrOBEX (Infrared Object Exchange protocol) [29] is defined by IrDA as an alternative to the HyperText Transport Protocol (HTTP) for embedded devices. IrOBEX targets memory-constrained embedded devices, which have slower processing speeds. Whereas HTTP makes a single request and a single reply, IrOBEX allows devices to break up requests and replies into smaller chunks. By breaking up the requests into smaller chunks of data, IrOBEX allows the data to be processed as it is received and allows a request or reply to be aborted.

IrOBEX, like HTTP, is transport neutral. In other words, IrOBEX works over almost any other transport layer protocol. Whereas the initial implementations of IrOBEX used Infrared as the transport, there are presently implementations of IrOBEX that are running over TCP, serial, and RFCOMM connections. Because IrOBEX may run over different transports and can break up requests and replies, IrOBEX may be optimized to a specific transport protocol. What does this mean? Every

IrOBEX packet is segmented to fit within each transport layer packet. This allows for efficient use of bandwidth.

IrOBEX has become even more popular since the Bluetooth SIG licensed the protocol from IrDA. When the protocol is used with Bluetooth wireless technology, the *Ir* is dropped, and the protocol is referred to as *OBEX*. (From this point forward, *OBEX* and *IrOBEX* are used interchangeably.) The Bluetooth SIG defined OBEX as one of the protocols in the Bluetooth protocol stack. OBEX sits on the RFCOMM protocol. The Bluetooth SIG went a step farther. The SIG realized that OBEX is an excellent building block protocol from which to create Bluetooth profiles. To facilitate building new profiles, the Bluetooth SIG defined the GOEP [3] to be the profile that defines how OBEX works within the Bluetooth environment.

The OBEX API defined in JABWT is an optional API. This means that the OBEX API may be implemented within a device that supports the Bluetooth APIs, but just because a device supports the Bluetooth APIs does not imply that it supports the OBEX APIs. This allows the OBEX API to be included in devices that do not support the Bluetooth APIs. The OBEX API is independent of the Bluetooth APIs.

So why would a developer use OBEX on a device that has RFCOMM, L2CAP, or TCP/IP? OBEX is a structured protocol that allows separation of data and the attributes of data. Using OBEX allows clear definition of one request from another. Using protocols such as RFCOMM or TCP/IP requires the applications to know how data is sent and when to send the reply. OBEX hides this within the protocol. OBEX is like the Extensible Markup Language (XML). It provides structure to the data sent whereas RFCOMM and TCP/IP simply send bytes.

5.1.1 Use Cases

OBEX can be used for a variety of purposes. The protocol is being used in PDAs as a way to exchange electronic business cards. OBEX also has been used to synchronize embedded devices with desktop computers. The OBEX API defined for the Java programming language is intended to allow OBEX to be used for an even wider range of applications.

Provisioning

A common problem for MIDP devices, such as cell phones, is how to get the MIDlets onto the device to run. (i.e., how do you provision

MIDlets?) OBEX is an ideal protocol for provisioning. One tool can be written that provides for over-the-air provisioning. Over-the-air provisioning is the act of retrieving MIDlets from a centralized server. OBEX allows the service provider to speed up the transmission of MIDlets over the air, which saves the user money. OBEX also provides ways to recover from a lost connection. In other words, the user does not have to retrieve the entire MIDlet if the connection to the server is lost. The user simply retrieves the remaining chunks of data.

With the introduction of Bluetooth wireless technology, the software kiosk is another way to provision MIDlets to user devices. In this approach, a user approaches a software kiosk and establishes an OBEX connection with the software kiosk over RFCOMM. The user finds the MIDlets he or she wants to download. These MIDlets could be purchased and then downloaded to the user's device.

Printing

J2ME has begun to be used by businesses as a way to keep in touch with employees. Being able to send and retrieve e-mail is now possible. Being able to update and check an employee's calendar and "to do" list also is possible. There is one drawback to using a J2ME device for these tasks. Most devices have a very limited screen size; therefore users find it quite helpful for those devices to send e-mail or the calendar to a printer. Up to this point, the J2ME space contained devices that could talk back only with a central server. With the introduction of JABWT to J2ME, any two devices can talk. Sending documents to print is a natural use of OBEX. The Bluetooth SIG has released the Basic Printing Profile, which uses OBEX [27].

5.1.2 Protocol Description

OBEX is built on six basic operations: CONNECT, SETPATH, GET, PUT, ABORT, and DISCONNECT. The client initiates every operation with a request and waits for the server to send its response. Every OBEX session begins with a CONNECT request from the client to the server. (Although the IrOBEX specification defined a connectionless OBEX, it is not described here. The OBEX API defined by JABWT does not address this type of OBEX.) Every session ends with a DISCONNECT request. Between the CONNECT and DISCONNECT requests, the client may send any number of SETPATH, GET, ABORT, or PUT requests. The

ABORT request is a special type of request. It ends a PUT or GET operation before the operation ends. (A PUT/GET operation is made of multiple PUT or GET requests and replies.)

Within each request and reply, OBEX headers may be sent. The
OBEX specification defines a list of common headers. The common
headers include but are not limited to:

- NAME, which specifies the name of the object
- LENGTH, which specifies the length of the object
- TYPE, which specifies the Multipurpose Internet Mail Extensions
  (MIME) type of the object
- COUNT, which is used by a CONNECT request to specify the
  number of objects to send or receive
- DESCRIPTION, a short description of the object
- HTTP, which specifies an HTTP header
- BODY, which specifies part of the object
- END OF BODY, which specifies the last part of the object

The OBEX specification defines how these common headers are
encoded. For example, the NAME header must be a Unicode string.
The BODY and END OF BODY headers are used to send or retrieve
objects from a server via PUT or GET requests. The END OF BODY
signals to the receiver that this is the last chunk of the object. In addition to the common headers, the specification also allows 64 user-
defined headers. The specification breaks these headers into four
groups of 16 headers. Each group represents a different type of data.
There are groups for Unicode strings, 4-byte unsigned integers, single
bytes, and byte sequences.

The OBEX specification defines two additional special operations:
the PUT-DELETE and CREATE-EMPTY operations. The PUT-DELETE
operation is a PUT operation with a NAME header and no BODY header.
This operation is used to tell the server to delete the object with the
specified name. The CREATE-EMPTY operation also is a PUT operation,
but the CREATE-EMPTY operation contains a NAME and an END OF
BODY header with no data. The CREATE-EMPTY operation signals to
the server to create the object with the specified name with nothing in
the object.

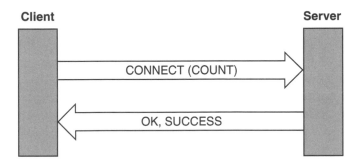

Figure 5.1 OBEX CONNECT operation.

5.1.3 Example Session

Every OBEX session begins with the client issuing a CONNECT request. If the client wants, the client can include additional headers to send to the server. When the server receives the request, the server processes the headers and decides whether it will accept the connection request. If the server accepts the request, the server responds with an OK, SUCCESS response code. If the server rejects the request, the server responds with one of the HTTP response codes that specify why the request was not accepted. In the example in Figure 5.1, the client issues the CONNECT request and sends the COUNT header to the server to specify the number of objects to be transferred. The server processes the request and replies with the SUCCESS, OK response code.

After the connection is established, the client may want to change to a different location on the server. The client is able to change folders by using the SETPATH operation. The client sends the SETPATH operation and specifies the name of the directory to change to by using the NAME header. When the server receives the request, it may decide to allow or not allow the change. The server can deny the request for a variety of reasons, including using the NOT FOUND response if the folder does not exist on the server.

Even though the server was not able to fulfill the SETPATH operation, the session is still active and the client may continue to make requests to the server. For example, the client may want to send a file to the server. To do this, the client issues a PUT request. If the file is large,

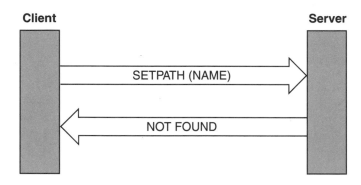

Figure 5.2   OBEX SETPATH Operation.

the client may need to break the file up into smaller chunks to send to the server. If this is the case, the client sends the initial PUT request with a NAME header, to specify the name of the file, and the BODY header containing the first chunk of the file. When the server receives this request, the server stores the first chunk of the file and replies with a CONTINUE response. When the client receives the CONTINUE response, the client sends the next chunk of the file via another PUT request with the BODY header. After storing this part of the file, the server sends another CONTINUE response. This back and forth continues until the last chunk of data is sent to the server. For the last chunk of the file, the client again sends a PUT request, but the client includes the data in an END OF BODY header rather than a BODY header. This header signals to the server that this is the last piece of the file. After the server receives notice from the client that no more data will be sent, the server responds with an OK, SUCCESS response code. When the client receives this response code, the client knows that the object was successfully sent to the server.

To end the OBEX session, the client must issue a DISCONNECT request. Usually, a DISCONNECT request does not contain any additional headers, but OBEX does not restrict headers from being included in the DISCONNECT request. When it receives a DISCONNECT request, the server frees any resources that it may have allocated and sends an OK, SUCCESS response to the client. When the client receives this response, the OBEX session has ended.

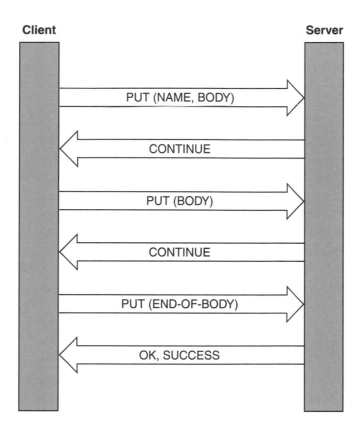

Figure 5.3   OBEX PUT operation.

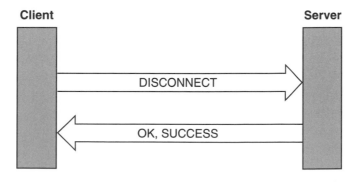

Figure 5.4   OBEX DISCONNECT operation.

It is important to remember that when the OBEX session has ended, the physical connection between the two devices may not have been closed. The transport protocol also must be disconnected. How or when this is done is not specified by the OBEX specification.

5.2 API Capabilities

The OBEX API is quite different from most existing OBEX implementations, which provide only a high-level interface to the protocol. For example, Palm developers can use an API for OBEX that allows a user to send a business card or receive an appointment but not to control how the data was sent. Control of the specifics of the transaction is not available. The Java OBEX API provides a low-level interface. The low-level interface gives developers more control over each request and reply, adding a new layer of complexity.

Although the OBEX API provides greater access to the protocol, the OBEX API hides some of the details of the protocol from developers. The OBEX API handles all the translation of OBEX headers to their corresponding byte representation. The API also hides some of the details of the CONNECT request. For example, the OBEX API implementation handles the negotiation of OBEX packet sizes. Because the packet size is not available to an application developer, the OBEX API implementation handles converting requests into multiple packets for PUT and GET requests. This allows an application to simply send the BODY data while relying on implementation of the API to convert the BODY data into different packets.

To make it easier to learn, the OBEX API was based on other Java APIs with which many developers are familiar. The client API is designed from the combination of the `javax.microedition.io.ContentConnection` interface and the `javax.microedition.io.DatagramConnection` interface from the GCF. GET, PUT and CREATE-EMPTY operations use the `javax.obex.Operation` interface, which extends the `ContentConnection` interface. The CONNECT, SETPATH, PUT-DELETE, and DISCONNECT operations work as the `DatagramConnection` interface does. For sending a message with the `DatagramConnection`, a `javax.microedition.io.Datagram` object must be created and used as the argument to the `send()` method of the `DatagramConnection` interface. Similarly, for sending OBEX headers, a `javax.obex.HeaderSet` object must be created and passed to the

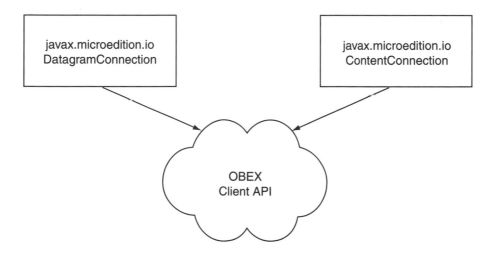

Figure 5.5   OBEX client API resulted from the combination of two connection types.

connect(), setPath(), delete(), and disconnect() methods of the javax.obex.ClientSession interface.

For an OBEX server, the OBEX API combines concepts from the javax.microedition.io.StreamConnectionNotifier interface and the Java servlet API. The server API, like the client API, is based on the GCF. After a SessionNotifier object is created by calling Connector.open(), acceptAndOpen() is called with a javax.obex. ServerRequestHandler object. The ServerRequestHandler class is similar to the java.servlet.http.HttpServlet class. The ServerRequestHandler class defines methods for each type of OBEX request that a server may receive, such as onConnect(), onDisconnect(), onPut(), onGet(), onDelete(), and onSetPath(). Only requests to which a server wants to respond must be implemented.

The OBEX API also provides a mechanism for OBEX authentication. OBEX authentication works via a challenge and response scheme using two OBEX headers. The AUTHENTICATION_CHALLENGE header is sent when an application on one device wants to authenticate an application on another device. When a device receives an AUTHENTI-CATION_CHALLENGE header, it combines the shared secret or password with the 16-byte challenge received in the AUTHENTICA-TION_CHALLENGE header. The Message Digest 5 (MD5) hash algo-rithm is applied to the combined password and challenge. The resulting

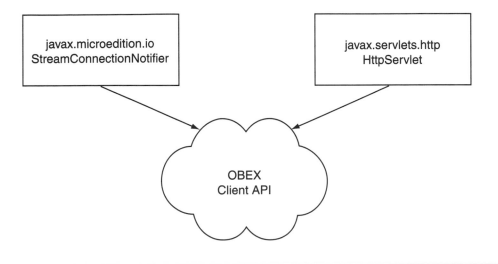

Figure 5.6   OBEX server API was created by combining two well known APIs.

value is returned in an AUTHENTICATION_RESPONSE header. When
the challenger receives the AUTHENTICATION_RESPONSE header, the
challenger combines the 16-byte challenge sent in the original
AUTHENTICATION_CHALLENGE header and the shared secret and
applies the MD5 hash algorithm. The resulting value is compared with
the value received in the AUTHENTICATION_RESPONSE header. If the
two values are equal, the other device is authenticated.

OBEX authentication is different from Bluetooth authentication.
Bluetooth authentication authenticates two Bluetooth devices to each
other. OBEX authentication authenticates two users or applications to
each other. Although Bluetooth authentication is handled at the
Bluetooth stack and radio layer, OBEX authentication is handled at the
application layer. OBEX authentication and Bluetooth authentication
can be used at the same time.

The OBEX API uses an API similar to the J2SE authentication API
for OBEX authentication. The OBEX API defines the `javax.obex.`
`Authenticator` interface. When an AUTHENTICATION_CHALLENGE
header is received, the `onAuthenticationChallenge()` method
is called. This method returns a `javax.obex.Password-`
`Authentication` object with the user name and password pair that will
be used in creating the AUTHENTICATION_RESPONSE. When

an AUTHENTICATION_RESPONSE header is received, the onAuthenticationResponse() method is called. The shared secret or password is returned from the onAuthenticationResponse() method. The OBEX API implementation handles all the hashing of challenges/passwords and validation of the authentication request.

5.3 Programming with the API

The OBEX API is built on the GCF defined in CLDC. The OBEX API adds three new interfaces that extend the javax.microedition. io.Connection interface. The javax.obex.ClientSession interface is returned from Connector.open() when a client connection string is provided. The javax.obex.SessionNotifier interface is returned from the Connector.open() method for server connections. Finally, the javax.obex.Operation interface is used to process PUT and GET requests. The javax.obex.Operation interface hides the back and forth nature of the PUT and GET requests (Figure 5.7).

In addition to these new interfaces, the OBEX API defines the javax.obex.Authenticator and javax.obex.HeaderSet interfaces. The Authenticator interface is implemented by applications that want to handle authentication challenges and responses (OBEX authentication is fully explained in section 5.3.5). The HeaderSet interface encapsulates a set of OBEX headers. All OBEX headers except

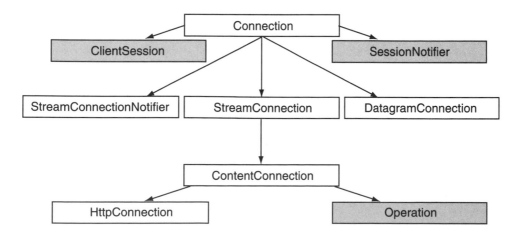

Figure 5.7   GCF with OBEX API

for the BODY, END-OF-BODY, CONNECTION-ID, AUTHENTICA-
TION_CHALLENGE, and AUTHENTICATION_RESPONSE headers can be
set in a `HeaderSet` object. OBEX headers not set within the `HeaderSet`
interface can be set and retrieved by other methods.

The OBEX API introduces three new classes. The
`javax.obex.PasswordAuthentication` class keeps user name and
password pairs for OBEX authentication. The `javax.obex.`
`ResponseCodes` class defines all the valid response codes that a server
may send to a client. Finally, servers extend the `javax.obex.`
`ServerRequestHandler` class. This class defines the methods called
when the server receives different OBEX requests.

5.3.1 Establishing a Connection

For a client or a server to use the OBEX API, the client or server must
first provide a connection string to `Connector.open()`. The OBEX API
uses the same connection URL definition as the CLDC specification:

```
{scheme}:[{target}][{params}]
```

The OBEX connection string is slightly different from the connection
strings defined in MIDP and MIDP 2.0. Because OBEX can be used
with a number of different transports, the connection string needs to
specify the transport protocol in addition to specifying OBEX. The
transport protocol is specified within the {scheme}. With the exception of OBEX over RFCOMM, the connection string defined by the
OBEX API is

```
{transport}obex://{target}{params}
```

If TCP/IP is the transport protocol used for an OBEX connection, the
{scheme} is `tcpobex`. When opening a client connection to a server,
the {target} is the IP address and port number of the server. When
opening a server connection, the {target} is just the port number of
the server. In the TCP/IP case, there are no {params} defined for a client
or server connection.

If RFCOMM is the transport protocol, the connection string does
not follow this rule. This is because the GOEP is the realization of

OBEX in the Bluetooth specification; therefore the {scheme} for OBEX over RFCOMM connections is `btgoep`. The {target} is the Bluetooth address and RFCOMM channel number to establish a client connection. For server connections, the {target} is the UUID of the service. All the valid {params} for RFCOMM are valid for OBEX over RFCOMM (see Table 4.1 for the list of valid {params} for RFCOMM).

Some example client connection strings are

btgoep://00802d5b12af:1;authenticate=yes

tcpobex://163.10.70.75:1505

irdaobex://discover;ias=MyAppOBEX,OBEX,OBEX:IrXfer;

See the JAWBT specification [20] for an explanation of the connection string for OBEX over IRDA.

Some server connection strings are

btgoep://localhost:1233212ADBAA9324BAFE23331231222C

tcpobex://:1801

irdaobex://localhost.0200

After `Connector.open()` is called with a client connection string, a `ClientSession` object is returned. A transport connection is been established by a call to `Connector.open()`, but an OBEX layer connection has not yet been established. To establish an OBEX layer connection, `ClientSession.connect()` must be called. Before the transport layer connection is closed, `ClientSession.disconnect()` must be called to close the OBEX layer connection.

On the server side, the `SessionNotifier` object returned by `Connector.open()` is used to accept connections from clients by calling `acceptAndOpen()` on the `SessionNotifier` object. The `acceptAndOpen()` method takes a `ServerRequestHandler` argument and an optional `Authenticator` argument. A developer creates a new class that extends the `ServerRequestHandler` class and implements the methods for the type of requests the developer would like the server to handle. For example, `onConnect()` should be implemented for CONNECT requests and `onGet()` for GET requests. The call to `acceptAndOpen()` does not return until a client connects. The `acceptAndOpen()` method returns a `Connection` object representing the transport layer connection to the client.

5.3.2 Manipulating OBEX Headers

OBEX communicates all of its information within headers. JABWT allows headers to be written and read via different methods based on the header. Of all the valid headers, the BODY, END-OF-BODY, AUTHENTICATION_CHALLENGE, AUTHENTICATION_RESPONSE, and CONNECTION-ID headers have specific methods that allow developers to access them. All other headers can be accessed through the HeaderSet interface.

Developers are not allowed to define their own implementation for the HeaderSet interface. Instead, developers use implementations of the interface found within the API implementation. OBEX clients use the createHeaderSet() method defined in the ClientSession interface. On the other hand, OBEX servers are passed HeaderSet implementations when they override an onXXX() method in the ServerRequestHandler class (see section 5.3.4 for more information on how to implement an OBEX server).

Once a HeaderSet object is created or received, it is very easy to access different headers. Within the HeaderSet interface are constants defined for most of the headers in the OBEX specification. In addition to these constants are 64 user-defined headers that can be used. To set a header in the object, call the setHeader() method with the header identifier and the header's value. The header's value must be of the type specified in the OBEX API. Table 5.1 is the full list of headers that can be set with setHeader(), their meaning according to the OBEX specification [29], and the type of object to use. For example, the COUNT header must be set with a java.lang.Long object, and the NAME header must be set with a java.lang.String. If setHeader() is called with a different type, IllegalArgumentException is thrown. Likewise, to retrieve a header, use the getHeader() method with the header identifier. The getHeader() method also returns an object of the type specified in Table 5.1.

Although some headers, such as NAME and COUNT, have a specific meaning, 64 headers are defined in OBEX that have no general meaning according to the OBEX specification. These are the user-defined headers. These headers should be used by applications to exchange data if the data does not fall into one of the defined OBEX headers.

The HeaderSet interface also provides a getHeaderList() method. This method returns an array of integers that represent the

Table 5.1 OBEX Header Constants in the `HeaderSet` Interface, Their Meaning, and Their Type

Value	Meaning	Type
COUNT	Used by CONNECT to specify the number of objects to be communicated during the session	`java.lang.Long`
NAME	Name of the object	`java.lang.String`
TYPE	MIME type of the object	`java.lang.String`
LENGTH	Size of the object	`java.lang.Long`
TIME_ISO_8601	Time stamp of the object (recommended header to use to time stamp an object)	`java.util.Calendar`
TIME_4_BYTE	Time stamp of the object	`java.util.Calendar`
DESCRIPTION	Brief description of the object	`java.lang.String`
TARGET	Target OBEX service	`byte[]`
HTTP	Specifies an HTTP header	`byte[]`
WHO	OBEX service processing the request	`byte[]`
OBJECT_CLASS	OBEX object class of the object	`byte[]`
APPLICATION_PARAMETER	Application-specific parameter	`byte[]`
48 to 63 (0×30 to 0×3F)	User-defined headers to send a string	`java.lang.String`
112 to 127 (0×70 to 0×7F)	User-defined headers to send a byte array	`byte[]`
176 to 191 (0×B0 to 0×BF)	User-defined headers to send a byte	`java.lang.Byte`
240 to 255 (0×F0 to 0×FF)	User-defined headers to send an unsigned integer in the range of 0 to 2^{32} to 1	`java.lang.Long`

header identifiers set within the `HeaderSet` object. The `getHeaderList()` method never returns `null`. If no headers are available via the `getHeaders()` method, `getHeaderlist()` returns an empty array. This method allows a developer to find all the headers included in a request or a reply without calling `getHeader()` on every header specified in the `HeaderSet` interface.

Five OBEX headers are handled differently. The BODY and END OF BODY headers are manipulated via input and output streams from an `Operation` object. The AUTHENTICATION_CHALLENGE and AUTHEN-TICATION_RESPONSE headers are accessed via the `Authenticator` interface. The CONNECTION-ID header can be retrieved and set through the `getConnectionID()` and `setConnectionID()` methods of `ClientSession` and `ServerRequestHandler`.

The CONNECTION-ID header is unique within OBEX. The CON-NECTION-ID header is used to differentiate multiple services provided by a single OBEX notifier object. If the CONNECTION-ID header is set in the OBEX API, the header is included in every packet sent by the API implementation.

5.3.3 Sending a Request to the Server

After establishing a transport layer connection to a server through `Connector.open()`, the client must first issue a CONNECT request to the server to establish the OBEX layer connection. The client sends a CONNECT request by calling `connect()`. Within the CONNECT request, the client may include any headers by passing the headers to `connect()`. A `HeaderSet` object is returned from `connect()`. This `HeaderSet` object allows the client to get the headers received from the server and the response code. To access the response code sent by the server, the client calls the `getResponseCode()` method. The `getResponseCode()` method returns one of the response codes defined in the `ResponseCodes` class. If the server responds with `OBEX_HTTP_OK`, the OBEX layer connection has been established. The server can send headers in the response.

The following code establishes a transport layer connection to the server and then an OBEX connection. As part of the OBEX CONNECT request, the COUNT header and a user-defined header are sent. Next the `connectToServer()` method verifies that the connection has been accepted. If the server denies the connection, the `connectToServer()` method retrieves the DESCRIPTION header to find out the reason for the failure.

```
ClientSession connectToServer(String connString) throws
  IOException {

  // Establish the transport layer connection
  ClientSession conn =
    (ClientSession)Connector.open(connString);

  // Create the HeaderSet object to send to the server
  HeaderSet header = conn.createHeaderSet();
```

```
// Set the headers to send to the server
header.setHeader(HeaderSet.COUNT, new Long(3));
header.setHeader(0x30, "New OBEX Connections");

HeaderSet response = conn.connect(header);

// Verify that the server accepted the connection
if (response.getResponseCode() !=
  ResponseCodes.OBEX_HTTP_OK) {

    try {
      conn.close();
    } catch (Exception e) {
    }

    // The connection was rejected by the server so
    // throw an IOException.
    throw new IOException("Connection rejected (0x" +
        Integer.toHexString(response.getResponseCode()) +
        ": " + (String)response.getHeader(
        HeaderSet.DESCRIPTION) +
        ")");
}

  return conn;
}
```

The delete() and disconnect() methods work in a similar way. The setPath() method works slightly differently. In a SETPATH request, the NAME header is used to specify to which directory to move. In addition to passing in the NAME header in the HeaderSet argument, any additional headers can be used. The setPath() method also takes two boolean arguments. The first argument is set to true if the server should move up one directory before moving to the directory specified by NAME. (This is similar to a cd.. in DOS.) The second argument, create, is set to true if the directory should be created if it does not exist. If the create argument is set to false, an error should occur if the client tries to move to a directory that does not exist. The following code moves to the directory specified by folderName.

```
void moveToDirectory(ClientSession conn, String folderName)
  throws IOException {
```

```
// Specify the directory to move to
HeaderSet header = conn.createHeaderSet();
header.setHeader(HeaderSet.NAME, folderName);

// Change to the directory specified. Do not backup
// one directory
// (second argument) and do not create it if it does
// not exist (third argument).
HeaderSet reply = conn.setPath(header, false, false);

// Validate that the server moved to the specified
// directory
switch (reply.getResponseCode()) {
case ResponseCodes.OBEX_HTTP_OK:
  // The request succeeded so simply return from this
  // method
  return;
case ResponseCodes.OBEX_HTTP_NOT_FOUND:
  // There was no directory with the name so throw an
  // IOException
  throw new IOException("Invalid directory");
default:
  // The request failed for some other reason, so
  // throw a generic
  // IOException
```

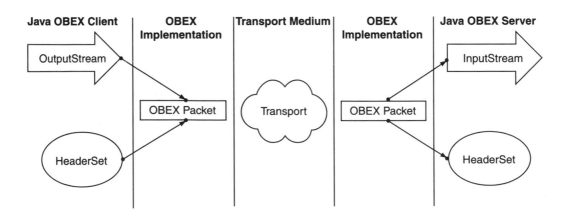

Figure 5.8 PUT request that combines `OutputStream` and `HeaderSet` into an OBEX packet.

```
      throw new IOException(
        "Move to directory request failed");
    }
  }
```

The GET and PUT operations work differently. Because PUT and GET requests pass body data between client and server, the put() and get() methods return an `Operation` object. To retrieve body data, open the `InputStream` or `DataInputStream` by using the `openInputStream()` and `openDataInputStream()` methods, respectively. On the other hand, the `OutputStream` and `DataOutputStream` returned by `openOutputStream()` and `openDataOutputStream()`, respectively, allow a client to send body data to the server. The OBEX implementation converts the BODY and non-BODY data headers to and from packets.

Sending and retrieving data must follow a set of rules depending on the type of OBEX request. Even though multiple packets can be

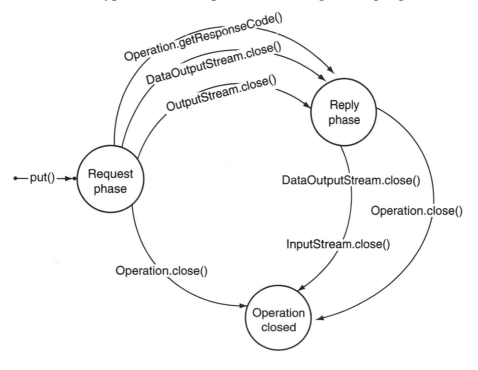

Figure 5.9 Phases of a PUT request.

exchanged, PUT and GET operations are still broken into requests and responses. During the request portion of the PUT and GET operation, the operation may write to the `OutputStream` or `DataOutputStream`. During the PUT or GET response, BODY data may be read from the `InputStream` or `DataInputStream`.

For PUT requests, closing the `OutputStream` or `DataOutputStream` ends the request portion of the operation. Calling `getResponseCode()` also causes the `OutputStream` to close and thus ends the PUT request and starts the response portion of the operation. It should be noted that calling `read()` on the `InputStream` before closing the `OutputStream` or before calling `getResponesCode()` causes the application to hang because the BODY data will not be sent until the response portion of the operation. The response portion starts when the `OutputStream` is closed or `getResponseCode()` is called.

The following code is an example of a PUT operation that sends an object to the server. The code also sends the TYPE and LENGTH headers in the PUT request.

```
void sendBytes(ClientSession conn, String type, byte[] data)
  throws IOException {

  // Set the headers in the HeaderSet to send to the
  // server
  HeaderSet header = conn.createHeaderSet();
  header.setHeader(HeaderSet.TYPE, type);
  header.setHeader(HeaderSet.LENGTH, new
    Long(data.length));

  // Issue the PUT request to the server
  Operation op = conn.put(header);

  // Send the BODY data to the server
  OutputStream out = op.openOutputStream();
  out.write(data);
  out.close();

  // Verify that the server accepted the object
  if (op.getResponseCode() != ResponseCodes.OBEX_HTTP_OK) {
    op.close();
    throw new IOException("Request failed");
  }
  op.close();
}
```

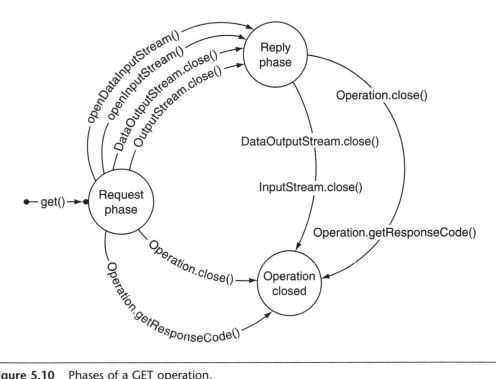

Figure 5.10 Phases of a GET operation.

GET operations work slightly differently from PUT operations. For GET operations, a call to openInputStream() or openDataInputStream() causes the request portion to end. If getResponseCode() is called during a GET operation, the InputStream is closed, and no further BODY data can be read. Therefore do not call getResponseCode() until all the BODY data sent by the server is read.

The following method retrieves an object from the server using a GET operation.

```
byte[] getBytes(ClientSession conn, String name) throws
    IOException {

  // Create the request to send to the server
  HeaderSet header = conn.createHeaderSet();
  header.setHeader(HeaderSet.NAME, name);

  // Send the request to the server
  Operation op = conn.get(header);
```

```
// Retrieve the bytes from the server
InputStream input = op.openInputStream();

// Read the data from the server until the end of
// stream is reached
ByteArrayOutputStream out = new ByteArrayOutputStream();
int data = input.read();
while (data != -1) {
    out.write(data);
    data = input.read();
}
input.close();

// Verify that the whole object was received
int responseCode = op.getResponseCode();
op.close();
switch(responseCode) {
    case ResponseCodes.OBEX_HTTP_OK:
        return out.toByteArray();
    case ResponseCodes.OBEX_HTTP_NOT_FOUND:
    case ResponseCodes.OBEX_HTTP_NO_CONTENT:
        // Since nothing was found, return null
        return null;
    default:
        throw new IOException("Request Failed");
    }
}
```

A client can end a PUT and GET request during the operation by calling the `abort()` method. The `abort()` method sends an ABORT request to the server and signals to the server the request should not be processed. The `abort()` method closes the `InputStream`, `OutputStream`, and `Operation` object. If the operation has already ended, the `abort()` method throws an `IOException`.

5.3.4 Receiving a Request from a Client

OBEX servers are similar to Java servlets once the transport layer connection is established. HTTP servlets extend `HttpServlet`; OBEX servers extend the `ServerRequestHandler` class. Unlike `HttpServlet`, the `ServerRequestHandler` class does not require any methods to be over-

Table 5.2 How OBEX Requests Are Translated to Methods by the JABWT Implementation

OBEX Request	`ServerRequestHandler` Method	Default Return Value
CONNECT	`onConnect()`	`OBEX_HTTP_OK`
SETPATII	`onSetPath()`	`OBEX_HTTP_NOT_IMPLEMENTED`
GET	`onGet()`	`OBEX_HTTP_NOT_IMPLEMENTED`
PUT	`onPut()`	`OBEX_HTTP_NOT_IMPLEMENTED`
DELETE	`onDelete()`	`OBEX_HTTP_NOT_IMPLEMENTED`
DISCONNECT	`onDisconnect()`	`OBEX_HTTP_OK`

ridden. OBEX servers need only to override the methods for the type of client requests the server would like to handle. For example, if the OBEX server wants only to process CONNECT, SETPATH, and PUT requests, the server needs only to override the `onConnect()`, `onSetPath()`, and `onPut()` methods. If the client makes a DELETE or GET request, the implementation on the server side would automatically respond with the `OBEX_HTTP_NOT_IMPLEMENTED` response code. Table 5.2 shows how OBEX requests are received by an application and how the implementation will respond if the method is not overridden.

The `onConnect()`, `onDelete()`, and `onDisconnect()` methods allow servers to respond to OBEX CONNECT, DELETE, and DISCONNECT requests, respectively. All three methods have two arguments. The first argument provides the headers sent from the client. The second argument provides the `HeaderSet` to set headers in the reply. The `onConnect()` and `onDelete()` methods both return the response code to send in the reply as specified in the `ResponseCodes` class. The `onDisconnect()` method returns nothing because a DISCONNECT request must send an `OBEX_HTTP_OK` response.

The following example code processes an OBEX CONNECT request. First, the COUNT and 0x30 user-defined headers are retrieved. If they exist in the request, the connection is accepted, otherwise the connection is rejected. If the connection is rejected, the description header specifies the cause of the rejection.

```
public int onConnect(HeaderSet request, HeaderSet reply) {
   try {
     // Retrieve the expected headers
     Long count = (Long) request.getHeader(HeaderSet.COUNT);
```

```
String conName = (String)request.getHeader(0x30);

if ((count == null) || (conName == null)) {
  reply.setHeader(HeaderSet.DESCRIPTION,
    "Required headers missing");
  return ResponseCodes.OBEX_HTTP_BAD_REQUEST;
}

return ResponseCodes.OBEX_HTTP_OK;
} catch (IOException e) {
  reply.setHeader(HeaderSet.DESCRIPTION,
    "IOException: " + e.getMessage());
  return ResponseCodes.OBEX_HTTP_INTERNAL_ERROR;
}
}
```

The onSetPath() method works similarly to onConnect(), onDisconnect(), and onDelete() methods with one exception. As part of a SETPATH request, the client may specify creation of the directory if it does not exist and backing up one directory before moving to the directory specified by the NAME header. The onSetPath() method has two boolean arguments to pass these values from the client's request to the server.

The onGet() and onPut() methods work differently. These methods have only a single argument, an Operation object. The Operation object provides access to the BODY header through the InputStream and OutputStream. Unlike Operation objects returned by the client's get() and put(), Operation objects received via the server's onGet() and onPut() methods do not have any special ordering rules. (For example, an Operation object received as an argument in onGet() may read from the InputStream first or it may write to the OutputStream first.) The Operation getResponseCode() and abort() methods throw an IOException if called on the server. If the server receives an ABORT from the client, the Operation is closed, and all the methods on the closed Operation throw an IOException.

In addition to BODY headers, GET and PUT operations can use additional headers. These headers can be retrieved via the getReceivedHeaders() method. This method returns a HeaderSet object containing all the latest headers received. Because GET and PUT operations may require multiple request and reply packets within a single operation, the same header may be sent multiple times. The getReceivedHeaders() method returns the HeaderSet object containing only the latest headers received. To send headers, a HeaderSet object must be created by calling the ServerRequestHandler.createHeaderSet() method. After the HeaderSet object is created, all headers that will be sent in the reply should be set. After the values are set, the headers are sent when the HeaderSet object is passed to the sendHeaders() method.

The following code reads the data sent to the server via a PUT request and stores it in a Record Management System (RMS) RecordStore.

```
public int onPut(Operation op) {
  int response = ResponseCodes.OBEX_HTTP_OK;

  try {
    // Retrieve the NAME header
    HeaderSet headers = op.getReceivedHeaders();
    String name = (String)headers.getHeader(HeaderSet.NAME);

    // Read the data from the input stream
    ByteArrayOutputStream out = new
      ByteArrayOutputStream();
    InputStream in = op.openInputStream();
    byte[] data = new byte[100];
    int length = in.read(data);
    while (length != -1) {
      out.write(data, 0, length);
      length = in.read(data);
    }
    in.close();

    // Open the RecordStore with the name from the NAME
    // header
    RecordStore store = RecordStore.openRecordStore(name,
      true);

    data = out.toByteArray();
    store.addRecord(data, 0, data.length);

    // Close the RecordStore
    store.closeRecordStore();
  } catch (Exception e) {
    HeaderSet header = createHeaderSet();
```

```
      header.setHeader(HeaderSet.DESCRIPTION,
        e.getMessage());
      try {
        op.sendHeaders(header);
      } catch (Exception ex) {
      }

      response = ResponseCodes.OBEX_HTTP_INTERNAL_ERROR;
    }

    // Close the Operation
    try {
      op.close();
    } catch (Exception e) {
    }

    return response;
  }
```

The OBEX API implementation verifies that the response code is valid before it is sent to the client. The implementation changes the response code to `OBEX_HTTP_INTERNAL_ERROR` if the onXXX() method returns something other than a response code specified in the `ResponseCodes` class. If an uncaught exception is received by the implementation, the implementation changes the response code to `OBEX_HTTP_INTER-NAL_ERROR`.

5.3.5 Using OBEX Authentication

OBEX authentication works via a challenge and response mechanism. To authenticate the other end of an OBEX connection, an AUTHENTICA-TION_CHALLENGE header is sent with a challenge. To respond to an authentication request, an AUTHENTICATION_RESPONSE header is sent with a hash of the challenge and password and an optional user name. Even though authentication usually occurs during a CONNECT request, OBEX authentication can occur at any time during an OBEX session. Before OBEX authentication is used, an `Authenticator` must be created and set via a call to `ClientSession.setAuthenticator()` or `SessionNotifer.acceptAndOpen()`. If no `Authenticator` is specified for a client or server, any authentication requests or replies will fail.

To send an AUTHENTICATION_CHALLENGE header, simply call the `createAuthenticationChallenge()` method on a `HeaderSet`

object that will be used in a request or a reply. The
createAuthenticationChallenge() method allows a developer to
specify which user name and password to include via a description
parameter. The method also allows the developer to specify whether a
user name is required (second argument) and whether full access will be
granted if the authentication succeeds (third argument).

The following code is an example of a client sending an authentication challenge to the server. It sets the Authenticator and issues an
authentication challenge within a CONNECT request. The following code
must set the Authenticator to handle the authentication response
header from the server. (The ClientAuthenticator class is defined later
in this chapter.)

```
ClientSession connectToServer(String connString) throws
   IOException {

  // Create the transport layer connection to the server
  ClientSession conn = (ClientSession)
    Connector.open(connString);

  // Set the AUTHENTICATION_CHALLENGE header to send to
  // the server.
  // The second argument to createAuthenticationChallenge()
  // specifies
  // that a user name is required. The third argument
  // specifies
  // whether full access will be granted.
  HeaderSet request = conn.createHeaderSet();
  request.createAuthenticationChallenge(
    "Test Password", true, false);

  // Set the Authenticator to respond to the
  // Authentication Response
  // header
  conn.setAuthenticator(new ClientAuthenticator());

  // Connect to the server
  HeaderSet reply = conn.connect(request);

  // Verify that the server accepted the connection
  if (reply.getResponseCode() !=
    ResponseCodes.OBEX_HTTP_OK) {
    conn.close();
```

```
        throw new IOException("Connection Failed (" +
          Integer.toHexString(reply.getResponseCode()) + ")");
      }
      return conn;
    }
```

To respond to an authentication challenge, an OBEX server must specify the `Authenticator` in the call to `acceptAndOpen()`. The code below sets the Authenticator to handle the authentication headers in this way. (The `ServerAuthenticator` class is defined later in this chapter.)

```
SessionNotifier waitForConnection(String connString)
  throws IOException {

  // Establish the server connection object
  SessionNotifier notifier = (SessionNotifier)
    Connector.open(connString);

  // Wait for the client to connect
  notifier.acceptAndOpen(new RequestHandler(), new
    ServerAuthenticator());

  return notifier;
}
```

When the server receives a CONNECT request with an AUTHENTICA-TION_CHALLENGE header, the `onAuthenticationChallenge()` method is called on the `Authenticator` object specified in `acceptAndOpen()`. The `onAuthenticationChallenge()` method is written as part of an implementation of the `Authenticator` interface and must return the user name and password to the implementation via a `PasswordAuthentication` object. The code below shows this process.

```
public class ServerAuthenticator implements Authenticator {
  public ServerAuthenticator() {
  }

  /**
   * When an AUTHENTICATION_CHALLENGE header is received,
   * pass the user name
   * and password back to the implementation.
   *
   * @param description specifies which password to use
```

```
 * @param isUserIDRequired true if the user name is
 * required; false if the
 * user name is not required
 * @param isFullAccess true if full access will be
 * granted; false if full
 * access will not be granted
 * @return the user name and password or null if the
 * description does not
 * specify "Test Password"
 */
public PasswordAuthentication onAuthenticationChallenge(
  String description, boolean isUserIDRequired,
  boolean isFullAccess) {

  if (description.equals("Test Password")) {
    return new PasswordAuthentication(
      new String("Bob").getBytes(),
      new String("GoodPassword").getBytes());
  }

  return null;
}

public byte[] onAuthenticationResponse(byte[] username) {
  return null;
}
}
```

After calling onAuthenticationChallenge, the OBEX API implementation on the server then invokes the onConnect() method. This allows the server to include additional headers in the reply or reject the connection.

```
public class RequestHandler extends
  ServerRequestHandler {

public RequestHandler() {
}

/**
 * Accept the connection. This method is called each
   time a CONNECT request is received.
 *
 * @param request ignored
```

```
 * @param reply set the COUNT header
 * @return always return OBEX_HTTP_OK
 */
public int onConnect(HeaderSet request, HeaderSet
    reply) {
  reply.setHeader(HeaderSet.TYPE, "text/text");
  return ResponseCodes.OBEX_HTTP_OK;
}
}
```

After the server sends the response in an AUTHENTICATION_RESPONSE header, the client's OBEX API implementation invokes the `onAuthenticationResponse()` method on the client's `Authenticator` object. The `onAuthenticationResponse()` method allows the client to pass the OBEX API implementation the correct password. After the OBEX API implementation receives a non-null password, the implementation validates the password. If the password is valid, the `connect()` method returns the HeaderSet received from the server. If the `onAuthenticationResponse()` method returns `null`, the authentication fails. If the authentication fails because null is returned or the wrong password was supplied, the call to `connect()` throws an `IOException` specifying that the authentication failed. The following code processes an AUTHENTICATION_RESPONSE header.

```
public class ClientAuthenticator implements Authenticator {

  public ClientAuthenticator() {
  }

  /**
   * Validates the password by returning the valid password.
   * @param username the user name provided; null if no
   * user name was
   * included in the header
   * @return the password for the user name specified;
   * null if the user name
   * or password is not valid
   */
  public byte[] onAuthenticationResponse(byte[]
    username) {

      // Checks to see if the only valid user name was
      // provided, otherwise
```

```
      // fail the authentication request by returning null
      if ((username == null) || (!new
        String(username).equals("Bob"))) {
        return null;
      }
      return new String("GoodPassword").getBytes();
  }

  public PasswordAuthentication onAuthenticationChallenge(
      String description, boolean isUserIDRequired,
      boolean isFullAccess) {
      return null;
  }
}
```

When a server wants to authenticate a client, the preceding process is followed, with two exceptions. First, an onXXX() method, such as onConnect() or onPut(), must add the AUTHENTICATION_CHALLENGE header by calling createAuthenticationChallenge() and return the OBEX_HTTP_UNAUTHORIZED response code. Second, the OBEX API implementation invokes the onAuthenticationFailure() method of the ServerRequestHandler specified instead of throwing an IOException as the client implementation does if the authentication fails. (Here's a tip: If a server uses OBEX authentication, it is easier to detect authentication failures if a new ServerRequestHandler object is passed to acceptAndOpen() for each connection.)

5.4 Summary

OBEX was defined by IrDA and adopted by the Bluetooth SIG. The GOEP defines OBEX within the Bluetooth world. Many different profiles have been defined on top of GOEP. For Bluetooth devices, OBEX uses the RFCOMM protocol as the transport protocol.

OBEX is built on a request and response scheme. The client drives the connection by issuing requests to the server. The server can accept or reject the request using any of the HTTP response codes. CONNECT, PUT, GET, SETPATH, DELETE, CREATE-EMPTY, and DISCONNECT are the valid operations that may be performed by a client. A client session begins with a CONNECT request and ends with a DISCONNECT request. Between the CONNECT and DISCONNECT request, any number of PUT, GET, SETPATH, DELETE, and CREATE-EMPTY operations can occur. All data is sent within OBEX headers. Any of these headers can be included in any of the operations.

OBEX provides a structured way to send data between embedded devices. Although RFCOMM works by sending bytes between devices via a stream, OBEX sends logical objects, not Java objects, between devices. By using OBEX, a developer does not need to worry about adding structure to a stream of bits. The developer needs to worry only about which headers to send and retrieve.

The OBEX API defined within JABWT is a separate API from the Bluetooth API. For this reason, the OBEX API was designed to be transport neutral. The OBEX API is built on the GCF defined by CLDC. The connection string passed to `Connector.open()` specifies which transport to use. For client connections, a `ClientSession` object is returned. A `SessionNotifier` object is returned for server connections.

With the `ClientSession` object returned by `Connector.open()`, `HeaderSet` objects can be created to send headers in any request. After `Connector.open()` is called, only the transport layer connection has been established. To establish an OBEX session, the `connect()` method is called. If the server accepts the connection request, the `put()`, `get()`, `setPath()`, or `delete()` method can be called to issue the associated request to the server. After the client finishes communicating with the server, the `disconnect()` method should be called to end the OBEX session and should be followed by the `close()` method to close the transport layer connection.

OBEX server connections work slightly differently. To process requests from a client, the server application must provide a class that extends the `ServerRequestHandler` class to the `SessionNotifier`'s `acceptAndOpen()` method. Requests from the client are passed back to the OBEX server via events to the `ServerRequestHandler` class. The `onConnect()`, `onPut()`, `onGet()`, `onSetPath()`, `onDelete()`, and `onDisconnect()` methods are called when the associated request is received from the client. Within the onXXX() method, the server can set any headers to send in the reply along with the response code.

OBEX provides a mechanism for authentication. This method is different from Bluetooth authentication. OBEX authentication uses a challenge and response scheme. Within the OBEX API, authentication starts with the `Authenticator` interface. When an authentication challenge or response is received, the appropriate method is called in the `Authenticator` object specified to the JABWT implementation. The JABWT implementation handles the details of packaging the response and determining whether the response was correct.

6 Device Discovery

CHAPTER

This chapter covers the following topics:

- Retrieving information on the local device
- Why is device discovery needed?
- Making a device discoverable
- Retrieving devices without an inquiry
- How to start an inquiry
- Changing security on a link
- Working with remote devices

6.1 Overview

Because the typical Bluetooth radio is part of a mobile device, a Bluetooth device must be able to dynamically locate devices within the area. A Bluetooth device must also be able to determine what services are on the devices found. The Bluetooth specification separates discovery of devices and discovery of services into separate processes. In the device discovery process, the local Bluetooth device finds the other Bluetooth devices in the area. In the service discovery process, the Bluetooth device determines which services the other devices have running on them.

In Bluetooth terms, device discovery is known as an *inquiry*. When a Bluetooth device issues an inquiry, the other devices in the area respond to the inquiry requests depending on their discoverable mode. These devices respond with their Bluetooth address and class of device record. The Bluetooth address is a 6-byte unique identifier assigned to every Bluetooth device by the manufacturer. The class of device record describes the type of Bluetooth device and provides a general indication of the types of services available on the device.

At the time of publication, the Bluetooth SIG had defined two types of inquiries: general and limited. A general inquiry is used to find all the Bluetooth devices in an area. A limited inquiry is used to find all devices in an area that are discoverable for only a limited length of time. A general inquiry is similar to asking all people in a room to say their names. A limited inquiry is similar to asking all people in a room to say their names only if they are accountants. Which devices respond to an inquiry request depends on the discoverable mode of the device. A Bluetooth device can be general, limited, or not discoverable. A general discoverable device responds only to general inquiries. Limited discoverable devices respond to general and limited inquiries. A device cannot respond to any inquiries if it is not discoverable.

During a general inquiry, the device performing the inquiry asks all the devices in the area to respond to a general inquiry request. Only

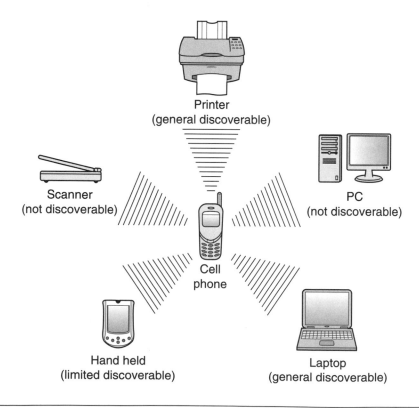

Figure 6.1   Cell phone performs a general inquiry.

devices that are limited or general discoverable respond to the request. For example, in Figure 6.1, the cell phone issues the general inquiry request. Although they may receive the request, the PC and scanner do not respond to the request because they are in the not discoverable mode (Figure 6.2.). The remaining devices in the area do respond to the cell phone with their Bluetooth addresses and class of device record.

6.2 API capabilities

JABWT provides two approaches to device and service discovery. First, JABWT provides methods that allow full control over device and service discovery. The second approach leaves the device and service discovery up to the JABWT implementation. This separation was created to allow the developers to develop Bluetooth profiles with the API and to

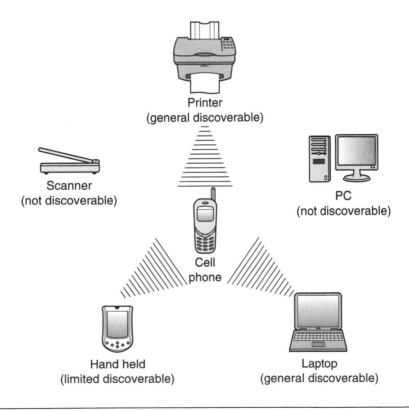

Printer
(general discoverable)

Scanner
(not discoverable)

PC
(not discoverable)

Cell
phone

Hand held
(limited discoverable)

Laptop
(general discoverable)

Figure 6.2 All general and limited discoverable devices respond to a general inquiry.

optimize their applications while also allowing developers to quickly get a Bluetooth application up and running. (The second approach is presented in Section 7.3.8.)

Device discovery starts with the JABWT application specifying the type of inquiry to perform, either general or limited. (Additional inquiry types are possible but have yet to be defined by the Bluetooth SIG.) The API returns each device found during an inquiry back to the application as the device is found via a `deviceDiscovered()` event. The device found and the class of device record of the remote device are returned.

The class of device record specifies the type of device responding and the services available on the device. The class of device record is made of the major service class, major device class, and minor device class. The major service class defines the services available on a device. The following list defines all the major service classes defined by the Bluetooth SIG when this book was published.

- Positioning
- Networking
- Capturing
- Object Transfer
- Audio
- Information
- Limited Discoverable
- Rendering
- Telephony

A device can have multiple major *service* classes. In other words, a device can have an audio and a telephony service running on it at the same time, which makes the major service class audio and telephony. The major device class and minor device class describe the physical type of device of which the Bluetooth radio is a part. A device can have only a single major *device* class. The Bluetooth SIG has defined the following major device classes:

- Computer (e.g., desktop, notebook, PDA, organizers)
- Phone (e.g., cellular, cordless, pay phone, modem)
- LAN/network access point
- Audio/video (e.g., headset, speaker, stereo, video display)

- Peripheral (e.g., mouse, joystick, keyboard)
- Imaging (e.g., printing, scanner, camera, display)
- Miscellaneous

The minor device class is defined on the basis of the major device class. The list of all the minor device classes is available from the Bluetooth SIG [30]. The minor device class is simply a more specific description of the device. For example, a device can be classified as an imaging device. The minor device class specifies whether the device is a camera, scanner, or printer. This system allows developers to perform service searches on only the devices that fit their needs. In the example, the developer is able to eliminate the camera and scanner devices from the service search if the developer is looking for a printing service.

JABWT provides a simpler approach to retrieving remote devices that eliminates the need for performing a complete inquiry. When it performs an inquiry, an application must wait eight to ten seconds for a 95% chance of finding all the devices in the area. In addition to taking time, an inquiry is power consuming, which is a major concern for embedded, battery-powered devices. To minimize the need for an inquiry, JABWT allows an application to retrieve without performing an inquiry a list of devices that would "likely" be in an area. These devices are called *predefined*. There are two types of predefined devices: pre-known and cached. Pre-known devices are devices with which the local device frequently interacts. Pre-known devices are set in the BCC. (Section 3.2 provides a full description of the BCC.) For example, a PDA frequently synchronizes with a desktop computer. The user of the PDA would specify the desktop computer as a pre-known device. A pre-known device does not guarantee that the device is currently reachable or available, but it does give an educated guess. The second type of device that can be retrieved without an inquiry is a cached device. Cached devices are Bluetooth devices found with a previous inquiry. The inquiry does not have to be performed by this application. The cached devices might have been found by a previous inquiry performed by another application on this same Bluetooth device.

6.3 Programming with the API

The `LocalDevice` class provides access to the local Bluetooth device. There is only a single `LocalDevice` object for the entire JABWT implementation. This `LocalDevice` object provides methods of retrieving information on the local device and a gateway for starting the different discovery processes.

6.3.1 Accessing the Local Device

Retrieving information and manipulating a local Bluetooth device begin with retrieving the `LocalDevice` object. The `LocalDevice` class has a private constructor, which prevents an application from creating a new `LocalDevice` object on its own. For an application to retrieve the `LocalDevice` object for the JABWT implementation, the application calls the `LocalDevice.getLocalDevice()` method. The `getLocalDevice()` method may throw a `BluetoothStateException` if the Bluetooth stack or radio is not working properly.

Once the `LocalDevice` has been retrieved, more information can be gathered on the local device, such as the device's Bluetooth address, friendly name, current discoverable mode, and class of device record. The `getBluetoothAddress()` method returns the device's address. The `getFriendlyName()` method returns the device's user-friendly name or returns null if the name could not be retrieved. The `getDiscoverable()` method returns the local device's current discoverable mode. The `DiscoveryAgent` class contains constants for general discoverable (`GIAC`, which stands for General Inquiry Access Code), limited discoverable (`LIAC`, which stands for Limited Inquiry Access Code), and not discoverable (`NOT_DISCOVERABLE`). Other discoverable modes are possible but have not been defined by the Bluetooth SIG. The `getDiscoverable()` method returns the actual value of the other discoverable modes if the local device is in the mode. Finally, the class of device record can be retrieved by means of the `getDeviceClass()` method. The `getDeviceClass()` method returns null if the class of device record could not be retrieved. (Section 6.3.4 describes manipulating the class of device record through a `DeviceClass` object.)

The `LocalDevice` class has a method for requesting a different discoverable mode. The `setDiscoverable()` method takes the requested discoverable mode as an argument. The discoverable mode can be `DiscoveryAgent.GIAC`, `DiscoveryAgent.LIAC`, `DiscoveryAgent.NOT_ DISCOVERABLE`, or any discoverable mode in the range 0x9E8B00 to 0x9E8B3F. The `setDiscoverable()` method returns `true` if the discoverable mode changes to the requested mode. This method returns `false` if the BCC denies the request or the local device does not support the requested discoverable mode. The `setDiscoverable()` method throws a `BluetoothStateException` if the requested change cannot occur at this time because the device is in a state that does not allow the change.

What happens when one device asks for limited discoverable while another asks for general discoverable? This is left up to the BCC. The JSR-82 specification does not place requirements on how the BCC resolves conflicting discoverable requests. The possible approaches include but are not limited to the following:

1. The first requested discoverable mode is honored until the application ends.

2. The last request is always honored.

3. One discoverable mode has a higher priority than another. For example, general discoverable has a higher priority than limited discoverable. Not discoverable is the lowest priority. A request to a higher priority is honored, whereas a request for a lower priority is denied.

The `LocalDevice` class also has the `getProperty()` method for retrieving additional information on the capabilities of the Bluetooth radio and stack. The `LocalDevice.getProperty()` method works similarly to the `System.getProperty()` method. The `LocalDevice.getProperty()` method takes, as a `String`, the specific property whose value is to be retrieved. The `getProperty()` method returns the value of the property as a `String`. Table 6.1 lists all the properties available through the `getProperty()` method. A JABWT implementation can add parameters to the `getProperty()` method but must support at a minimum all the properties in Table 6.1. The argument is case sensitive.

To show how to use these methods within an application, the `BluetoothInfoMIDlet` follows. The `BluetoothInfoMIDlet` displays a `Form` with the Bluetooth address, friendly name, current discoverable mode, and all the properties of the local Bluetooth device. The first step to creating the MIDlet is creating the `BluetoothInfoMIDlet` class and adding code to its `startApp()` method to display a `Form`. The next step is to add an exit `Command` to the `Form` to destroy the MIDlet.

Table 6.1   Properties Available through `LocalDevice.getProperty`

Property	Description	Valid Value
bluetooth.api.version	The version of the JABWT that is supported. This property does not relate to the Bluetooth specification number.	"1.0" for the current version of the JABWT
bluetooth.master.switch	Is master/slave switch allowed?	"true" or "false"
bluetooth.sd.attr.retrievable.max	Maximum number of service attributes to be retrieved per service record.	A base 10 integer (e.g., "1", "2")
bluetooth.connected.devices.max	Maximum number of connected devices supported.	A base 10 integer (e.g., "1", "2")
bluetooth.l2cap.receiveMTU.max	Maximum ReceiveMTU size in bytes supported in L2CAP.	A base 10 integer (e.g., "1", "2")
bluetooth.sd.trans.max	Maximum number of concurrent service discovery transactions.	A base 10 integer (e.g., "1", "2")
bluetooth.connected.inquiry.scan	Can the local device respond to an inquiry request while the device has established a link to another device?	"true" or "false"
bluetooth.connected.page.scan	Can the local device accept a connection from a new remote device if it is already connected to another remote device?	"true" or "false"
bluetooth.connected.inquiry	Can the local device start an inquiry while it is connected to another device?	"true" or "false"
bluetooth.connected.page	Can the local device establish a connection to a remote device if the local device is already connected to another device?	"true" or "false"

```java
package com.jabwt.book;

import java.lang.*;
import javax.microedition.midlet.*;
import javax.microedition.lcdui.*;
import javax.bluetooth.*;

public class BluetoothInfoMIDlet extends BluetoothMIDlet {
  /**
   * Called when the MIDlet is started to display the
   * properties of the
   * MIDlet on a Form.
   */
  public void startApp() throws
    MIDletStateChangeException {
    Display currentDisplay = Display.getDisplay(this);

    Form infoForm = new Form("Device Info");
    currentDisplay.setCurrent(infoForm);

    // Add the exit command and set the listener
    infoForm.addCommand(new Command("Exit",
      Command.EXIT, 1));
    infoForm.setCommandListener(this);
  }
}
```

Now that the `BluetoothInfoMIDlet` has been created, the `getBluetoothInfo()` method is added. The `getBluetoothInfo()` method retrieves the Bluetooth device information and displays it on the screen. This method first retrieves the `LocalDevice` object. Next, the Bluetooth address is retrieved and displayed on the screen. Before the user-friendly name returned from `getFriendlyName()` is displayed, the `getBluetoothInfo()` method must verify that null was not returned. If null was returned, the appropriate message is added to the `Form`; otherwise, the user-friendly name is displayed. A switch statement is used to display the discoverable mode to resolve the value of the discoverable mode with its associated name. Finally, each of the properties available via the `LocalDevice.getProperty()` method is retrieved and appended to the Form. The values returned from

`getProperty()` do not need to be checked for null because these
values are required to be part of the JABWT implementation.

```
public class BluetoothInfoMIDlet
  extends BluetoothMIDlet {

  public void startApp() throws
    MIDletStateChangeException {
    Display currentDisplay = Display.getDisplay(this);

    Form infoForm = new Form("Device Info");
    currentDisplay.setCurrent(infoForm);

    getBluetoothInfo(infoForm);

    // Add the exit command and set the listener
    infoForm.addCommand(new Command("Exit",
      Command.EXIT, 1));
    infoForm.setCommandListener(this);
  }

  /**
   * Displays the Bluetooth device information on the
   * screen.
   * @param f the Form to display the information on
   */
  private void getBluetoothInfo(Form f) {
    LocalDevice local = null;

    // Retrieve the local Bluetooth device object
    try {
      local = LocalDevice.getLocalDevice();
    } catch (BluetoothStateException e) {
      f.append("Failed to retrieve the local device (" +
        e.getMessage() + ")");
      return;
    }

    // Retrieve the Bluetooth address
    f.append("Address: " + local.getBluetoothAddress());
```

```
f.append("\n");

// Retrieve the Bluetooth friendly name
String name = local.getFriendlyName();
if (name == null) {
  f.append("Name: Failed to Retrieve");
} else {
  f.append("Name: " + name);
}
f.append("\n");

// Retrieve the current discoverable mode
int mode = local.getDiscoverable();
StringBuffer text = new StringBuffer(
  "Discoverable Mode: ");
switch (mode) {
  case DiscoveryAgent.NOT_DISCOVERABLE:
    text.append("Not Discoverable");
    break;
  case DiscoveryAgent.GIAC:
    text.append("General");
    break;
  case DiscoveryAgent.LIAC:
    text.append("Limited");
    break;
  default:
    text.append("0x");
    text.append(Integer.toString(mode, 16));
    break;
}
f.append(text.toString());
f.append("\n");

// Retrieve all the default properties
// and display them on the screen.
f.append("API Version: " +
  local.getProperty("bluetooth.api.version"));
f.append("\n");
f.append("Master Switch Supported: " +
  local.getProperty("bluetooth.master.switch"));
f.append("\n");
```

```
        f.append("Max Attributes: " +
          local.getProperty(
            "bluetooth.sd.attr.retrievable.max"));
        f.append("\n");
        f.append("Max Connected Devices: " +
          local.getProperty(
            "bluetooth.connected.devices.max"));
        f.append("\n");
        f.append("Max Receive MTU: " +
          local.getProperty(
            "bluetooth.l2cap.receiveMTU.max"));
        f.append("\n");
        f.append("Max Service Discovery Transactions: " +
          local.getProperty("bluetooth.sd.trans.max"));
        f.append("\n");
        f.append("Connection Options\n");
        f.append(" Inquiry Scan Supported: " +
          local.getProperty(
            "bluetooth.connected.inquiry.scan"));
        f.append("\n");
        f.append(" Page Scan Supported: " +
          local.getProperty(
            "bluetooth.connected.page.scan"));
        f.append("\n");
        f.append(" Inquiry Supported: " +
          local.getProperty("bluetooth.connected.inquiry"));
        f.append("\n");
        f.append(" Page Supported: " +
          local.getProperty("bluetooth.connected.page"));
        f.append("\n");
    }
}
```

The BluetoothInfoMIDlet displays a great deal of information about the local Bluetooth device and its JABWT implementation. Figure 6.3 shows a screen shot of the BluetoothInfoMIDlet running.

Simple Device Discovery

JABWT provides device and service discovery capabilities via the DiscoveryAgent class and the DiscoveryListener interface. Each

Figure 6.3 `BluetoothInfoMIDlet` running in J2ME Wireless Toolkit (emulation only).

device has a single `DiscoveryAgent` object. The `DiscoveryAgent` provides methods to start device and service searches. The `DiscoveryListener` interface is used by the `DiscoveryAgent` to pass devices and services back to the application as they are found. This `DiscoveryAgent` object is retrieved from the local device via the `LocalDevice.getDiscoveryAgent()` method. The following method shows how to retrieve the `DiscoveryAgent` object for a Bluetooth device.

```
public static DiscoveryAgent getLocalDiscoveryAgent() {
  try {
    /*
     * Retrieve the local Bluetooth device object for
     * this device.
```

```
        * This method may throw a BluetoothStateException
        * if the local
        * device could not be initialized.
        */
       LocalDevice local = LocalDevice.getLocalDevice();
       DiscoveryAgent agent = local.getDiscoveryAgent();
       return agent;
    } catch (BluetoothStateException e) {
       return null;
    }
}
```

The getLocalDiscoveryAgent() method must catch a BluetoothStateException because LocalDevice.getLocalDevice() may throw it. Once the LocalDevice is retrieved, the call to getDiscoveryAgent() returns the DiscoveryAgent associated with the LocalDevice. Multiple calls to getDiscoveryAgent() return the same object.

The DiscoveryListener interface is the other intricate part of device and service discovery in the JABWT. The DiscoveryListener interface is implemented by an application to receive devices and service records as they are discovered. The interface also provides an application with a notification that the inquiry or service search has completed.

The easiest way to retrieve a list of RemoteDevices is using the retrieveDevices() method in the DiscoveryAgent class. The retrieveDevices() method returns the list of pre-known devices if the DiscoveryAgent.PREKNOWN argument is used and the list of cached devices if the DiscoveryAgent.CACHED option is set. Pre-known devices are devices with which the local device commonly interacts. Devices can be registered as pre-known in the BCC. There is no guarantee that a pre-known device is in the area or can be connected to. Cached devices are devices that have been found via a previous inquiry. How many devices are cached and for how long is implementation dependent. Because of these facts, there is no guarantee that a cached or pre-known device is currently available, but the retrieveDevices() method is a quick way to get to the service search phase.

To show how to use the retrieveDevices() method, the DiscoveryMIDlet is created to display all the pre-known and cached devices. To add this capability, the startApp() method creates a List and makes it the current displayable. The startApp() method calls the

Figure 6.4 `DiscoveryMIDlet` retrieving list of pre-known and cached devices (emulation only).

`addDevices()` method to retrieve the pre-known and cached devices to print out the Bluetooth addresses of each of these devices. To identify which devices are pre-known and which are cached, "-P" or "-C" is appended to each device's Bluetooth address to represent pre-known and cached, respectively. Figure 6.4 shows the `DiscoveryMIDlet` running within the J2ME Wireless Toolkit.

```
package com.jabwt.book;

import java.lang.*;
import java.util.*;
import java.io.*;
import javax.microedition.midlet.*;
```

```java
import javax.microedition.lcdui.*;
import javax.bluetooth.*;

public class DiscoveryMIDlet extends BluetoothMIDlet {
  /**
   * The List of remote devices
   */
  private List deviceList;

  /**
   * The DiscoveryAgent for the local device.
   */
  private DiscoveryAgent agent;

  /**
   * Retrieves the list of pre-known and cached devices.
   * Updates the
   * display to show the list of devices.
   */
  public void startApp() throws MIDletStateChangeException {
    // Create a new List and set it to the current
    // displayable
    deviceList = new List("List of Devices", List.IMPLICIT);
    deviceList.addCommand(new Command("Exit",
      Command.EXIT, 1));
    deviceList.setCommandListener(this);
    Display.getDisplay(this).setCurrent(deviceList);

    // Retrieve the DiscoveryAgent object. If
    // retrieving the local device causes a
    // BluetoothStateException, something is wrong so
    // stop the app from running.
    try {
      LocalDevice local = LocalDevice.getLocalDevice();
      agent = local.getDiscoveryAgent();
    } catch (BluetoothStateException e) {
      // Prevent the application from starting if the
      // Bluetooth device
      // could not be retrieved.
      throw new MIDletStateChangeException(
        "Unable to retrieve local Bluetooth device.");
    }
```

```
    addDevices();
  }
  /**
   * Updates the List of devices with the cached and
   * pre-known devices.
   */
  private void addDevices() {
    // Retrieve the pre-known device array and append the
    // addresses
    // of the Bluetooth device. If there are no pre-known
    // devices, move
    // on to cached devices.
    RemoteDevice[] list = agent.retrieveDevices(
      DiscoveryAgent.PREKNOWN);
    if (list != null) {
      for (int i = 0; i <list.length; i++) {
        String address = list[i].getBluetoothAddress();
        deviceList.insert(0, address + "-P", null);
      }
    }

    // Retrieve the cached device array and add the
    // addresses to the
    // list.
    list = agent.retrieveDevices(DiscoveryAgent.CACHED);
    if (list != null) {
      for (int i = 0; i < list.length; i++) {
        String address = list[i].getBluetoothAddress();
        deviceList.insert(0, address + "-C", null);

      }
    }
  }
}
```

6.3.2 Device Discovery via Inquiry

Starting an inquiry is more complicated than simply retrieving a list of
devices. An inquiry requires the Bluetooth radio to issue requests for all
devices in the area to respond according to their discoverable mode.

This process uses power and can prevent the radio from being used for other purposes. Before an application can request an inquiry, the application must implement the `DiscoveryListener` interface. This interface requires that the `deviceDiscovered()` and the `inquiryCompleted()` methods be implemented for device discovery. To actually start an inquiry, the `startInquiry()` method is used. The `startInquiry()` method takes, as arguments, the type of inquiry and an implementation of the `DiscoveryListener` interface.

JABWT provides constants for the two types of inquiries defined by the Bluetooth SIG. The `DiscoveryAgent.GIAC` inquiry type should be passed to `startInquiry()` for a general inquiry. A general inquiry locates all devices in the general or limited discoverable mode. For a limited inquiry, the `DiscoveryAgent.LIAC` inquiry type should be used. Again, a limited inquiry finds all devices in the area in the limited discoverable mode. A device is placed in the limited discoverable mode when it is discoverable for only a short time. In addition to general and limited inquiry, the Bluetooth SIG specified that other inquiry access codes may be defined in the range 0x9E8B00 to 0x9E8B3F in the future. Therefore, `startInquiry()` accepts any value in this range.

The `startInquiry()` method returns `true` if the inquiry is started. Because not all devices support all the inquiry access codes, the `startInquiry()` method returns `false` if a valid inquiry access code is provided but the code is not supported. Valid inquiry access codes are in the range 0x9E8B00 to 0x9E8B3F along with `GIAC` and `LIAC`. The `startInquiry()` method throws an `IllegalArgumentException` if an invalid inquiry access code is passed as an argument. The `startInquiry()` method throws a `BluetoothStateException` if the inquiry could not be started because the device is in a state that does not allow an inquiry to be completed. A device may be in such a state when the device is already performing an inquiry or when the local device is already connected to another device.

After starting the inquiry using `startInquiry()`, JABWT returns devices to the application via `deviceDiscovered()` events. A `deviceDiscovered()` event occurs every time a remote Bluetooth device is found by the Bluetooth radio. The `deviceDiscovered()` event provides the `RemoteDevice` object and associated `DeviceClass` object each time the event occurs. The `RemoteDevice` object provides the Bluetooth address of a remote Bluetooth device along with methods to retrieve the friendly name and security controls for the remote device. The

DeviceClass object contains the class of device of the RemoteDevice. (The DeviceClass object is explained further in Section 6.3.4).

JABWT provides a way to cancel an inquiry. An application may want to cancel an inquiry once it finds a specific Bluetooth device or if the application is paused or destroyed. The cancelInquiry() method cancels an inquiry. To prevent one application from canceling the inquiry of another Bluetooth application, the cancelInquiry() method takes one parameter, the DiscoveryListener object used when the inquiry was started. The cancelInquiry() method returns true if the inquiry was canceled. If cancelInquiry() returns false, an inquiry could not be found associated with the DiscoveryListener provided, so no inquiry is canceled.

To notify the application that the inquiry has been completed, the inquiryCompleted() event was added to JABWT. The inquiryCompleted() event provides the reason the inquiry ended as an argument to the method. The DiscoveryListener.INQUIRY_COM-PLETED reason is specified if the inquiry completes normally. The DiscoveryListener.INQUIRY_TERMINATED reason is passed as part of the inquiryCompleted() event if the inquiry was canceled by the application using the cancelInquiry() method. The call to cancelInquiry() is a non-blocking call. The inquiryCompleted() event occurs independently of the cancelInquiry() method ending. Finally, the inquiryCompleted() event receives a DiscoveryListener.INQUIRY_ERROR reason if an error occurs during processing of the inquiry.

The following code shows a simple MIDlet that starts an inquiry and displays all the devices that respond to the inquiry request. The Bluetooth address of each device is displayed in a List. When the inquiry ends and the inquiryCompleted() method is called, an Alert appears to notify the user that the inquiry has ended. If an error occurs during processing of the MIDlet, an Alert is displayed to the user to notify the user of the error.

```
public class DiscoveryMIDlet extends BluetoothMIDlet
  implements DiscoveryListener {

    /**
     * Retrieves the list of pre-known and cached
     * devices. Updates the
```

```
   * display to show the list of devices.
   */
  public void startApp() throws
    MIDletStateChangeException {
      // Create a new List and set it to the current
      // displayable
      deviceList = new List("List of Devices",
        List.IMPLICIT);
      deviceList.addCommand(new Command("Exit",
        Command.EXIT, 1));
      deviceList.setCommandListener(this);
      Display.getDisplay(this).setCurrent(deviceList);

      // Retrieve the DiscoveryAgent object. If
      // retrieving the local device causes a
      // BluetoothStateException, something is wrong
      // so stop the app from running.
      try {
        LocalDevice local = LocalDevice.getLocalDevice();
        agent = local.getDiscoveryAgent();
      } catch (BluetoothStateException e) {
        // Prevent the application from starting if
        // the Bluetooth device
        // could not be retrieved.
        throw new MIDletStateChangeException(
          "Unable to retrieve local Bluetooth device.");
      }

      addDevices();

      try {
        agent.startInquiry(DiscoveryAgent.GIAC, this);
      } catch (BluetoothStateException e) {
        throw new MIDletStateChangeException(
          "Unable to start the inquiry");
      }
  }

  ...

  /**
```

```
 * Called each time a new device is discovered.
 * This method prints the device's Bluetooth
 * address to the screen.
 *
 * @param device the device that was found
 * @param cod the class of device record
 */
public void deviceDiscovered(RemoteDevice device,
  DeviceClass cod) {
    String address = device.getBluetoothAddress();
    deviceList.insert(0, address + "-I", null);
}

/**
 * Called when an inquiry ends. This method
 * displays an Alert to notify the user the inquiry
 * ended. The reason the inquiry ended is displayed
 * in the Alert.
 *
 * @param type the reason the inquiry completed
 */
public void inquiryCompleted(int type) {
    Alert dialog = null;

    // Determine if an error occurred. If one did
    // occur display an Alert
    // before allowing the application to exit.
    if (type != DiscoveryListener.INQUIRY_COMPLETED) {
      dialog = new Alert("Bluetooth Error",
        "The inquiry failed to complete normally",
          null, AlertType.ERROR);
    } else {
        dialog = new Alert("Inquiry Completed",
          "The inquiry completed normally", null,
            AlertType.INFO);
    }

    dialog.setTimeout(Alert.FOREVER);
    Display.getDisplay(this).setCurrent(dialog);
}
```

Figure 6.5 `DiscoveryMIDlet` after discovering devices via an inquiry (emulation only).

```
public void servicesDiscovered(int transID,
  ServiceRecord[] record) {
}
public void serviceSearchCompleted(int transID, int
  type) {
}
```
}

Most of the `DiscoveryMIDlet` code is required by the MIDP specification. The important parts of the code are found in the `startApp()`, `deviceDiscovered()`, and `inquiryCompleted()` methods. The inquiry is started with `startInquiry()` in the `startApp()` method so that it occurs each time the MIDlet is made active. If started in the constructor, the inquiry occurs only when the MIDlet is created. If a `Bluetooth-`

StateException occurs during retrieval of the LocalDevice object or the start of the inquiry, the startApp() method throws a MIDlet-StateChangeException to notify the KVM that the MIDlet is not able to run correctly. This procedure simplifies the user experience by allowing the KVM to handle the user interaction in the case of this type of error.

The deviceDiscovered() and inquiryCompleted() methods must be implemented because the DiscoveryMIDlet implements the DiscoveryListener interface. The deviceDiscovered() method is important because this is the method used to pass the remote devices found in the inquiry back to the MIDlet. For the purpose of this MIDlet, all this method does is get the remote device's Bluetooth address and add it to the List. (Figure 6.5 shows the DiscoveryMIDlet running.) The inquiryCompleted() method verifies that the inquiry completed successfully. If the inquiry did not complete properly, an Alert is displayed to the user to notify the user of the error. If the inquiry did complete properly, an Alert saying so is displayed to the user.

Because the user may exit from the MIDlet before the inquiry ends, code must be added to cancel the inquiry. Therefore the commandAction() method is modified to call cancelInquiry(). Because calling cancelInquiry() when no inquiry is occurring does nothing, the commandAction() method calls cancelInquiry() every time the user exits from the MIDlet.

```
public class DiscoveryMIDlet extends BluetoothMIDlet
  implements DiscoveryListener {

    ...

    /**
     * Called when a Command is selected. If it is an
     * Exit Command, then the
     * MIDlet will be destroyed.
     *
     * @param c the Command that was selected
     * @param d the Displayable that was active when
     * the Command was selected
     */
    public void commandAction(Command c, Displayable d) {
        if (c.getCommandType() == Command.EXIT) {
            // Try to cancel the inquiry.
```

```
        agent.cancelInquiry(this);

        notifyDestroyed();
    }
  }
}
```

6.3.3   Retrieving Information from a Remote Device

A number of methods provide additional information about a remote
device. Before any of these methods can be called, a RemoteDevice
object must be created. There is no public constructor for the
RemoteDevice class, so an application cannot directly instantiate a new
RemoteDevice object. The application must use one of the three ways to
get a RemoteDevice object. First, RemoteDevice objects are created in
the device discovery process. RemoteDevice objects are passed to the
application as arguments via deviceDiscovered() events.

   Second, a class that extends the RemoteDevice class can be
written and instantiated by an application. The following code does
just this.

```
package com.jabwt.book;

import javax.bluetooth.*;

public class MyRemoteDevice extends RemoteDevice {

    /**
     * Creates a new RemoteDevice object based upon the
     * address provided.
     *
     * @param address the Bluetooth address
     */
    public MyRemoteDevice(String address) {
        super(address);
    }
}
```

The address provided in the constructor must be 12 hex characters with
no preceding "0x." If the address is the same as that of the local device
or if it contains non-hex characters, the constructor throws an
IllegalArgumentException. If the address string is null, the con-

structor throws a `NullPointerException`. After instantiating a new `MyRemoteDevice` object, an application can call any of the `RemoteDevice` methods.

The third and final way to get a `RemoteDevice` object is using the `RemoteDevice.getRemoteDevice()` static method. The `getRemoteDevice()` method takes, as an argument, a Bluetooth connection to a remote device. The `getRemoteDevice()` method returns a `RemoteDevice` object representing the device to which the Bluetooth connection is connected. The `getRemoteDevice()` method throws an `IOException` if the connection is closed. The method throws an `IllegalArgumentException` if the connection is not a Bluetooth connection object or if the connection object is a notifier object.

After the `RemoteDevice` object is retrieved, the `getBluetoothAddress()`, `isTrustedDevice()`, and `getFriendly-Name()` methods can be invoked. The `getBluetoothAddress()` method returns the Bluetooth address of the remote device. The `getFriendlyName()` method in the `RemoteDevice` class is different from the `getFriendlyName()` of the `LocalDevice` method. The `getFriendlyName()` method of the `RemoteDevice` class takes a boolean argument that specifies whether the JABWT implementation should always retrieve the friendly name from the remote device or if it should retrieve the name only if the friendly name for the remote device is not known. Retrieving the friendly name requires the local device to establish a link to the remote device to retrieve the name. Because the friendly name on a device rarely changes, using a cached value if one exists eliminates the need to establish the link to the remote device. The `getFriendlyName()` method throws an `IOException` if the remote device could not be contacted to retrieve the friendly name.

Bluetooth security can be specified after a connection is established by means of the `RemoteDevice` class. The `RemoteDevice` class provides methods for authenticating, encrypting, and authorizing a connection after a connection has been established to a remote device by the `authenticate()`, `encrypt()`, and `authorize()` methods, respectively.

The `authenticate()` method authenticates the remote device represented by the `RemoteDevice` object. The `authenticate()` method requires an existing connection to the `RemoteDevice`. If no connection exists, the `authenticate()` method throws an `IOException`. Calling `authenticate()` can cause a pairing to occur if the remote and local devices have not paired previously. The `authenticate()` method returns `true` if the remote device is authenticated;

otherwise, it returns `false`. If the remote device has already been authenticated, the `authenticate()` method returns immediately with the value `true`. In other words, once a link has been authenticated, JABWT does not try to authenticate the remote device again until the link is destroyed and a new one is created.

The `encrypt()` method works slightly differently. It allows encryption on a connection to be turned on and off. This method takes two parameters: the connection to change the encryption on and a boolean specifying whether encryption should be turned on or off. The `Connection` object passed to encrypt must be to the same remote Bluetooth device the `RemoteDevice` object is representing. The `Connection` object must also be a RFCOMM, L2CAP, or OBEX over RFCOMM connection. Like `authenticate()`, the `encrypt()` method returns `true` if the change succeeds and `false` if it fails.

Changing the encryption on a link is more complicated than simply authenticating a link. The request to turn on encryption can fail for a variety of reasons. First, encryption requires the link to be authenticated. If the authentication or pairing fails, then the request to turn on encryption also fails. Second, the remote device may not support or may not want encryption enabled on the link. Third, the BCC may not allow encryption on the link.

Turning off encryption is even more complicated because turning off encryption actually makes the link less secure. A request to turn off encryption may fail for two reasons. First, the remote device may require that encryption be enabled on the link. Second, the BCC may not allow encryption to be turned off. This may be a system-wide policy, or another application may be running on the device that requires the link to be encrypted. For all of these reasons, a call to `encrypt()` should be considered a request and its return value checked.

The final method in the `RemoteDevice` class that allows a change in the security of a connection is the `authorize()` method. Recall that authorization is done on a connection basis as opposed to a link basis. The `authorize()` method takes the `Connection` object to authorize. Because authorization requires a link to be authenticated, a call to `authorize()` can cause authentication and pairing if these events have not occurred on the link. After it has been verified that the link has been authenticated, the `authorize()` method requests the BCC to authorize the connection. The `authorize()` method returns `true` if the connection is authorized and `false` if the connection is not authorized.

The `RemoteDevice` class has three methods that allow an application to determine the security level on a connection. The `isAuthenticated()` and `isEncrypted()` methods return `true` if the link to the remote device has been authenticated or encrypted, respectively. Both methods return `false` if the requested security is not enabled or if there is no link between the two devices. The `isAuthorized()` method works slightly differently. This method takes the `Connection` object to check for authorization. The `isAuthorized()` method returns `true` if the connection has been authorized and `false` if it has not been authorized.

Finally, the `RemoteDevice` class contains a method that allows an application to determine whether a device is a trusted device. The `isTrustedDevice()` method returns `true` if the `RemoteDevice` object represents a trusted device. A trusted device is a device that always passes authorization. This condition is set and maintained by the BCC.

6.3.4 Using the `DeviceClass` Class

The `DeviceClass` is a unique object. It provides three methods to access the class of device record. The class of device record specifies the physical type of the device and the general services it provides. The `getServiceClasses()` method retrieves the list of all service classes on the device. Each time a service registers itself with a device, the type of service is specified in the class of device record. This procedure allows another device to identify whether a remote device may have a service it is looking for. For example, if an application is looking for a printing service, the application should look for a device that has a rendering service class. This eliminates the overhead of performing a service search on a device that does not have the requested service.

The `getServiceClasses()` method returns an integer representing all the major service classes available on a device. (The Bluetooth SIG in the Bluetooth Assigned Numbers document [30] defines the major service classes.) Because a device can have multiple service classes, the Bluetooth SIG defines a service class by setting a bit in the class of device record. For example, bit 18 is set for the rendering service class. If a device has a rendering and an audio service, bits 18 and 21 are set. In this situation, `getServiceClasses()` returns an integer with bits 18 and 21 set or the value 18874368 (0x1200000). To determine whether a device has a rendering service, bit 18 must be isolated. The following code provides a way of doing this.

```
boolean checkForRenderingService(DeviceClass d) {
    // The Rendering service bit is bit 18. Setting bit
    // 18 produces the
    // number 0x40000.
    if ((d.getServiceClasses() & 0x40000) != 0) {
        return true;
    } else {
        return false;
    }
}
```

The `checkForRenderingService()` method isolates the rendering service bit by performing an AND on the service class of the device and a number with only bit 18 set. If the result of this AND is zero, then bit 18 is not set, and a rendering service is not available on the device. Table 6.2 lists the major service classes currently defined by the Bluetooth SIG, the bit number of the service class, and the integer value of setting only that bit. The Bluetooth SIG may add service classes in the future. Application developers should use the major service class cautiously because it gives only an indication of the types of services available on a device.

Table 6.2 Major Service Classes Defined by the Bluetooth SIG

Service Class	Type of Service	Bit Number	Hex Value
Limited Discoverable Mode	Device is in the limited discoverable mode	13	0x2000
Positioning	Location identification	16	0x10000
Networking	LAN, ad hoc, etc.	17	0x20000
Rendering	Printing, speaker, etc.	18	0x40000
Capturing	Scanner, microphone, etc.	19	0x80000
Object Transfer	V-inbox, v-folder, etc.	20	0x100000
Audio	Speaker, microphone, headset service, etc.	21	0x200000
Telephony	Cordless telephony, modem, headset service, etc.	22	0x400000
Information	Web server, Wireless Application Protocol (WAP) server, etc.	23	0x800000

Table 6.3 Major Device Classes Defined by the Bluetooth SIG

Major Device Class	Example	Hex Value
Computer	Desktop, noteboook, PDA, organizer	0x100
Phone	Cellular, cordless, pay phone, modem	0x200
LAN/network access point		0x300
Audio/video	Headset, speaker, stereo, video display, VCR	0x400
Peripheral	Mouse, joystick, keyboard	0x500
Imaging	Printer, scanner, camera, display	0x600
Miscellaneous	All other devices	0x000

The major device class is different from the service classes. The major device class reports the physical type of device to which the Bluetooth radio is connected. Because a device cannot have more then one major device class, there is no need to check a bit. The getMajorDeviceClass() returns the major device class value. At present, the Bluetooth SIG has defined seven major device classes. Table 6.3 lists all major device classes defined by the Bluetooth SIG at the time of publication of this book. The following code shows how simple it is to check for the major device class.

```
boolean checkForImaging(DeviceClass d) {
    if (d.getMajorDeviceClass() == 0x600) {
        return true;
    } else {
        return false;
    }
}
```

The minor device class returned via the getMinorDeviceClass() method must be interpreted on the basis of the major device class. Each major device class has a list of minor device classes that specify more information about the specific device. For example, the minor device class specifies whether a device with the computer major device class is a desktop, notebook, or PDA. The full listing of minor device classes for each major device class is available in the Bluetooth Assigned Numbers document [30].

6.4 Summary

Device discovery is a key part of any JABWT application. In Bluetooth terms, device discovery is known as *inquiry.* There are two types of inquiry: general and limited. Devices respond to inquiry requests according to their discoverable mode. There are three types of discoverable mode: not discoverable, limited discoverable, and general discoverable. When a device issues a general inquiry, all devices that are limited and general discoverable respond. When a device performs a limited inquiry, only devices that are limited discoverable respond.

All device and service discovery is started with the `DiscoveryAgent` class. The `DiscoveryAgent` class provides two different methods for discovering devices. The `retrieveDevices()` method allows applications to retrieve a list of devices found via a previous inquiry or a list of devices with which the local device frequently communicates. The `startInquiry()` method actually performs an inquiry. As devices are found, they are passed back to the application via `deviceDiscovered()` events. In addition to the devices, `deviceDiscovered()` events also pass back the class of device record. The class of device record contains information on the type of device and the services available on the device.

This chapter shows how to retrieve additional information on local and remote devices. The `LocalDevice` class provides methods that allow the applications to request the current discoverable mode, retrieve the friendly name of the local device, and retrieve information on the JABWT implementation. The `RemoteDevice` class provides similar methods for retrieving additional information on the remote device. The `RemoteDevice` class also provides methods for setting and retrieving different security settings on the link to the remote device.

7 Service Discovery

This chapter covers the following topics:

- What is a Bluetooth service?
- What is a service record?
- How to perform a service search
- Retrieving additional service record attributes
- Using the simple device and service discovery API
- What is service registration?
- How are service records created and added to the SDDB?
- How are service records modified by server applications?
- What is a connect-anytime service and how does it differ from a run-before-connect service?

7.1 Overview

After the devices in an area are discovered, the next step before connecting to a device is finding the services a device has running on it. Unlike device discovery, the service discovery process involves only a single pair of devices (Figure 7.1). The service discovery process requires the device searching for services to ask a device with services whether it has a service defined by a service record that has a specific set of attributes. If a remote device has a service with the attributes specified, the remote device returns the service record describing the service. The service record has multiple attributes. These attributes provide additional information on a specific service. These attributes may contain anything, including information on how to connect to the service.

Service discovery follows the client-server model. A service discovery client issues a service search request to a service discovery server. The

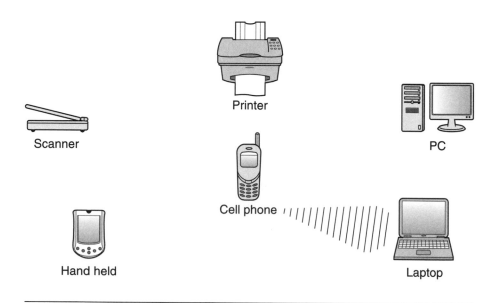

Figure 7.1   Unlike an inquiry, a service search is between only two devices.

service discovery server determines whether the server has any services that meet the search criteria. For a server to know what services are available, each service registers with a service discovery database (SDDB) kept by the Bluetooth stack. When it receives a service search request, the server searches the SDDB for the specified service.

Chapter 3 lists the typical responsibilities of a Bluetooth server application:

1. Creating a service record that describes the service offered by the application

2. Adding the service record to the server's SDDB to make potential clients aware of this service

3. Registering the Bluetooth security measures associated with a service

4. Accepting connections from clients that request the service offered

5. Updating the service record in the SDDB if characteristics of the service change

6. Removing or disabling the service record in the SDDB when the service is no longer available

Responsibilities 1, 2, 5, and 6 compose a subset of the server responsibilities having to do with advertising a service to client devices. We call this subset *service registration*. This chapter describes the process of service registration with JABWT and the process of service discovery with JABWT. Server responsibility 3, which involves security, is discussed in Chapter 4. Server responsibility 4, which involves accepting client connections, is discussed in Chapter 4 for serial port servers and Chapter 5 for OBEX servers. Chapter 8 discusses the process of accepting client connections for L2CAP servers.

7.1.1 Key Concepts

A service record answers the following questions:

- What kind of service does this server application offer?
- How does a client connect to this service?

Figure 3.3 is an overview of the components involved in service registration and service discovery. Service records and the Service Discovery Protocol (SDP) are described in great detail in Part E of the Bluetooth specification v1.1 [1]. However, the JABWT specification is the first standard API for Bluetooth service registration. The following questions about service registration were left unanswered by the Bluetooth specification:

- How are service records created?
- How are service records added to the SDDB so clients can discover them?
- How are service records modified?
- How are service records removed from the SDDB (or otherwise disabled) so clients can no longer discover them?

The Bluetooth specification did not define requirements in these areas because a standardized approach to service registration was not required for ensuring interoperability of Bluetooth devices from different manufacturers. Consequently, the mechanics of service registration were left for Bluetooth stack implementations to define. The result was a variety of different APIs for accomplishing service registration. The standard API defined by JABWT service registration makes it possible to write Bluetooth server applications that are portable across all JABWT implementations. JABWT service registration also potentially serves as a model for Bluetooth APIs in other programming languages.

7.1.2 Services Defined by Bluetooth Profiles

The Bluetooth SIG has provided profile specifications [3] that describe standardized services. Examples of some of these services are LAN access services, file transfer services, business-card exchange services, and synchronization services. Additional profiles describing standardized services were developed after the Bluetooth profiles specification v1.1 [3]. For example, three printing profiles were defined that offer various forms of printing services [7, 27, 28].

If a service is defined by a Bluetooth profile, then the profile specification describes the requirements for the service record, device security, device discoverable modes, and so on. If you want to claim that your service implements a Bluetooth profile, you have to qualify your application through the Bluetooth qualification process [10].

7.1.3 Custom Services

Developers can define their own Bluetooth server applications beyond and independently of those specified in the Bluetooth profiles and make these services available to remote clients. Applications that do not claim to provide a service described in a Bluetooth profile do not need to undergo the Bluetooth qualification process. Custom services have a great deal more latitude about how they are implemented than do Bluetooth profile implementations. The developers of custom services provide the software for both communicating Bluetooth devices. The server application can be tailored to particular characteristics of the client implementation. This process is different from that for servers for Bluetooth profiles, which must be written to work with many different implementations of the client application.

7.2 API capabilities

Once a list of devices has been retrieved via device discovery, the next step for a Bluetooth application is determining which applications or services are available on the remote Bluetooth device. JABWT provides a nonblocking way to retrieve all service records that meet a specific set of requirements on a remote Bluetooth device. A service record describes a service and is made of a set of attributes. Attributes specify how to connect to a service, the name of the service, a description of the service, and other useful information. When an application searches for a service, the application provides a set of UUIDs to search for. (A UUID is a bit sequence that uniquely identifies a characteristic of a service.) UUIDs are used to describe attributes of a service. Some UUIDs are specified by the Bluetooth specification. Other UUIDs are defined on a service-by-service basis. JABWT provides a way to specify a set of attributes to retrieve once a service is found. When a service is found that contains all the UUIDs specified, the service's service record is returned via a `servicesDiscovered()` event.

To provide a simple way to get a JABWT application up and running, JABWT defines a method that performs both device and service discovery while hiding the details of both capabilities. The `selectService()` method allows an application to specify a single UUID, which is used to locate the requested service on a remote device. The `selectService()` method returns a connection string that can be used by `Connector.open()` to connect to the service found. This is a blocking method and can take longer than 10 seconds in some situations. Therefore an application should invoke this method in a separate thread to prevent the application from appearing frozen to the user.

7.2.1 Run-before-Connect Services

Ordinarily, a server application must be running and ready to accept connections before a client attempts to make a connection to the server. Server applications that have this requirement are called *run-before-connect services* in the JABWT specification. Figure 7.2 is a Unified Modeling Language (UML) sequence diagram that illustrates the messages involved in service registration for a run-before-connect service. Each arrow in the sequence diagram is a message. The top-to-bottom ordering of the arrows indicates the time sequence of the messages. The boxes at the top of the vertical *lifelines* indicate the objects that send or receive the messages. (If these diagramming conventions are unfamiliar, a description of UML sequence diagrams can be found in Fowler and

Scott [31].) In Figure 7.2 the boxes are all Java objects created by a JABWT program with the exception of the SDDBRecord. The SDDBRecord is a service record in the SDP server's database. The SDDBRecord is not directly accessible by a JABWT application.

Figure 7.2 illustrates the answers that JABWT offers to the following questions about Bluetooth service records for run-before-connect services:

- How are service records created?

- How are service records added to the SDDB so clients can discover them?

- How are service records removed from the SDDB (or otherwise disabled) so clients can no longer discover them?

The methods `open()`, `acceptAndOpen()`, and `close()` shown in Figure 7.2 are part of the GCF defined by CLDC [13]. These methods are used by a variety of J2ME applications for I/O operations. The basic approach taken by JABWT is to add additional behavior to these GCF methods so that service records are automatically created and then automatically added and removed from the SDDB, as follows:

- `Connector.open(String url)` creates a Bluetooth service record if the parameter `url` starts with btspp://localhost:, btgoep://localhost:, or btl2cap://localhost:.

- The first time an `acceptAndOpen()` message is sent to the notifier, a copy of the service record is added to the SDDB.

- When a `close()` message is sent to the notifier, the service record is removed from the SDDB or disabled. (The "X" at the bottom of the SDDBRecord timeline in Figure 7.2 is sequence diagram notation for deleting an object.)

One consequence of the JABWT approach is that in many cases the server application can rely only on the automatic behavior of the JABWT implementation and does not need to contain any code to explicitly manipulate service records.

7.2.2 Servers Are Usually Discoverable

The GAP specification [3] describes several modes of operation that characterize Bluetooth devices. Chapter 6 describes the discoverable

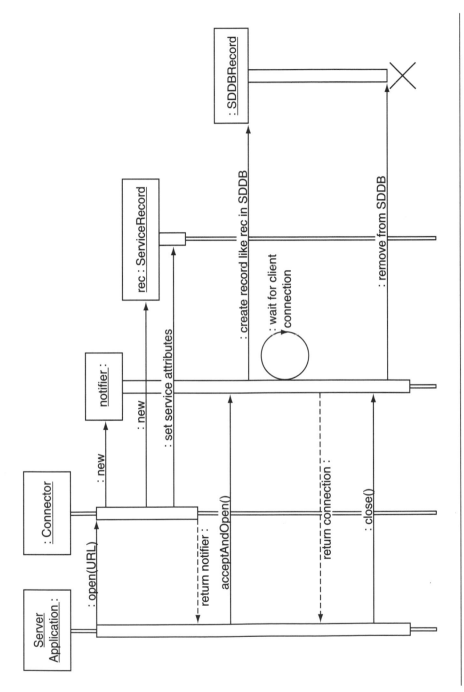

Figure 7.2 Life cycle of a service record for a run-before-connect service.

mode that determines whether the local device will respond to an inquiry conducted by a remote device. Most server applications want the local device to be in either general discoverable or limited discoverable mode so clients can find them and access their service. JABWT server applications can request that the device be made discoverable by means of the instance method `LocalDevice.setDiscoverable()`, with an argument of either `DiscoveryAgent.GIAC` or `DiscoveryAgent.LIAC`.

There are some scenarios in which it makes sense for a server to be nondiscoverable. These scenarios require that the clients have some advance knowledge about the existence of the server device and its Bluetooth address. For example, users who own a PC and a PDA that both have Bluetooth wireless technology might want their server applications to be accessible only to their own devices. If server applications are run on both the PC and the PDA, users can make those services available only to their own devices by

- Making the PC nondiscoverable using the BCC on the PC
- Making the PDA nondiscoverable using the BCC on the PDA
- Making the PDA a pre-known device for the PC using the BCC on the PC
- Making the PC a pre-known device for the PDA using the BCC on the PDA

Because device users may have their own reasons for making the local device nondiscoverable, the JABWT implementation is not the final authority on whether the device will enter a discoverable mode. The implementation makes a request to the BCC to make the local device discoverable, but this request might not be satisfied if the device user has chosen to make the local device nondiscoverable (see Chapter 3).

7.2.3 Register a Service

This section describes the service records automatically created by the JABWT implementation for server applications. These service records allow clients to find the service and make a connection to the server. In many cases, these automatically generated service records are sufficient, and the server application does not need to take any other action.

These descriptions of the default service records are provided so that developers

- Can decide whether these service records are sufficient to advertise their services, and
- Can determine how to modify the service records when modifications are necessary

Service Records for Serial Port

Table 7.1 illustrates the service record automatically created by the JABWT implementation when a server application executes the following statement:

```
Connector.open("btspp://localhost:68EE141812D211D78EED00B0D
              03D76EC;name=SPPEx");
```

The Bluetooth Profiles specification [3] contains a template for the service record used by the SPP. The JABWT implementation uses this template to create a service record and inserts the appropriate value for the RFCOMM server channel identifier into the service record. The result is a minimal but sufficient service record.

The service record in Table 7.1 shows four (attribute ID, attribute value) pairs. Each pair describes one attribute of the service. The shaded rows in Table 7.1 are the attribute IDs and the unshaded rows are the attribute values. The Bluetooth SDP uses a value between 0 and 2^{16}-1 (65535) to represent each attribute ID in a service record, and these are shown in Table 7.1 as hexadecimal numbers. For example, the attribute ID 0x0001 indicates the ServiceClassIDList attribute ID, one of the attribute IDs defined by the Bluetooth SDP specification [1]. Table 7.2 provides a list of the most common attribute IDs defined in the Bluetooth Assigned Numbers [30].

Each attribute value is a DataElement. A DataElement is a self-describing data structure that contains a type and a value. For example, the third attributeValue in the service record in Table 7.1 is a simple DataElement with type String and value "SPPEx." The value "SPPEx" is extracted by the JABWT implementation from the parameter "name=SPPEx" in the connection string. The JABWT implementation uses this string "SPPEx" to construct a DataElement of type String. This

Table 7.1   Service Record Created by `Connector.open("btspp://localhost:…")`

ServiceClassIDList<0x0001>

DataElement(type = DATSEQ,

        DataElement(type = UUID,

                UUID(68EE141812D211D78EED00B0D03D76EC)

                        —from the connection string)

        DataElement(type = UUID,

                UUID(SerialPort<0x1101>)))

ProtocolDescriptorList<0x0004>

DataElement(type = DATSEQ,

        DataElement(type = DATSEQ,

                DataElement(type = UUID,

                        UUID(L2CAP<0x0100>)))

        DataElement(type = DATSEQ,

                DataElement(type = UUID,

                      UUID(RFCOMM<0x0003>))

                DataElement(type = U_INT_1,

                      1   —server channel identifier.

                          —Assigned by the stack;

                          —added to the service record

                          —by JABWT)))

ServiceName<0x0100>

—Name of the service in the primary language of the service record

DataElement(type = STRING,

        "SPPEx" —from "name=SPPEx" in the connection string)

```
ServiceRecordHandle<0x0000>

DataElement(type = U_INT_4,

            12345 —value assigned by the SDP Server)
```

DataElement is then used as the ServiceName attribute of the service record.

A DataElement may be one of the following types.

- Null
- Integer (1, 2, 4, 8, and 16 byte)
- Unsigned integer (1, 2, 4, 8, and 16 byte)
- URL
- UUID
- String
- Boolean
- DATALT—Data element alternative
- DATSEQ—Data element sequence

Three data element types require further explanation: UUID, data element sequence, and data element alternative.

A data element sequence is a list of data elements in which all elements are part of the definition. In other words, a data element sequence is an all-inclusive set of data elements. A data element alternative, on the other hand, is a data element whose value is a list of data elements of which any one may be selected. Put slightly differently, a data element alternative is a set of data elements of which any one of the values may be used.

The first attribute value in Table 7.1 contains the thirty-two–digit hexadecimal number `68EE141812D211D78EED00B0D03D76EC`. This number is also extracted from the connection string. The number is used to create a 128-bit UUID and then is wrapped in a DataElement of type UUID. UUIDs are used extensively in creating service records, and their meaning varies depending on where they are used in the service record. In this case, the UUID represents one of the ServiceClasses in the ServiceClassIDList. ServiceClasses are very important in identifying

Table 7.2 Some Service Record Attribute IDs Defined by Bluetooth Assigned Numbers

Name	ID	Type	Description
ServiceRecordHandle	0x0000	32-bit unsigned integer	Uniquely identifies each service on a device.
ServiceClassIDList	0x0001	A data element sequence of UUIDs	Defines the service classes that describes the service. The service classes are defined by the Bluetooth SIG.
ServiceID	0x0003	UUID	Uniquely identifies the service instance associated with this service record.
ProtocolDescriptorList	0x0004	A data element sequence of data element sequences of UUID and optional parameters	Describes the protocols to use to connect to the service.
ServiceInfoTimeToLive	0x0007	32-bit unsigned integer	Defines the length of time this service record is valid and will remains unchanged.
ServiceAvailability	0x0008	8-bit unsigned integer	Describes the relative availability of the service to accept additional connections.
BluetoothProfileDescriptorList	0x0009	A data element sequence of data element sequence pairs	Specifies all the profiles this service implements.
DocumentationURL	0x000A	URL	A URL that points to the documentation for the service.
IconURL	0x000C	URL	A URL that points to an icon that may be used to represent the service.
ServiceName	0x0100	String	The name of the service in the primary language of this service record.
ServiceDescription	0x0101	String	A description of the service in the primary language of this service record.

services. For example, each Bluetooth profile is associated with a particular ServiceClass UUID. If a client wants to find the service record for a particular JABWT server application, it can search for the ServiceClass UUID used by that server application.

The other service class in the ServiceClassIDList is the 16-bit UUID, 0x1101, which identifies this as a serial port service record. This list of two service classes summarizes the type of service being offered. Because this attribute value represents a list of service classes, the two DataElements that represent individual service classes are wrapped in another DataElement that represents the entire list (or sequence) of service classes. This wrapper DataElement for the list has type DATSEQ, which is an abbreviation for DataElement Sequence.

In the ServiceClassIDList attributeValue in Table 7.1 we see both 16-bit and 128-bit UUIDs. Although a Bluetooth UUID always represents a 128-bit value, the Bluetooth specification defines both 16-bit and 32-bit "short forms" or aliases for some common 128-bit Bluetooth UUIDs. For example, the Serial Port Service Class ID, 0000**1101**00001000800000805F9B34FB, is a 128-bit UUID that has a 16-bit short form 0x1101. It takes fewer bits to store and transmit a service record when these short form UUIDs are used, so the short forms are generally used when they are available. The short-form UUIDs are defined by the Bluetooth Assigned Numbers [30].

A 16-bit UUID can be converted to a 128-bit UUID by means of the following formula:

$$UUID_{128} = (UUID_{16} * 2^{96}) + 0x00000000000001000800000805F9B34FB$$

Table 7.3 shows examples of the use of this formula to convert from a 16-bit UUID to a 128-bit UUID.

Table 7.3 Examples of Conversion from a 16-Bit UUID to a 128-Bit UUID

Mnemonic	16-Bit UUID	128-Bit UUID
RFCOMM	0x0003	0x0000**0003**00001000800000805F9B34FB
BNEP	0x000F	0x0000**000F**00001000800000805F9B34FB
L2CAP	0x0100	0x0000**0100**00001000800000805F9B34FB
OBEXObjectPush	0x1105	0x0000**1105**00001000800000805F9B34FB

The ProtocolDescriptorList attribute value has the most complicated structure of the four attributes shown in Table 7.1. The ProtocolDescriptorList describes how clients can connect to the service described by the service record. It lists the protocol stack needed to communicate with the service and any protocol-specific parameters needed to uniquely address the service. In the example shown in Table 7.1, a connection to this serial port service can be made by means of a stack of protocols that consists of the L2CAP layer and the RFCOMM layer. The implication is that the server application communicates directly with RFCOMM. Server channel 1 has been assigned to the server application by the Bluetooth stack, and this channel identifier is included in the service record so clients know the proper channel identifier to use to make a connection to the service.

The structure of the ProtocolDescriptorList is a list of lists with one sublist for every stack layer involved in the communications. So conceptually this looks like ((L2CAP), (RFCOMM, 1)), where parentheses are used as shorthand for a DataElement of type DATSEQ. The first element (L2CAP) indicates that L2CAP is the lowest protocol layer used to access this service. Strictly speaking, other Bluetooth stack protocols below L2CAP are involved, but stack layers below L2CAP are not included in SDP service records. The second element, (RFCOMM, 1), consists of two elements. The first element is the name of the next higher layer protocol, RFCOMM. The second element is a protocol-specific parameter, 1, which is the RFCOMM server channel identifier.

The list-of-lists structure is represented in the service record as an attribute value with structure

```
DataElement(type = DATSEQ,
            DataElement(type = DATSEQ, …)
            DataElement(type = DATSEQ, …))
```

Short-form UUIDs are used to represent the protocols L2CAP and RFCOMM. A DataElement of type U_INT_1 represents the server channel identifier 1 used by RFCOMM. This type of DataElement describes an unsigned integer of size 1 byte. In addition to the U_INT_1 type, there are DataElements types for signed and unsigned integers that are 1, 2, 4, 8, or 16 bytes long.

The third attribute shown in Table 7.1, ServiceName, has already been discussed. Its value is a DataElement of type String with value

"SPPEx." The Bluetooth SDP specification defines the ServiceName attribute as a brief string representing the service suitable for display to the device user.

The fourth service attribute shown in Table 7.1 is the ServiceRecordHandle. This is a required attribute for every service record and plays an important role in the implementation of Bluetooth service discovery. However, the ServiceRecordHandle should be considered internal bookkeeping irrelevant to JABWT applications. JABWT applications may not modify this attribute. For this reason, the ServiceRecordHandle attribute is omitted from the rest of the tables describing service records in this book.

The SDP specification [1] describes the binary format used to transmit (attribute ID, attribute value) pairs from a service record over the air to another Bluetooth device. However, JABWT applications do not see that binary representation. Table 7.1 provides a representation of a service record that maps more directly onto the Java objects visible to JABWT applications. Table 7.1 refers to the JABWT classes `DataElement` and `UUID`.

Service Records for L2CAP

As an alternative to serial port communications using `btspp`, JABWT server applications can communicate using L2CAP or OBEX. Servers that use these protocols need service records different from the one shown for `btspp`. Again, the JABWT implementation is responsible for automatically creating the service records. L2CAP is described in Chapter 8. A server's call to `Connector.open()` using the following `btl2cap` connection string creates a service record like the one shown in Table 7.4:

```
"btl2cap://localhost:BA661F1C148911D783C300B0D03D76EC;
        name=An L2CAP Server"
```

There are several differences between Table 7.1 and Table 7.4:

- SerialPort has been removed from the ServiceClassIDList.
- RFCOMM has been removed from the ProtocolDescriptorList.
- The value of the Protocol/Service Multiplexer (PSM), 0x1001, is included as an L2CAP parameter in the ProtocolDescriptorList.

Table 7.4   A Service Record Created by `Connector.open("btl2cap://localhost:…")`

ServiceClassIDList<0x0001>
DataElement(type = DATSEQ,
DataElement(type = UUID,
UUID(BA661F1C148911D783C300B0D03D76EC)
—from the connection string))
ProtocolDescriptorList<0x0004>
DataElement(type = DATSEQ,
DataElement(type = DATSEQ,
DataElement(type = UUID,
UUID(L2CAP<0x0100>))
DataElement(type = U_INT_2,
0x1001 –Protocol/Service Multiplexer.
–Assigned by the stack;
–filled in by JABWT)))
ServiceName<0x0100>
DataElement(type = STRING,
"An L2CAP Server" –from "name=An L2CAP Server"
–in the connection string)

Because L2CAP servers talk directly to the L2CAP layer in the Bluetooth stack, L2CAP is the last element in the ProtocolDescriptorList that describes the sequence of protocol layers that must be traversed to reach this server application. The protocol and service multiplexer parameter is required because L2CAP is a multiplexing layer, so multiple applications may be interacting with the L2CAP layer on the server device. The PSM value in the service record enables L2CAP to identify the particular application or protocol above L2CAP that will provide the service described by the service record. L2CAP uses the PSM value to set up an L2CAP channel to the correct application when a client connects to this service (see Chapter 8).

As was the case for the SPP, the JABWT implementation adds all the mandatory service attributes of the service record for L2CAP. The result is a minimal, but sufficient, service record.

Service Records for OBEX over RFCOMM

A third option for a Bluetooth server application is to use OBEX for communications. The following statement is an example of a connection string used for OBEX over RFCOMM:

```
"btgoep://localhost:0E18AE04148A11D7929B00B0D03D76EC;
        name=An OBEX Server"
```

The abbreviation `goep` in the protocol `btgoep` refers to the Generic Object Exchange Profile [3], which is the base Bluetooth profile shared by all of the Bluetooth OBEX profiles. The relation between OBEX and the GOEP profile is similar to the relation between the RFCOMM protocol and the SPP.

This call to `Connector.open("btgoep://localhost:…")` creates a service record like the one shown in Table 7.5. There are only a few differences between this service record and the one shown in Table 7.1 for `btspp`. In Table 7.5 the service record contains OBEX as the last item in its ProtocolDescriptorList. This indicates that the server application talks directly to the OBEX layer of the Bluetooth stack. Another difference between Table 7.5 and Table 7.1 is that ServiceClassIDList in Table 7.5 does not include the SerialPort service class ID included for `btspp`.

Table 7.6 summarizes the three different protocols used by Bluetooth servers and the `Connector.open()` methods used to create service records for all three protocols. As shown in Table 7.6, the `Connector.open()` method is primarily defined in the CLDC specification [13]. Whereas CLDC provides the primary specification for the behavior of the `Connector.open()` method, the JABWT specification describes the valid `url` arguments for Bluetooth servers and the behavior of `Connector.open()` in creating Bluetooth service records.

Add the Service Record to the SDDB

Although the `Connector.open()` methods in Table 7.6 create a minimal service record for run-before-connect services, that service

Table 7.5 A Service Record Created by `Connector.open("btgoep://localhost:…")`

ServiceClassIDList<0x0001>

DataElement(type = DATSEQ,
        DataElement(type = UUID,
                UUID(0E18AE04148A11D7929B00B0D03D76EC)
                  —from the connection string))

ProtocolDescriptorList<0x0004>

DataElement(type = DATSEQ,
    DataElement(type = DATSEQ,
        DataElement(type = UUID,
            UUID(L2CAP<0x0100>)))
    DataElement(type = DATSEQ,
        DataElement(type = UUID,
            UUID(RFCOMM<0x0003>))
        DataElement(type = U_INT_1,
            20 –server channel identifier))
    DataElement(type = DATSEQ,
        DataElement(type = UUID,
            UUID(OBEX<0x0008>))))

ServiceName<0x0100>

DataElement(type = STRING,
    "An OBEX Server" –from "name=" in
        –the connection string)

record is not yet visible to client devices. The server that created the service record can access it and make modifications to it if desired. However, it is possible only for clients of run-before-connect services to connect after the server calls `acceptAndOpen()`. For this reason, the JABWT implementation adds a service record to the SDDB only the first time the server calls one of the `acceptAndOpen()` methods in Table 7.7.

Table 7.6   Methods That Create a Service Record

Protocol	Interface	Methods	Specification
btspp	Connector	open(url)	CLDC
		open(url,mode)	
		open(url,mode,timeout)	
btl2cap	Connector	open(url)	CLDC
		open(url,mode)	
		open(url,mode,timeout)	
btgoep	Connector	open(url)	CLDC
		open(url,mode)	
		open(url,mode,timeout)	

Once the service record is in the SDDB, client applications can discover that service record and attempt to connect to the server application.

A RFCOMM service can accept multiple connections from different clients by calling `acceptAndOpen()` repeatedly for the same notifier. Each client accesses the same service record and connects to the service using the same RFCOMM server channel. If the underlying Bluetooth system does not support multiple connections, then the implementation of `acceptAndOpen()` throws a `BluetoothStateException`. L2CAP and OBEX over RFCOMM services also can accept multiple clients.

A `ServiceRegistrationException` is thrown by all of the `acceptAndOpen()` methods in Table 7.7 if they fail to add a service record to the SDDB.

Remove the Service Record from the SDDB

Once the notifier associated with a run-before-connect service is closed, it is no longer possible to call `acceptAndOpen()` to accept another client connection. For this reason, the JABWT implementation removes the service record from the SDDB or disables the service record. Table 7.8 shows the different types of notifiers that add this behavior to the `close()` method inherited from the GCF interface `javax.microedition.io.Connection`.

Table 7.7 Methods That Add Service Records to the SDDB

Protocol	Interface	Methods	Specification
btspp	StreamConnectionNotifier	acceptAndOpen()	CLDC
btl2cap	L2CAPConnectionNotifier	acceptAndOpen()	JABWT
btgoep	SessionNotifier	acceptAndOpen(handler)	JABWT
		acceptAndOpen(handler, authenticator)	

Table 7.8 Methods That Remove or Disable Service Records

Protocol	Interface	Methods	Specification
btspp	StreamConnectionNotifier	close()	CLDC
btl2cap	L2CAPConnectionNotifier	close()	CLDC
btgoep	SessionNotifier	close()	CLDC

7.2.4 Modifications to Service Records

In many cases, it is desirable to modify the service record created by the JABWT implementation. For example, if your service corresponds to a Bluetooth profile, you will have to modify the service record so that the record conforms to the requirements of the profile. Even if you are writing a custom application and are not required to have a standardized service record, you may want to modify your service record to provide various kinds of useful information to potential clients. Many optional attributes are defined in Part E of the Bluetooth SDP specification [1] that server applications can use to describe the properties of their service. It is also possible to add application-specific, user-defined attributes to the service record that are not defined by the Bluetooth specification.

Figure 7.3 adds JABWT methods for modifying service records to the sequence diagram shown in Figure 7.2. The LocalDevice class provides a getRecord() method that a server application can use to obtain

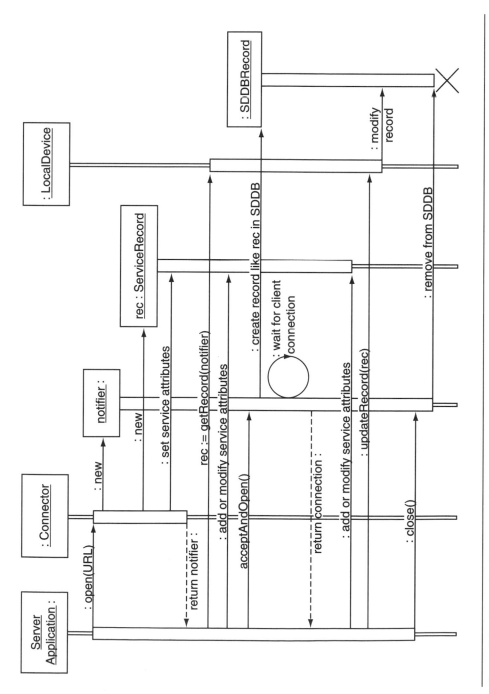

Figure 7.3 Example of server modifying its service record.

its `ServiceRecord`. The server can modify the `ServiceRecord` object by adding or modifying attributes using `ServiceRecord.set-AttributeValue()`. As shown in Figure 7.3, any modifications the server application makes to its `ServiceRecord` before calling `acceptAndOpen()` for the first time will be reflected in the service record added to the SDDB by `acceptAndOpen()`.

Any changes made to the service record object by a JABWT application after the first call to `acceptAndOpen()` are not reflected in the service record in the SDDB seen by clients. This is because the service record in the SDDB is essentially a copy of the service record Java object at the time of the first call to `acceptAndOpen()`. To modify service records already in the SDDB, JABWT provides the instance method `LocalDevice.updateRecord(serviceRecord)`.

7.2.5 Device Service Classes

As described in Chapter 6, clients can consult the `DeviceClass` of any device they discover to determine what kind of device has been found (e.g., phone, PDA, or PC). The `DeviceClass` also indicates the major service classes offered by the discovered device (e.g., rendering, telephony, or information). This means there are two different ways in which a server application describes the service it offers:

- By adding a service record to the SDDB
- By activating major service class bits in the `DeviceClass`

The server application can use the `setDeviceServiceClasses()` method of `ServiceRecord` to turn on some of the service class bits of the device to reflect the new service being offered. A server application is not required to use the `setDeviceServiceClasses()` method. However, it is recommended that a server use the method to describe its service in terms of the major service classes. Keeping the major service classes up to date reduces the likelihood that clients will erroneously skip over this device when looking for a service.

The `close()` message also causes the JABWT implementation to deactivate any service class bits that were activated by `setDeviceServiceClasses()`, unless another service whose notifier is not yet closed also activated some of the same bits.

7.3 Programming with the API

The programming examples in this chapter are divided into examples of service registration and examples of service discovery. Sections 7.3.1 through 7.3.4 provide examples of service registration. These sections show examples of the use of methods for creating and modifying service records. The examples in these sections are all server applications. These servers simply create a service record and add it to the SDDB. No client applications are needed to illustrate this behavior. Not all of the code needed to produce a running application is presented in the text. The complete code is available in Appendix A. Sections 7.3.5 through 7.3.8 provide examples of service discovery. These sections extend the DiscoveryMIDlet that was introduced in Chapter 6 to discover various aspects of the service defined in Section 7.3.2.

7.3.1 Automatic Generation of Service Records

In this first example, the server application makes no modifications to the service record. This is the simplest case. Figure 7.4 shows the output produced by the DefaultBtsppRecordMIDlet. The display shows the connection string that clients can use to connect to this server:

btspp://0080375a0000:1

The display also shows that the service record for the server has five service attributes and lists their attribute IDs as hex numbers.

The DefaultBtsppRecordMIDlet implements the Runnable interface. The run() method first calls the method askToBe-GeneralDiscoverable() defined in the DefaultBtsppRecord-Server class to attempt to make the server device general discoverable. The run() method calls the method defineDefaultBtsppService() to create the service record and define the StreamConnection-Notifier. The new service record is obtained from the LocalDevice, and a brief description of the service record is appended to a display Form, output. Finally, the run() method calls the acceptClient-Connections() method defined in the DefaultBtsppRecordServer class. This method adds the service record to the SDDB and waits for client connections.

Figure 7.4 Example Code Displays Information about the Default Service Record (emulation only).

```
public class DefaultBtsppRecordMIDlet extends MIDlet
  implements Runnable, CommandListener {

  StreamConnectionNotifier notifier;
  /* The form displayed to the user. */
  private Form output;

  ...

  public void run() {
    LocalDevice theRadio;

    // Define the serial port service and create the notifier
    try {
      theRadio = LocalDevice.getLocalDevice();
```

```
            server = new DefaultBtsppRecordServer();
            server.askToBeGeneralDiscoverable(theRadio);
            notifier = server.defineDefaultBtsppService();
        } catch (IOException e) {
            output.append("Unable to start server (IOException: " +
                e.getMessage() + ")");
            return;
        }

        if (notifier != null) {
            ServiceRecord record = theRadio.getRecord(notifier);
            output.append("URL=" + server.getURL(record));
            output.append(server.describeAttributes(record));
        } else {
            output.append("Unable to start server");
            return;
        }

        // Use the notifier to establish serial port connections
        server.acceptClientConnections(notifier);
    }
}
```

Now that we have seen the overall flow of execution defined by the
`DefaultBtsppRecordMIDlet`, we will examine the `DefaultBtspp-RecordServer` class. The `askToBeGeneralDiscoverable()` method
uses the `setDiscoverable()` method to request that the device be
made general discoverable. This enables client devices that do device
discovery with the GIAC mode to find the server device. If
`setDiscoverable()` returns `false`, indicating that the request was
not granted, or if it throws an exception, the server just proceeds. Any
clients that know the Bluetooth address for this server can access this
service even if the device is not discoverable. For example, clients that
include the server device among their pre-known devices can access the
server (see Chapter 6).

The `defineDefaultBtsppService()` method calls `Connector.open(connString)` to create a `StreamConnectionNotifier`. That
same call also creates a default `btspp` service record such as the one
shown in Table 7.1 and associates it with the notifier.

```
public class DefaultBtsppRecordServer {
    boolean stop = false;
```

```java
void askToBeGeneralDiscoverable(LocalDevice dev) {
  try {
    /* Request that the device be made discoverable */
    dev.setDiscoverable(DiscoveryAgent.GIAC);
  } catch(BluetoothStateException ignore) {
    /* discoverable is not an absolute requirement */
  }
}
public StreamConnectionNotifier
  defineDefaultBtsppService() {
    StreamConnectionNotifier notifier;

    String connString =
      "btspp://localhost:" +
        "68EE141812D211D78EED00B0D03D76EC;" +
      "name=SPPEx";
    try {
      notifier =
        (StreamConnectionNotifier)
          Connector.open(connString);
    } catch (IOException e){
      return null;
    }
    return notifier;
}
public String getURL(ServiceRecord record) {
    String url =
      record.getConnectionURL(
        ServiceRecord.NOAUTHENTICATE_NOENCRYPT,
        false);
    if (url != null) {
      return url.substring(0, url.indexOf(";"));
    } else {
      return "getConnectionURL()=null";
    }
}
public String describeAttributes(ServiceRecord
  record) {
    int[] attributeIDs = record.getAttributeIDs();
    StringBuffer strBuf = new StringBuffer(100);
    strBuf.append("\n").append(Integer.toString(
      attributeIDs.length));
```

```
        strBuf.append(" Attributes: ");
        for (int i = 0; i < attributeIDs.length; i++) {
          strBuf.append("<0x");
          strBuf.append(Integer.toHexString(attributeIDs[i]));
          strBuf.append(">\n");
        }
        return strBuf.toString();
    }
    public void acceptClientConnections(
      StreamConnectionNotifier notifier) {
      if (notifier == null) {
        return;
      }
      try {
        while (!stop) {
          StreamConnection clientConn = null;
          /*
           * acceptAndOpen() waits for the next client to
           * connect to this service. The first time through
           * the
           * loop, acceptAndOpen() adds the service record to
           * the SDDB and updates the service class bits
           * of the device.
           */
          try {
            clientConn =
              (StreamConnection)notifier.acceptAndOpen();
          } catch (ServiceRegistrationException e1) {
          } catch (IOException e) {
            continue;
          }
          /*
           * Code to communicate to a client over clientConn
           * would go here.
           */
        }
      } finally {
          try {
            shutdown(notifier);
          } catch (IOException ignore) {
          }
      }
```

```
  }

  public void shutdown(StreamConnectionNotifier notifier)
  throws IOException {

    stop = true;
    notifier.close();

  }

}
```

The `getURL()` method returns a connection string that clients can use to connect to the `DefaultBtsppRecordServer`. The `getURL()` method calls the JABWT `getConnectionURL()` method to get the connection string, and then the string is shortened for display by removing the parameter list. As shown in Figure 7.4, the result is `btspp://0080375a0000:1`, where `0080375a0000` is the Bluetooth address of the local device, and 1 is the server channel identifier. Typically, clients send the `getConnectionURL()` message to a service record obtained during service discovery to obtain a connection string to connect to that service. Here we send the same message to the server's own service record to obtain the connection string for display by the `DefaultBtsppRecordMIDlet`.

The `describeAttributes()` method uses the JABWT method `getAttributesIDs()` to obtain an array of the attribute IDs that are part of the new service record. The `describeAttributes()` method returns a string that includes the number of attributes in this array and the hexadecimal values of the attribute IDs. The `DefaultBtsppRecordMIDlet` displays this string on the user interface. These attribute IDs can be compared with the ones shown for the default `btspp` service record in Table 7.1. The `DefaultBtsppRecordMIDlet` displays the attribute IDs in Table 7.1. (Some JSR-82 implementations do not return a ServiceRecordHandle, 0x0000.) One additional attribute, ServiceRecordState 0x002, might also be displayed. The Bluetooth stack may add the ServiceRecordState attribute to a service record to make it easier for clients to determine whether that service record has changed. If the value of the ServiceRecordState attribute has not changed since the last time it was checked, the client knows that none of the attributes in the service record have changed.

The last method defined in `DefaultBtsppRecordServer` is `acceptClientConnections()`. This method calls `acceptAndOpen()`, which adds the service record to the SDDB, where it will be visible to clients. The `acceptAndOpen()` method then blocks and waits for a client to connect. Once a client makes a connection, the `acceptAndOpen()` method returns a `StreamConnection` that the server can use to communicate with that client using RFCOMM (see Chapter 4).

7.3.2 Modifying a Service Record

This section illustrates how a server can modify its service record by adding additional service attributes. Suppose we want to create the service record shown in Table 7.9 for a two-person Bluetooth game. The JABWT implementation automatically adds the first three attributes shown in Table 7.9 when it creates the service record. The last three attributes must be added by the server application. Two of the service attributes added, ServiceDescription and DocumentationURL, are standard attributes defined in the SDP specification [1, Part E]. A ServiceDescription is a brief description of the service (fewer than 200 characters). The DocumentationURL provides a pointer to a Web page for detailed documentation of the service. The third attribute added, 0x2222, is a nonstandard, application-specific service attribute. This attribute shows the highest score achieved to date by the user of this device. Clients might use this attribute to select a suitable opponent for the game or to assign handicaps.

The `defineGameService()` method shown below illustrates how the service record shown in Table 7.9 can be created by a server application. The statement

```
notifier = (StreamConnectionNotifier)
   Connector.open(connString)
```

creates the service record and returns a notifier cast to a `StreamConnectionNotifier`. The notifier is used to access the new service record by the statement

```
ServiceRecord record = localDev.getRecord(notifier);
```

The `defineGameService()` method then adds three additional service attributes to the service record before that record is made visible to clients. The method `setAttributeValue()` is used to add each attribute to the service record.

Table 7.9   The Service Record for a Bluetooth Game

ServiceClassIDList<0x0001>

DataElement(type = DATSEQ,

        DataElement(type = UUID,

                UUID(0FA1A7AC16A211D7854400B0D03D76EC))

        DataElement(type = UUID,

                UUID(SerialPort<0x1101>)))

ProtocolDescriptorList<0x0004>

DataElement(type = DATSEQ,

        DataElement(type = DATSEQ,

                DataElement(type = UUID,

                        UUID(L2CAP<0x0100>)))

        DataElement(type = DATSEQ,

                DataElement(type = UUID,

                        UUID(RFCOMM<0x0003>))

                DataElement(type = U_INT_1,

                        3 –server channel identifier)))

ServiceName<0x0100>

DataElement(type = STRING,

        "A Bluetooth Game")

ServiceDescription<0x0101>

        DataElement(type = STRING,

                "This game is fun! It is for two people.

                You can play it on your cell phones.")

DocumentationURL<0x000A>

    –Where to find documentation

DataElement(type = URL,

       "http://www.gameDocsOnSomeWebPage.com")

<0x2222>

    –An application-specific attribute for the highest score in the game

DataElement(type = U_INT_4,

      10000)

```
public StreamConnectionNotifier
  defineGameService(LocalDevice localDev, long highScore) {

  StreamConnectionNotifier notifier;

  String connString =
    "btspp://localhost:0FA1A7AC16A211D7854400B0D03D76EC;" +
    "name=A Bluetooth Game";
  try {
    notifier =
      (StreamConnectionNotifier)Connector.open(connString);
  } catch (IOException e2){
    return null;
  }
  ServiceRecord record = localDev.getRecord(notifier);
  // Add optional ServiceDescription attribute; attribute
  // ID 0x0101.
  record.setAttributeValue(0x0101,
    new DataElement(DataElement.STRING,
    "This game is fun! It " +
    "is for two people. " +
    "You can play it on " +
    "your cell phones."));

  // Add optional DocumentationURL attribute; attribute ID
  // 0x000A.
  record.setAttributeValue(0x000A,
    new DataElement(DataElement.URL,
    "http://" +
    "www.gameDocsOnSomeWebpage.com"));
  /*
```

```
 * Add an application-specific attribute for the highest
 * score achieved by this player to date.
 */
record.setAttributeValue(0x2222,
  new DataElement(DataElement.U_INT_4,
  highScore));
  return notifier;
}
```

When the server does `acceptAndOpen()`, the service record added to the SDDB has the additional service attributes added by the `defineGameService()` method. When using application-specific service attributes, keep in mind that the Bluetooth specification reserves certain attribute ID values. Attribute IDs in the range 0x000D to 0x01FF are reserved and should not be used.

7.3.3 Support for String Attributes in Several Languages

Table 7.10 shows how Bluetooth service records can include strings in more than one language. In addition to the ServiceName and ServiceDescription attributes shown in Table 7.9, three service attributes have been included in the service record. Two of these attributes provide the ServiceName and ServiceDescription in French. The third attribute, the LanguageBaseAttributeIDList, describes the two languages used in this service record and provides the information needed to differentiate the English strings from the French strings.

To support use of multiple languages in service records, the Bluetooth SDP uses a base-plus-offset scheme for all service attributes of type string. In the service record shown in Table 7.10, the base for English service attributes is 0x0100. The base for French service attributes is 0x0120. The SDP specification [1] defines the ServiceDescription as having an offset of 0x0001. This means the attribute ID of the ServiceDescription in English in this service record is given by the English base plus offset; or

0x0100 + 0x0001 = 0x0101

The attribute ID of the ServiceDescription in French is given by the French base plus offset, or

0x0120 + 0x0001 = 0x0121

ServiceName is defined as having an offset of 0x0000, so the ServiceName in English has attribute ID

0x0100 + 0x0000 = 0x0100

The ServiceName in French has attribute ID

0x0120 + 0x0000 = 0x0120

The LanguageBaseAttributeIDList contains the attribute ID base for each language. LanguageBaseAttributeIDList is an optional service attribute. However, if a service record were to use more than one language, it would be very difficult for applications to use the other languages without knowing the attribute ID base value for the other languages. The attributeValue for the LanguageBaseAttributeIDList is a list, or DATSEQ, of DataElements of type U_INT_2, that is, of type unsigned 2-byte integer.

The elements of the LanguageBaseAttributeIDList are implicitly grouped into triplets, where each triplet is for a particular language. The first element of the triplet is the language code as standardized by ISO 639 [32]. For English, this code is "en"; for French, it is "fr." The second element of the triplet is the character encoding used for the language. Unicode Transformation Format 8 (UTF-8) is an example of character encoding. The Internet Assigned Numbers Authority maintains a standard list of character encodings [33]. Each encoding in the standard has a MIBenum value; for example, UTF-8 is 0x006A (decimal 106). The MIBenum value of the character encoding is the second element in each triplet contained in the LanguageBaseAttributeIDList. The third element of each triplet is the attribute ID base value for the triplet's language.

The base values used in the third element of each triplet are not standardized. The service records in an SDDB may use different base values for the same language. The only rules are the following:

- The attribute ID base for the primary language used in a particular service record must be 0x0100.

- If there is a LanguageBaseAttributeIDList in the service record, the first language in this list must use the attribute ID base 0x0100; that is, the first language must be the primary language.

The attribute ID base used for a second language is not standardized; that is, we chose the value of 0x0120 for the base value for French in Table 7.10. In selection of base values, care must be taken to avoid

Table 7.10   Selected Attributes from a Service Record with English and French Strings.

...
ServiceName<0x0100>   –Name of the service in the primary language of the service record
DataElement(type = STRING,   "A Bluetooth Game" –from "name=" in the connection string)
ServiceDescription<0x0101>   –Description of the service in the primary language

DataElement(type = STRING,
            "This game is fun! It is for two people.
            You can play it on your cell phones.")

ServiceName<0x0120>   –Name of the service in French
DataElement(type = STRING,   "Jeu de Bluetooth")
ServiceDescription<0x0121>   –Description of the service in French

DataElement(type = STRING,
            "Ce jeu est amusant ! Il se joue à deux. Vous pouvez
            y jouer sur vos téléphones mobiles.")

LanguageBaseAttributeIDList<0x0006>   –Describe the languages used in the service record

DataElement(type = DATSEQ,
            DataElement(type = U_INT_2,
                        0x656E –ASCII for "en", English)
            DataElement(type = U_INT_2,
                        0x006A –the MIBenum for UTF-8)

```
DataElement(type = U_INT_2,
                  0x0100 –attribute ID base for English)
DataElement(type = U_INT_2,
                  0x6672 –ASCII for "fr", French)
DataElement(type = U_INT_2,
                  0x006A –the MIBenum for UTF-8)
DataElement(type = U_INT_2,
                  0x0120 –attribute ID base for French))
```

conflicts with the attribute IDs defined by the Bluetooth Assigned Numbers. One recommendation is to choose attribute ID base values so that the sum of base value plus offset falls either in the range 0x0100 to 0x01FF or in the range 0x0900 to 0xFFFF. The same recommendation applies to user-defined, service-specific attributes with string values.

7.3.4 Service Records for Bluetooth Profiles

The Bluetooth Profiles specification [3] describes a number of common tasks that will be accomplished with Bluetooth wireless technology. The profiles document lists requirements that help in achieving interoperability between devices with independent implementations of these standardized tasks. Developers who intend to implement one of these Bluetooth profiles with their JABWT application need to study the specification [3] closely so that their applications can pass any Bluetooth qualification tests for the profile and can successfully interoperate with other devices that also support the profile.

The profile specifications place requirements on both client and server roles for each profile. Part of the requirements for servers is a specification of what the service record will look like for the profile service. As an example, Table 7.11 shows the service record for the Object Push Profile from the Bluetooth profiles specification [3]. This format is followed by all of the Bluetooth profiles.

The Object Push Profile describes how electronic business cards and other similar objects can be transmitted between Bluetooth devices by means of OBEX. The server in the Object Push Profile is called a Push Server, and the client is called a Push Client. As Table 7.11 shows, the

Table 7.11   Service Record Defined by the Bluetooth Object Push Profile

Item	Definition	Type	Value	AttrID	Status	Default Value
ServiceClassIDList				0x0001	Mand.	
ServiceClass #0	UUID for OBEXObjectPush"	UUID	0x1105		Mand.	0x1105
ProtocolDescriptorList				0x0004	Mand.	
Protocol ID #0	UUID for L2CAP protocol	UUID	0x0100		Mand.	0x0100
Protocol ID #1	UUID for RFCOMM protocol	UUID	0x0003		Mand.	0x0003
Parameter #0	Server channel	UINT8	varies		Mand.	varies
Protocol ID #2	UUID for OBEX	UUID	0x0008		Mand.	0x0008
ServiceName	Displayable Text name	String	varies	0x0000 + base	Opt.	"OBEX Object Push"
BluetoothProfile DescriptorList				0x0009	Opt.	
Profile ID #0	Supported profile	UUID	0x1105			0x1105
Version #0	Profile version	UINT16	0x0100			0x0100
Supported Formats List	Supported Formats List	Data Element Sequence of UINT8	Formats: 0x01 = vCard 2.1 0x02 = vCard 3.0 0x03 = vCal 1.0 0x04 = iCal 2.0 0x05 = vNote 0x06 = vMessage 0xFF = any type of object.	0x0303	Mand.	

UUID with short form 0x1105 is defined as the Service Class ID for Push Servers that conform to the Object Push Profile. Push Clients can look for service records that contain this UUID to identify Push Servers that have demonstrated they meet the requirements of the Object Push Profile.

The Status column in Table 7.11 indicates service record entries that are mandatory (Mand.) and entries that are optional (Opt.) according to the Bluetooth specification.

The UUID values in the Value and Default Value columns shown in Table 7.11 are obtained from the Bluetooth Assigned Numbers [30]. The service attribute ID values in the AttrID column also are obtained from the Bluetooth Assigned Numbers. The version of Table 7.11 in the Object Push Profile specification does not contain these values explicitly but instead refers to the assigned numbers.

The service record in Table 7.11 can be translated into the same notation used earlier in this chapter to describe the `btspp`, `btl2cap`, and `btgoep` service records. That translation is shown in Table 7.12. The translation is straightforward for the most part. However, the two notations use different units (bits versus bytes) when describing types for numbers. Table 7.11 from the Bluetooth profiles specification uses `Uint8` and `Uint16`, which refer to unsigned 8-bit and 16-bit integers. Table 7.12, on the other hand, uses `U_INT_1` and `U_INT_2` for these same two quantities. Table 7.12 uses the names of JABWT constants for all the "type =" entries. The `javax.bluetooth.DataElement` constants `U_INT_1` and `U_INT_2` refer to 1-byte and 2-byte integers. The representations in Table 7.11 and Table 7.12 are equivalent but use different units (bits versus bytes) when describing the type of a number.

There are several points to observe about Table 7.12. In addition to the familiar attributes ServiceClassIDList, ProtocolDescriptorList, and ServiceName are several attributes that we have not seen before. Table 7.12 includes a BluetoothProfileDescriptorList, which is an attribute used to declare that this service conforms to version number 1.00 of the Object Push Profile. The service records for Bluetooth profiles commonly include a BluetoothProfileDescriptorList attribute, although that attribute usually is optional. The short-form UUID for OBEXObjectPush, 0x1105, is used in the BluetoothProfileDescriptorList to designate the Object Push Profile. Because this UUID also is used in the

Table 7.12 Service Record for an OBEX Object Push Server

ServiceClassIDList<0x0001>

DataElement(type = DATSEQ,
            DataElement(type = UUID,
                        UUID(OBEXObjectPush<0x1105>)
                        —Object Push UUID))

ProtocolDescriptorList<0x0004>

DataElement(type = DATSEQ,
            DataElement(type = DATSEQ,
                        DataElement(type = UUID,
                                    UUID(L2CAP<0x0100>)))
            DataElement(type = DATSEQ,
                        DataElement(type = UUID,
                                    UUID(RFCOMM<0x0003>))
                        DataElement(type = U_INT_1,
                                    4 –server channel identifier))
            DataElement(type = DATSEQ,
                        DataElement(type = UUID,
                                    UUID(OBEX<0x0008>)))

ServiceName<0x0100>
DataElement(type = STRING,   "OBEX Object Push Server")
BluetoothProfileDescriptorList<0x0009>

DataElement(type = DATSEQ,
            DataElement(type = DATSEQ,
                        DataElement(type = UUID,
                                    UUID(OBEXObjectPush<0x1105>))
                        DataElement(type = U_INT_2,
                                    0x0100 – version 1.00)))

Supported Formats List<0x0303>

DataElement(type = DATSEQ,
       DataElement(type = U_INT_1,
                  0x01 – vCard 2.1)
       DataElement(type = U_INT_1,
                  0x02 – vCard 3.0))

ServiceClassIDList, this marks the second appearance of this same UUID in the service record.

Table 7.12 also includes one attribute, Supported Formats List, that is unique to the Object Push Profile. The Supported Formats List attribute describes the different object formats supported by this Push Server. The Supported Formats List entry in Table 7.11 describes the different object formats recognized by the Object Push Profile. In Table 7.12, the two formats for electronic business cards have been specified. The Object Push Profile requires that Phone Book applications support data exchange using the vCard 2.1 content format [34].

The following example code shows how a server application can create an Object Push service record. After `Connector.open()` is used to create the service record, the `defineObjectPushService()` method adds the BluetoothProfileDescriptorList attribute to the service record by calling the application method `setBluetoothProfileList()`. The code for this method is presented later. It is followed by code that adds the Supported Formats List attribute to the service record to declare that this server understands the vCard 2.1 and 3.0 formats.

```
/**
 * Create the service record for an OBEX Object Push
 * server as defined
 * by the Bluetooth Object Push profile.
 */
public SessionNotifier defineObjectPushService() {

  SessionNotifier notifier;
  // The UUID 00001105000... is the long-form UUID for the
  // short form 0x1105 defined for the Object Push
  // service ID by
  // assigned numbers.
```

```
String connString =
  "btgoep://localhost:" +
    "0000110500001000800000805F9B34FB;" +
  "name=OBEX Object Push Server";

// Connector.open() assigns a RFCOMM server channel
// and creates a service record using this channel.
try {
  notifier =
    (SessionNotifier)Connector.open(connString);
} catch (ServiceRegistrationException e1) {
  // The open method failed because unable to obtain
  // an RFCOMM
  // server channel.
  return null;
} catch (IOException e2){
  // The open method failed due to another IOException
  return null;
}

try {
  localDev = LocalDevice.getLocalDevice();
} catch (BluetoothStateException e) {
  return null;
}
ServiceRecord record = localDev.getRecord(notifier);

// Add the optional service attribute
// BluetoothProfileDescriptorList
ServiceRecordUtilities.setBluetoothProfileList(record,
  0x1105, 0x0100);
DataElement objFormatsDE = new
  DataElement(DataElement.DATSEQ);
// supported format 0x01 = vCard 2.1
objFormatsDE.addElement(new
  DataElement(DataElement.U_INT_1, 0x01));
// supported format 0x02 = vCard 3.0
objFormatsDE.addElement(new
  DataElement(DataElement.U_INT_1, 0x02));
// Add mandatory Supported Formats List, attribute ID
// 0x0303
record.setAttributeValue(0x0303, objFormatsDE);
```

```
// An Object Push Server provides an Object Transfer
// service.
// Bit 20 of the Class of Device is for Object Transfer.
record.setDeviceServiceClasses(0x100000);
return notifier;
}
```

Table 7.12 shows that the Object Push service record has the following ServiceClassIDList:

DataElement(type = DATSEQ,
        DataElement(type = UUID,
                UUID(OBEXObjectPush<0x1105>)
                        —-Object Push UUID))

This step is accomplished by the method `defineObject-PushService()` by using the connection string:

```
String connString =
        "btgoep://localhost:" +
        "0000110500001000800000805F9B34FB;" +
        "name=OBEX Object Push Server";
```

The JABWT implementation inserts the UUID from the connection string into the ServiceClassIDList of the service record. Although there is a short form UUID of 0x1105 for the OBEXObjectPush service class, we have used the long form in the connection string. The reason is that a UUID in a connection string is always interpreted as a 128-bit UUID. This means that 1105 would be interpreted as the 128-bit UUID 00000000000000000000000000001105 not as the 128-bit UUID 0000110500001000800000805F9B34FB.

In the example code, the `defineObjectPushService()` method uses the `setDeviceServiceClasses()` method of the `ServiceRecord` interface to describe the object transfer major service class provided by the server application

```
record.setDeviceServiceClasses(0x100000);
```

The specification of the Object Push Profile requires that the Push Server indicate that it offers this object transfer service in its device class. A server uses the `setDeviceServiceClasses()` method to associate the `ServiceRecord` with all of the major service classes that describe that service. Later, when a server first calls `acceptAndOpen()`, both its service record and its major service class bits are made visible to client devices. In the case of the major service classes, `acceptAndOpen()` performs a logical OR of the current settings of the service class bits of the device with the major service classes declared by the `setDeviceServiceClasses()` method. This OR operation might activate additional service class bits that indicate new capabilities for the device.

The `defineObjectPushService()` method makes a static method call to create the BluetoothProfileDescriptorList. The code for that static method is shown below. It creates the DataElement structure required for the BluetoothProfileDescriptorList attribute by the Object Push Profile. This method uses the `DataElement.addElement()` method to assemble DataElements of type DATSEQ. One `DataElement` of type DATSEQ is used for the pair of profile and version number. Another `DataElement` of type DATSEQ is used for the list of pairs. In this case, there is only one pair in the list of pairs (Table 7.12).

```
public class ServiceRecordUtilities {
  public static final int ATT_ID_BLUETOOTH_PROFILE_LIST =
    0x0009;

  /**
   * Sets the value of the BluetoothProfileDescriptorList
   * attribute to
   * be the profile represented by a short-form UUID value
   * and version number.
   * @param record The service record to be modified
   * @param profileUuidValue The short-form UUID for the
   * profile from the Bluetooth Assigned Numbers
   * @param version The version of the profile this
   * service conforms to.
   * The format is 0xMMmm where MM is the
   * major version
   * number and mm is the minor version number.
   */
  public static void setBluetoothProfileList(
    ServiceRecord record,
    long profileUuidValue,
    int version) {
    UUID profileUuid = new UUID(profileUuidValue);
```

```
DataElement profileUuidDE = new
  DataElement(DataElement.UUID,
              profileUuid);
DataElement versionDE = new
  DataElement(DataElement.U_INT_2, version);
DataElement profileVersionPairDE
  = new DataElement(DataElement.DATSEQ);
DataElement profileDescriptorDE = new
  DataElement(DataElement.DATSEQ);

// Create a pair with profile UUID and profile version
profileVersionPairDE.addElement(profileUuidDE);
profileVersionPairDE.addElement(versionDE);

// Add the pair to the list of profiles
profileDescriptorDE.addElement(profileVersionPairDE);

// Set the BluetoothProfileDescriptorList to a DATSEQ data
// element containing the UUID-version pair for this
// profile.
record.setAttributeValue(ATT_ID_BLUETOOTH_PROFILE_LIST,
                         profileDescriptorDE);
  }
}
```

7.3.5 Service Discovery

Service discovery within Bluetooth wireless technology can be as complicated or as simple as desired. Like an inquiry, service discovery is a non-blocking request. As service records are discovered, they are passed to the application as events. Also like an inquiry, an event occurs at the end of the service search to notify the application that the service search has been completed. Unlike an inquiry, many devices support multiple service searches at any one time. The number of service searches that the local device supports can be retrieved via a Bluetooth device property. The "bluetooth.sd.trans.max" property can be retrieved via the `LocalDevice.getProperty()` method to determine the maximum number of concurrent service searches.

For the local device to search for a service on a remote device, the local device sends a list of UUIDs to search for to the remote device. The remote device checks all the service records on it for all of the UUIDs sent to it. For every service record that has all the UUIDs, the remote device sends back the ServiceRecordHandle and the requested attributes for that service record.

Starting a service search on a remote device begins with the `DiscoveryAgent.searchServices()` method. The `search-Services()` method takes four arguments. The first argument is the list of attributes to retrieve in any service record that meets the other search criteria. By default, the `searchServices()` method retrieves the ServiceRecordHandle, ServiceClassIDList, ServiceRecordState, ServiceID, and ProtocolDescriptorList attributes. These attributes are known as the *default attributes*. If the attributes list argument is null, only the default attributes are retrieved. If a list of attributes is provided, the default attributes are retrieved in addition to the list provided. With the default attributes, the application has enough information to establish a connection to the service. Additional attributes may be retrieved if additional information about the service is needed. The second argument, the list of UUIDs to search for, specifies all the UUIDs that must exist in a service to be retrieved. The more complete this list of UUIDs, the less likely it is that a service record will contain all of these UUIDs. The third argument, the remote device to search, is a `RemoteDevice` object received via an inquiry or a call to `retrieveDevices()`. The final argument is the `DiscoveryListener` object that will be notified when the services are discovered.

The `searchServices()` method returns the transaction ID for the service search if the device is able to start the service search. The transaction ID allows an application to cancel the search, identify which search located a service, and determine when a specific search is completed. The `searchServices()` method may throw a `BluetoothStateException` if the local device has reached the maximum number of service searches or if the current service search could not be started.

As services are discovered, they are sent to the `Discovery-Listener` via the `servicesDiscovered()` method. The transaction ID of the service search along with all the service records found during the search also is provided. The `servicesDiscovered()` method can be called multiple times for a single service search request. The service records are returned as an array of `ServiceRecord` objects. Each of these `ServiceRecord` objects contains all the attributes requested in the call to `searchServices()` along with the default attributes.

Table 7.13 Status Codes for Service Searches

Completion Status	Reason
SERVICE_SEARCH_COMPLETED	At least one service record was found and the search completed normally.
SERVICE_SEARCH_TERMINATED	The service search was canceled by a call to cancelServiceSearch().
SERVICE_SEARCH_ERROR	An error occurred during the service search.
SERVICE_SEARCH_NO_RECORDS	No records were found during the service search.
SERVICE_SEARCH_DEVICE_NOT_REACHABLE	The RemoteDevice specified to searchServices() could not be reached (i.e., a connection could not be established to the remote device).

When the service search is completed, the serviceSearch-Completed() method is called. The serviceSearchCompleted() method provides the transaction ID of the search that ended and a completion status code. Table 7.13 lists all the completion status codes and what those codes mean.

Like an inquiry, a service search can be canceled with the cancelServiceSearch() method. The cancelServiceSearch() method takes as an argument the transaction ID of the service search to cancel. The method returns true if the search was canceled. Canceling the search also causes a serviceSearchCompleted() event to occur with the SERVICE_SEARCH_TERMINATED status code. If the method returns false, either the service search has already ended or the transaction ID is not valid.

Returning to the DiscoveryMIDlet introduced in Chapter 6, the next step is to search for services. The DiscoveryMIDlet will be modified to search for the Bluetooth game service defined earlier in this chapter. To determine which device to search, the DiscoveryMIDlet waits until the user selects a Bluetooth device from a List. The DiscoveryMIDlet then searches the device specified for the UUID defined by the Bluetooth game service. After retrieving all the services that use this UUID, the DiscoveryMIDlet displays the name of each service. Before starting the service search, the DiscoveryMIDlet must be modified to maintain a list of the `RemoteDevice` objects found via device discovery and to keep track of when the device is in an inquiry.

```java
public class DiscoveryMIDlet extends BluetoothMIDlet
  implements DiscoveryListener {

    ...

    /**
     * Keeps track of the RemoteDevice objects.
     */
    private Vector deviceVector;
    /**
     * Specifies if an inquiry is currently occurring.
     */
    private boolean isInInquiry;

    ...

    public void startApp() throws MIDletStateChangeException {
      isInInquiry = false;
      // Create a new List and set it to the current
      // displayable
      deviceList = new List("List of Devices", List.IMPLICIT);
      deviceList.addCommand(new Command("Exit",
        Command.EXIT, 1));
      deviceList.setCommandListener(this);
      Display.getDisplay(this).setCurrent(deviceList);

      // Retrieve the DiscoveryAgent object. If the
      // retrieving the
      // local device causes a BluetoothStateException,
      // something is wrong
      // so stop the app from running.
      try {
        LocalDevice local = LocalDevice.getLocalDevice();
        agent = local.getDiscoveryAgent();
      } catch (BluetoothStateException e) {
        throw new MIDletStateChangeException(
          "Unable to retrieve local Bluetooth device.");
      }

      deviceVector = new Vector();
      addDevices();
```

```
    try {
      agent.startInquiry(DiscoveryAgent.GIAC, this);
    } catch (BluetoothStateException e) {
      throw new MIDletStateChangeException(
        "Unable to start the inquiry");
    }

    isInInquiry = true;
  }

  public void deviceDiscovered(RemoteDevice device,
    DeviceClass cod) {
    String address = device.getBluetoothAddress();
    deviceList.insert(0, address + "-I", null);
    deviceVector.insertElementAt(device, 0);
  }

  public void inquiryCompleted(int type) {
    isInInquiry = false;

    Alert dialog = null;

    // Determine if an error occurred. If one did occur
    // display an Alert
    // before allowing the application to exit.
    if (type != DiscoveryListener.INQUIRY_COMPLETED) {
      dialog = new Alert("Bluetooth Error",
        "The inquiry failed to complete normally", null,
        AlertType.ERROR);
    } else {
      dialog = new Alert("Inquiry Completed",
        "The inquiry completed normally", null,
          AlertType.INFO);
    }

    dialog.setTimeout(Alert.FOREVER);
    Display.getDisplay(this).setCurrent(dialog);
  }

  private void addDevices() {
    // Retrieve the pre-known device array and append the
    // addresses
    // of the Bluetooth device. If there are no pre-know
    // devices, move on to cached devices.
    RemoteDevice[] list =
      agent.retrieveDevices(DiscoveryAgent.PREKNOWN);
```

```
      if (list != null) {
        for (int i = 0; i < list.length; i++) {
          String address = list[i].getBluetoothAddress();
          deviceList.insert(0, address + "-P", null);
          deviceVector.insertElementAt(list[i], 0);
        }
      }
      // Retrieve the cached device array and append the
      // addresses to the
      // list.
      list = agent.retrieveDevices(DiscoveryAgent.CACHED);
      if (list != null) {
        for (int i = 0; i < list.length; i++) {
          String address = list[i].getBluetoothAddress();
          deviceList.insert(0, address + "-C", null);
          deviceVector.insertElementAt(list[i], 0);
        }
      }
    }
  }
}
```

Now that the DiscoveryMIDlet keeps track of each RemoteDevice object found and when the MIDlet is performing an inquiry, the DiscoveryMIDlet can be modified to perform a service search. The service search is started when a user selects one of devices displayed on the screen. Because many Bluetooth devices cannot start service searches while the device is performing an inquiry, the inquiry is canceled if one is occurring before the search is started.

```
public class DiscoveryMIDlet extends BluetoothMIDlet
  implements DiscoveryListener {

  ...

  /**
   * The List of service records that were found.
   */
  private List serviceRecordList;

  ...

  public void commandAction(Command c, Displayable d) {
```

```
    if (c.getCommandType() == Command.EXIT) {
  if (isInInquiry) {
      // Try to cancel the inquiry.
        agent.cancelInquiry(this);
  }

  notifyDestroyed();
} else if (c == List.SELECT_COMMAND) {
  // Since the deviceList is currently visible, the user
  // must
  // have selected a device to search so display the
  // serviceRecordList screen.
  serviceRecordList = new List("Services Found",
    List.IMPLICIT);
  serviceRecordList.addCommand(new Command("Exit",
    Command.EXIT, 1));
  serviceRecordList.setCommandListener(this);

  Alert splash = null;

  // If an inquiry is presently occurring, cancel the
  // inquiry
  // before starting the service search. Otherwise,
  // start the
  // service search
  if (isInInquiry) {
    agent.cancelInquiry(this);

    splash = new Alert("Cancel Inquiry",
      "Ending the inquiry and starting the service search",
      null, AlertType.INFO);
  } else {
    splash = new Alert("Starting Search",
      "Starting the service search",
      null, AlertType.INFO);

    startServiceSearch();
  }

  splash.setTimeout(2000);
  Display.getDisplay(this).setCurrent(splash,
    serviceRecordList);
  }
}
/**
```

```
     * Starts the service search.
     */
    private void startServiceSearch() {

        try {
          // Search for the Bluetooth Game service record and
          // retrieve
          // the name attribute in addition to the default
          // attributes.
          UUID[] uuidList = new UUID[1];
          uuidList[0] = new
            UUID("0FA1A7AC16A211D7854400B0D03D76EC", false);
          int[] attrList = new int[1];
          attrList[0] = 0x100;
          // The RemoteDevices are in the deviceVector in the
          // same order as
          // they are on the screen so getting the index
          // allows us to
          // retrieve the correct RemoteDevice object.
          int index = deviceList.getSelectedIndex();
          RemoteDevice d =
            (RemoteDevice)deviceVector.elementAt(index);

          int id = agent.searchServices(attrList, uuidList,
            d, this);
        } catch (BluetoothStateException e) {
          Alert error = new Alert("Error",
            "Unable to start the service search (" +
              e.getMessage() +
            ")", null, AlertType.ERROR);
          error.setTimeout(Alert.FOREVER);
          Display.getDisplay(this).setCurrent(error, deviceList);
        }
    }

    public void inquiryCompleted(int type) {
        isInInquiry = false;

        Alert dialog = null;

        // Determine if an error occurred. If one did occur
        // display an Alert
        // before allowing the application to exit.
        if (type != DiscoveryListener.INQUIRY_COMPLETED) {
```

```
    // If the device inquiry was terminated, then the
    // user must have
    // selected a Remote Device to perform a service
    // search on so
    // start the service search.
    if (type == DiscoveryListener.INQUIRY_TERMINATED) {
      startServiceSearch();

      return;
    } else {
        dialog = new Alert("Bluetooth Error",
          "The inquiry failed to complete normally", null,
          AlertType.ERROR);
      }
  } else {
    dialog = new Alert("Inquiry Completed",
      "The inquiry completed normally", null,
      AlertType.INFO);
  }
  dialog.setTimeout(Alert.FOREVER);
  Display.getDisplay(this).setCurrent(dialog);
 }
}
```

The startServiceSearch() method is called from two different parts of the previous code. The startServiceSearch() method is called from the commandAction() method if an inquiry is not in progress. If an inquiry is in progress, the commandAction() method cancels the inquiry and the startServiceSearch() method is called from the inquiryCompleted() method when the cancel is processed.

The startServiceSearch() method starts the service search. This method performs a service search for the Bluetooth game service described earlier in this chapter. When a service is found with the Bluetooth game service's UUID, the 0x100 attribute also is retrieved. This is the ServiceName attribute ID as defined by the Bluetooth SIG. (This is used later in this chapter.)

Even though the startServiceSearch() method starts the search, the DiscoveryMIDlet does not do anything with the services that it finds at present. Therefore the servicesDiscovered() method is modified to display the number of service records returned to the DiscoveryMIDlet. The serviceSearchCompleted() method is also modified to display a message to the user when the service search ends.

```
public class DiscoveryMIDlet extends BluetoothMIDlet
  implements DiscoveryListener {

  ...

    public void servicesDiscovered(int transID,
      ServiceRecord[] record) {
      serviceRecordList.insert(0,
        Integer.toString(record.length), null);
    }

    /**
     * Called when the service search has ended. Displays a
     * message to the
     * user that the service search completed and specifies
     * if the search
     * completed normally.
     *
     * @param transID the transaction ID
     * @param type specifies how the service search completed
     */
    public void serviceSearchCompleted(int transID, int type) {
      Alert dialog = null;

      // Determine if an error occurred. If one did occur
      // display an Alert
      // before allowing the application to exit.
      if (type !=
        DiscoveryListener.SERVICE_SEARCH_COMPLETED) {
        dialog = new Alert("Bluetooth Error",
          "The service search failed to complete normally",
            null,
            AlertType.ERROR);
      } else {
        dialog = new Alert("Service Search Completed",
          "The service search completed normally", null,
            AlertType.INFO);
      }
      dialog.setTimeout(Alert.FOREVER);
      Display.getDisplay(this).setCurrent(dialog);
    }
  }
```

7.3.6 Working with Service Records

After a `ServiceRecord` is retrieved from a service search, the next step is to determine whether the service described by the `ServiceRecord` is the desired service. Once the service is determined to be the desired service, the `getConnectionURL()` method can be called to retrieve the connection string that establishes a connection to the service. This connection string may then be passed to `Connector.open()` to establish the connection. The `getConnectionURL()` method also allows the application to specify the security requirements of the connection and whether the local device is the master or the slave (see section 4.3 for more information on Bluetooth security).

Before calling `getConnectionURL()`, the application must determine whether the `ServiceRecord` describes the service desired. This step highlights the need to be as specific as possible when determining the list of UUIDs to search for. Being as specific as possible minimizes the need to do additional work to determine whether the `ServiceRecord` returned is for the desired service. In most situations, a complete list of UUIDs used in the service search eliminates the need for additional verification. When the service record is discovered in this situation, all that is required is calling the `getConnectionURL()` method to begin using the service.

There are situations that require additional verification or determination. For example, if the local device is able to locate two instances of the same service, the local device could connect to the service that is currently less busy. The application may also want to request additional information that allows the user of the application to determine which service to use.

To actually access the values of each of the attributes, the `getAttributeValue()` method should be used. The `getAttribute-Value()` method returns the attribute value of the attribute ID specified or null if the attribute ID is not in this service record. The value of an attribute is encapsulated in the `DataElement` class. The `DataElement` class provides accessor methods to determine the type of the data element and its value. Table 7.14 lists the different types of data elements and how these types relate to the `DataElement` class.

Before the value of a data element is retrieved, the `getDataType()` method should be called to verify the data type of the value. This step should always be done before retrieving the value of a

Table 7.14   Bluetooth Data Element Types and Their Associated Java Types

Bluetooth Type	DataElement Data Type	Java Type	Method for Retrieving Value from DataElement
Null	NULL	Represents a `null` value	None
Unsigned integer (1 byte)	U_INT_1	`long` value in the range of 0 to 255	`getLong()`
Unsigned integer (2 bytes)	U_INT_2	`long` value in the range of 0 to 2^{16}-1	`getLong()`
Unsigned integer (4 bytes)	U_INT_4	`long` value in the range of 0 to 2^{32}-1	`getLong()`
Unsigned integer (8 bytes)	U_INT_8	`byte[]` value in the range of 0 to 2^{64}-1	`getValue()`
Unsigned integer (16 bytes)	U_INT_16	`byte[]` value in the range of 0 to 2^{128}-1	`getValue()`
Integer (1 byte)	INT_1	`long` value in the range –128 to 127	`getLong()`
Integer (2 bytes)	INT_2	`long` value in the range -2^{15} to 2^{15}-1	`getLong()`
Integer (4 bytes)	INT_4	`long` value in the range -2^{31} to 2^{31}-1	`getLong()`
Integer (8 bytes)	INT_8	`byte[]` value in the range -2^{63} to 2^{63}-1	`getValue()`
Integer (16 bytes)	INT_16	`byte[]` value in the range -2^{127} to 2^{127}-1	`getValue()`
URL	URL	`java.lang.String`	`getValue()`
UUID	UUID	`javax.bluetooth.UUID`	`getValue()`
Boolean	BOOL	`boolean`	`getBoolean()`
String	STRING	`java.lang.String`	`getValue()`
Data element sequence	DATSEQ	`java.util.Enumeration`	`getValue()`
Data element alternative	DATALT	`java.util.Enumeration`	`getValue()`

data element because calling the wrong method on a `DataElement` object causes a `ClassCastException` to be thrown.

To show how to use `DataElement`s and `ServiceRecord`s, we are modifying the `DiscoveryMIDlet` to display the ServiceName attribute value for each service record found. This is done by modifying the `servicesDiscovered()` method. First, the `servicesDiscovered()` method retrieves the `DataElement` for the ServiceName attribute. Before the string contained in the `DataElement` is extracted , the `getDataType()` method must be called to determine the type of attribute value stored in the `DataElement` object. After it is verified that the data element is a string, the value of the data element is displayed.

```
public class DiscoveryMIDlet extends BluetoothMIDlet
    implements DiscoveryListener {

  ...

  /**
   * The service records that were found in the last
   * service search.
   */
  private Vector serviceRecordVector;

  ...

  /**
   * Called each time a service is discovered. Retrieve
   * the name attribute
   * from the service record and display it on the
   * screen. Add the service
   * record to the service record Vector for later.
   *
   * @param transID the transaction ID
   * @param record the service records that were found
   */
  public void servicesDiscovered(int transID,
      ServiceRecord[] record) {

    // Process each service record individually
    for (int i = 0; i < record.length; i++) {

      //Retrieve the name attribute from the service record
      DataElement nameElement =
        (DataElement)record[i].getAttributeValue(0x100);

      // The name attribute is only valid if it exists and
      // is a string
      // If either of these conditions fail, move on to the
      // next service record.
      if ((nameElement != null) &&
        (nameElement.getDataType() == DataElement.STRING)) {

        //Retrieve the name and display it on the screen.
```

```
            String name = (String)nameElement.getValue();
            serviceRecordList.insert(0, name, null);

            serviceRecordVector.insertElementAt(record[i], 0);
          }
        }
      }

      ...

      private void startServiceSearch() {
        serviceRecordVector = new Vector();

        try {
          // Search for the Bluetooth Game service record and
          // retrieve
          // the name attribute in addition to the default
          // attributes.
          UUID[] uuidList = new UUID[1];
          uuidList[0] = new UUID(
            "0FA1A7AC16A211D7854400B0D03D76EC", false);
          int[] attrList = new int[1];
          attrList[0] = 0x100;

          // The RemoteDevices are in the deviceVector in the
          // same order as
          // they are on the screen so getting the index
          // allows us to
          // retrieve the correct RemoteDevice object.
          int index = deviceList.getSelectedIndex();
          RemoteDevice d =
            (RemoteDevice)deviceVector.elementAt(index);

          int id = agent.searchServices(attrList, uuidList, d,
            this);
        } catch (BluetoothStateException e) {
          Alert error = new Alert("Error",
            "Unable to start the service search (" +
            e.getMessage() +
            ")", null, AlertType.ERROR);
          error.setTimeout(Alert.FOREVER);

          Display.getDisplay(this).setCurrent(error, deviceList);
        }
      }
    }
```

In addition to displaying the service name of each service discovered, every `ServiceRecord` object returned to the application is stored in a `Vector` so that additional information can be gathered from the service record later.

7.3.7 Retrieving Additional Attributes after Service Discovery

The `getAttributeIDs()` method returns the IDs of all the attributes that have been retrieved from the remote device. This method does not return all the attributes defined in the service record on the remote device. Why would a `ServiceRecord` that has been discovered not have all the attributes of the service record on the remote device? The answer is simple. To reduce the amount of data actually sent over the air. If there is no intention to actually use an attribute, there is no reason to retrieve the attribute.

Sometimes the local device needs an attribute only in specific instances. JABWT provides a way to retrieve these attributes after the service search has been completed. For retrieving additional attributes, the `populateRecord()` method is called with the list of additional attributes to retrieve. The `populateRecord()` method returns `true` if some or all of the attributes specified are retrieved. The method may also throw an `IOException` if the remote device that has the service described by the `ServiceRecord` cannot be reached or the service is no longer available.

The `populateRecord()` method goes over the air to retrieve these additional attributes. Unlike `searchServices()`, which issues a request and then returns, a call to `populateRecord()` does not return until it fails or the information is retrieved. Because the `populateRecord()` method blocks, be aware of where this method is called. Calling the method within an event handler can affect the user's experience.

To show how to use the `populateRecord()` method, we modify the `DiscoveryMIDlet` to retrieve the ServiceDescription attribute. This procedure requires a few modifications to the `DiscoveryMIDlet`. Because it implements `Runnable` through the `BluetoothMIDlet` class, the `DiscoveryMIDlet` must have a `run()` method. When a user selects a service name from the List displayed on the screen, a new thread is created for the `DiscoveryMIDlet` that retrieves the ServiceDescription attribute by means of the `populateRecord()` method.

```
public class DiscoveryMIDlet extends BluetoothMIDlet
  implements DiscoveryListener {

...

public void commandAction(Command c, Displayable d) {
  if (c.getCommandType() == Command.EXIT) {
    if (isInInquiry) {
      // Try to cancel the inquiry.
      agent.cancelInquiry(this);
    }

    notifyDestroyed();
  } else if (c == List.SELECT_COMMAND) {
    // Determine if the deviceList is the one that was
    // selected.
    if (d == deviceList) {
      // Since the deviceList is currently visible, the
      // user must
      // have selected a device to search so display the
      // serviceRecordList screen.
      serviceRecordList = new List("Services Found",
        List.IMPLICIT);
      serviceRecordList.addCommand(new Command("Exit",
        Command.EXIT, 1));
      serviceRecordList.setCommandListener(this);

      Alert splash = null;

      // If an inquiry is presently occurring, cancel
      // the inquiry
      // before starting the service search. Otherwise,
      // start the
      // service search
      if (isInInquiry) {
        agent.cancelInquiry(this);

        splash = new Alert("Cancel Inquiry",
          "Ending the inquiry and starting the service"
            + "search",
          null, AlertType.INFO);
      } else {

        splash = new Alert("Starting Search",
          "Starting the service search",
```

```
                  null, AlertType.INFO);

            startServiceSearch();

        }

      splash.setTimeout(2000);
      Display.getDisplay(this).setCurrent(splash,
        serviceRecordList);

        } else {
          // Since the serviceRecordList is presently being
          // displayed,
          // get the description attribute for the service
          // that was
          // selected.
          new Thread(this).start();
        }
      } else {
        // The user must have selected the Back command. So
        // display the
        // names of all the services that were found.
        serviceRecordList = new List("Services Found",
          List.IMPLICIT);
        serviceRecordList.addCommand(new Command("Exit",
          Command.EXIT, 1));
        serviceRecordList.setCommandListener(this);

        for (int i = 0; i < serviceRecordVector.size(); i++) {
          // Services were only added to the
          // serviceRecordVector if
          // they had a valid name attribute. Therefore,
          // there is no need
          // to test the nameElement.
          ServiceRecord record =
            (ServiceRecord)serviceRecordVector.elementAt(i);
          DataElement nameElement =
            (DataElement)record.getAttributeValue(0x100);
          String name = (String)nameElement.getValue();

          serviceRecordList.insert(0, name, null);
        }
        Display.getDisplay(this).setCurrent(
          serviceRecordList);
```

```
        }
    }
    /**
     * This thread is started when the user selects a
     * service name. This
     * thread retrieves the description of the service and
     * displays the
     * description on the screen.
     */
    public void run() {
      Alert error = null;

      try {
        // Identify the service record selected by the user
        int index = serviceRecordList.getSelectedIndex();
        ServiceRecord record =
          (ServiceRecord)serviceRecordVector.elementAt(index);

        // Retrieve the description attribute from the
        // remote device
        int[] attrList = new int[1];
        attrList[0] = 0x101;

        if (record.populateRecord(attrList)) {

          // Retrieve the description data element and
          // verify that it
          // exists and is a String
          DataElement descriptionDataElement =
            record.getAttributeValue(0x101);
          if ((descriptionDataElement != null) &&
              (descriptionDataElement.getDataType() ==
            DataElement.STRING)) {

            // Display the description on the screen
            String description =
              (String)descriptionDataElement.getValue();

            Form descriptionForm = new Form(
              "Service Description");
            descriptionForm.append(description);
            descriptionForm.addCommand(new Command("Exit",
              Command.EXIT, 1));
            descriptionForm.addCommand(new Command("Back",
              Command.OK, 1));
```

```
        descriptionForm.setCommandListener(this);
        Display.getDisplay(this).setCurrent(
          descriptionForm);
        return;
      }
    }
    error = new Alert("Error",
      "Failed to retrieve the description of this service",
      null, AlertType.ERROR);
  } catch (IOException e) {
    error = new Alert("Error",
      "Failed to retrieve the description (IOException: " +
      e.getMessage() + ")", null, AlertType.ERROR);
  }
  // Display the error message on the screen
  error.setTimeout(2000);
  Display.getDisplay(this).setCurrent(error);
  }
}
```

Note that in the `run()` method, the ServiceDescription attribute is not simply retrieved and displayed. Like the ServiceName attribute displayed on the screen previously, the `DataElement` returned for the ServiceDescription attribute is inspected to determine whether the `DataElement` represents a String. Also, the return value of `populateRecord()` is checked to verify that the ServiceDescription attribute was retrieved.

In addition to starting the thread that retrieves the ServiceDescription attribute, the `commandAction()` method is modified to allow the user to return to the list of service names after retrieving the service description. This procedure allows the user to retrieve the ServiceDescription attribute of other services that were found during the service search.

7.3.8 Simple Device and Service Discovery

To make things easier for developers, the `selectService()` method combines the process of device and service discovery. The `selectService()` method returns a connection string that can be used by `Connector.open()` to connect to the service. If a service cannot be found

that meets the requirements of the search, selectService() returns
null. The selectService() method has three arguments. The first argument is the UUID to search for in the ServiceClassIDList attribute. The
second argument specifies the minimum security requirements needed for
the connection. The third argument specifies whether the local device
needs to be the master of this connection.

```
Connection getConnection(String uuidValue) throws
  IOException {
  String connString;

  try {
    // Retrieve the LocalDevice and DiscoveryAgent objects.
    LocalDevice local = LocalDevice.getLocalDevice();
    DiscoveryAgent agent = local.getDiscoveryAgent();

    // Retrieve the connection string to the service
    UUID searchUUID = new UUID(uuidValue, false);
    connString = agent.selectService(searchUUID,
      ServiceRecord.NOAUTHENTICATE_NOENCRYPT, false);

  } catch (BluetoothStateException e) {
    throw new IOException("BluetoothStateException: " +
      e.getMessage());
  }

  if (connString == null) {
    throw new IOException(
      "Failed to locate a device with the UUID " +
      uuidValue);
  }
  return Connector.open(connString);
}
```

The getConnection() method uses the selectService() method to
locate a service using the UUID value specified. If a service is found, the
code calls Connector.open() to establish a connection to the service
found. If a service is not found, the code throws an IOException to
signal that a connection could not be established.

JABWT does not specify how selectService() finds a device
with the service requested. Therefore an inquiry can occur during
the call to selectService(). Because of this possibility, the
selectService() method should be called in a separate thread

because an inquiry can last 10 seconds or more. This procedure prevents the application from appearing frozen while the `selectService()` method is called.

Generating a UUID for Your Service

For testing your server application, you can make up an arbitrary series of hexadecimal digits for the UUID needed in the server's connection string. However, when you are ready to package your application, you should provide a UUID that is truly unique so that clients can use this UUID to locate your server application on Bluetooth devices. For example, the `defineGameService()` method shown earlier in this chapter used the UUID `0FA1A7AC16A211D7854400B0D03D76EC`. A process has been specified for generating UUIDs that have a very high probability of being unique [35]. This process generates a UUID using a timestamp and the Ethernet address of the computer used to generate the UUID. It would have been useful to provide a method for generating UUID as part of the JABWT. However, this UUID-generating method would have been used only during development and would not have been used for actually running JABWT applications. This method was omitted from the API to keep the JABWT implementation as small as possible for J2ME devices.

Several utilities are available for generating UUIDs. These utilities tend to be operating system specific because of the need to access the Ethernet card address. On Windows, UUIDs can be generated with the tool `Guidgen.exe` that comes with Microsoft® Visual Studio®. On Linux a `uuidgen` function is available as part of the e2fsprogs package for second extended (ext2) Linux file systems. For example, the command

```
uuidgen -t
```

returns a result such as the following:

```
0fa1a7ac-16a2-11d7-8544-00b0d03d76ec
```

The last twelve hexadecimal digits are the network card address. As can be seen from the example output from `uuidgen`, it is conventional to include hyphens between certain digits of a UUID. However, hyphens are not allowed in the String representations of JABWT UUIDs; the hyphens must be removed before the UUID can be used in a JABWT connection string.

The Bluetooth SIG has reserved a range of UUIDs for use by the Bluetooth specifications. This reserved range starts at the Bluetooth base value of `00000000-0000-1000-8000-00805F9B34FB` and includes all 2^{32} values up to `FFFFFFFF-0000-1000-8000-00805F9B34FB`. Applications should use values in this range only for the purposes described in the Bluetooth specifications.

7.3.9 Connect-Anytime Services

Some devices may provide a capability for starting selected server applications on demand when a client application attempts to connect to a server application not currently running. Server applications with this capability are called *connect-anytime services* in the JABWT specification. Section 7.2.1 discusses run-before-connect services. This section discusses connect-anytime services. An implementation of JABWT need not support both run-before-connect services and connect-anytime services. In fact, the first JABWT implementations support only run-before-connect services.

Connect-anytime services were described in the JABWT specification with the idea that they would take advantage of the MIDP 2.0 [26] capabilities for automatic startup of server MIDlets when clients attempt to connect. The relevant MIDP 2.0 class is `javax.microedition.io.PushRegistry`. JABWT does not explicitly mention any of the MIDP 2.0 mechanisms for automatically starting applications, because the JABWT specification was finalized before the proposed MIDP 2.0 APIs could be discussed publicly under the rules of the Java Community Process.

The run-before-connect service illustrated in Figure 7.2 is a proven scheme with demonstrated implementations. By contrast, the connect-anytime service sketched in Figure 7.5 is currently unproved, and the details remain to be worked out.

In Figure 7.5 the service record is added to the SDDB when the server application is first installed on the device. The service record remains visible to clients as long as the application has not been totally removed from the device. When a client discovers the service record and attempts to connect with a server installed but not currently running, the application management system starts the server application and hands off the client connection to the server. Clients need to do nothing special to connect to a connect-anytime service that is not currently running. A client simply retrieves the service record of the

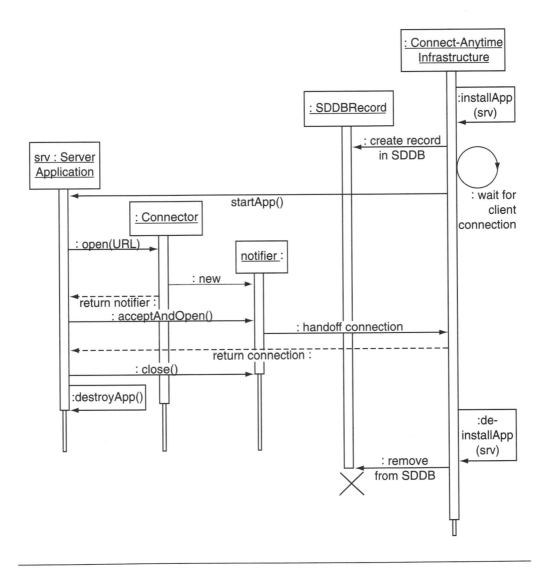

Figure 7.5   Lifecycle of a service record for a connect-anytime service.

connect-anytime service from the server and then attempts to connect using the `Connector.open()` string in the usual way.

There are several potential advantages of connect-anytime services. Device users frequently are responsible for starting run-before-connect services. This requires effort on the users' part, and they may sometimes forget to start a service. Connect-anytime services may be easier for users because users have only to start the client, and then the server will be started automatically. The infrastructure for connect-anytime services is likely to ask user permission before starting up a service, but granting this permission should be easier for users than initiating the server startup process on their own. Also, if a device provides several services, it may be less computationally expensive to have the connect-anytime infrastructure listening for all service requests than it is to have all of the services running at all times.

Although Figure 7.5 shows the service record for a connect-anytime service being added to the SDDB at application installation, that is only one possibility. The JABWT specification provides a fair amount of latitude for when service records for connect-anytime services are actually added to the SDDB. The key point is that JABWT allows an option whereby clients can connect to a service not currently running, if it is possible to start the server application to complete the connection.

7.4 Summary

A Bluetooth client application communicates with a Bluetooth server application on another device to use the services provided by the server. Service discovery is the process of identifying the services offered by nearby Bluetooth devices by retrieving their service records. This chapter describes the JABWT methods used for locating service records that contain a particular collection of UUIDs and for retrieving some of the attributes of those service records.

Service registration is the process of creating a service record describing a service and adding it to the SDDB, where it can be discovered by clients. For many server applications, developers do not need to be concerned about service records. The JABWT implementation creates and registers a service record automatically. This service record advertises the service to potential clients and provides the information needed to construct a connection string that clients can use to access the service. In many cases, this automatically generated service record is sufficient.

In cases in which the automatically generated service record is inadequate, JABWT provides capabilities that allow developers to modify the service records. This chapter describes the service records automatically generated by JABWT and the procedure for modifying those service records when necessary.

8 L2CAP

CHAPTER

This chapter covers the following topics:

- What is L2CAP?
- What kinds of applications are appropriate for L2CAP communications?
- What support for L2CAP communications does JABWT provide?
- How is an L2CAP channel configured by a JABWT application?
- Why do L2CAP applications need to provide flow control?

8.1 Overview

L2CAP stands for *logical link control and adaptation protocol*. L2CAP is a multiplexing layer that allows several higher-level protocols or applications to use Bluetooth communications. Figure 8.1 shows where L2CAP fits in the Bluetooth protocol stack. The figure shows a common hardware configuration with separate host hardware and a Bluetooth radio module. In this configuration, the L2CAP layer is on the host side of the HCI. Also in this configuration, L2CAP uses HCI to communicate with the baseband layer in the Bluetooth radio module. All Bluetooth data communications use L2CAP, but Bluetooth voice communications do not.

As Figure 8.1 shows, several protocols sit on top of the L2CAP layer and use L2CAP to provide access to the Bluetooth hardware in the Bluetooth radio module. The SDP and the RFCOMM protocol are two of these higher-level protocols. JABWT provides access to both SDP and RFCOMM. Chapter 7 describes how JABWT applications use the SDP protocol to discover service records. Chapter 4 describes how JABWT applications use the RFCOMM protocol for serial port communications.

JABWT does not provide access to the other two protocols shown above L2CAP in Figure 8.1. TCS binary defines the call-control signaling that establishes speech and data calls between Bluetooth devices. The BNEP [6] is an optional protocol developed after Bluetooth specification version 1.1 but based on the 1.1 version of the specification. The BNEP can be used to transmit IP packets over L2CAP and supports the PAN profile [36].

The PAN profile is one of three Bluetooth profiles that provide access to the Internet for Bluetooth devices. Two other profiles for Internet access are the LAN Access Profile [3] and the Dial-up Networking Profile [3]. The LAN Access Profile and the Dial-up Networking Profile use the RFCOMM protocol rather than the BNEP as their entry point into the Bluetooth protocol stack. The LAN Access Profile addresses the case in which a data terminal such as a laptop uses Bluetooth wireless technology to communicate with a LAN access point that serves as a gateway to a LAN. This is one of the use cases also addressed by the PAN profile. The PAN profile supersedes the LAN Access Profile, so the LAN Access Profile is now considered obsolete. The Dial-up Networking Profile describes the case in which a data terminal such as a laptop uses Bluetooth wireless technology to communicate with a cell phone or modem that provides a dial-up connection to a LAN.

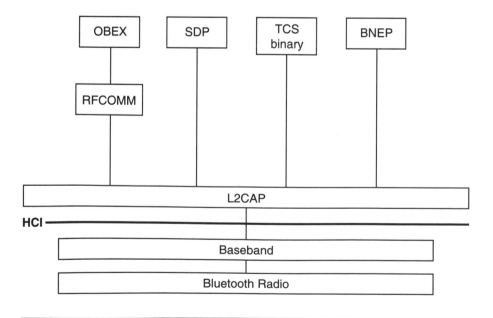

Figure 8.1   Position of L2CAP in the Bluetooth stack.

8.1.1   L2CAP Channels and L2CAP Packets

Figure 8.2 illustrates the multiplexing service that L2CAP provides. The left side of Figure 8.2 represents one Bluetooth device, and the right side represents another Bluetooth device. On the left side, an L2CAP server application and the RFCOMM protocol both are using L2CAP to provide Bluetooth communications. L2CAP establishes L2CAP channels that connect these higher-level entities to their counterparts on the remote device. In Figure 8.2, two L2CAP channels are represented. One L2CAP channel runs between the L2CAP server application and the L2CAP client application. Another L2CAP channel runs between the RFCOMM protocol layers on the two devices. In Figure 8.2 these L2CAP channels are represented as highways. The arrows traveling over the highways represent L2CAP packets. L2CAP provides full-duplex communications, so the L2CAP packets can travel in both directions.

The length of the arrow represents the size of the L2CAP packet. There is a limit to the size of the L2CAP packet that can be transferred over a particular L2CAP channel in a particular direction. This limit is called the *maximum transmission unit* (MTU). In Figure 8.2, the arrows heading to the L2CAP client are longer than the arrows heading from

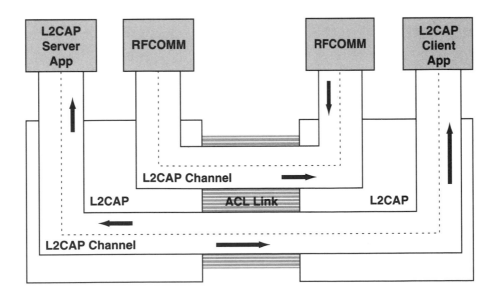

Figure 8.2   L2CAP channels transmit L2CAP packets to multiple destinations.

the L2CAP client. This configuration is intended to suggest that the MTU for the L2CAP packets received by the L2CAP client is larger than the MTU for packets received by the L2CAP server. When the L2CAP channel is established, the MTU values for travel in both directions are negotiated by the two L2CAP components. Section 8.2.3 provides additional details about MTUs.

Figure 8.2 shows the ACL link between the two devices. The baseband layer of the protocol stack establishes the ACL link. There is exactly one ACL link between two Bluetooth devices communicating with each other. The ACL link and the baseband functions provide the infrastructure needed to support the high-level, "logical" abstractions of L2CAP channels and L2CAP packets that L2CAP presents to higher-level protocols and applications.

L2CAP packets have to be converted into one or more baseband packets for transmission over the ACL link. The receiving device then reassembles these baseband packets into L2CAP packets. There are various sizes of baseband packets, but the largest payload is 339 bytes. This is much smaller than the largest payload possible for an L2CAP packet, 65,535 bytes. Because baseband packets are much smaller than packet sizes used by higher-level protocols and applications, the segmentation and reassembly process hides the details about Bluetooth baseband packets from the higher levels of the stack and from applications. By presenting abstractions such as L2CAP channels and L2CAP packets to higher levels, L2CAP makes it easier for higher-level protocols and applications to use Bluetooth communications. This adaptation function is one of the important contributions of L2CAP.

The L2CAP channels shown in Figure 8.2 are what are known as *connection-oriented channels*. They support L2CAP packet transmission in both directions, and the L2CAP packets transmitted are intended for use only by the single device at the other end of the ACL link. L2CAP also provides *connectionless channels*. Connectionless channels allow only one-way traffic, and they are intended for broadcasting L2CAP packets to a group of nearby devices. JABWT provides no support for connectionless channels.

8.1.2 Reasons for Using L2CAP

A number of Bluetooth protocols are defined on top of the L2CAP protocol. Figure 8.1 shows four of these protocols: RFCOMM, SDP, TCS binary, and BNEP. However, the number of these protocols keeps growing as new Bluetooth profiles are developed that define new protocols based on L2CAP. The first column of Table 8.1 lists the current Bluetooth protocols that are layered on top of L2CAP. (Additional protocols and profiles are currently under development by the Bluetooth SIG.) The second column of Table 8.1 lists the current Bluetooth profiles that use the protocol listed in the first column. The Bluetooth protocols and profiles above the line dividing Table 8.1 are candidates for implementation with the JABWT L2CAP API. The profiles below the line that use the RFCOMM protocol are candidates to be implemented with the JABWT RFCOMM API. The JABWT service discovery API provides the key capabilities of the SDAP, so there should be no need to use JABWT to implement the SDAP.

The protocols and profiles above the line in Table 8.1 do not use RFCOMM or OBEX, so if they can be implemented at all with JABWT,

Table 8.1 Protocols and Profiles above Line Are Candidates for L2CAP API

Protocols That Use L2CAP Directly	Profiles Using the Protocol
Telephony Control Protocol Specification (TCS-BIN) [1]	Cordless Telephony Profile [3]
	Intercom Profile [3]
Bluetooth Network Encapsulation Protocol (BNEP) [6]	Personal Area Networks [36]
	Extended Service Discovery Profile [37]
Hardcopy Control Channel [7]	Hardcopy Cable Replacement Profile [7]
Hardcopy Notification Channel [7]	Hardcopy Cable Replacement Profile
Audio/Video Control Transport Protocol [8]	Audio/Video Remote Control Profile [38]
Audio/Video Distribution Transport Protocol [9]	Generic Audio/Video Distribution Profile [39]
	Advanced Audio Distribution Profile [40]
RFCOMM [1]	Serial Port Profile [3]
	Dial-up Networking Profile [3]
	FAX Profile [3]
	Headset Profile [3]
	Hands-Free Profile [41]
Service Discovery Protocol [1]	Service Discovery Application Profile [3]

they will use the L2CAP API. Because JABWT does not provide an interface to all of the L2CAP features, it may not be possible to implement all of the protocols and profiles in Table 8.1 with JABWT. For example, the first protocol in the table, TCS-BIN makes use of both connection-oriented and connectionless L2CAP channels. Because JABWT does not support connectionless L2CAP channels, it would not be possible to implement all of the TCS-BIN protocol with JABWT.

In the case of TCS-BIN, the JSR-82 expert group made an explicit decision that telephony control would likely be provided by device manufacturers, so it was not necessary for JABWT to provide an API that could be used to implement TCS-BIN. However, the other protocols and profiles above the line were defined by the Bluetooth SIG after definition of JABWT, which was based on the 1.1 version of the Bluetooth specification. Consequently, it may or may not be possible to implement these protocols and profiles with JABWT. Developers have to study the specifications carefully and assure themselves that JABWT support for L2CAP is sufficient to implement a particular protocol and profile.

For example, JABWT and the Bluetooth audio/video profiles have incompatible requirements regarding flush timeout. The baseband layer, a layer below L2CAP in the Bluetooth stack (Figure 8.1), offers the option of retransmitting packets until they are received successfully. The retransmit option is controlled by a parameter called *flush timeout,* which indicates how long the baseband attempts to retransmit a packet before giving up and flushing the packet. JABWT currently requires that L2CAP communications use a flush timeout of 0xFFFF, which means that baseband should never give up. The baseband should continue to retransmit until either the packet is acknowledged or the ACL link terminates. On the other hand, the Bluetooth audio/video profiles specify that applications using the audio/video profiles be allowed to set the value of flush timeout. These audio/video profiles recommend that small values should be used for flush timeout. Small values for flush timeout help ensure that most of the L2CAP bandwidth is devoted to the initial transmission of audio/video data and that retransmission is minimized. The next revision of the JABWT specification is expected to remove the requirement for using a flush timeout of 0xFFFF. The revised JABWT specification could introduce a way for applications to request a particular flush timeout. This would remove the current obstacle to using JABWT to implement the audio/video profiles.

In addition to the standardized applications defined as Bluetooth profiles, custom applications based on the L2CAP API are possible. In the case of custom applications, JABWT developers have a choice about whether to use the L2CAP API, the RFCOMM API, or the OBEX API. For most custom applications, the stream-oriented APIs provided by the higher-level protocols RFCOMM and OBEX would have advantages. However, if a custom application requires control over which bytes are sent together in a single packet, then the L2CAP API is the best choice. This might be the case if the application needs to define a new packet-based protocol analogous to the packet-based protocols listed in the first column of Table 8.1. If a stream-based protocol can be used, RFCOMM and OBEX are better options. OBEX itself is a good example of a stream-based protocol [1, 29] that can be defined over RFCOMM.

8.2 API Capabilities

This section describes the support that JABWT provides for L2CAP communications. The Java interfaces defined by JABWT for L2CAP are described. Examples of connection strings used to open an L2CAP connection are provided. Guidelines are proposed for configuring L2CAP channels with MTU parameters in connection strings and for selecting appropriate sizes for the byte arrays used to send and receive L2CAP packets. Issues related to flow control are discussed.

8.2.1 JABWT for L2CAP

Figure 8.3 shows the two interfaces defined in JABWT for L2CAP communications, L2CAPConnection and L2CAPConnectionNotifier. An L2CAP server uses an L2CAPConnectionNotifier to wait for an L2CAP client to establish a connection. The notifier then returns an L2CAPConnection object to provide access to the L2CAP channel between the client and the server. The L2CAPConnection interface can be used to send data between the client and the server using the L2CAP protocol.

When an L2CAP client is successful in opening a connection to an L2CAP server, the result returned from Connector.open() is an L2CAPConnection that gives the client access to the L2CAP channel. Again, the client uses the L2CAPConnection to send and receive data.

The L2CAP client does not use the `L2CAPConnectionNotifier` interface.

For serial port (RFCOMM) communications, the JABWT specification did not need to define any new classes or interfaces beyond those in the GCF defined by CLDC [13]. GCF already provided the stream-oriented interfaces `StreamConnection` and `Stream-ConnectionNotifier`. However, these CLDC interfaces were not useful for L2CAP because L2CAP communications are based on packets not on streams.

CLDC has a `DatagramConnection` interface that is packet oriented rather than stream oriented, and `DatagramConnection` was considered for possible use with L2CAP. As it turns out, `send()` and `receive()` methods were defined for `L2CAPConnection`. `DatagramConnection` has these same methods, but the method arguments are different. For `DatagramConnection` these methods take a `Datagram` argument, whereas the arguments to the `L2CAPConnection` versions of the methods are byte arrays. Each `Datagram` object sent over a `DatagramConnection` contains a destination address, because each `Datagram` can be going to a different recipient. However, this overhead associated with `Datagram` is not needed for L2CAP packets. Each `L2CAPConnection` instance defines a unique sending application and a unique receiving application. Because the address information is contained in the connection, there is no need to provide an address as part of the argument to `send()` or `receive()`.

The `receive()` method blocks until either an L2CAP packet is read or the L2CAP channel is closed. The `ready()` method defined by the `L2CAPConnection` interface makes it possible to check whether a call to `receive()` will block. The `ready()` method returns `true` if an L2CAP packet is available to be read immediately by `receive()` without blocking.

8.2.2 Open an L2CAP Connection

Here are some examples of legal arguments to `Connector.open()` for L2CAP clients:

```
"btl2cap://0050CD00321B:1001"
"btl2cap://0050CD00321B:1001;receiveMTU=512"
"btl2cap://0050CD00321B:1001;receiveMTU=512;"
  + "transmitMTU=512"
```

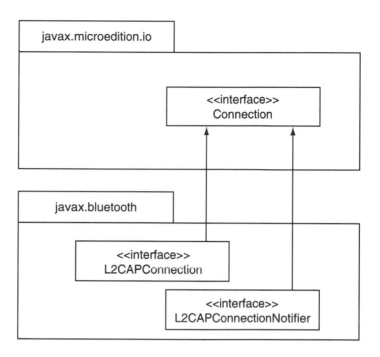

Figure 8.3 JABWT defines two interfaces for L2CAP communications.

```
"btl2cap://0050CD00321B:1001;authenticate=true;"
  + "encrypt=true"
"btl2cap://0050CD00321B:1001;master=true"
```

The protocol name `btl2cap` is "bee tee *el* two cap," not "bee tee *one* two cap." The entry `0050CD00321B` in these examples is the Bluetooth address of the server device. The entry 1001 in these examples is the PSM value for the server application. The PSM is obtained from the service record. The PSM tells the L2CAP layer on the remote device which server application the client wants as the destination of the new L2CAP channel. Higher-level protocols such as RFCOMM and SDP have L2CAP PSM values permanently assigned to them. A PSM has to be dynamically generated for an application, and it is possible that a different PSM will be assigned to the same server application the next time it starts up. This situation is similar to that of `btspp` server channel identifiers, which can vary from device to device and can even vary over time for the same service. One difference between PSMs and service channel identifiers in JABWT is that PSMs in `btl2cap` connection strings are interpreted as hexadecimal numbers, whereas service channel identifiers in `btspp` and `btgoep` connection strings are interpreted as decimal numbers.

The security parameters `authenticate` and `encrypt` are familiar from Chapter 4. The parameter `master` used to request the master role in the resulting Bluetooth network also is familiar. The parameters `receiveMTU` and `transmitMTU` are unique to L2CAP. The parameter `receiveMTU` indicates the size in bytes of the payload of the largest L2CAP packet that the client is willing to receive from the server. The parameter `transmitMTU` indicates the size in bytes of the payload of the largest L2CAP packet that the client will send to the server. These parameters are discussed further in the next section.

L2CAP client applications typically get a connection string from one of the instance methods:

- `ServiceRecord.getConnectionURL(int requiredSecurity, boolean master)`

- `DiscoveryAgent.selectService(UUID uuid, int security, boolean master)`

However, if either of the parameters `transmitMTU` or `receiveMTU` is to be used, it must be appended to the Strings returned from these methods. There is no option to include these MTU parameters in the arguments to the methods as there is for the security parameters and the master parameter.

Here are some examples of legal arguments to `Connector.open()` for L2CAP servers:

```
"btl2cap://localhost:9C68A2AA1EC011D79E6C00B0D03D76EC"
"btl2cap://localhost:9C68A2AA1EC011D79E6C00B0D03D76EC;"
                         + "name=L2CAPEx"
"btl2cap://localhost:9C68A2AA1EC011D79E6C00B0D03D76EC;"
                         + "receiveMTU=512"
"btl2cap://localhost:9C68A2AA1EC011D79E6C00B0D03D76EC;"
                         + "receiveMTU=512;"
                         + "transmitMTU=1024"
"btl2cap://localhost:9C68A2AA1EC011D79E6C00B0D03D76EC;"
                         + "authenticate=true;"
```

```
                                          +  "encrypt=true;"
                                          +  "authorize=true"
     "btl2cap://localhost:9C68A2AA1EC011D79E6C00B0D03D76EC;"
                                          +  "master=true"
```

The only new parameters for L2CAP servers are `receiveMTU` and `transmitMTU`. They have the same meaning for the server as they do for the client. A PSM value is not part of the server's connection string. The PSM is generated automatically and inserted into the service record by the JABWT implementation. This is similar to the situation for `btspp` servers, in which the server channel identifier also is automatically generated and inserted into the service record (see Chapter 7).

8.2.3 L2CAP Channel Configuration

There may be a limit on the size of L2CAP payload the Bluetooth stack can receive or the size of payload a JABWT application is prepared to receive. The largest L2CAP packet payload the Bluetooth stack can receive is returned by `LocalDevice.getProperty("bluetooth.l2cap.receiveMTU.max")`.

The application should decide whether it wants to handle payloads as large as the stack can handle or something smaller. The answer is likely to depend on the nature of the application and the Java heap space expected to be available to applications.

On the basis of these considerations, the application can communicate `receiveMTU` to the remote device when it creates a connection using the `receiveMTU` parameter, `Connector.open("btl2cap://...;receiveMTU=1024")`.

For some applications it is important to be able to send L2CAP packets up to a particular size. For example, the BNEP needs to be able to transmit the maximum Ethernet packet payload, 1500 bytes, plus all of the associated BNEP headers in a single L2CAP packet. Consequently, BNEP needs to be able to send L2CAP packets with payloads of at least 1691 bytes [6]. This requirement on the size of outgoing L2CAP packets can be declared by a JABWT application with the connection string parameter `transmitMTU=1691`.

In general, it is better not to specify `receiveMTU` or `transmitMTU` values in the connection string unless absolutely necessary. MTU values are assigned automatically if no MTU values are mentioned in the connection string. The automatic assignment usually is the default MTU of 672 defined by the L2CAP specification. However, there are cases, such as the BNEP case discussed earlier, in which setting a particular value is required.

The documentation on MTUs can be confusing. Many of the details about `receiveMTU` and `transmitMTU` in the JABWT specification [20] are relevant only to implementers of the JABWT specification. The Bluetooth L2CAP specification [1] describes MTUs from the point of L2CAP. However, L2CAP allows a back-and-forth negotiation process for the MTU values for an L2CAP connection that does not really apply to JABWT applications. The `receiveMTU` and `transmitMTU` values specified in connection strings by JABWT applications should not be viewed as initial proposals in a back-and-forth negotiation. Instead they should be viewed as non-negotiable requirements.

For application developers, we boil down the essentials about MTUs to four rules for code development and one potential pitfall to be aware of even if all four rules are followed.

MTU Rule 1

The values for `receiveMTU` and `transmitMTU` in your L2CAP connection string must be no smaller than `L2CAPConnection.MINIMUM_MTU`, which is 48, the minimum MTU allowed by the Bluetooth L2CAP specification. The values for `receiveMTU` and `transmitMTU` also must be no larger than 65,535, the maximum payload size in an L2CAP packet.

MTU Rule 2

The value for `receiveMTU` in your L2CAP connection string must be smaller than or equal to `LocalDevice.getProperty("bluetooth. l2cap.receiveMTU.max")`, the largest L2CAP packet that can be received by the Bluetooth stack on the device on which your application is currently running. Applications can use this property at runtime to tailor their MTU values to the limits of any Bluetooth stack in use.

MTU Rule 3

For transmitting outgoing packets over an L2CAP connection with `send(byte[] outBuf)`, the byte array `outBuf` must be no larger than

L2CAPConnection.getTransmitMTU(). If outBuf is larger than this, bytes are discarded before the L2CAP packet is sent. If transmitMTU was declared in the L2CAP connection string, then getTransmitMTU() has that same value.

MTU Rule 4

To receive incoming packets with receive(byte[] inBuf), allocate a byte array of size L2CAPConnection.getReceiveMTU().

If you use an inBuf smaller than L2CAPConnection.get-ReceiveMTU(), any bytes received in the L2CAP packet that do not fit in inBuf are discarded. If receiveMTU was declared in the L2CAP connection string, you could allocate a byte array of size receiveMTU. However, if the remote device declares a transmitMTU in its connection string that is smaller than receiveMTU, then L2CAPConnection.get-ReceiveMTU() could be smaller than receiveMTU. It never is larger than receiveMTU.

If you follow all four MTU rules, it is still possible that at runtime a particular L2CAP client and server will be unable to form a connection because of incompatible MTU values. For example, suppose Application A specifies MTU values in its connection string as follows:

```
"btl2cap://...;receiveMTU=receiveMTU_A;transmitMTU=
    transmitMTU_A"
```

Also, suppose Application B specifies MTU values in its connection string as follows:

```
"btl2cap://...;receiveMTU=receiveMTU_B;transmitMTU=
    transmitMTU_B)"
```

MTU Mismatch Pitfall

The applications fail to connect because of inappropriate MTU values,

- If the largest packet Application A will send, $transmitMTU_A$, is larger than the largest packet Application B can receive, $receiveMTU_B$, or

- If the largest packet Application B will send, $transmitMTU_B$, is larger than the largest packet Application A can receive, $receiveMTU_A$

The basic problem that leads to the MTU mismatch pitfall is that the L2CAP protocol does not provide any way to inquire at runtime about the MTU requirements of the remote device other than trying to make a connection and seeing whether you succeed. (Server applications can use custom service attributes in their service records to communicate their MTU requirements, but we are not aware of any precedent for doing this in the Bluetooth profiles.)

If you are writing both the client and server applications, you can avoid this pitfall by not specifying MTU values at all in the connection string or by making $transmitMTU_A$ = $receiveMTU_B$ and $receiveMTU_A$ = $transmitMTU_B$. If you have to interoperate with a variety of implementations, and they use different MTU values, the best strategy is to omit the `transmitMTU` parameter from your connection string. By omitting a `transmitMTU`, you avoid a mismatch with the `receiveMTU` of the remote device.

Omitting a `receiveMTU` in your connection string does not provide the same benefit. The L2CAP channel configuration process requires that each application propose an MTU value for incoming L2CAP packets. If there is no `receiveMTU` in the connection string, then the JABWT implementation supplies a value for `receiveMTU` by using the constant `L2CAPConnection.DEFAULT_MTU`, which has the value 672.

8.2.4 No Flow Control in L2CAP

L2CAP does not provide any flow control mechanism nor does it provide any mechanism for ensuring reliable transmission of L2CAP packets. The baseband layer, which is below L2CAP in the Bluetooth stack, provides flow control for the ACL link as a whole. Unfortunately, it is not sufficient to rely on the flow control provided by the lower baseband level. The problem is that L2CAP is a multiplexing layer that provides multiple L2CAP channels headed to multiple higher-level protocols or applications. In cases in which L2CAP packets arrive faster than they can be processed by one of the higher-level protocols and applications, the L2CAP buffers fill up. When buffers are going to overflow, the only options available to L2CAP are the following:

- Let the lower-level flow-control mechanisms kick in and shut off all incoming packets over this ACL link. Baseband flow-control shuts off L2CAP packets over all the L2CAP channels, not just the L2CAP channels that are having trouble keeping up.

- Discard some L2CAP packets because there is no room for them in the L2CAP buffers. The lower stack layers will not retransmit these packets, because they have already been acknowledged as successfully received.

Simply discarding L2CAP packets is an unattractive option that would lead to data corruption or hung communications. However, the other option whereby the lower-level flow control shuts off all of the L2CAP channels can lead to deadlock in certain situations. The same problem of a multiplexing layer over a reliable communication layer arises in infrared data communications. The deadlock scenario for the IrDA protocol stack is discussed by Williams and Millar [42].

A summary of the deadlock scenario in L2CAP terms is as follows: Suppose a higher-level application uses two L2CAP channels. One of the L2CAP channels is used as a data channel, and the other L2CAP channel is used as a signaling channel. It is possible that the L2CAP buffers are overflowing because the application is waiting to receive an L2CAP packet on the signaling channel before it processes the packets on the data channel. If this is the case, and if baseband flow control shuts off the entire ACL link, then the L2CAP packet on the signaling channel cannot get through. The application continues to wait for this packet, so it does not process the packets on the data channel. However, processing packets on the data channel is the only thing that will free L2CAP buffers and get packets flowing again on the ACL link.

Because L2CAP has no flow control, the protocols and profiles that use L2CAP communications need to have their own mechanisms for flow control. For example, the RFCOMM protocol offers a credit-based flow control mechanism. The Hardcopy Cable Replacement Profile [7], which is one of three Bluetooth profiles for printing, also uses a credit-based flow control mechanism. The Bluetooth Extended Service Discovery Profile [37] uses an end-to-end window flow control mechanism.

If a flow control mechanism were to be added to L2CAP, it would not be necessary for every protocol and profile based on L2CAP to provide its own flow control. For this reason, there is a good chance that the Bluetooth SIG will provide a version of L2CAP with flow control in an upcoming version of the Bluetooth specification.

8.2.5 Types of Applications Using L2CAP

L2CAP applications can be implementations of standard Bluetooth profiles, or they can be nonstandardized, custom applications. The issues that come up are somewhat different depending on which kind of application is planned.

Implementing Bluetooth Profiles Using L2CAP

Certain Bluetooth profiles use L2CAP as their entry point into the Bluetooth protocol stack. Developers who intend to implement one of these Bluetooth profiles with JABWT applications need to study the profile specifications closely so that their applications can pass any Bluetooth qualification tests [10] for this profile and can successfully interoperate with other devices that support these profiles.

Some Bluetooth profiles place requirements on MTU values configured for L2CAP channels. For example, the Hardcopy Cable Replacement Profile establishes two L2CAP channels: a control channel and a data channel. The profile requires that the MTU for the control channel be at least 128 bytes in both directions. The profile recommends that the MTU for the data channel be larger than the minimum (48 bytes) but does not require a particular value.

Implementing Custom Applications Using L2CAP

L2CAP applications that do not claim to conform to a Bluetooth profile do not need to undergo the Bluetooth qualification process. However, developers planning a custom application will still benefit from studying the Bluetooth profiles that use L2CAP. These profiles provide useful examples of how to best use L2CAP.

You should consider how your application will provide flow control. Several flow control schemes have been adopted by the Bluetooth profiles and protocols. For example, SDP entails a simple scheme that requires that only one SDP request from an SDP client to an SDP server can be outstanding at any point in time. Until the server responds to this request, the client is not allowed to issue another request over this same L2CAP channel.

Other current approaches for flow control over L2CAP are referenced in Section 8.2.4. It is worth consulting those references to see what options are available.

8.3 Programming with the API

This section shows example code for MIDP applications that use JABWT L2CAP communications. The example code illustrates the use of JABWT and some design considerations for L2CAP applications. Not all of the code needed to produce a running application is presented here. The complete code is available in Appendix A.

8.3.1 Example: Echo L2CAP Packets

The example code shows both an L2CAP server and an L2CAP client. The L2CAP server echoes back any L2CAP packets sent by the L2CAP client. The client sends 50,000 bytes in a series of L2CAP packets. The size of the packets sent by the client is determined by the value of `getTransmit-MTU()` for the connection. The payload of every packet the server receives is immediately sent back to the client. Both the client and the server keep a count of the total number of bytes sent or received over this connection. This byte count is reported when the packet exchange is complete.

We first look at the MIDlet method `openL2CAPConnection()`, which computes the connection string for either the server or the client and then starts it running. This method takes as arguments `receiveMTU` and `transmitMTU` and two boolean arguments that indicate whether those arguments should be added as parameters to the connection string. There is also an argument indicating whether a client or a server should be started. In the case in which a client should be started, `openL2CAPConnection()` uses the `selectService()` method to obtain a connection string for a server application. The `selectService()` method attempts to find a server application that uses a particular UUID in its service record. Having computed the connection string in the `url` variable, the `openL2CAPConnection()` method starts a thread to execute the client. In the case in which the method is starting a server, computing the connection string is just a matter of concatenating strings for the `btl2cap` scheme, a UUID for the ServiceClassID (see Chapter 7), and any MTU parameters.

```
void openL2CAPConnection(boolean isClient,
                    boolean receiveMTUInput,
                    int receiveMTU,
                    boolean transmitMTUInput,
                    int transmitMTU) {
```

```
String url = null;
String paramString = "";

if (receiveMTUInput) {
  paramString += ";receiveMTU=" + receiveMTU;
}
if (transmitMTUInput) {
  paramString += ";transmitMTU=" + transmitMTU;
}
if (isClient) {
  displayField.setText(
    "searching, please wait...");
  DiscoveryAgent agent =
    device.getDiscoveryAgent();
  try {
    url
        = agent.selectService(uuid,
            ServiceRecord.NOAUTHENTICATE_NOENCRYPT,
              false);
  } catch (BluetoothStateException e) {
    displayError("Error",
                "BluetoothStateException: " +
                e.getMessage());
  }
  if (url == null) {
    displayError("Error",
                "failed to find server!");
    return;
  }
  url += paramString;
  new L2capClient(this).start(url);
} else {
  url = "btl2cap://localhost:" + uuid.toString();
  url += paramString;
  new L2capServer(this).start(url);
}
}
```

The `L2capServer` runs in its own thread, and it establishes an `L2CAPConnection` in its `run()` method.

```java
public class L2capServer extends EchoParticipant
    implements Runnable {
  L2capMtuMIDlet parent;
  private String url;

  public L2capServer(L2capMtuMIDlet parent) {
    this.parent = parent;
    this.out = parent.displayField;
  }

  public void start(String url) {
    this.url = url;
    new Thread(this).start();
  }

  public void run() {
    LocalDevice device = null;
    L2CAPConnectionNotifier notifier = null;
    try {
      device = LocalDevice.getLocalDevice();
      /* Request that the device be made discoverable */
      device.setDiscoverable(DiscoveryAgent.GIAC);
    } catch(BluetoothStateException e) {
      parent.displayError("Error",
                          "BluetoothStateException: " +
                          e.toString());
      return;
    }
    try {
      notifier = (L2CAPConnectionNotifier)
        Connector.open(url);
    } catch (IllegalArgumentException e) {
      parent.displayError("Error",
                          "IllegalArgumentException in " +
                          " Connector.open()");
    } catch (IOException e) {
      parent.displayError("Error",
                          "IOException: " +
                          e.getMessage());
    }
```

```
   if (notifier == null) {
     return;
       }
   try {
     out.setLabel("["+url+"]");
     for (;;) {
       L2CAPConnection conn = notifier.acceptAndOpen();
       echoReceivedL2capPackets(conn);
       conn.close();
     }
   } catch(IOException e) {
     parent.displayError("Error",
                           "IOException: " +
                           e.getMessage());
   } catch (IllegalArgumentException e) {
     parent.displayError("Error",
                           "IllegalArgumentException: " +
                           e.getMessage());
   }
  }
}
```

The statement that creates the L2CAPConnectionNotifier is

```
notifier = (L2CAPConnectionNotifier)Connector.open(url);
```

This statement also creates an L2CAP service record (see Chapter 7). The `openL2CAPConnection()` method described above provides the `url`. Its value in this first example is

```
"btl2cap://localhost:9C68A2AA1EC011D79E6C00B0D03D76EC;"
                          + "receiveMTU=672;transmitMTU=672"
```

If the `url` argument to `Connector.open()` violates either MTU Rule 1 or MTU Rule 2, then this statement throws an `IllegalArgument-Exception`. There is code for exception handling in `L2capServer` to catch the `IllegalArgumentException`. It is unusual to provide an exception handler for an unchecked Java exception such as this, but it has advantages for demonstrating the results of MTU rule violations as described in the next section.

The statement that adds the service record to the SDDB and waits for a client to connect is

```
L2CAPConnection conn = notifier.acceptAndOpen();
```

If this statement does not throw an exception, it returns an instance of an `L2CAPConnection`, which provides access to the L2CAP channel between the `L2capServer` and the `L2capClient`.

The definition of the `echoReceivedL2capPackets()` method that actually sends and receives the bytes is described below in the `EchoParticipant` class. The `L2capServer` extends the `EchoParticipant` class, so it inherits this method.

The code for the `L2capClient` is shown next. Here the key statement in the `run()` method is

```
conn = (L2CAPConnection)Connector.open(url);
```

Again, the `openL2CAPConnection()` method provides the `url`; its value varies with the Bluetooth device address of the server and the PSM assigned to the server application. In this first example it has the value

```
"btl2cap://0050CD00321B:1001;authenticate=false;"
  + "encrypt=false;master=false;"
  + "receiveMTU=672;transmitMTU=672"
```

The `Connector.open(url)` statement attempts to form an L2CAP connection to the echo service described by the `url` argument.

```
public class L2capClient extends EchoParticipant
    implements Runnable {
  L2capMtuMIDlet parent;
  private String url;

  public L2capClient(L2capMtuMIDlet parent) {
    this.parent = parent;
    this.out = parent.displayField;
  }

  public void start(String url) {
    this.url = url;
```

```
      new Thread(this).start();
    }

    public void run() {
      L2CAPConnection conn = null;
      out.setLabel("["+url+"]");
      try {
        conn = (L2CAPConnection)Connector.open(url);
      } catch (IllegalArgumentException e) {
        parent.displayError("Error",
                            "IllegalArgumentException in "
                            + "Connector.open()\n"
                            + e.getMessage());
      } catch (BluetoothConnectionException e) {
        String problem = "";
        if (e.getStatus() ==
          BluetoothConnectionException.UNACCEPTABLE_PARAMS)
          {problem = "unacceptable parameters\n";
        }
        parent.displayError("Error",
                            "BluetoothConnectionException: "
                             + problem + "msg=" +
                             e.getMessage() +
                            "\nstatus= " + e.getStatus());
      } catch (IOException e) {
        parent.displayError("Error",
                            "IOException: " + e.getMessage());
      }
      if (conn == null) {
        return;
      }
      try {
        sendL2capPacketsForEcho(conn);
        conn.close();
      } catch (IOException e) {
        parent.displayError("Error",
                            "IOException: " + e.getMessage());
      }
    }
  }
```

If a connection cannot be formed between the L2CAP client and the L2CAP server because of incompatible MTU values (see the MTU mismatch pitfall in Section 8.2.3) then a `Bluetooth-ConnectionException` is thrown with a status of `Bluetooth-ConnectionException.UNACCEPTABLE_PARAMS`. The error handling code for the `L2capClient` class checks for a `Bluetooth-ConnectionException` with that status. The `Bluetooth-ConnectionException` class defines five other constants in addition to `UNACCEPTABLE_PARAMS`. These constants describe different reasons that a connection attempt might fail. As shown in the example code, the `getStatus()` method is used to retrieve the constant that applies to a particular exception.

Once the `L2CAPConnection` is established, it is passed to the method `sendL2capPacketsForEcho()`, which sends and receives the bytes over the L2CAP channel. The `sendL2capPacketsForEcho()` method is inherited from `EchoParticipant`, which is the next class we examine. This class has two methods. The method `sendL2cap-PacketsForEcho()` is used by the client for generating the L2CAP packets. The method `echoReceivedL2capPackets()` is used by the server for echoing back the bytes received from the client.

```
public class EchoParticipant {

    protected StringItem out;
    private int bytesToSend = 100000;

    void sendL2capPacketsForEcho(L2CAPConnection conn)
      throws IOException {

      byte[] sbuf = new byte[conn.getTransmitMTU()];
      byte[] rbuf = new byte[conn.getReceiveMTU()];
      for (int i=0; i < sbuf.length; i++) {
        sbuf[i] = (byte)i;
      }
      int count = 0;
      long start = System.currentTimeMillis();
      while (count < bytesToSend) {
        conn.send(sbuf);
        count += sbuf.length;
        count += conn.receive(rbuf);
```

```
    /* Display the bytes sent and received so far */
    out.setText(Integer.toString(count));
  }
  /* Let the echoer know we are done sending bytes */
  conn.send("DONE".getBytes());
  conn.receive(rbuf);
  long end = System.currentTimeMillis();
  out.setText("Done (transferred "+count+" bytes)\n"
            + "Elapsed time " + (end - start)/1000
            + "sec");
}
void echoReceivedL2capPackets(L2CAPConnection conn)
  throws IOException {

  byte[] ibuf = new byte[conn.getReceiveMTU()];
  int bytesIn;
  int count = 0;
  for (;;) {
    bytesIn = conn.receive(ibuf);
    byte[] obuf = new byte[bytesIn];
    System.arraycopy(ibuf, 0, obuf, 0, bytesIn);
    conn.send(obuf);
    if ((bytesIn == 4) && (new
      String(obuf)).equals("DONE")) {break;}
    count += 2 * bytesIn;
    /* Display the bytes received and sent so far */
    out.setText(Integer.toString(count));
  }
  out.setText("Done (transferred " + count + " bytes)");
  }
}
```

The key parts of both methods are the statements that send and receive L2CAP packets. The method sendL2capPacketsForEcho() does

```
conn.send(sbuf);
```

followed by

```
count += conn.receive(rbuf);
```

The method `echoReceivedL2capPackets()` reverses the order of these operations.

The method `sendL2capPacketsForEcho()` follows MTU Rule 3, which limits the size of packets sent to a maximum of `getTransmitMTU()`. This is shown in the two statements

```
byte[] sbuf = new byte[conn.getTransmitMTU()];
```

and

```
conn.send(sbuf);
```

The method `sendL2capPacketsForEcho()` also follows MTU Rule 4, which recommends allocating a byte array of size `getReceiveMTU()` to receive incoming packets:

```
byte[] rbuf = new byte[conn.getReceiveMTU()];
```

and

```
count += conn.receive(rbuf);
```

The method `echoReceivedL2capPackets()` also follows MTU Rules 3 and 4, although this is more difficult to see for MTU Rule 3. The relevant statements are

```
bytesIn = conn.receive(ibuf);
byte[] obuf = new byte[bytesIn];
  ...
conn.send(obuf);
```

The size of the byte array sent is based on the size of the byte array received. How do we know that the byte array `obuf` in `conn.send(obuf)` is not larger than `transmitMTU`? Because all MTU values are specified as 672 bytes in both the server and client connection strings, we know that the packet received will not be larger than 672 bytes. We can conclude that `obuf`, the byte array sent, also will be no larger than 672 bytes.

The client knows it is finished sending packets when its count exceeds 100,000 bytes. The `L2capClient` sends a special 4-byte packet corresponding to the ASCII values for the character string "DONE" to inform the L2capServer that the client is finished sending bytes.

8.3.2 User Interface for MTU Values

The example code in this section extends the L2CAP echo program of the previous section with a user interface that lets you enter values for receiveMTU and transmitMTU for both the L2CAP server and the L2CAP client. These MTU values are then used in the connection strings. If an empty value is provided for one of these MTU values, that is, if the field in the user interface is cleared, the corresponding MTU parameter is not included in the connection string passed to Connector.open(). This user interface makes it easy to try various combinations of MTUs to see the effect of MTU Rules 1 and 2 and the MTU mismatch pitfall discussed in Section 8.2.3. This user interface also makes it possible to experience the effect of MTU size on the time required for the client and server to transmit 100,000 bytes over L2CAP.

Figure 8.4 shows the user interface for entering MTU values. Both the server and the client use the same user interface. Figure 8.4 (a) shows the first screen, which allows the user to enter a value for receiveMTU. Figure 8.4 (b) shows the second screen, which allows the user to enter a value for transmitMTU. The values shown in Figure 8.4 are compatible because transmitMTU ≤ receiveMTU for L2CAP packets sent from the client to the server.

The method getReceiveMTUFromUser() shown below creates the display shown in Figure 8.4 (a) for entering a value for receiveMTU. The constant L2CAPConnection.MINIMUM_MTU is used to display the lower bound on legal input values. The LocalDevice property bluetooth.l2cap.receiveMTU.max is used to display the upper bound on legal input values. The constant L2CAPConnection.DEFAULT_MTU is provided as the starting value of the input field.

```
private void getReceiveMTUFromUser(boolean isClient) {
  String maxRecMTUPlus1;
  String maxRecMTU
    = LocalDevice.getProperty(
      "bluetooth.l2cap.receiveMTU.max");
  if (maxRecMTU == null) {
    maxRecMTUPlus1 = "Unknown";
  } else {
```

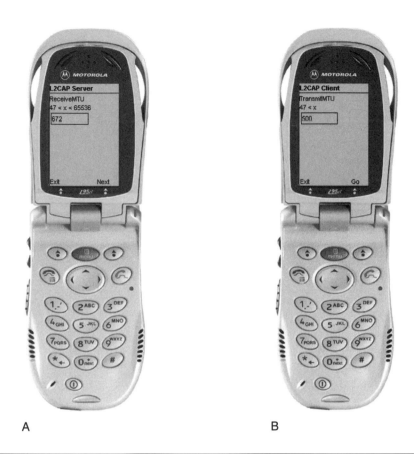

A   B

Figure 8.4 User interface for MTU experiments. (A) A `receiveMTU` of 672 bytes is entered for the server. (B) A `transmitMTU` of 500 bytes is entered for the client (emulation only).

```
/* Get (max + 1) for display of (min - 1) < x <
(max + 1) */
maxRecMTUPlus1
    = (new Integer(Integer.parseInt(maxRecMTU) +
    1)).toString();
}
String initialMTU
  = Integer.toString(L2CAPConnection.DEFAULT_MTU);
receiveMTUForm = new Form(isClient ? "L2CAP Client" :
  "L2CAP Server");
String recMtuFieldLabel
```

```
        = "ReceiveMTU \n" + (L2CAPConnection.MINIMUM_MTU
            - 1) + " < x < " + maxRecMTUPlus1;
    receiveMTUForm.append(new TextField(recMtuFieldLabel,
        initialMTU, 10, TextField.NUMERIC));
    receiveMTUForm.addCommand(new Command("Exit",
        Command.EXIT, 1));
    receiveMTUForm.addCommand(new Command("Next",
        Command.ITEM, 1));
    receiveMTUForm.setCommandListener(this);
    display.setCurrent(receiveMTUForm);
}
```

We can cause problems for the `L2capServer` if we enter the following MTU values in the user interface:

Client: `receiveMTU=500`, `transmitMTU=672`

Server: `receiveMTU=672`, `transmitMTU=500`

These values avoid the MTU mismatch pitfall, so the connection is formed. The client sends 672-byte L2CAP packets to the server. The server can receive these packets because 672 bytes is the same as the server's `receiveMTU`. However, when the server attempts to echo the bytes back to the client, a 672-byte packet is larger than the server's `transmitMTU` of 500 bytes.

There are several options for dealing with this problem. For the sake of simplicity, we adopt an approach that does only one `send(outBuf)` for each `receive(inBuf)` and uses an `outBuf` of size `transmitMTU`. The extra 172 bytes are not echoed back to the client. This allows us to have just one `send()` for every `receive()` and keeps the example code a little simpler. In theory, using an `outBuf` of 672 bytes with all the received bytes should lead to the same result as using an `outBuf` of size `transmitMTU`. The excess 172 bytes should be automatically discarded by the JABWT implementation. However, this would violate MTU Rule 3. Following MTU Rule 3 here makes it clear in the code that the failure to echo all the bytes is intentional.

The shaded statements below show the changes made to the method `echoReceivedL2capPackets()` shown in Section 8.3.1. The shaded statements limit the number of bytes echoed from each incoming L2CAP packet to just `transmitMTU` bytes.

```
void echoReceivedL2capPackets(L2CAPConnection conn)
  throws IOException {

  byte[] ibuf = new byte[conn.getReceiveMTU()];

  int transmitMTU = conn.getTransmitMTU();

  int bytesIn;

  int bytesOut;

  int count = 0;
  for (;;) {
    bytesIn = conn.receive(ibuf);

    bytesOut = Math.min(bytesIn, transmitMTU);
    byte[] obuf = new byte[bytesOut];
    System.arraycopy(ibuf, 0, obuf, 0, bytesOut);

    conn.send(obuf);
    if ((bytesIn == 4) && (new String(obuf)).equals
      ("DONE")) {
        break;}

    count += bytesIn + bytesOut;

    /* Display the bytes received and sent so far */
    out.setText(Integer.toString(count));
  }
  out.setText("Done (transferred " + count + " bytes)");
}
```

8.3.3 L2CAP Clients and Servers Have the Same Capabilities

The example code in this chapter might leave the erroneous impression that L2CAP server applications have to be passive and are incapable of initiating communications. This is not the case. Although the client initiates the L2CAP connection, once that connection is formed, both sides have access to an instance of an L2CAPConnection, so both sides have the same capabilities. Clients and servers can both send packets whenever they want to. An easy experiment that illustrates this point is to exchange these two statements in the example code:

```
sendL2capPacketsForEcho(conn);
```

and

```
echoReceivedL2capPackets(conn);
```

This exchange changes the example code so that instead of the server echoing the packets sent by the client, the client echoes the packets sent by the server.

8.3.4   Flow Control

L2CAP provides no flow control, so Bluetooth protocols and profiles that use L2CAP typically provide their own flow control. Let's consider the echo example of this chapter from the point of view of flow control. Suppose the client device is capable of sending L2CAP packets much faster than the server device is capable of echoing them back. Because our example code waits for a packet to be returned before it tries to send the next packet, the client is paced by the server's ability to echo the packets. This should keep the client from getting ahead of the server and overflowing the server's buffers.

However, suppose that instead of a symmetric, two-way echoing application, the data transfer is one way. In that case, a different flow control scheme is required. In addition to the L2CAP packets that transmit data and travel in one direction it would be necessary to send back L2CAP packets containing control signals to stop and start the data flow.

The next code example illustrates a one-way data transfer using a credit-based flow control scheme.

The code for the complete example is too lengthy to be shown here, so only selected methods involved with credit-based flow control are shown. The complete code is available in Appendix A. Credit-based flow control is used in the Bluetooth specification for RFCOMM and the Hardcopy Cable Replacement Profile. In the credit-based flow control scheme illustrated in this example, the L2CAP server starts by issuing four credits to the L2CAP client. The client can send as many L2CAP packets as it has credits, so the client can then send four packets to the L2CAP server. When the client's credit count reaches zero, the client must stop sending L2CAP packets and wait for additional credits from the server.

In the `CreditBased1WayXfer` class shown below, the key section that accomplishes the flow control is

```
if (availableCredits > 0) {
    conn.send(sbuf);
    availableCredits--;
```

The L2CAP client can use the JABWT `send()` method to send an L2CAP packet to the server as long as it has available credits. However, each packet sent uses up a credit. When the credits reach zero, the L2CAP client has to stop sending data until more credits are received.

```
public class CreditBased1WayXfer {

    // number of L2CAP packets the receiver has
    // authorized to be sent
    int availableCredits;
    protected StringItem out;
    private int bytesToSend = 50000;

    void sendL2capPackets(L2CAPConnection conn) throws
      IOException {

      boolean sentDone = false;
      byte[] sbuf = new byte[conn.getTransmitMTU()];
      int receiveMTU = conn.getReceiveMTU();
      byte[] rbuf = new byte[receiveMTU];
      for (int i=0; i < sbuf.length; i++) {
        sbuf[i] = (byte)i;
      }
      int count = 0;
      long start = System.currentTimeMillis();
      //listen for credits authorizing sending packets
```

```
      receiveCredits(conn, receiveMTU);
      while (count < bytesToSend) {
          if (availableCredits > 0) {
              conn.send(sbuf);
              availableCredits--;
              count += sbuf.length;
              // Display the number of bytes sent so far
              out.setText(Integer.toString(count));
          }
          maybeReceiveCredits(conn, receiveMTU);
      }
      // Let the receiver know we are done sending bytes
      while (!sentDone) {
          if (availableCredits > 0) {
              conn.send("DONE".getBytes());
              sentDone = true;
          } else {
              maybeReceiveCredits(conn, receiveMTU);
          }
      }
      long end = System.currentTimeMillis();
      out.setText("Done (transferred "+count+" bytes)\n"
              + "Elapsed time " + (end -
              start)/1000 + "sec");
  }
}
```

The `sendL2capPackets()` method above uses the two application
methods `receiveCredits()` and `maybeReceiveCredits()` to listen
for L2CAP packets that deliver additional credits from the server. The
definition of the `receiveCredits()` method is shown next. This
method reads an L2CAP packet from the server and interprets the byte
array in that packet as an integer. That integer is added to
`availableCredits` to increase the credits available for use by the
client.

```
  // Read an L2CAP packet. If it has four bytes, then
  // interpret those
```

```
// bytes as new credits for sending L2CAP packets.
void receiveCredits(L2CAPConnection conn,
  int receiveMTU) {
    int incomingBytes;
    int newCredits;
    byte[] rbuf - new byte[receiveMTU];
    try {
        incomingBytes = conn.receive(rbuf);
    } catch (IOException ignore) {
      return;
    }
    // assume four bytes are used to encode new
    // credits
    if (incomingBytes != 4) {
        return;
    }
    availableCredits +=
      CreditBased1WayXfer.byteArray2Int(rbuf);
}

// Convert a four-byte array to an int. The byte
// array is assumed
// to have a big Endian byte order.
public static int byteArray2Int(byte[] argBytes) {
    int result = 0;
    // big-endian conversion
    for (int i = 0, j = 0; i < 4; i++, j++) {
        result = result + (((int)argBytes[i] << 24)
                            >>> (j * 8));
    }
    return result;
}
```

The L2CAP server issues an additional credit to the client only when the server frees up buffer space to hold one additional L2CAP data packet. It is unclear how long it takes the server to process one of the previously sent L2CAP packets, free up the space needed to receive another packet from the client, and send an L2CAP packet back to the client to issue the additional credit. Because `receiveCredits()` uses the blocking JABWT method `receive()` to read an L2CAP packet from the server, there is always the risk that a call to `receive()` can become stuck waiting for this L2CAP packet from the server. The credit-based flow control scheme is meant to block only when the client has no more credits, so we want the client to listen for additional credits without blocking.

The key to keeping the client from getting stuck in `receive()` is to use the JABWT `ready()` method to test whether an L2CAP packet is available for the client to read. If `ready()` returns `true`, `receive()` returns an L2CAP packet without blocking. The client's `maybeReceiveCredits()` method is shown next. It uses the `ready()` method to check for additional credits issued by the server without blocking.

```
// If there is an L2CAP packet waiting to be read,
// then call
// receiveCredits. Otherwise return without
// blocking.
void maybeReceiveCredits(L2CAPConnection conn,
    int receiveMTU) {
  try {
    if (conn.ready()) {
      receiveCredits(conn, receiveMTU);
    }
  } catch (IOException ignore) {
  }
}
```

All of the example code we have looked at so far for credit-based flow control has been client code. The L2CAP server in this example has two threads: one thread to move the L2CAP packets received from the client to a buffer storage location and a second thread to process the buffered L2CAP packets and issue credits.

The `receiveL2capPackets()` method shown next is used in the thread that receives the incoming L2CAP packets and stores them. It is derived from the `echoReceivedL2capPackets()` used in the echo examples earlier in this chapter. The `receiveL2capPackets()` method has been modified to store the bytes obtained from an L2CAP packet sent by the client to one of four `L2capPacketBuffers` maintained

by the server. An `L2capPacketBuffer` has room to store
`getReceiveMTU()` bytes. These bytes are processed later by the second
thread. The code in `echoReceivedL2capPackets()` for counting
incoming bytes and for echoing those bytes back to the client has been
removed from `receiveL2capPackets()`.

```java
public class CreditBased1WayXfer {
...

    void receiveL2capPackets(L2CAPConnection conn,
                             L2capBuffers buffers,
                             CreditIssuer issuer)
                                throws IOException {

        byte[] ibuf = new byte[conn.getReceiveMTU()];
        L2capPacketBuffer packetBuffer;
        int transmitMTU = conn.getTransmitMTU();
        int bytesIn;

        for (;;) {
            packetBuffer =
              buffers.nextAvailablePacketBuffer();
            if (packetBuffer != null) {
              bytesIn = conn.receive(ibuf);
              packetBuffer.storeBytes(ibuf, bytesIn);
              if ((bytesIn == 4) &&
                  (new String(ibuf, 0,
                    bytesIn)).equals("DONE")) {
                      break;
              }
            } else {
              if (conn.ready()) {
                System.out.println("Should not get here. No " +
                            "L2capPacketBuffer " +
                            "available " +
                            "to receive incoming " +
                            "packet.");
              }
            }
```

```
    }
    issuer.setDoneProcessing();
    out.setText("Done (transferred " + issuer.count +
      " bytes)");
  }
...
}
```

The following example code shows the `run()` method for the
`CreditIssuer` thread that processes the buffered packets and issues
credits to the client. The first thing that happens in the
`CreditIssuer.run()` method is that an L2CAP packet is sent to the
client containing a number represented as a byte array. The number in
the L2CAP packet is the number of starting credits that the server issues
to the client. This number is determined by the number of client
packets that the server has buffer space available to receive.

The `CreditIssuer` then continuously loops over the buffers to
process any packets that have been received and stored there by the
other server thread. The only processing of packets done in the example
is to count the number of bytes in each packet and keep a total count of
bytes received from the client over this L2CAP channel.

```
public class CreditIssuer implements Runnable {

...

  public void run() {

    L2capPacketBuffer packetBuffer;
    int freedBuffers;
    //Issue one credit for each L2capPacketBuffer
    int totalCredits =
        L2capBuffers.NUMBER_OF_PACKET_BUFFERS;
    byte[] issueCreditsPacketPayload =
      CreditBased1WayXfer.int2ByteArray(totalCredits);
    try {
      conn.send(issueCreditsPacketPayload);
    } catch (IOException e) {
      System.out.println("IOException when issuing "
        + "initial credits");
```

```
            return;
        }
    while (!doneProcessing) {
        freedBuffers = 0;
        while ((packetBuffer =
                    buffers.nextUsedPacketBuffer())
                != null) {
            count += packetBuffer.getNumBytesStored();
            packetBuffer.eraseStoredBytes();
            freedBuffers++;
        }

        if (freedBuffers > 0) {
            try {
                conn.send(CreditBased1WayXfer.int2ByteArray(
                    freedBuffers));
            } catch (IOException e) {
                System.out.println("IOException " +
                    e.getMessage());
            }
        }
        try {
            Thread.sleep(sleepTime);
        } catch (InterruptedException ignore) {
        }
    }
}
...
}
```

After the bytes in a buffered L2CAP packet have been counted,
the CreditIssuer thread calls the application method erase-
StoredBytes() to make this L2capPacketBuffer available to store
future L2CAP packets. CreditIssuer keeps track of how many
buffers it has freed up and uses the following statement to send an
L2CAP packet to the client to issue one additional credit for each
buffer freed:

```
conn.send(CreditBased1WayXfer.int2ByteArray(
        freedBuffers));
```

The statement `Thread.sleep(sleepTime)` at the bottom of the `while` loop makes it possible to introduce an arbitrary delay into the `CreditIssuer` thread. Experimenting with various delays shows how credit-based flow control adjusts the client's data-transmission rate to match the server's packet-processing rate.

8.4 Summary

L2CAP is one of three APIs for Bluetooth communication that are available to JABWT applications. JABWT provides a packet-based API for L2CAP as opposed to the stream-based APIs available for serial port and OBEX.

L2CAP communications are the right choice for an application if

- The application implements a Bluetooth profile that uses the L2CAP protocol and that Bluetooth profile does not use one of the higher-level protocols RFCOMM or OBEX, or

- The application implements a new custom protocol that is packet oriented

The `L2CAPConnection` interface provides methods for sending and receiving L2CAP packets over an L2CAP channel. Applications can use the connection string parameters `receiveMTU` and `transmitMTU` to define their requirements for maximum payload sizes of the L2CAP packets. This chapter presents four rules regarding MTU values for use in JABWT programs.

L2CAP provides no flow control, so JABWT applications that use the L2CAP API need to provide their own flow control. Without some form of flow control, L2CAP applications could encounter packet loss or deadlock. This chapter provides example code for two flow control schemes:

- Simple flow control that waits for a response to packet n before sending packet $n + 1$

- Credit-based flow control

9 CHAPTER Example Applications

This chapter covers the following topics:

- Writing a MIDlet that uses the Bluetooth APIs
- Writing a MIDlet that uses the OBEX APIs

9.1 Overview

Now that JABWT has been introduced, what can a developer do with the APIs? This chapter contains two sample applications that show the API in use. These examples show how to use JABWT within an MIDP application (i.e., MIDlet). Because peer-to-peer gaming will most likely be one of the first uses of JABWT, the first application is an implementation of a simple game of tic-tac-toe using RFCOMM to allow a user to compete against an opponent. The second application is a simple messaging application. In this application, an OBEX client can send messages to and retrieve messages from an OBEX messaging server.

To develop MIDlets with JABWT, a J2ME development tool must be used with a Bluetooth development kit. There are a variety of J2ME development tools. The oldest is the J2ME Wireless Toolkit from Sun Microsystems. The J2ME Wireless Toolkit is available free from Sun at java.sun.com. Most Bluetooth development kits require purchasing expensive hardware, but developers are able to get up and running quickly and inexpensively by using a software simulator. One available from Rococo Software is called the Impromptu Simulator. A trial version is available at www.rococosoft.com. This trial version allows developers to try out JABWT. The following code has been tested in this environment.

(This chapter contains a large amount of code. Added or changed code appears on a gray background. The original, unshaded code is provided for context.)

9.2 Tic-Tac-Toe MIDlet

The mobile gaming industry is likely to be one of the first groups of developers to use JABWT. Despite its simplicity, the Tic-Tac-Toe MIDlet that follows is a good example of a mobile game that uses JABWT. The Tic-Tac-Toe MIDlet contains the main `TicTacToeMIDlet` class along with the `TTTGame`, `TTTCanvas`, `PauseCanvas`, and `PauseTimerTask` classes. All five classes work together to enable a user to play a game of tic-tac-toe with a friend.

The `TicTacToeMIDlet` class is the MIDlet run by the KVM. This class also implements the `CommandListener` interface for handling requests to start and exit the game. The `TTTGame` class runs in a separate thread and handles communication between devices. Depending on what the user selects, this thread either creates a service record and registers it with the Bluetooth stack or performs device and service discovery to find an opponent to play. The `TTTCanvas` class handles the display of the game board. The `PauseCanvas` class is a helper class that displays a splash screen while the application processes a request from the user. The `PauseCanvas` class accepts a message in parts and displays one part of the message every second. This gives the appearance that the MIDlet is doing something when there is nothing to display. For example, the `PauseCanvas` class is displayed when device and service discovery is taking place. The `PauseTimerTask` class works with the `PauseCanvas` class to notify the `PauseCanvas` class to repaint the screen.

9.2.1 Defining the `TicTacToeMIDlet`

Overview

The `TicTacToeMIDlet` class extends the `MIDlet` class. It is the main class for the tic-tac-toe game. The class implements the `CommandListener` interface to respond to `Command` events from the user. In particular, these `Command` events signal the start or end of a game. Because the `TicTacToeMIDlet` class extends `MIDlet`, it implements the `startApp()`, `pauseApp()`, and `destroyApp()` abstract methods. These methods do nothing. The constructor on the other hand, retrieves the `Display` for this MIDlet and creates the exit `Command` button. The constructor also creates the initial screen for display to the user. The first screen allows the user to select whether to join a game or start a new game.

The only other method in the `TicTacToeMIDlet` class is the `commandAction()` method. This method must be implemented because the class implements the `CommandListener` interface. This method is called each time the user selects a `Command`. When `commandAction()` is called by the underlying system, the method first checks to see whether the exit `Command` has been selected. If it has, the MIDlet is destroyed, and the game ends. If the exit `Command` has not been selected, the `commandAction()` method starts a new game thread because the user has selected the start `Command`.

Implementation

After operation of the tic-tac-toe game has been defined, the next step is to start coding the main MIDlet. First, define an empty MIDlet with the proper imports.

```java
package com.jabwt.book;

import java.lang.*;
import java.io.*;
import java.util.*;
import javax.microedition.midlet.*;
import javax.microedition.lcdui.*;
import javax.microedition.io.*;
import javax.bluetooth.*;

/**
 * The TicTacToeMIDlet allows two users to
 * play a game of
 * Tic-Tac-Toe against each other. One user will start a
 * new game while the
 * other user searches for an existing game. When both
 * users establish a
 * connection, the game starts.
 */
public class TicTacToeMIDlet extends MIDlet {
  /**
   * Creates the Tic-Tac-Toe MIDlet. This constructor sets
   * the initial
   * display to the user.
   */
  public TicTacToeMIDlet() {
```

```
   }
   /**
    * Called when the MIDlet is started.
    *
    * @exception MIDletStateChangeException never thrown
    */
   public void startApp() throws MIDletStateChangeException {
   }
   /**
    * Called when the MIDlet is paused.
    */
   public void pauseApp() {
   }
   /**
    * Called when the MIDlet is destroyed.
    *
    * @param unconditional ignored
    */
   public void destroyApp(boolean unconditional) {
   }
}
```

Before a user is able to start playing an opponent, one device must discover the other device and establish a connection to it. Because this MIDlet works as a client and a server, there are two options for figuring out who the server and who the client are. The first option is to do device and service discovery. If no device is found with the tic-tac-toe game service, this `TicTacToeMIDlet` acts as the server. If a device is found, this `TicTacToeMIDlet` acts as the client. The second option is more straightforward. It asks the user to act as the client or as the server. Because the second option is more straightforward, we use this approach.

The following code creates a `Form` that allows the user to select whether the user's device is client or server. To make this request more user-friendly, the user is asked to create a new game (act as the server) or join an existing game (act as the client).

```
public class TicTacToeMIDlet extends MIDlet {
   /**
    * The display for this MIDlet.
    */
   public Display theDisplay;
```

```java
/**
 * Determines if a new game should be started or if the
 * MIDlet needs to find a game to join.
 */
private ChoiceGroup gameType;

/**
 * The exit command.
 */
public Command exitCommand;

/**
 * Creates the Tic-Tac-Toe MIDlet. This constructor
 * creates the initial display to the user.
 */
public TicTacToeMIDlet() {

    // Retrieve the display for this MIDlet
    theDisplay = Display.getDisplay(this);
    exitCommand = new Command("Exit", Command.EXIT, 1);

    // Set up the initial screen for the MIDlet
    createStartScreen();
}

/**
 * Creates the initial screen that starts the game.
 */
public void createStartScreen() {
    // Set up the initial screen for the MIDlet
    Form firstScreen = new Form("JABWT Tic-Tac_Toe");
    firstScreen.append("Welcome to JABWT Tic-Tac-Toe");
    gameType = new ChoiceGroup(null, ChoiceGroup.EXCLUSIVE);
    gameType.append("Start a new Game", null);
    gameType.append("Join an Existing Game", null);
    gameType.setSelectedIndex(0, true);
    firstScreen.append(gameType);
    firstScreen.addCommand(new Command("Start", Command.OK,
        1));
    firstScreen.addCommand(exitCommand);
    theDisplay.setCurrent(firstScreen);
}
...
}
```

The previous code gives a user two options, to play the game or to exit the MIDlet. To differentiate these requests, two different `Commands` are created. Because it is the `CommandListener` for the first screen, the `TicTacToeMIDlet` must implement the `commandAction()` method. This method exits the `MIDlet` if the "Exit" `Command` is selected. If the start `Command` is selected, the game is started. Before the game is started, the game class must be written (see Section 9.2.3).

```
public class TicTacToeMIDlet extends MIDlet implements
  CommandListener {

  ...

  /**
   * The CommandListener for exit commands.
   */
  public CommandListener theListener;
```

Figure 9.1   First Screen of the Tic-Tac-Toe MIDlet (emulation only).

```
/**
 * Creates the initial screen that starts the game.
 */
public void createStartScreen() {
  // Set up the initial screen for the MIDlet
  Form firstScreen = new Form("JABWT Tic-Tac_Toe");
  firstScreen.append("Welcome to JABWT Tic-Tac-Toe");
  gameType = new ChoiceGroup(null, ChoiceGroup.EXCLUSIVE);
  gameType.append("Start a new Game", null);
  gameType.append("Join an Existing Game", null);
  gameType.setSelectedIndex(0, true);
  firstScreen.append(gameType);
  firstScreen.addCommand(new Command("Start",
    Command.OK, 1));
  firstScreen.addCommand(exitCommand);
  firstScreen.setCommandListener(this);
  theListener = this;
  theDisplay.setCurrent(firstScreen);
}

...

/**
 * Called each time a command is selected. This method
 * should only be
 * called to start the game or to exit. If exit is
 * selected, the
 * MIDlet is destroyed. Otherwise,
 * depending on which
 * element in the ChoiceGroup is selected,
 * this method either
 * starts a thread to wait for another
 * MIDlet to connect or
 * starts a thread to find another MIDlet to
 * play.
 *
 * @param c the Command that was selected
 *
 * @param d the current Displayable
 */
public void commandAction(Command c, Displayable d) {
  // Determine if the exit command was selected
  if (c == exitCommand) {
```

```
      // End the game
      notifyDestroyed();
   } else {
      /*
       * TODO: Start the game
       */
   }
}
   ...
}
```

The createStartScreen() method is complete for most purposes, but one additional modification needs to be made to simplify future code. At present, the createStartScreen() method creates a Form and displays it to the user. On some occasions, an Alert may need to be displayed. The createStartScreen() method requires that a new parameter be added to represent the Alert. The createStartScreen() method sets this parameter to the current Displayable as long as it is not null.

```
public class TicTacToeMIDlet extends MIDlet implements
  CommandListener {

   ...
   /**
    * Creates the Tic-Tac-Toe MIDlet. This constructor will
    * create
    * the initial display to the user.
    */
   public TicTacToeMIDlet() {
     // Retrieve the display for this MIDlet
     theDisplay = Display.getDisplay(this);
     exitCommand = new Command("Exit", Command.EXIT, 1);
     // Set up the initial screen for the MIDlet
     createStartScreen(null);
   }
   /**
    * Creates the initial screen that starts the game.
    *
    * @param alert the Alert before changing
    * to the initial
```

```
          * screen
          */
         public void createStartScreen(Alert alert) {
             // Set up the initial screen for the MIDlet
             Form firstScreen = new Form("JABWT Tic-Tac_Toe");
             firstScreen.append("Welcome to JABWT Tic-Tac-Toe");
             gameType = new ChoiceGroup(null, ChoiceGroup.EXCLUSIVE);
             gameType.append("Start a new Game", null);
             gameType.append("Join an Existing Game", null);
             gameType.setSelectedIndex(0, true);
             firstScreen.append(gameType);
             firstScreen.addCommand(new Command("Start", Command.OK,
                 1));
             firstScreen.addCommand(exitCommand);
             firstScreen.setCommandListener(this);

             theListener = this;

             if (alert == null) {
                 theDisplay.setCurrent(firstScreen);
             } else {
                 theDisplay.setCurrent(alert, firstScreen);
             }
         }
     ...
     }
```

9.2.2 The `PauseCanvas` and `PauseTimerTask` Helper Classes

Overview

The `PauseCanvas` class is a utility class that provides a splash screen to the user. The `PauseCanvas` displays an array of `Strings`. After each second, an index, the `messageIndex`, is incremented by one until the full message is displayed. The `PauseCanvas` does this by creating a `TimerTask` to go off every second within the `PauseCanvas` constructor. This `TimerTask` increments the `messageIndex` and repaints the `PauseCanvas`. When the `PauseCanvas` is no longer displayed to the user, the `hideNotify()` method is called, and the `TimerTask` is canceled. The `PauseCanvas` provides a way for a game to work in the background without freezing the screen.

The `PauseTimerTask` class extends the `TimerTask` class and works closely with the `PauseCanvas` class. The `run()` method is called after every second. This method increments the `messageIndex` of the `PauseCanvas` and causes the `PauseCanvas` to be repainted.

Implementation

The `PauseCanvas` class extends the `Canvas` class to allow the `PauseCanvas` class to draw directly on the screen via the `paint()` method. When the class is loaded, the height and width of the screen are retrieved via the `getHeight()` and `getWidth()` methods. These values are cached so that multiple calls to these methods are not needed. The constructor for the `PauseCanvas` class takes the message to display as an argument in a `String` array. This allows the developer to specify the locations of breaks between words without requiring additional processing.

```
package com.jabwt.book;

import java.lang.*;
import java.util.*;
import javax.microedition.lcdui.*;
  /**
   * The PauseCanvas class provides a screen
   * that displays a
   * message to the user and makes it appear like the
   * MIDlet is
   * doing something by displaying the message in parts.
   */
public class PauseCanvas extends Canvas {
    /**
     * The height of the display.
     */
    private final int HEIGHT = getHeight();
    /**
     * The width of the display.
     */
    private final int WIDTH = getWidth();
    /**
     * The components of the message to display. Each
     * element is displayed to
     * the screen starting with index 0.
```

```
 */
 private String[] message;
 /**
  * Creates a PauseCanvas that displays
  * the message provided.
  *
  * @param m the message to display to the screen; the
  * message
  * must not be null and must have at
  * least one element
  */
 public PauseCanvas(String[] m) {
   // Set up the message
   message = new String[m.length];
   System.arraycopy(m, 0, message, 0, m.length);
 }
 /**
  * Called each time the screen should be repainted.
  * This method displays
  * the message up to the index specified by
  * messageIndex.
  *
  * @param g used to write the message to the screen
  */
 public void paint(Graphics g) {
 }
}
```

Because the PauseCanvas must be updated every second, a TimerTask must be created to repaint the PauseCanvas after every second. The PauseTimerTask class sends this repaint request. Changing the display necessitates an index for tracking the number of the strings in the array that should be displayed. The PauseTimerTask updates this index each time the timer goes off. The PauseTimerTask also repaints the PauseCanvas to update the screen to the user. The PauseTimerTask is created and started when the PauseCanvas is made visible via the showNotify() method.

```
public class PauseCanvas extends Canvas {

   ...
```

```
/**
 * Tracks which elements in the message
 * array should be
 * displayed.
 */
private int messageIndex;

/**
 * The timer used to change the display periodically.
 */
private PauseTimerTask task;

/**
 * Creates a PauseCanvas that displays the
 * message provided.
 *
 * @param m the message to display to the screen; the
 * message
 * must not be null and must have at least
 * one element
 */
public PauseCanvas(String[] m) {

  // Set up the message
  message = new String[m.length];
  System.arraycopy(m, 0, message, 0, m.length);
  // Start by displaying the full message on the first
  // repaint
  messageIndex = message.length - 1;
}

/**
 * Called when this PauseCanvas is made
 * visible. This method
 * creates and starts a new PauseTimerTask.
 */
public void showNotify() {

  // Starts the timer to periodically change the screen
  task = new PauseTimerTask(this);
  new Timer().scheduleAtFixedRate(task, 1500, 1000);
}

    ...

/**
```

```
 * The PauseTimerTask class is used to
 * force the
 * PauseCanvas to repaint periodically.
 * This class also sets
 * which components of the message specified to
 * PauseCanvas
 * should be displayed.
 */
class PauseTimerTask extends TimerTask {
  /**
   * The canvas that is repainted periodically.
   */
  private PauseCanvas parent;
  /**
   * Creates a PauseTimerTask to be used
   * with the
   * PauseCanvas specified.
   *
   * @param p the canvas to repaint
   */
  public PauseTimerTask(PauseCanvas p) {
     parent = p;
  }
  /**
   * Called each time the timer goes off. This method
   * will increment the index
   * into the message array and then repaint the
   * PauseCanvas specified in the constructor.
   */
  public void run() {
     parent.messageIndex++;
     parent.repaint();
  }
}
}
```

Now that the `PauseTimerTask` is repainting the canvas after every second, the `PauseCanvas` class must be modified to draw the message to the screen. To do this, the `paint()` method begins by repainting the background. Next, the `paint()` method draws the message on the canvas.

```
public class PauseCanvas extends Canvas {
    private static final int COLOR_WHITE = 0xFFFFFF;
    private static final int COLOR_BLACK = 0x000000;

    ...

    /**
     * Called each time the screen should be repainted. This
     * method will display the message up to the index
     * specified by messageIndex.
     *
     * @param g used to write the message to the screen
     */
    public void paint(Graphics g) {
        int textX = WIDTH / 2;
        int textY = 10;

        // Clear the screen, fill screen with background
        g.setColor(COLOR_WHITE);
        g.fillRect(0, 0, WIDTH, HEIGHT);

        // Set the message color to be black
        g.setColor(COLOR_BLACK);

        // Write each element to the screen up to the
        // messageIndex
        messageIndex = messageIndex % message.length;
        for (int i = 0; i <= messageIndex; i++) {
            g.drawString(message[i], textX, textY, Graphics.TOP |
                Graphics.HCENTER);
            textY += 15;
        }
    }
    ...
}
```

At this point, the PauseCanvas repeatedly updates the screen with a message. When the PauseCanvas class is no longer visible, there is no reason for the timer to continue to go off and repaint the screen. The PauseCanvas is notified via the hideNotify() method that it is no longer currently visible. At this point, the PauseCanvas stops the TimerTask.

```
public class PauseCanvas extends Canvas {
  ...
  /**
   * Called when the canvas is no longer displayable.
   * This method stops the
   * timer.
   */
  public void hideNotify() {
    task.cancel();
  }

  ...
}
```

9.2.3 Creating the Game Thread

Overview

The `TicTacToeMIDlet` class creates the `TTTGame` class when a new game is started. A new game is started when the user selects to join an existing game or start a new game. If the user selects to join a game, the `run()` method creates a `PauseCanvas` object to display a message while the method attempts to find an opponent by calling the `selectService()` method of the local `DiscoveryAgent`. If no service is found, then an `Alert` is displayed notifying the user that a game could not be found. If a service is found, the `run()` method connects to the service. After connecting to the service, the method creates a `TTTCanvas` object and makes it the currently displayed `Canvas`.

If the user selects to create a new game, the `run()` method still creates a `PauseCanvas` object with a message and sets it to the current display. It does not perform a device or service search. The `run()` method creates a service record and waits for an opponent to join. The `run()` method creates the service record by calling `Connector.open()` and then calling `acceptAndOpen()` on the `StreamConnection-Notifier` object returned from `Connector.open()`. Once an opponent connects, the `run()` method creates a `TTTCanvas` object and sets it to the current display.

After the connection is established, the `run()` method reads an opponent's moves from the connection to the opponent. The method also opens an `OutputStream` that the `TTTCanvas` class uses to send moves made by the user to the opponent's device.

Implementation

The TTTGame class is the game thread that handles the communication and actions within the game. Because it must run as a separate thread, the TTTGame class implements the Runnable interface. This interface requires that the run() method be defined. Before the run() method is called, the constructor must be invoked to create a new TTTGame object. The constructor takes a boolean argument, which specifies whether the TTTGame should start as a server or as a client. The TTTGame starts when the thread is started, but that comes later.

```java
package com.jabwt.book;

import java.lang.*;
import java.io.*;
import javax.bluetooth.*;
import javax.microedition.lcdui.*;
import javax.microedition.io.*;

/**
 * This class is used to play a game of Tic-Tac-Toe.
 */
public class TTTGame implements Runnable {
  /**
   * The parent MIDlet for this game. The parent provides
   * access to the
   * current Display and game canvas.
   */
  private TicTacToeMIDlet parent;

  /**
   * Specifies if the game should act as a client or a server
   */
  private boolean isServer;

  /**
   * Creates a TTTGame object that starts the
   * game as either a
   * client or server.
   *
   * @param isServer true if the game should
   * start as the
   * server; false if the game should start
   * as the client
```

```
 * @param parent the parent MIDlet to this game
 */
public TTTGame(boolean isServer, TicTacToeMIDlet parent) {
  this.isServer = isServer;
  this.parent = parent;
}

/**
 * Called when the thread is started. This is the main
 * method of the
 * thread. This thread determines if a new game should
 * be started or a
 * game should be found and joined. It then performs
 * the action that was requested.
 */
public void run() {

}
}
```

Now that the `TTTGame` class exists, the game can be started in the `TicTacToeMIDlet` class. The game is started when the user selects whether to start a new game or to join a game. The following code starts the game appropriately.

```
public class TicTacToeMIDlet extends MIDlet implements
  CommandListener {

  ...

  /**
   * The Tic-Tac-Toe Game object.
   */
  public TTTGame theGame;

  ...

  /**
   * Called each time a command is selected. This method
   * should only be
   * called to start the game or to exit. If exit is
   * selected, the
   * MIDlet is destroyed. Otherwise,
   * depending on which
   * element in the ChoiceGroup is selected,
   * this method either
```

```
 * starts a thread to wait for another
 * MIDlet to connect or
 * starts a thread to find another MIDlet to
 * play.
 *
 * @param c the Command that was selected
 *
 * @param d the current Displayable
 */
public void commandAction(Command c, Displayable d) {
  // Determine if the exit command was selected
  if (c == exitCommand) {
    // End the game
    notifyDestroyed();
  } else {
    // Start the game
    theGame = new TTTGame(gameType.isSelected(0), this);
    new Thread(theGame).start();
  }
 }
}
```

Once the game thread has started, the `run()` method is executed. Before
an attempt is made to locate a device to connect to or wait for a connection from an opponent, a splash screen is displayed to the user by means
of the `PauseCanvas` class. This splash screen allows the user to end the
game by selecting the exit `Command` added to the `Canvas`. Depending on
the user's selection, a different message is displayed on the screen.

```
public class TTTGame implements Runnable {
  ...
  /**
   * Called when the thread is started. This is the main
   * method of the
   * thread. This thread determines if a new game should
   * be started or a
   * game should be found and joined. It then performs
   * the action that was requested.
   */
public void run() {
    createSplashScreen();
```

```
      }
      /**
       * Uses the PauseCanvas class to display a
       * splash screen to
       * the user before the game is able to begin. The message
       * to display is
       * dependent on whether or not the local device should
       * act as the server.
       */
      private void createSplashScreen() {
        String[] message;

        // Create a unique message depending on if the game
        // should start a
        // new game (server) or join an existing game (client)
        if (isServer) {

          // Set up the message to display to the user to
          // explain the game
          // is waiting for an opponent to connect
          message = new String[5];
          message[0] = "Waiting";
          message[1] = "on an";
          message[2] = "Opponent";
          message[3] = "to Join";
          message[4] = "the Game";
        } else {

          // Set up the message that states that this game is
          // looking for
          // an opponent
          message = new String[3];
          message[0] = "Searching";
          message[1] = "for a Game";
          message[2] = "to Join";
        }
        // Create the canvas and set it to the current display
        PauseCanvas canvas = new PauseCanvas(message);
        canvas.addCommand(parent.exitCommand);
        canvas.setCommandListener(parent.theListener);
        parent.theDisplay.setCurrent(canvas);
        canvas.repaint();
      }
    }
```

Now that the display is set for the user, the `TTTGame` thread must prepare for a game. If the user has selected to create a new game, the `TTTGame` thread must create an RFCOMM server to which another `TicTacToeMIDlet` can connect. In this situation, the `TTTGame` thread must first make the device general discoverable to allow another `TicTacToeMIDlet` to find it. After the device is set to general discoverable, the `TTTGame` thread creates a `StreamConnectionNotifier` object by calling `Connector.open()`. Because a game of tic-tac-toe does not require any security, no security requirements are specified in the call to `Connector.open()`. After calling `Connector.open()`, the thread calls `acceptAndOpen()`. This step makes the device connectable, registers the service record in the service record database, and allows another `TicTacToeMIDlet` to connect to this game.

The following code defines a method used whenever an error occurs. This method displays an alert to the user and then closes the MIDlet.

```java
public class TTTGame implements Runnable {

    /**
     * The connection to the opponent.
     */
    private StreamConnection conn;

    ...

    /**
     * Called when the thread is started. This is the main
     * method of the
     * thread. This thread determines if a new game should
     * be started or a
     * game should be found and joined. It then performs
     * the action that was requested.
     */
    public void run() {

        createSplashScreen();

        // Determine if this game should start as a server or
        // a client
        if (isServer) {
            // Wait for another TicTacToeMIDlet to connect to
            // this one to
            // start the game
            conn = waitForConnection();
```

```
      } else {
        /*
         * TODO: Handle when the game should start as a client
         */
      }

      try {
        conn.close();
      } catch (IOException e) {
      }
    }

    /**
     * Makes the device general discoverable and then waits
     * for another
     * TicTacToeMIDlet to connect.
     *
     * @return the connection to the opponent
     */
    private StreamConnection waitForConnection() {
      // Make the device discoverable, create the server and
      // wait for a connection
      StreamConnectionNotifier notifier = null;
      try {
        LocalDevice theRadio = LocalDevice.getLocalDevice();
        theRadio.setDiscoverable(DiscoveryAgent.GIAC);
        notifier = (StreamConnectionNotifier)Connector.open(
        "btspp://localhost:8a02dc796f3141f1b83096cc0ac738cf");
        conn = notifier.acceptAndOpen();
      } catch (Exception e) {

        // Reclaim any used resources
        try {
          notifier.close();
        } catch (Exception ex) {
        }
        try {
          conn.close();
        } catch (Exception ex) {
        }
          displayError("Error", "Unable to wait for a " +
            "connection (" +
            e.getClass().getName() + ": " + e.getMessage());
```

```
            return null;
        }

        return conn;
    }
    /**
     * Displays an error Alert to the user and go back to
     * the MIDlet start screen.
     *
     * @param title the title of the Alert
     *
     * @param msg the message to include in the
     * Alert
     */
    private void displayError(String title, String msg) {
        // Display the error message
        Alert error = new Alert(title, msg, null,
          AlertType.ERROR);
        error.setTimeout(Alert.FOREVER);

        parent.createStartScreen(error);
    }
```

```
    ...
}
```

Now that code has been added that allows a game to be created, the next step is to add code to join a game. The `connectToServer()` method completes device discovery and service search and establishes a connection to the service discovered. To simplify the device discovery and service search, the `connectToServer()` method uses `DiscoveryAgent.selectService()`. Because this code is executing in a separate thread, the blocking call to `selectService()` is not noticed by the user. If no service is found, an error message is displayed to the user, and the thread ends. After a service to which to connect is located, a connection is established to the service by calling `Connector.open()`.

```
public class TTTGame implements Runnable {

    ...
```

```java
/**
 * Called when the thread is started. This is the main
 * method of the
 * thread. This thread determines if a new game should
 * be started or a
 * game should be found and joined. It then performs
 * the action that was
 * requested.
 */
public void run() {

  createSplashScreen();

  // Determine if this game should start as a server or
  // a client
  if (isServer) {

    // Wait for another TicTacToeMIDlet to connect to
    // this one to
    // start the game
    conn = waitForConnection();
  } else {

    // Establish a connection to a TicTacToeMIDlet in
    // the area.
    conn = connectToServer();
    if (conn == null) {
      return;
    }
  }
}

/**
 * Locates another device running the Tic-Tac-Toe game
 * and establishes
 * a connection to the game.
 *
 * @return a connection to another
 * TicTacToeMIDlet;
 * null if a connection could not be
 * established to another
 * TicTacToeMIDlet
 */
```

```
      private StreamConnection connectToServer() {

        Connection conn;

        // Locate another TicTacToeMIDlet that has started a
        // game to
        // connect to
        try {
          LocalDevice local = LocalDevice.getLocalDevice();
          DiscoveryAgent agent = local.getDiscoveryAgent();
          String connString = agent.selectService(
            new UUID("8a02dc796f3141f1b83096cc0ac738cf",
            false), ServiceRecord.NOAUTHENTICATE_NOENCRYPT,
            false);

        // Verify that a game to join was found
        if (connString == null) {
            displayError("Error",
              "Unable to locate a game to join");
            return null;
        }

        // Establish a connection to the device and game that
        // was found
        conn = Connector.open(connString);
      } catch (BluetoothStateException e) {
        displayError("Bluetooth Error",
          "Unable to establish a " +
          "connection to another game." +
            "(BluetoothStateException: " +
          e.getMessage() + ")");
        return null;
      } catch (IOException e) {
        displayError("IO Error", "Unable to establish a " +
          "connection to another game. (IOException: " +
          e.getMessage() + ")");
        return null;
      }

      return (StreamConnection)conn;
    }
    ...
}
```

9.2.4 Playing the Game

Overview

The `TTTCanvas` class draws the tic-tac-toe display and handles user input. To handle the user input, the `keyPressed()` method is implemented. This method is called each time the user presses a key on the mobile device. Each of the squares that make up the tic-tac-toe board are numbered from 1 to 9. When the user presses a key, the `keyPressed()` method translates the key number and calls `recordMove()`. The `recordMove()` method verifies that a move request is valid. A valid request is a move to an empty square. The method records the move. After the move is recorded, the screen is repainted, and the method checks to see whether the move is a winning move. If the move is a winner, an `Alert` is displayed indicating as such.

The `paint()` method is the other major method in the `TTTCanvas` class. The `paint()` method draws the board on the screen.

Implementation

Before we are able to play the game, the user display must be created. The `TTTCanvas` class provides this display. The `TTTCanvas` class constructor takes in the `TTTGame` associated with this `Canvas`. This step allows the `TTTCanvas` object to communicate with the `TTTGame` object. The `TTTCanvas` draws the tic-tac-toe game board by extending the `Canvas` class and implementing the `paint()` method. The `paint()` method draws the tic-tac-toe game board and keeps track of the moves of both players. To keep track, an integer array is created that records each move. The value zero represents an empty square. A value of one represents a square that the user has selected, and a value of negative one represents a square selected by the opponent.

For performance reasons, the `TTTCanvas` retrieves the width and height of the screen when the class is loaded. This eliminates the need to retrieve the width and height each time `paint()` is called.

```
package com.jabwt.book;

import java.lang.*;
import javax.microedition.lcdui.*;

/**
```

```
 * The TTTCanvas controls the display and
 * helps play the
 * tic-tac-toe game.
 */
public class TTTCanvas extends Canvas {
  private static final int COLOR_WHITE = 0xFFFFFF;
  private static final int COLOR_RED = 0xFF0000;
  private static final int COLOR_BLUE = 0x0000FF;
  /**
   * The height of the display.
   */
  private final int HEIGHT = getHeight();
  /**
   * The width of the display.
   */
  private final int WIDTH = getWidth();
  /**
   * The parent MIDlet to this canvas.
   */
  private TicTacToeMIDlet parent;
  /**
   * The game board. 0 stands for empty slot. 1 for this
   * player's
   * move, -1 for the opponent's move.
   */
  private int[] board;
  /**
   * The game that is being played
   */
  private TTTGame theGame;
  /**
   * Creates a TTTCanvas object and
   * initializes the game.
   *
   * @param game the TTTGame thread running the game
   *
   * @param p the parent MIDlet for this canvas
   */
  public TTTCanvas(TTTGame game, TicTacToeMIDlet p) {
```

```
    board = new int[9];
    parent = p;
    // Initialize the game board
    for (int i = 0; i < board.length; i++) {
      board[i] = 0;
    }
    theGame = game;
  }
  /**
   * Called each time the screen should be repainted.
   * This method draws the
   * game screen and labels the X's and O's according to
   * the player's moves.
   *
   * @param g the interface to draw to the screen
   */
  public void paint(Graphics g) {
      // Paint the background
      g.setColor(COLOR_WHITE);
      g.fillRect(0, 0, WIDTH, HEIGHT);

      // Draw the game board
      g.setColor(COLOR_RED);

      g.fillRect(WIDTH / 3, 0, 5, HEIGHT);
      g.fillRect((WIDTH * 2) / 3, 0, 5, HEIGHT);
      g.fillRect(0, HEIGHT / 3, WIDTH, 5);
      g.fillRect(0, (HEIGHT * 2) / 3, WIDTH, 5);
  }
}
```

Now that the game board has been drawn, the TTTGame must be connected with the TTTCanvas. The TTTGame must also set the TTTCanvas to the current Displayable. The following code does this. The code also gets the input and output streams to communicate with the opponent. The OutputStream needs to be a package access member variable to allow the TTTCanvas to send the user's move to the opponent. The InputStream does not need to be a member variable because the TTTCanvas does not need to read from it. The run() method reads all the opponent's moves and passes them to the TTTCanvas.

Because tic-tac-toe is a turn-based game, one player must be selected to make the first move. For this tic-tac-toe game, the MIDlet that creates a new game goes first. The MIDlet that joined the game waits for the first move from the MIDlet that created the game.

```
public class TTTGame implements Runnable {

    /**
     * The Canvas that draws the game board and the moves
     */
    private TTTCanvas theCanvas;

    /**
     * The OutputStream to send moves over.
     */
    OutputStream output;

    /**
     * Keeps track of whose turn it is.
     */
    boolean myTurn;

    ...

    /**
     * Called when the thread is started. This is the main
     * method of the
     * thread. This thread determines if a new game should
     * be started or a
     * game should be found and joined. It then performs
     * the action that was requested.
     */
    public void run() {
    createSplashScreen();

    // Determine if this game should start as a server or a
    // client
    if (isServer) {

        // Wait for another TicTacToeMIDlet to connect to this
        // one to
        // start the game
        conn = waitForConnection();

        myTurn = true;

    } else {

        // Establish a connection to a TicTacToeMIDlet in the
        // area.
```

Figure 9.2 Screenshot of the TTTCanvas (emulation only).

```
    conn = connectToServer();
    if (conn == null) {
      return;
    }

    myTurn = false;
  }

  InputStream input = null;
  try {
    input = conn.openInputStream();
    output = conn.openOutputStream();
  } catch (IOException e) {
    displayError("IO Error",
      "An error occurred while opening " +
      "the input and output streams" +
```

```
      "(IOException: " + e.getMessage() + ")");
   try {
     conn.close();
   } catch (Exception ex) {
   }
   return;
}

// Create the game Canvas and set it to the current
// display
theCanvas = new TTTCanvas(this, parent);
parent.theDisplay.setCurrent(theCanvas);
theCanvas.addCommand(parent.exitCommand);
theCanvas.setCommandListener(parent.theListener);
theCanvas.repaint();
   try {
     input.close();
     output.close();
     conn.close();
   } catch (IOException e) {
   }
}

...
}
```

The next step is to begin to process input from the user. (To make the code more simplistic and because this is not a book on MIDP, this MIDlet is written so that it interfaces with the user via key presses rather than pointer presses.) Each square on the board is numbered from 1 to 9 across and down as on the keypad of a phone. The user selects the box in which to make a move. This information is received by the keyPressed() method of TTTCanvas. The keyPressed() method verifies that it is this user's turn. The method records the move and sends it to the opponent via the output member variable of TTTGame. After the move is sent, the keyPressed() method makes it the opponent's turn. It also notifies the TTTGame object to allow the TTTGame to wait for the opponent to make a move.

The paint() method is also modified so that the color changes according to whose turn it is. The paint() method also contains code that updates the tic-tac-toe board with Xs and Os. For this game, Xs and

Os are replaced with red and blue squares. If the square has yet to be taken by one of the players, the `paint()` method ignores the square.

```java
public class TTTCanvas extends Canvas {

  ...

  /**
   * Called each time the screen should be repainted.
   * This method draws the
   * game screen and labels the X's and O's according to
   * the player's moves.
   *
   * @param g the interface to draw to the screen
   */
  public void paint(Graphics g) {

    // Paint the background
    g.setColor(COLOR_WHITE);
    g.fillRect(0, 0, WIDTH, HEIGHT);
    // Draw the game board
    if (theGame.myTurn) {
      g.setColor(COLOR_RED);
    } else {
      g.setColor(COLOR_BLUE);
    }

    g.fillRect(WIDTH / 3, 0, 5, HEIGHT);
    g.fillRect((WIDTH * 2) / 3, 0, 5, HEIGHT);
    g.fillRect(0, HEIGHT / 3, WIDTH, 5);
    g.fillRect(0, (HEIGHT * 2) / 3, WIDTH, 5);

    // Fill in with the moves that have occurred.
    for (int i = 0; i < 3; i++) {
      for (int j = 0; j < 3; j++) {
        int index = (i * 3) + j;

        switch (board[index]) {
        case 1:
          // This is my square so set it to red
          g.setColor(COLOR_RED);
          g.fillRect((j * (WIDTH / 3)) + 5, (i * (HEIGHT /
            3)) + 5,
            (WIDTH / 3) - 5, (HEIGHT / 3) - 5);
          break;
```

```
      case -1:
        // This is my opponent's square so set it to blue
        g.setColor(COLOR_BLUE);
        g.fillRect((j * (WIDTH / 3)) + 5, (i * (HEIGHT /
          3)) + 5,
          (WIDTH / 3) - 5, (HEIGHT / 3) - 5);
        break;

      default:
        break;
      }
    }
  }
}

/**
 * Called each time a key is pressed. This method
 * records the move and
 * repaints the screen.
 *
 * @param keyNum the key that was pressed
 */
public void keyPressed(int keyNum) {
  boolean isValid;

  // Verify that it was my turn to move. Do nothing if
  // it is
  // my opponent's turn
  if (theGame.myTurn) {

    // Record the key press in the proper space if the
    // space is empty
    switch (keyNum) {
    case KEY_NUM1:
      isValid = recordMove(0, true);
      break;
    case KEY_NUM2:
      isValid = recordMove(1, true);
      break;
    case KEY_NUM3:
      isValid = recordMove(2, true);
      break;
    case KEY_NUM4:
      isValid = recordMove(3, true);
```

```
            break;
        case KEY_NUM5:
          isValid = recordMove(4, true);
          break;
        case KEY_NUM6:
          isValid = recordMove(5, true);
          break;
        case KEY_NUM7:
          isValid = recordMove(6, true);
          break;
        case KEY_NUM8:
          isValid = recordMove(7, true);
          break;
        case KEY_NUM9:
          isValid = recordMove(8, true);
          break;
        default:
          // An invalid key was pressed so ignore it
          return;
    }
    if (!isValid) {
      return;
    }

    try {
      theGame.output.write(keyNum - KEY_NUM1);
      theGame.output.flush();
    } catch (Exception e) {
    }

    synchronized (theGame) {
      theGame.notifyAll();
    }
  }
}
/**
 * Verifies that the space is empty and then records the move.
 *
 * @param key the key number that was pressed
 *
 * @param myMove true if it was this
 * player's move;
 * false if the other player made the move
```

```
 *
 * @return true if the move was a valid move; false if the
 * move was not valid
 */
public boolean recordMove(int key, boolean myMove) {
  if (board[key] == 0) {
    if (myMove) {
      board[key] = 1;
    } else {
      board[key] = -1;
    }

    repaint();
    return true;
  }

  return false;
}
}
```

Now that one player can make a move and send it to the other player, the other player must read the move and update the board. The TTTGame object does this. The TTTGame object reads from the InputStream the square that has been selected. Next, the move is recorded by the TTTCanvas object, and the TTTCanvas is repainted. Finally, the TTTGame object waits on itself until the current user presses a key and sends it to the other player. One special case must be considered. The MIDlet that starts the game gets the first move; therefore this MIDlet needs to wait for the first move to occur before it starts to read from the InputStream. The following code does this.

```
public class TTTGame implements Runnable {

  ...

  /**
   * Called when the thread is started. This is the main
   * method of the
   * thread. This thread determines if a new game should
   * be started or a
   * game should be found and joined. It then performs
   * the action that was
   * requested.
```

```
      */
    public void run() {
      createSplashScreen();
      // Determine if this game should start as a server or
      // a client
      if (isServer) {
        // Wait for another TicTacToeMIDlet to connect to
        // this one to
        // start the game
        conn = waitForConnection();

        myTurn = true;
      } else {
        // Establish a connection to a TicTacToeMIDlet in
        // the area.
        conn = connectToServer();
        if (conn == null) {
          return;
        }
        myTurn = false;
      }
      InputStream input = null;
      try {
        input = conn.openInputStream();
        output = conn.openOutputStream();
      } catch (IOException e) {
        displayError("IO Error",
          "An error occurred while opening " +
          "the input and output streams (IOException: " +
          e.getMessage() + ")");

        try {
          conn.close();
        } catch (Exception ex) {
        }
        return;
      }
  }
  // Create the game Canvas and set it to the current display
  theCanvas = new TTTCanvas(this, parent);
  parent.theDisplay.setCurrent(theCanvas);
```

```
theCanvas.addCommand(parent.exitCommand);
theCanvas.setCommandListener(parent.theListener);
theCanvas.repaint();
```

```
    // If it is my turn, wait until the TTTCanvas
    // Records the first move
    if (myTurn) {
      synchronized (this) {
        try {
          this.wait();
        } catch (Exception e) {
        }
      }
    }
    // Continue processing until the game is over and the
    // connection is
    // closed
    try {
      for (;;) {
        myTurn = false;
        int id = (int)input.read();

        if (id == -1) {
            displayError("IO Error", "The connection has been " +
              "closed by your opponent. The game is over.");
            break;
        }
        theCanvas.recordMove(id, false);

        myTurn = true;

        // Wait until the user makes a move
        synchronized (this) {
            try {
              this.wait();
            } catch (Exception e) {
            }
        }
      }
    } catch (Exception e) {
      displayError("Error",
        "An error occurred while communicating with your " +
          "opponent(" +
```

```
        e.toString() + ")");
    } finally {
    try {
        input.close();
        output.close();
        conn.close();
    } catch (Exception ex) {
    }
    }
  }
}
```

The `TicTacToeMIDlet` is almost complete. Both `TicTacToeMIDlets` can communicate and send their moves back and forth, but the goal of the game is to identify the first player to get three in a row. The `isWinner()` method checks the board to determine whether there are three in a row in any direction. The `isWinner()` method is called each time a move is made. Once a winner is identified, an `Alert` is used to notify the player. Because it needs to be called on each move, the `isWinner()` method is added to the `recordMove()` method introduced previously. The `recordMove()` method updates the board and then calls the `isWinner()` method.

```
public class TTTCanvas extends Canvas {

  ...

  /**
   * Determines if this move created a winning pattern.
   *
   * @return true if their is a winner;
   * false if there is no winner yet.
   */
  public boolean isWinner() {
    // Look for three in a row across
    for (int i = 0; i < 9; i += 3) {
      if ((board[i] != 0) && (board[i] == board[i + 1]) &&
        (board[i + 1] == board[i + 2])) {

        return true;
      }
    }
```

```
// Look for three in a row down
for (int i = 0; i < 3; i++) {
  if ((board[i] != 0) && (board[i] == board[i + 3]) &&
     (board[i] == board[i + 6])) {

    return true;
  }
}

// Check for the crosses
if ((board[4] != 0) && (((board[0] == board[4]) &&
   (board[4] == board[8])) ||
   ((board[2] == board[4]) && (board[4] == board[6])))) {

  return true;
}

return false;
}
```

```
/**
 * Verifies that the space is empty and then records
 * the move.
 * If the space is not empty, this method will not do
 * anything.
 *
 * @param key the key number that was pressed
 *
 * @param myMove true if it was this
 * player's move;
 * false if the other player made the move
 *
 * @return true if the move was a valid move; false
 * if the
 * move was not valid
 */
public boolean recordMove(int key, boolean myMove) {
  if (board[key] == 0) {
    if (myMove) {
      board[key] = 1;
    } else {
      board[key] = -1;
    }
```

```
      repaint();
```
```
      // Determine if there is a winner on this move
      if (isWinner()) {

        // Display a message to say there is a winner
        Alert winnerScreen;
        if (myMove) {
          winnerScreen = new Alert("Game Over",
           "You just won!", null, AlertType.INFO);
        } else {
          winnerScreen = new Alert("Game Over",
            "Sorry, you got beat.", null, AlertType.INFO);
        }
        winnerScreen.setTimeout(Alert.FOREVER);
        parent.createStartScreen(winnerScreen);
      }
```
```
      return true;
    }
    return false;
  }
}
```

At present, the TTTGame thread never ends. It is stuck in the *for* loop
until the remote end closes the Connection. To allow the game to end,
the isWinner() method is reused, and the *for* loop needs to be changed
to a *while* loop. A check for isWinner() must be done immediately
after the call to recordMove(). This check determines whether the
opponent has made the winning move. Now, the TTTGame thread continues to execute until there is a winner.

```
public class TTTGame implements Runnable {

  ...
  /**
   * Called when the thread is started. This is the main
   * method of the
   * thread. This thread determines if a new game should
   * be started or a
   * game should be found and joined. It then performs
   * the action that was
```

```
 * requested.
 */
public void run() {
  createSplashScreen();

  // Determine if this game should start as a server or
  // a client
  if (isServer) {

    // Wait for another TicTacToeMIDlet to connect to
    // this one to
    // start the game
    conn = waitForConnection();

    myTurn = true;
  } else {

    // Establish a connection to a TicTacToeMIDlet in
    // the area.
    conn = connectToServer();
    if (conn == null) {
      return;
    }

    myTurn = false;
  }

  InputStream input = null;
  try {
    input = conn.openInputStream();
    output = conn.openOutputStream();
  } catch (IOException e) {
    displayError("IO Error",
      "An error occurred while opening " +
      "the input and output streams (IOException: " +
      e.getMessage() + ")");

    try {
    conn.close();
    } catch (Exception ex) {
    }
    return;
  }

  // Create the game Canvas and set it to the current
  // display
```

```
theCanvas = new TTTCanvas(this, parent);
parent.theDisplay.setCurrent(theCanvas);
theCanvas.addCommand(parent.exitCommand);
theCanvas.setCommandListener(parent.theListener);
theCanvas.repaint();

// If it is my turn, wait until the TTTCanvas records
// the first move
if (myTurn) {
  synchronized (this) {
    try {
      this.wait();
    } catch (Exception e) {
    }
  }
}

// Continue processing until the game is over and the
// connection is
// closed
try {
  while (!theCanvas.isWinner()) {
    myTurn = false;
    int id = (int)input.read();

    if (id == -1) {
      displayError("IO Error",
        "The connection has been " +
        "closed by your opponent. The game is over.");
      break;
    }
    theCanvas.recordMove(id, false);

    // Determine if this move won the game
    if (theCanvas.isWinner()) {
      break;
    }

    myTurn = true;
    // Wait until the user makes a move
    synchronized (this) {
      try {
        this.wait();
      } catch (Exception e) {
```

```
            }
          }
        }
      } catch (Exception e) {
          displayError("Error",
            "An error occurred while communicating with" +
              " your opponent(" +
            e.toString() + ")");
      } finally {
        try {
          input.close();
          output.close();
          conn.close();
        } catch (Exception ex) {
        }
      }
    }

    ...
}
```

At this point, the `TicTacToeMIDlet` can be played against an opponent. Only one problem exists in the code. What happens when there is a tie, as often is the case in this game? One final method must be added to determine whether a tie exists. The `isTie()` method checks to see whether all of the squares have been taken. If there are no empty squares, the `isTie()` method returns true.

```
public class TTTCanvas extends Canvas {
    ...
    /**
     * Determine if there is a tie. A tie exists if all the
     * squares have been
     * selected.
     *
     * @return true if all of the squares have
     * been selected;
     * otherwise false
     */
    public boolean isTie() {
```

```
      for (int i = 0; i < 9; i++) {
        if (board[i] == 0) {
          return false;
        }
      }

      return true;
    }
  }
```

This procedure requires two additional checks in the `TTTGame run()` method. These checks display a message to the user and take the user back to the start if a tie occurs.

```
public class TTTGame implements Runnable {

  ...

  /**
   * Called when the thread is started. This is the main
   * method of the
   * thread. This thread determines if a new game should
   * be started or a
   * game should be found and joined. It then performs
   * the action that was
   * requested.
   */
  public void run() {
    createSplashScreen();

    // Determine if this game should start as a server or
    // a client
    if (isServer) {

      // Wait for another TicTacToeMIDlet to connect to
      // this one to
      // start the game
      conn = waitForConnection();

      myTurn = true;
    } else {

    // Establish a connection to a TicTacToeMIDlet in
    // the area.
    conn = connectToServer();
```

```
      if (conn == null) {
        return;
      }
    myTurn = false;
  }
  InputStream input = null;
  try {
    input = conn.openInputStream();
    output = conn.openOutputStream();
  } catch (IOException e) {
    displayError("IO Error",
      "An error occurred while opening " +
      "the input and output streams (IOException: " +
      e.getMessage() + ")");
    try {
      conn.close();
    } catch (Exception ex) {
    }
    return;
  }

  // Create the game Canvas and set it to the current
  // display
  theCanvas = new TTTCanvas(this, parent);
  parent.theDisplay.setCurrent(theCanvas);
  theCanvas.addCommand(parent.exitCommand);
  theCanvas.setCommandListener(parent.theListener);
  theCanvas.repaint();

  // If it is my turn, wait until the TTTCanvas records
  // the first move
  if (myTurn) {
    synchronized (this) {
      try {
        this.wait();
      } catch (Exception e) {
      }
    }
  }

  // Continue processing until the game is over and the
  // connection is
  // closed
```

```
try {
    while (!theCanvas.isWinner()) {
      myTurn = false;
      int id = (int)input.read();

      if (id == -1) {
        displayError("IO Error",
          "The connection has been " +
          "closed by your opponent. The game is over.");
        break;
      }
      theCanvas.recordMove(id, false);

      // Determine if this move won the game
      if (theCanvas.isWinner()) {
        break;
      }

      // Determine if this move caused a tie
      if (theCanvas.isTie()) {
        displayError("Tie",
          "There is no winner. This game " +
          "is a tie.");
        break;
      }

      myTurn = true;

      // Wait until the user makes a move
      synchronized (this) {
        try {
          this.wait();
        } catch (Exception e) {
        }
      }

      // Determine if this move caused a tie
      if (theCanvas.isTie()) {
        displayError("Tie",
          "There is no winner. This game " +
          "is a tie.");
        break;
      }
    }

  } catch (Exception e) {
```

```
        displayError("Error",
          "An error occurred while communicating with" +
            " your opponent(" +
          e.toString() + ")");
    } finally {
      try {
        input.close();
        output.close();
        conn.close();
      } catch (Exception ex) {
      }
    }
  }

  ...
}
```

9.3 OBEX Application Download

The OBEX message application is a client-server application made of a pair of MIDlets. The OBEX message application allows a client to send and retrieve messages from a server. This application provides no security or authentication but simply illustrates the use of the OBEX API.

The OBEX `MessageClient` allows a user to send and retrieve messages from a server. The `MessageClient` requires the user to select a user name. After choosing a user name, the user may select to send or retrieve a message. If the user selects to send a message, the user enters the user name of the recipient and the message to send. An OBEX PUT operation is used to send the message to the server. If the user selects to retrieve a message, the `MessageClient` MIDlet retrieves the message from the server and displays the message to the user. The OBEX GET operation is used to retrieve the message.

The OBEX `MessageServer` MIDlet accepts connections from OBEX `MessageClient` MIDlets. When the client sends a message via a PUT operation, the `MessageServer` stores the message in a `Vector` with the user name of the recipient. On the other hand, the `MessageServer` searches for a message with the user name sent by the client and finds a message for that user. The `MessageServer` then sends the message in the reply.

9.3.1 The Message Server Application

Overview

The `MessageServer` MIDlet receives and sends messages at the request of the `MessageClient`. Each message is represented by an object of type `Message` and is stored in a `Vector`. The `run()` method, which is part of the `MessageServer` class because the class implements the `Runnable` interface, simply creates a `SessionNotifier` object and repeatedly calls `acceptAndOpen()`. For each call of `acceptAndOpen()`, a new `RequestHandler` object is created and passed to the `acceptAndOpen()` method to process requests from the client. When the user is finished using the server, the server is shut down by means of selection of the Exit command on the MIDlet display.

For OBEX CONNECT requests, the `RequestHandler` class does not override the `onConnect()` method because no additional processing is needed for CONNECT requests except to accept the connection. The default implementation of the `javax.obex.ServerRequest-Handler` class is all that is needed.

The client uses PUT requests to send messages to the server. When a PUT request is received, the `onPut()` method is called. The `onPut()` method first retrieves the NAME header. If no NAME header is received, the method returns the `OBEX_HTTP_BAD_REQUEST`. If the NAME header is received, the `InputStream` is opened on the `Operation` argument, and the message is read. After the entire message is read, a new `Message` object is created and added to the `Vector` of all messages. Before the method returns with `OBEX_HTTP_OK`, the `InputStream` and `Operation` objects are closed.

The client issues a GET request to retrieve a message from the server. For GET requests, the `onGet()` method first retrieves the NAME header to determine the name of the user whose message is to be retrieved. If no NAME header is received, the `onGet()` method returns with the `OBEX_HTTP_BAD_REQUEST` response code. The `onGet()` method next searches for a message with the user name specified. The method performs this search by traversing the `Vector` of `Message` objects until a message for the user name is found. If no message is found, the method returns `OBEX_HTTP_NOT_FOUND`. Otherwise, the `onGet()` method sends the message found to the client by writing it to the `OutputStream` of the `Operation` object provided as an argument. After the message is written to the `OutputStream` and the

`OutputStream` and `Operation` objects are closed, the `onGet()` method finally returns `OBEX_HTTP_OK`.

For OBEX DISCONNECT requests, the `onDisconnect()` method is not overridden because the server does not need to do any additional processing when the client disconnects from the server.

Creating the Base Application

The `MessageServer` is a MIDlet that stores messages sent to another user and replies with a message when requested. The `MessageServer` must implement the `Runnable` interface so that it can have one thread processing requests from clients and one thread handling UI events. This mechanism allows a user to track the server because the server prints log messages on the screen. This factor is important with an embedded device because there is no way to print log information on standard out. The `MessageServer` class also must implement the `CommandListener` interface to allow a user to stop the server and exit the MIDlet.

The following code creates the skeleton of the `MessageServer` MIDlet. It starts the server thread and allows the user to stop the server. Within the `MessageServer` constructor, a `Vector` is created to log messages, and a `Form` is created to which to log messages. After the `Form` is created, the `MessageServer` constructor adds an exit `Command` to the `Form` and starts the processing thread. The `startApp()` method then sets the `Form` to the current displayable. Because the `MessageServer` implements the `CommandListener` interface, the `MessageServer` receives any `Command` event. The only `Command` event possible is the exit `Command`. The `MessageServer` is destroyed if the `commandAction()` method is called.

```
package com.jabwt.book;

import java.lang.*;
import java.io.*;
import java.util.*;
import javax.microedition.io.*;
import javax.microedition.midlet.*;
import javax.microedition.lcdui.*;
import javax.bluetooth.*;
import javax.obex.*;
```

```java
/**
 * The MessageServer class allows a client to send to and
 * receive messages
 * from other clients.
 */
public class MessageServer extends MIDlet implements
  Runnable,
  CommandListener {

  /**
   * Keeps all the messages sent to different users.
   */
  private Vector msgList;

  /**
   * The form displayed to the user.
   */
  private Form output;

  /**
   * Creates a MessageServer object and
   * starts the server
   * thread.
   */
  public MessageServer() {
    msgList = new Vector();

    output = new Form("OBEX Message Server");
    output.addCommand(new Command("Exit", Command.EXIT, 1));
    output.setCommandListener(this);

    new Thread(this).start();
  }

  /**
   * Called each time the MIDlet is started. This method
   * sets the current
   * display to the logging form.
   *
   * @exception MIDletStateChangeException never occurs
   */
  public void startApp()
    throws MIDletStateChangeException {
    Display currentDisplay = Display.getDisplay(this);
```

```
    currentDisplay.setCurrent(output);
  }
  public void pauseApp() {
  }
  public void destroyApp(boolean unconditional) {
  }
  /**
   * The OBEX message server will wait and accept
   * connections from clients
   * to send and retrieve messages.
   */
  public void run() {
  }
  /**
   * Called each time a command occurs. The only command is
   * the Exit command.
   * This method will destroy the MIDlet.
   *
   * @param c ignored
   * @param d ignored
   */
  public void commandAction(Command c, Displayable d) {
    notifyDestroyed();
  }
}
```

Before the server can start processing requests from clients, a class that extends the ServerRequestHandler class must be created. The RequestHandler class fulfills this role. It processes requests from clients. The RequestHandler class is modified later in this chapter to handle PUT and GET requests.

```
package com.jabwt.book;

import java.lang.*;
import java.io.*;
import java.util.*;
import javax.obex.*;

/**
```

```
 * The RequestHandler class handles requests
 * from the OBEX
 * client to store and retrieve messages for a specific user.
 */
public class RequestHandler extends ServerRequestHandler {
  /**
   * The list of messages stored by the server
   */
  public Vector msgList;
  /**
   * Creates a RequestHandler object with the
   * specified
   * Vector which will be used to store and retrieve
   * messages.
   *
   * @param list the Vector used to store and
   * retrieve
   * messages
   */
  public RequestHandler(Vector list) {
    msgList = list;
  }
}
```

Next, the server thread is updated to receive connections from clients. First, the SessionNotifier object is created by calling Connector.open(). After the SessionNotifier object is created, a log message is added to the Form. Next, a forever loop is entered. Within the loop, a new RequestHandler object is created and used to call acceptAndOpen() on the SessionNotifier object. If an I/O error occurs during the call to acceptAndOpen(), the server thread ends, and a message is appended to the current Form. The commandAction() method also is updated. If the user selects to close the MessageServer MIDlet, the SessionNotifier object is closed before the MIDlet is destroyed.

```
public class MessageServer extends MIDlet implements
  Runnable,
  CommandListener {
```

```
/**
 * The connection string to use with
 * Connector.open().
 */
public static final String CONNECTION_STRING =
  "btgoep://localhost:750ef04247a54693b6384708eb87ec5e";
/**
 * The server object used to accept connections.
 */
private SessionNotifier notifier;
```

...

```
/**
 * The OBEX message server will wait and accept
 * connections from clients
 * to send and retrieve messages.
 */
public void run() {
    // Create the server connection object and make the
    // local device general discoverable
    try {
      LocalDevice local = LocalDevice.getLocalDevice();
      local.setDiscoverable(DiscoveryAgent.GIAC);
      notifier = (SessionNotifier)
        Connector.open(CONNECTION_STRING);
    } catch (IOException e) {
      output.append("Unable to start server (IOException: " +
        e.getMessage() + ")");
      return;
    }

    output.append("Started Server");

    while (true) {
      // Accept a connection from a client
      RequestHandler server = new RequestHandler(msgList);
      try {
        notifier.acceptAndOpen(server);
      } catch (IOException e) {
        output.append(
          "Unable to accept a connection from a " +
```

```
              "client (IOException: " +
                e.getMessage() + ")");
          output.append("SHUTTING DOWN SERVER!");
          break;

        }
      }
    }
    /**
     * Called each time a command occurs. The only command
     * is the Exit
     * command. This method will destroy the MIDlet.
     *
     * @param c ignored
     * @param d ignored
     */
    public void commandAction(Command c, Displayable d) {
      try {
        notifier.close();
      } catch (Exception e) {
      }
      notifyDestroyed();
    }
}
```

Receiving Messages from the Client

The next step in writing the Message Server application is writing the code to receive messages from the client. The client sends a message to a single user by means of the PUT operation. The user name of the intended recipient of the message is sent within the NAME header. The message is sent via the BODY and END-OF-BODY headers. Before this situation is handled, a data structure to store the user name and message pair is created. The following code for the Message class holds the user name and message of a single message. Methods to access both member variables also are defined.

```
package com.jabwt.book;

import java.lang.*;

/**
 * The Message class provides a structure
 * for keeping the message
```

```
 * and user name combination.
 */
public class Message {
  /**
   * The user name the message is intended for.
   */
  private String userName;
  /**
   * The actual message.
   */
  private String message;
  /**
   * Creates a new Message for the user
   * specified with the text
   * specified.
   *
   * @param name the user the message is intended for
   *
   * @param msg the message that was sent
   */
  public Message(String name, String msg) {
    userName = name;
    message = msg;
  }
  /**
   * The user name the message was intended for.
   */
  public String getUserName() {
    return userName;
  }
  /**
   * The message for the user name.
   */
  public String getMessage() {
    return message;
  }
}
```

Because the PUT operation sends the message, the `onPut()` method is overwritten. Before the message is read, the user name is extracted from

the NAME header. If no user name is included, the `onPut()` method
returns the `OBEX_HTTP_BAD_REQUEST` error code because the request
was not complete. After the recipient's user name is read, the message is
read from the `InputStream` of the `Operation` object. After the
message is read, a new `Message` object is created and added to the
`Vector` of all messages. If an `Exception` occurs during processing of
the request, the `OBEX_HTTP_INTERNAL_ERROR` response code is
returned. Otherwise, the `OBEX_HTTP_OK` response code is returned.

```
public class RequestHandler extends ServerRequestHandler {

    ...

    /**
     * Called each time an OBEX PUT request is received.
     * This method will add
     * the message received in the BODY header for the user
     * specified in the
     * NAME header to the messages Vector.
     *
     * @param op the interface to the Operation
     *
     * @return the response code to send to the client
     */
    public int onPut(Operation op) {

      try {
        HeaderSet headers = op.getReceivedHeaders();
        String name =
          (String)headers.getHeader(HeaderSet.NAME);
        int msgSize = (int)((Long)headers.getHeader(
        HeaderSet.LENGTH)).longValue();
        if (name == null) {
          // If no NAME header is received, then it is not
          // a valid
          // request.
          return ResponseCodes.OBEX_HTTP_BAD_REQUEST;
        }

        InputStream input = op.openInputStream();
        byte[] data = new byte[msgSize];
        StringBuffer msg = new StringBuffer();
        // Read the BODY data / message
```

```
          int length = 0;
          int totalLength = 0;
          do {
            length = input.read(data);
            msg.append(new String(data, 0, length));
            totalLength += length;
          } while (totalLength != msgSize);

          input.close();

          // Add the message to the Vector
          msgList.addElement(new Message(name,
            msg.toString()));

          // Close the open connections
          op.close();
        } catch (Exception e) {
          return ResponseCodes.OBEX_HTTP_INTERNAL_ERROR;
        }
        return ResponseCodes.OBEX_HTTP_OK;
    }
}
```

Sending Messages to a Client

Because the GET operation is being used to retrieve messages from a server, the `onGet()` method must be overwritten within the `MessageServer` class. As in receiving a message from a client, the message server first retrieves the NAME header. If the NAME header is not present, the request cannot be completed, and an error return code is returned. The NAME header contains the name of the user trying to retrieve a message from the server. Next, the `onGet()` method steps through every message in the `msgList` `Vector` until a message is found for the user or the end of the `Vector` is reached. If the end of the `Vector` is reached and no `Message` is found for the user, the `OBEX_HTTP_NOT_FOUND` response code is returned. If a `Message` is found, the `onGet()` method opens the `OutputStream` of the `Operation` object and writes the message. If everything completes successfully, the `OBEX_HTTP_OK` response code signals to the client that a message has been found and returned. If an exception occurs during the processing of the `onGet()` method, the `OBEX_HTTP_INTERNAL_ERROR` response code is returned.

```
public class RequestHandler extends ServerRequestHandler {

  ...

  /**
   * Called each time an OBEX GET request is received.
   * This method will
   * will return a message in the BODY header for the
   * user specified. If no
   * message is found, this method will return a response
   * code of
   * OBEX_HTTP_NOT_FOUND.
   *
   * @param op used to retrieve the user name and send
   * the message
   *
   * @return the response code to send to the server;
   * OBEX_HTTP_OK if a message is sent in the
   * reply;
   * OBEX_HTTP_NOT_FOUND if no message could
   * be found for the
   * user specified; OBEX_HTTP_BAD_REQUEST if
   * no NAME is
   * specified; OBEX_HTTP_INTERNAL_ERROR if
   * another error
   * occurred.
   */
  public int onGet(Operation op) {

    try {
      // Retrieve the name of the user who is requesting
      // a message
      HeaderSet header = op.getReceivedHeaders();

      String name = (String)header.getHeader(HeaderSet.NAME);
      if (name == null ) {
        header = createHeaderSet();
        header.setHeader(HeaderSet.LENGTH, new Long(0));
        op.sendHeaders(header);
        op.close();

        return ResponseCodes.OBEX_HTTP_BAD_REQUEST;
      }
```

```
                  // Find a message for the user specified
                  int length = msgList.size();
                  Message temp = null;
                  for (int i = 0; i < length; i++) {

                    temp = (Message)msgList.elementAt(i);
                    if (temp.getUserName().equals(name)) {
                      break;
                    }
                    temp = null;
                  }
                  header = createHeaderSet();

                  // If no data is found, notify the client that no
                  // data was found
                  if (temp == null) {
                    header.setHeader(HeaderSet.LENGTH, new Long(0));
                    op.sendHeaders(header);

                    return ResponseCodes.OBEX_HTTP_NOT_FOUND;
                  }

                  header.setHeader(HeaderSet.LENGTH,
                    new Long(temp.getMessage().getBytes().length));
                  op.sendHeaders(header);

                  // Send the message back to the client
                  OutputStream out = op.openOutputStream();
                  out.write(temp.getMessage().getBytes());
                  out.flush();

                  // Close all the open resources
                  out.close();
                  op.close();

                  msgList.removeElement(temp);
                } catch (Exception e) {
                  return ResponseCodes.OBEX_HTTP_INTERNAL_ERROR;
                }

                return ResponseCodes.OBEX_HTTP_OK;
              }
            }
```

9.3.2   The Message Client Application

Overview

The MessageClient is a MIDlet that allows a user to send messages to and receive messages from a MessageServer. The MessageClient starts with the user specifying a user name. Because this application does not provide security, no password is provided. After the user name is received, the MessageClient attempts to find a MessageServer to which to connect. To keep things simple, the DiscoveryAgent. selectService() method is used to find a MessageServer. After the message server is found, the MessageClient connects to the MessageServer using Connector.open(). Once the transport layer connection is established, the MessageClient establishes an OBEX connection by calling ClientSession.connect().

After connecting to the server, the MessageClient creates a Form that allows the user to select between sending and receiving a message. If the user chooses to send a message, a new Form is created to allow the user to specify the user name and message. Once the user name and message are entered, the user selects the "Send" Command. After verifying that a user name and message have been entered, the MessageClient sends the message to the server using a PUT command. If the user selects to receive a message, the MessageClient issues a GET command with the user's user name. If there is a message on the server, the message is retrieved and displayed to the user in an Alert. If no messages are found on the server, an error message is displayed to the user.

At any time, the user can exit from the MessageClient MIDlet. When the user selects to exit, the MIDlet is destroyed. When the MIDlet is destroyed, the destroyApp() method is called. The connection to the server is disconnected and closed within the destroyApp() method.

Creating the Base MIDlet

The MessageClient MIDlet begins with the MessageClient constructor. The constructor retrieves the Display for the MIDlet. The startApp() method is called next by the Application Management engine within the KVM. Within the startApp() method, the login Form is created and set to the current Displayable.

To be notified when the user wants to log in, the `MessageClient`
class implements the `CommandListener` interface. This step requires
that the `MessageClient` class define the `commandAction()` method.
The `commandAction()` method first determines whether the "Exit"
`Command` or the "Login" `Command` has been selected by the user. If the
"Exit" `Command` has been selected, the MIDlet is destroyed by calling
`notifyDestroyed()`. If the user has selected the "Login" `Command`, the
`commandAction()` method first checks to see whether a user name has
been provided by the user. If the user name has not been provided, an
error `Alert` is displayed to the user. On the other hand, the client processing thread is started by the `commandAction()` method if the user
did enter a user name. The client-processing thread is defined within the
`MessageClient` class. Therefore the `MessageClient` class implements
the `Runnable` interface.

```
package com.jabwt.book;

import java.lang.*;
import java.io.*;
import javax.microedition.io.*;
import javax.microedition.midlet.*;
import javax.microedition.lcdui.*;
import javax.bluetooth.*;
import javax.obex.*;

/**
 * The MessageClient MIDlet allows a user to
 * send and retrieve
 * messages from a MessageServer MIDlet.
 */
public class MessageClient extends MIDlet implements
  CommandListener,
  Runnable {
  /**
   * The user name to use when communicating with the server.
   */
  private String userName;
  /**
   * The display for this MIDlet.
   */
  private Display theDisplay;
```

```
/**
 * Creates a MessageClient object and
 * retrieves the
 * Display for this MIDlet.
 */
public MessageClient() {
  theDisplay = Display.getDisplay(this);
}

/**
 * Called when the MIDlet is started. This method will
 * create the Login
 * Form and make it the current
 * Displayable.
 *
 * @exception MIDletStateChangeException never thrown
 */
public void startApp()
  throws MIDletStateChangeException {
  Form login = new Form("Login");
  login.append(new TextField("User Name", "", 10,
    TextField.ANY));
  login.addCommand(new Command("Login", Command.OK, 1));
  login.addCommand(new Command("Exit", Command.EXIT, 1));
  login.setCommandListener(this);

  theDisplay.setCurrent(login);
}

public void pauseApp() {
}
public void destroyApp(boolean unconditional) {
}

/**
 * Called when a Command is selected. If
 * the Exit
 * Command is selected, then the MIDlet is
 * destroyed. If the
 * Login Command (OK) is selected, the
 * method will verify
 * that the user name was entered and then start the
 * processing thread.
 *
```

```
    * @param c the Command that was selected
    * @param d the Displayable which the
    * Command
    * is attached to
    */
  public void commandAction(Command c, Displayable d) {
    switch (c.getCommandType()) {
    case Command.EXIT:
      notifyDestroyed();
      break;
    case Command.OK:

      // Retrieve the user name from the Form and verify
      // that a user
      // name has been entered
      TextField userTextField =
        (TextField)((Form)d).get(0);
      if (userTextField.getString().trim().equals("")) {
        Alert error = new Alert("Error",
          "Please enter a user name before continuing",
          null, AlertType.ERROR);
        error.setTimeout(Alert.FOREVER);
        theDisplay.setCurrent(error);
        return;
      }

      userName = userTextField.getString();

      new Thread(this).start();

      break;
    }
  }
  public void run() {
  }
}
```

Establishing a Connection to the Server

The run() method in the MessageClient class is responsible for locating a server and establishing a connection to the server. To keep the user updated on the progress of the run() method, a Form is created to log messages. After the Form is created and set to the current Displayable, the `DiscoveryAgent` is retrieved for the local Bluetooth device. The `selectService()` method is called on the `DiscoveryAgent` to retrieve a connection string to a `MessageServer`. (The `selectService()` method is used for simplicity's sake.)

After a `MessageServer` is found, the `run()` method connects to the `MessageServer` by calling `Connector.open()`. After a `ClientSession` object is retrieved, the `run()` method issues a CONNECT request by calling `connect()`. The `HeaderSet` returned by `connect()` is checked to determine whether the connection has been accepted by the server. If the `getResponseCode()` does not return `OBEX_HTTP_OK`, the connection to the server is closed, and an error message is displayed to the user.

For displaying the error message to the user, another method is added to the `MessageClient` class. The `displayError()` method creates a modal `Alert` with the title and error message provided to the method.

```
public class MessageClient extends MIDlet implements
  CommandListener,
  Runnable {

  /**
   * The connection to the message server.
   */
  private ClientSession conn;

  ...

  /**
   * Displays an error message to the user.
   *
   * @param title the title of the Alert
   * @param message the message to display to the user
   */
  private void displayError(String title, String message) {
    Alert error = new Alert(title, message, null,
      AlertType.ERROR);
    error.setTimeout(Alert.FOREVER);
    theDisplay.setCurrent(error);
  }

  /**
   * Searches for a MessageServer to connect to and
   * establishes an OBEX
   * connection to the MessageServer that is found.
```

```java
*/
public void run() {
  // Create a form to keep the user updated on the
  // progress of the thread
  Form f = new Form("Connecting...");
  f.append("Searching for Message Server...");
  f.addCommand(new Command("Exit", Command.EXIT, 1));
  f.setCommandListener(this);
  theDisplay.setCurrent(f);

  try {
    // Search for a MessageServer
    LocalDevice local = LocalDevice.getLocalDevice();
    DiscoveryAgent agent = local.getDiscoveryAgent();
    String connString = agent.selectService(
      new UUID("750ef04247a54693b6384708eb87ec5e",
        false),
      ServiceRecord.NOAUTHENTICATE_NOENCRYPT, false);

    if (connString == null) {
      f.append("Unable to find the message server");
      displayError("Error",
        "Unable to find a Message Server to connect to.");
      return;
    }

    f.append("Done\n");
    f.append("Connecting to Server...");

    // Establish a transport layer connection to the
    // MessageServer
    conn = (ClientSession)Connector.open(connString);

    f.append("Done\n");
    f.append("Establishing OBEX connection...");

    // Issue an OBEX CONNECT request
    HeaderSet header = conn.connect(null);
    if (header.getResponseCode() !=
      ResponseCodes.OBEX_HTTP_OK) {
    f.append("The connection was rejected");
    displayError("Rejected",
      "The connection has been rejected by the " +
        "server. (0x" +
```

```
                    Integer.toHexString(header.getResponseCode()) + ")");
             conn.close();
             conn = null;
             return;
         }
     } catch (Exception e) {
       f.append("An Error has occurred");
       displayError("Error",
         "An error occurred while trying to locate and " +
         "connect to " +
         "the Message Server (" + e.getClass().getName() +
         ": " +
         e.getMessage() + ")");
       if (conn != null) {
         try {
           conn.close();
         } catch (Exception ex) {
         }
         conn = null;
       }
       return;
     }
   }
}
```

Now that the MessageClient is connected to the MessageServer, the MessageClient displays a Form to the user so that the user can select to send or retrieve a message. The getNextOptionFromUser() method is created for this procedure. This method creates a new List and adds two list items from which to select. This method has one argument, an Alert, which is displayed before the List. This feature is used later. The getNextOptionFromUser() method is placed at the end of the run() method after the connection is established.

```
public class MessageClient extends MIDlet implements
  CommandListener,
  Runnable {

  ...

  /**
   * Creates a List that allows the user to
   * select to send a
```

```
 * message or retrieve a message. If the
 * dialog argument
 * is not null, the dialog Alert is
 * displayed before the
 * List is displayed.
 *
 * @param dialog the Alert to display
 * before the
 * List; if null no
 * Alert is
 * displayed
 */
private void getNextOptionFromUser(Alert dialog) {
  List requestForm = new List("Message Client",
    List.EXCLUSIVE);
  requestForm.append("Send a Message", null);
  requestForm.append("Receive a Message", null);
  requestForm.addCommand(new Command("Ok",
    Command.SCREEN, 1));
  requestForm.addCommand(new Command("Exit",
    Command.EXIT, 1));

  requestForm.setCommandListener(this);

  // Display the Alert before the List if it is not null
  if (dialog == null) {
    theDisplay.setCurrent(requestForm);
  } else {
    theDisplay.setCurrent(dialog, requestForm);
  }
}
```

```
/**
 * Searches for a MessageServer to connect to and
 * establishes an OBEX
 * connection to the MessageServer that is found.
 */
public void run() {
  // Create a form to keep the user updated on the
  // progress of the
  // thread
  Form f = new Form("Connecting...");
  f.append("Searching for Message Server...");
  f.addCommand(new Command("Exit", Command.EXIT, 1));
```

```
f.setCommandListener(this);
theDisplay.setCurrent(f);

try {
  // Search for a MessageServer
  LocalDevice local = LocalDevice.getLocalDevice();
  DiscoveryAgent agent = local.getDiscoveryAgent();
  String connString = agent.selectService(
    new UUID("750ef04247a54693b6384708eb87ec5e", false),
    ServiceRecord.NOAUTHENTICATE_NOENCRYPT, false);
  if (connString == null) {
    t.append("Unable to find the message server");
    displayError("Error",
      "Unable to find a Message Server to connect to.");
    return;
  }

  f.append("Done\n");
  f.append("Connecting to Server...");

  // Establish a transport layer connection to the
  // MessageServer
  conn = (ClientSession)Connector.open(connString);

  f.append("Done\n");
  f.append("Establishing OBEX connection...");

  // Issue an OBEX CONNECT request
  HeaderSet header = conn.connect(null);

  if (header.getResponseCode() !=
    ResponseCodes.OBEX_HTTP_OK) {
    f.append("The connection was rejected");
    displayError("Rejected",
      "The connection has been rejected by the " +
        "server. (0x" +
      Integer.toHexString(header.getResponseCode()) + ")");
    conn.close();
    conn = null;
    return;
  }

  // Allow the user to select what to do next
  getNextOptionFromUser(null);
} catch (Exception e) {
  f.append("An Error has occurred");
```

```
        displayError("Error",
          "An error occurred while trying to locate and" +
            " connect to " +
          "the Message Server (" + e.getClass().getName() +
            ": " +
          e.getMessage() + ")");
        if (conn != null) {
          try {
            conn.close();
          } catch (Exception ex) {
          }
          conn = null;
        }
        return;
      }
    }
}
```

Sending a Message to the Server

The sendMessage() method sends messages to the server via a PUT operation. The sendMessage() method takes, as arguments, the recipient of the message and the actual message. The sendMessage() method first creates a HeaderSet object and sets the recipient's user name to be the NAME header. Next, the LENGTH header is set to the length of the message to send. After the NAME and LENGTH headers are set, the sendMessage() method calls put() with this HeaderSet to create the Operation object for sending the message to the server. The sendMessage() method opens the OutputStream and writes the message to the output stream. After the message is written, the getResponseCode() method is called to determine whether the message was correctly received by the server. If the message is not sent to the server correctly, an error Alert is displayed to the user.

```
public class MessageClient extends MIDlet implements
  CommandListener,
  Runnable {
  ...

  /**
   * Sends the specified message to the specified name.
   *
   * @param name the name of the user to send to
```

```
       * @param message the message to send to the user
       */
      private void sendMessage(String name, String message) {
        Operation op = null;
        byte[] data = message.getBytes();
        Alert error = null;
        try {
          // Set the NAME header to the recipient's user name
          // and the
          // LENGTH header to the length of the message
          HeaderSet header = conn.createHeaderSet();
          header.setHeader(HeaderSet.NAME, name);
          header.setHeader(HeaderSet.LENGTH, new
            Long(data.length));

          op = conn.put(header);

          // Send the message to the server via the OutputStream
          OutputStream out = op.openOutputStream();
          out.write(data);
          out.flush();
          out.close();
          op.close();

          // Verify the response code
          int code = op.getResponseCode();
          if (code != ResponseCodes.OBEX_HTTP_OK) {
            error = new Alert("Request Rejected",
              "The server rejected the message. (0x" +
              Integer.toHexString(code) + ")", null,
                AlertType.ERROR);
            error.setTimeout(Alert.FOREVER);
          }
        } catch (IOException e) {
          error = new Alert("IO Error",
            "An IO error occurred while sending the " +
            "request to the server (" + e.getMessage() + ")", null,
            AlertType.ERROR);
          error.setTimeout(Alert.FOREVER);
        } finally {
          try {
            op.close();
          } catch (Exception e) {
```

```
        }
    }

    // Retrieve the next option from the user
    getNextOptionFromUser(error);
}
}
```

Now that it is able to send a message, the `MessageClient` must be able to get the message from the user. For getting the message from the user, a `Form` is displayed that allows the user to enter a user name and message. After entering the user name and message, the user can select to send the message using the "Send" `Command`. After the user chooses to send the message, the user name and message are read from the `Form`. If the user name is not specified, an error `Alert` is displayed. If a user name is specified, the `sendMessage()` method is called to send a message. At any time, the "Exit" `Command` can be selected to destroy the MIDlet. The "Exit" `Command` closes the connection to the server if one exists.

```
public class MessageClient extends MIDlet implements
  CommandListener,
  Runnable {

...

  /**
   * Called when a Command is selected. If
   * the Exit
   * Command is selected, then the MIDlet is
   * destroyed. If the
   * Login Command (OK) is selected, the
   * method will verify
   * that the user name was entered and then start the
   * processing thread.
   *
   * @param c the Command that was selected
   * @param d the Displayable which the
   * Command
   * is attached to
   */
  public void commandAction(Command c, Displayable d) {

    switch (c.getCommandType()) {
    case Command.EXIT:

        try {
```

```
          conn.close();
        } catch (Exception e) {
        }
    notifyDestroyed();
    break;
case Command.OK:

    // Retrieve the user name from the Form and verify
    // that a user
    // name has been entered
    TextField userTextField = (TextField)((Form)d).get(0);
    if (userTextField.getString().trim().equals("")) {
      Alert error = new Alert("Error",
        "Please enter a user name before continuing",
        null, AlertType.ERROR);
      error.setTimeout(Alert.FOREVER);
      theDisplay.setCurrent(error);
      return;
    }
    userName = userTextField.getString();

    new Thread(this).start();

    break;

case Command.SCREEN:
    List requestForm = (List)d;
    // Determine if the user wants to send a message or
    // retrieve a
    // message. If getSelectedIndex() is 0, then "Send a
    // Message"
    // was selected. Otherwise, retrieve a message.
    if (requestForm.getSelectedIndex() == 0) {

      Form sendForm = new Form("Send Msg");
      sendForm.append(new TextField("User", null, 10,
        TextField.ANY));
      sendForm.append(new TextField("Message", null, 250,
        TextField.ANY));

      sendForm.addCommand(new Command("Exit", Command.EXIT,
        1));
      sendForm.addCommand(new Command("Send", Command.ITEM,
        1));

      sendForm.setCommandListener(this);
```

```
                    theDisplay.setCurrent(sendForm);
        }
    break;
  case Command.ITEM:
    Form sendMessage = (Form)d;
    // Retrieve the user name and verify that one was
    // entered.
    TextField userName = (TextField)sendMessage.get(0);
    if (userName.getString().trim().equals("")) {
      displayError("Incomplete",
        "A user name must be specified to send a message");
      return;
    }
    TextField message = (TextField)sendMessage.get(1);
    sendMessage(userName.getString(), message.getString());
    break;
  }
 }
 ...
}
```

Retrieving a Message from the Server

The retrieveMessage() method is defined to use the get() method to retrieve a message from the server. Before get() is called, the retrieveMessage() method creates a new HeaderSet object and sets the name of the current user in the NAME header. The server uses this name to search for messages. The message is read from the InputStream of the Operation object. After the message is read, the response code is checked to determine whether the complete message has been sent. If the complete message has been sent and an OBEX_HTTP_OK response code is received, the message is displayed on the screen. If another response code is received, the appropriate error message is displayed.

The following code ties the procedure together by modifying the commandAction() method. If the user selects "Retrieve a Message," the retrieveMessage() method is called to retrieve the message.

```
public class MessageClient extends MIDlet implements
  CommandListener,
  Runnable {
```

```
...
/**
 * Retrieves a message for this user from the server.
 */
public void retrieveMessage() {
  Alert msg = null;
  try {
    // Specify the name of the user whose message should
    // be retrieved
    HeaderSet header = conn.createHeaderSet();
    header.setHeader(HeaderSet.NAME, userName);

    Operation op = conn.get(header);

    // Read the message from the InputStream. If an
    // error response
    // code was returned, the InputStream will be empty.
    StringBuffer buf = new StringBuffer();
    InputStream input = op.openInputStream();
    header = op.getReceivedHeaders();

    int size = (int)((Long)header.getHeader(
      HeaderSet.LENGTH)).longValue();

    // Read the message from the server
    byte[] data = new byte[size];
    int length = input.read(data);
    int temp = 0;
    int bytesRead = length;
    while (bytesRead != size) {
      buf = buf.append(new String(data, temp, length));
      temp = length;
      length = input.read(data);
      bytesRead += length;
    }
    buf = buf.append(new String(data, temp, length));

    input.close();

    // Check the response code to see if the whole
    // message was read
    int code = op.getResponseCode();
    switch (code) {

    // If the whole message was read, print the message
    // in an Alert
```

```
      case ResponseCodes.OBEX_HTTP_OK:
        msg = new Alert("Message", buf.toString(), null,
          AlertType.INFO);

        break;

      // No messages exist for this user on the server
      case ResponseCodes.OBEX_HTTP_NOT_FOUND:
        msg = new Alert("No Message",
          "No messages on the server",
          null, AlertType.INFO);

        break;

      // An error occurred so print out an error message
      default:
        msg = new Alert("Error",
          "As error occurred while communicating " +
          " with the server (" + Integer.toHexString(code)
          + ")",
          null, AlertType.INFO);

        break;
      }

      op.close();
    } catch (IOException e) {
      msg = new Alert("IO Error",
        "An IO error occurred while communicating " +
        "with server (IOException: " + e.getMessage() +
        ")", null,
        AlertType.INFO);
    }

    msg.setTimeout(Alert.FOREVER);

    getNextOptionFromUser(msg);
}
```

```
/**
 * Called when a Command is selected. If the Exit
 * Command is selected, then the MIDlet is
 * destroyed. If the
 * Login Command (OK) is selected, the
 * method will verify
 * that the user name was entered and then start the
 * processing thread.
```

```
*
* @param c the Command that was selected
* @param d the Displayable which the
* Command
* is attached to
*/
 public void commandAction(Command c, Displayable d) {
   switch (c.getCommandType()) {
   case Command.EXIT:
     notifyDestroyed();
     break;
   case Command.OK:
     // Retrieve the user name from the Form and verify
     // that a user
     // name has been entered
     TextField userTextField =
       (TextField)((Form)d).get(0);
     if (userTextField.getString().trim().equals("")) {
       Alert error = new Alert("Error",
         "Please enter a user name before continuing",
         null, AlertType.ERROR);
       error.setTimeout(Alert.FOREVER);
       theDisplay.setCurrent(error);
       return;
   }

   userName = userTextField.getString();

   new Thread(this).start();

   break;
 case Command.SCREEN:

 List requestForm = (List)d;

 // Determine if the user wants to send a message or
 // retrieve a
 // message. If getSelectedIndex() is 0, then "Send a
 // Message"
 // was selected. Otherwise, retrieve a message.
 if (requestForm.getSelectedIndex() == 0) {

   Form sendForm = new Form("Send Msg");
   sendForm.append(new TextField("User", null, 10,
```

```
      TextField.ANY));
    sendForm.append(new TextField("Message", null, 250,
      TextField.ANY));

    sendForm.addCommand(new Command("Exit", Command.EXIT,
      1));
    sendForm.addCommand(new Command("Send", Command.ITEM,
      1));

    sendForm.setCommandListener(this);

    theDisplay.setCurrent(sendForm);

  } else {
  // Retrieve a message from the server
  retrieveMessage();
  }

  break;

  case Command.ITEM:

    Form sendMessage = (Form)d;

    // Retrieve the user name and verify that one was entered.
    TextField userName = (TextField)sendMessage.get(0);
    if (userName.getString().trim().equals("")) {
        displayError("Incomplete",
          "A user name must be specified to send a message");
        return;
      }
      TextField message = (TextField)sendMessage.get(1);
      sendMessage(userName.getString(), message.getString());
      break;
    }
  }
  ...
}
```

9.4 Summary

This chapter provides two example applications. One example application, the tic-tac-toe game, shows how to use the Bluetooth API. The tic-tac-toe game uses the RFCOMM protocol to allow two people to play a simple game of tic-tac-toe. The second application uses the OBEX API to send and receive messages from a server application using OBEX over the RFCOMM transport protocol.

10 Implementing JABWT on a Device

CHAPTER

This chapter covers:

- The steps required to implement JABWT on a device
- Issues and requirements for implementing JABWT
- Technology Compatibility Kit (TCK) compliance

A specification becomes a standard only when it is implemented. Until then it is merely a .pdf file.

In the previous chapters we talk extensively about the JABWT specification and how to write applications using the API. But for these applications to run, there needs to be devices enabled with JABWT. In this chapter we discuss some of the issues related to implementing this API.

Who should implement JABWT?

- J2ME device manufacturers who plan to add Bluetooth wireless technology to their devices
- Bluetooth device manufacturers who want to extend the programming capability of their devices to the vast number of Java programmers

This API brings together two different worlds, Bluetooth wireless technology and Java technology, and unites the benefits of each.

There are several aspects to enabling a device with JABWT. An implementation depends on the components in the system, namely, the Bluetooth hardware, the Bluetooth stack, the operating system, the KVM, the CLDC implementation, and possibly other optional Java APIs or profiles. Because these components vary from device to device, the issues with JABWT implementation vary. Typically only selection of the

Bluetooth protocol stack and CLDC/KVM implementation influence the porting of JABWT to a device. For the device manufacturer today, there are a wide range of choices for each of these components. Therefore, instead of covering the minute details of porting for a particular set of components, this chapter highlights the main issues an implementer needs to think about while implementing JABWT on a device.

It is recommended that anyone attempting to port JABWT to a device understand the Bluetooth specification, the Bluetooth protocol stack, the Bluetooth radio hardware being used, and the KVM and CLDC on the device.

10.1 Porting Process

The general device and Bluetooth system requirements for implementing JABWT are discussed in Chapter 2. But each device being built has specific Bluetooth application and system requirements. Before starting the porting process of JABWT, an implementer has to make sure the JABWT hardware and system requirements are met in the device in question. The next steps are as follows:

1. Port a CLDC/KVM implementation (or CDC/JVM or J2SE + JSR-197 implementation)
2. Integrate a Bluetooth protocol stack and radio
3. Implement JABWT and the BCC
4. Run the TCK to check for compliance of the implementation to the JABWT specification.

How many of these steps are needed depends on the device used for the JABWT implementation. An implementer starting to create a JABWT device can begin with one of the following four categories:

Category 1: The device currently has neither J2ME nor native Bluetooth support. All four steps listed above have to be implemented.

Category 2: The device is currently a J2ME device but has no native Bluetooth support. Steps 2 through 4 are needed.

Category 3: The device has native Bluetooth support but is not J2ME enabled. Steps 1, 3, and 4 are needed.

Category 4: The device has J2ME and native Bluetooth support but does not have JABWT. Steps 3 and 4 are needed.

Figures 10.1 through Figure 10.4 illustrate these four categories. The above steps and categories assume a KVM-based machine with a non-Java interface to a native Bluetooth stack and no Java Native Interface (JNI) in the J2ME implementation. In the case of devices that have the Bluetooth protocol stack implemented completely in the Java programming language or have JNI, some of the components discussed in the next sections may not be applicable, but the general issues in the porting process are still applicable. This chapter attempts to cover the more difficult case, which is a device with a KVM implementation that has a C interface to a native Bluetooth stack and no JNI.

JABWT depends only on CLDC libraries. Generally, however, CLDC does not make a complete J2ME solution. Devices usually have one or more J2ME profiles to complete their functionality. MIDP is one such profile typically used in mobile phones. Mobile phones are expected to be one of the large-volume JABWT devices. Figure 10.1 shows the components of an implementation that has CLDC/MIDP, a native Bluetooth stack, native Bluetooth applications, and JABWT. Such a device would support a wide range of Bluetooth applications. For example, native Bluetooth applications would access the native Bluetooth protocol stack through the APIs provided directly by the stack. In addition, JABWT applications can access the Bluetooth

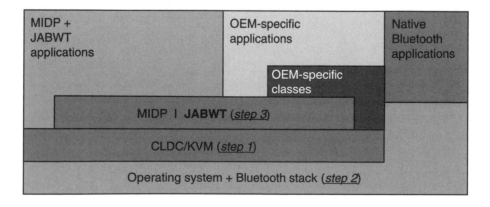

Figure 10.1 Components of JABWT device.

protocol stack using the APIs defined by the JSR-82 specification (shown as JABWT, next to MIDP in Figure 10.1).

The dependence of JABWT on CLDC is confined to the package `javax.microedition.io`. JSR-197 defines `javax.microedition.io` as an optional package in J2SE that will enable JABWT to be an optional package in J2SE also. With JSR-197, there are three choices for step 1 above: either port CLDC/KVM, or port CDC/JVM, or port J2SE + JSR-197.

Now let's look at each of the four steps in the porting process.

10.2 Steps 1 and 2: Adding J2ME and Bluetooth Support

To add Java technology to a device with native Bluetooth support (Figure 10.2), one has to port an appropriate Java virtual machine and set of class libraries to that device (step 1). Likewise, to add Bluetooth wireless technology to a J2ME device (Figure 10.3), one has to port a native Bluetooth protocol stack to the device (step 2). Implementation details of these two steps are beyond the scope of this book. These two steps can be performed in any order if not already done on the device. They are two independent porting efforts. When these two steps are completed, the architecture of the resulting device is similar to that shown in Figure 10.4.

If both step 1 and step 2 are needed, the JABWT implementation can be simplified by selection of a Bluetooth protocol stack and a KVM with appropriate features. Of all the modules, the KVM-stack interface is the most crucial; hence selecting the stack for the JABWT device is an important step. This issue is discussed next.

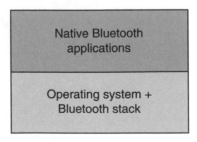

Figure 10.2 Components of a Native Bluetooth Device.

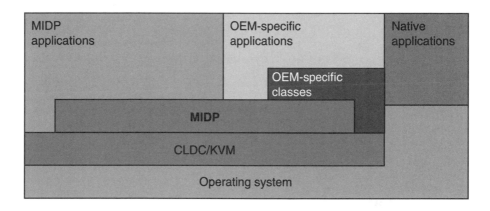

Figure 10.3 Components of MIDP device.

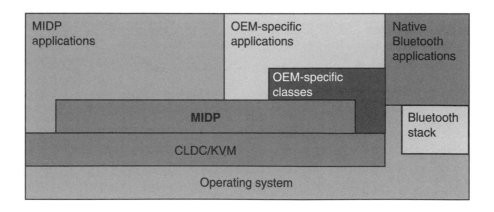

Figure 10.4 A device with MIDP and a native Bluetooth stack.

Stack Features That JABWT Requires

As stated in Chapter 2, the underlying Bluetooth protocol stack must be qualified in accordance with the Bluetooth Qualification Program for at least the GAP, SDAP, and SPP. Without these features in the stack, JABWT cannot be implemented. In addition, the interface between the

JABWT implementation and the Bluetooth protocol stack is simplified if the stack has the following features:

- Applications access the stack through a set of APIs.

- The stack supports asynchronous calls for all operations that may require a nontrivial amount of time for completion.

- Applications are notified of asynchronous events. The use of callback functions is the most common way of accomplishing this task, but it can also be performed through interrupts or application-level polling.

In selection of a stack for a JABWT device, these issues must to be taken into account. If the device already has a stack, these issues will help identify the necessary modifications or workarounds that may be required for completing the JABWT implementation.

A qualified stack generally has all the required functionality for a JABWT implementation. Going through all the required functionality would amount to listing the Bluetooth specification itself, but the key requirements of the stack are as follows:

1. The stack should provide APIs to perform RFCOMM connections, inquiry, and service discovery functions.

2. The stack should provide an API to add and delete service records.

3. The stack should give access to APIs for performing L2CAP connections. This is a key area because many stacks have L2CAP capabilities but do not provide a way of accessing them from outside the stack. The JABWT implementation must perform L2CAP functions directly.

4. The stack should provide the following security and support features:

   - Determine whether the given device is trusted

   - Authorize the given connection and remote device

   - Set the device PIN

   - Enable or disable encryption

   - Authenticate the remote device

   - Determine whether a given remote device has already been authenticated

- Determine whether a given connection has already been authorized
- Determine whether a given link is encrypted
- Get the user-friendly name of the local device
- Get the user-friendly name of the remote device
- Get the class of device information for the local device
- Change the discoverable mode of the local device
- Enable or disable the connectable mode for the local device
- Get the Bluetooth address of the local device

Other stack features that would make the porting effort easier are as follows:

1. The stack should provide callback functions for asynchronous event notification. Otherwise the KVM has to poll the stack, a process that affects performance of the JABWT implementation.

2. The stack should support asynchronous calls for time-consuming operations; otherwise the performance of the KVM will be affected. This subject is discussed in more detail in the Section 10.3.

3. Although not required by the JABWT specification, support for (a) sending HCI commands, (b) security modes 2 and 3, and (c) master/slave switching in the stack will simplify the JABWT implementation.

4. Good debugging capabilities should exist.

10.3 Step 3: Implementing JABWT

By accomplishing step 1 and step 2, one arrives at a device that has an implementation of J2ME and native Bluetooth support but does not have JABWT. Many such devices are available. These devices come with step 1 and step 2 completed. Figure 10.4 shows the components of such a device. Implementing JABWT on this device (step 3) would make this device a JABWT device as shown in Figure 10.1.

The implementation components from steps 1 through 3 are shown in Figure 10.5. The JABWT implementation consists of the Java

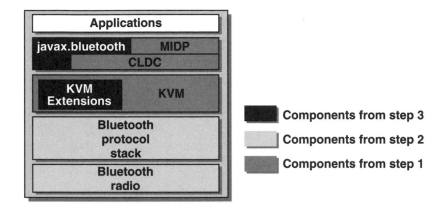

Figure 10.5   Implementation components.

libraries, `javax.bluetooth` and optionally `javax.obex` (not shown), and KVM extensions. The Java libraries layers most likely will not need to change for porting to a different stack or KVM. The components of the KVM extensions are shown in Figure 10.6.

The KVM and KVM operating system interface (KOSI) shown in Figure 10.6 are the native code part of the CLDC implementation. The components of the KVM extensions (i.e., Bluetooth KVM, Bluetooth-KOSI, and BCC) are part of the JABWT implementation. The KVM extensions provide the following:

- Native functions to make calls to the stack
- Event handling code to receive callbacks from the stack
- BCC to resolve conflicts between applications over device state and security measures
- Code to interface with the stack and manage data structures

Depending on the KVM, it may be necessary to modify the KOSI layer of CLDC. (If the J2ME implementation has a JNI interface, such modifications will not be necessary.)

Bluetooth-KVM

This module contains changes to the KVM to incorporate JABWT. This includes changes to the KVM for handling events from the Bluetooth

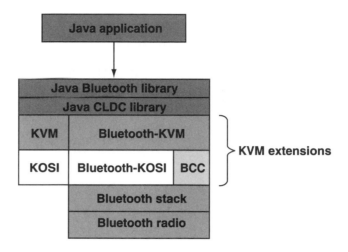

Figure 10.6 Components of KVM extensions.

protocol stack and additional native functions called by the Java libraries. This layer is stack independent but depends on the KVM. The details of this module depend on the architecture and design of the KVM used.

Bluetooth-KOSI

This layer is the interface layer between the KVM and the Bluetooth protocol stack. This layer is stack dependent and needs to be ported for each device with a different Bluetooth stack. The person implementing this layer needs a detailed understanding of the stack API and the stack event mechanism.

10.3.1 KVM-Stack Interface

Some of the key issues with implementing the Bluetooth-KVM and Bluetooth-KOSI modules are as follows:

- Managing connections. Managing the Java objects in the Bluetooth classes and the connections in the Bluetooth protocol stack is one of key issues in the KVM extensions. When a J2ME application makes a `Connector.open()` call to establish a connection, an appropriate Java object is created if the connection request is successful. The actual connection between Bluetooth devices is established within the Bluetooth protocol stack. It is up to the Bluetooth-KVM and Bluetooth-KOSI layers to maintain this association between the Java objects in the J2ME application and the actual Bluetooth connection within the protocol stack. This association must be maintained even if there are multiple and simultaneous connections.

- Event handling. In addition to transferring data between the Bluetooth Java libraries and the Bluetooth protocol stack, the native interface must be able to transfer event notifications from the protocol stack to the KVM, where it is processed. These events can be generated by the protocol stack in the local device or generated as a result of some operation performed by the remote device. These events happen asynchronously. Typical notification mechanisms are periodic polling by the KVM or KVM callback functions registered with the Bluetooth protocol stack. The latter is more efficient. Choosing a stack with that capability helps ease the JABWT port to a device. In this case the KVM registers with the Bluetooth protocol stack to receive events that provide the results to pass back to the application.

- Blocking and non-blocking stack calls. The layers above the KVM extensions are context switched by the KVM, and this feature enables different threads within J2ME to run. Even if one Java thread is blocked, the other Java threads continue to run. It is frequently the case, however, that the KVM itself is single threaded from the system software perspective. This means that if the Bluetooth-KOSI layer makes a blocking call to the Bluetooth stack, the entire J2ME engine blocks, and no threads run. The performance of the J2ME system suffers. Context switching in J2ME with single-threaded KVM is illustrated in Figure 10.7. Because of the nature of Bluetooth communications, many of the operations take a noticeable amount of time to complete. Limiting the blocking calls to the Bluetooth protocol stack is highly desirable in a JABWT implementation.

The following are possible blocking and non-blocking call scenarios. These issues are to be considered when porting to a Bluetooth stack or in selection of a Bluetooth stack for the JABWT device.

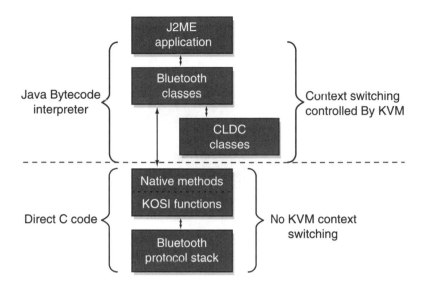

Figure 10.7 Context-switching in J2ME.

1. The JABWT application makes a blocking API call, and the KVM makes a blocking call to the stack. In this case both the application and the KVM block until the operation is complete. Operations such as these should be limited only to very fast stack calls, such as calls to get the name of the local device. An example of such a method in JABWT is the method `LocalDevice.getBluetoothAddress()`.

2. The JABWT application makes a non-blocking API call using the event-driven methods in the API. An example of such a method in JABWT is `DiscoveryAgent.searchServices()`, which uses a Java listener object to receive completed events. The KVM then registers with the Bluetooth stack to receive notification of events. Once this event is received, the KVM uses events in the Java API to return results to the application. Note: if a stack does not provide a non-blocking call for an event-driven method in JABWT, that stack is not a good stack to be used in a JABWT device.

3. The JABWT application makes a blocking call on an operation in which it would not be advisable to block the KVM (e.g., methods that access a remote device). Therefore the related call to the stack

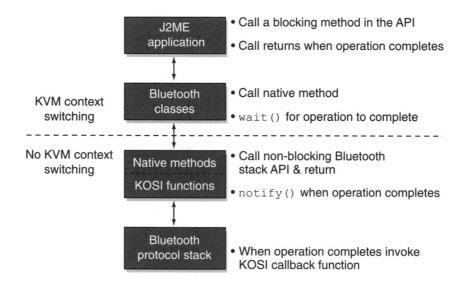

Figure 10.8   Not blocking the KVM.

that the KVM needs to make is a non-blocking call. Then the KVM extension modules should convert the blocking call from the application to an event-driven call. An example of this scenario is shown in Figure 10.8. One way to do the conversion is by using the Java methods `java.lang.Object.wait()` and `java.lang.Object.notify()`. In general, any JABWT method that requires Bluetooth communications over the air to remote devices should not block the KVM and is a potential target for such a conversion. Examples of such methods are `DiscoveryAgent.selectServices()`, `RemoteDevice.getBluetoothAddress()`, and `RemoteDevice.getFriendlyName(alwaysAsk)` when the input parameter `alwaysAsk` is `true`.

10.3.2 Implementing the BCC

The BCC is another component of the KVM extensions. As described in the JABWT specification, the BCC is entirely implementation dependent and would require some level of porting for each device, even if the KVM and stack are the same. The BCC serves the vital role of resolving conflicts between multiple applications that make conflicting requests to the Bluetooth protocol stack. For example, one application may request the Bluetooth stack to turn on encryption while another application may request encryption to be turned off. The BCC also sets and enforces device-wide security settings. Therefore, depending on the requirements of the final system, the scope of the BCC may range from something quite trivial to something very complex. The following is a list of key BCC design and implementation issues:

- Will there be a mix of non-J2ME and J2ME applications? If so, the BCC may have to reside in the protocol stack or be part of the operating system.

- Will there be a need to support a number of different security modes?

- Will the user have the capability of modifying the behavior of the BCC? If so, there may be a need to develop a UI of some sort for the BCC.

The simplest BCC implementation would consist of a set of static device policies and security settings that would always apply to all applications. However, a more sophisticated BCC may be required to support a more diverse range of applications and application requirements, thus increasing the complexity of the BCC.

10.3.3 OBEX Implementation

The OBEX API within JABWT is independent of the Bluetooth APIs. It is also an optional API. Thus a JABWT implementation can consist of only the Bluetooth APIs (`javax.bluetooth`) and not the OBEX APIs (`javax.obex`). Being transport independent makes it easy to implement the OBEX APIs on devices that do not have Bluetooth transports but have other transports (e.g., IrDA, USB) over which OBEX can be implemented.

The OBEX implementation can be in the Java language or be in a native implementation. Figure 10.9 shows the difference between the two implementations. There may be devices that already have native OBEX implementations. In this case, it may be better to implement the Java OBEX APIs defined in JABWT on top of the native implementation. On the other hand, an OBEX implementation in the Java programming language may help reduce the porting work when a manufacturer builds many different devices with OBEX capability.

Native OBEX Implementation

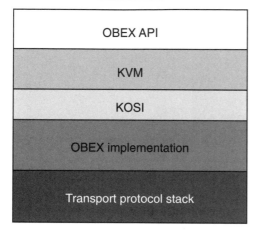

OBEX API
KVM
KOSI
OBEX implementation
Transport protocol stack

Java Implementation

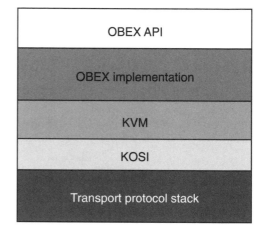

OBEX API
OBEX implementation
KVM
KOSI
Transport protocol stack

Figure 10.9   OBEX Implementations.

10.4 Step 4: TCK Compliance

A TCK is the suite of tests, tools, and documentation used to verify that an implementation is compliant with a Java API specification. All specifications defined under the JCP have a TCK. All independent implementations of these specifications must be tested for compliance by running the TCK. The procedure is black box API testing with minimal functional and stress testing. JABWT implementers can do additional functional and stress testing of their products. Only the JABWT implementation, not the applications written with JABWT, needs to be tested for TCK compliance. An application that runs on a compliant JABWT device should run on any compliant JABWT device provided the application is strictly written to the specification.

TCK compliance testing is different from the Bluetooth Qualification process. The Bluetooth Qualification process ensures that products comply with the Bluetooth specification. Although JSR-82 TCKs will be used to verify compliance of JABWT, the Bluetooth Qualification process would have to be used to qualify a Bluetooth profile written with JABWT. The Bluetooth profile is technically an application of JABWT; hence TCK compliance is not applicable.

The JSR-82 specification has two TCKs for determining the compliance of devices with the JABWT specification:

- The Bluetooth TCK tests the compliance of the Bluetooth API (`javax.bluetooth`) of JABWT
- The OBEX TCK tests the compliance of the OBEX API (`javax.obex`) of JABWT

These TCKs are a set of tests that can be inserted into Sun's CLDC TCK and JavaTest™ harness. They consist of test-case sources, test-case classes, and documentation. TCKs can be licensed from the JSR specification lead companies. Companies that lead a JSR must create a reference implementation (RI) and TCK for the specification developed. The RI and TCK must be made available for licensing. The RI and the TCKs for JSR-82 can be licensed from the JSR-82 specification lead company, Motorola. (Inquires about RI and TCKs can be sent to motorolajava@javaland.sps.mot.com). The CLDC TCK can be licensed from Sun Microsystems. Before claiming compliance or compatibility to the JSR-82 specification, companies implementing the JABWT APIs must use the JSR-82 TCK to demonstrate that their implementations conform to the specification. All tests in the JSR-82 TCK have to run and pass on the product before the product can be claimed as JABWT compliant or compatible.

TCK Setup and Configuration

The JABWT TCKs use the same client-server design as the CLDC TCK does, which includes the JavaTest framework. The TCK server runs the JavaTest application, and a TCK client device runs the CldcAgent application.

Figure 10.10 shows the setup for the JSR-82 TCK test. The JABWT implementation being tested on the TCK client device interacts with a second Bluetooth device running an application designed specifically to participate in the JABWT TCK test. This test application is called the TCK Agent, and the JSR-82 TCK setup requires the use of a TCK Agent to interact in a predetermined manner with the CldcAgent application running on the TCK client. Figure 10.10 shows the TCK Agent and the CldcAgent and indicates that the TCK Agent has been added to the

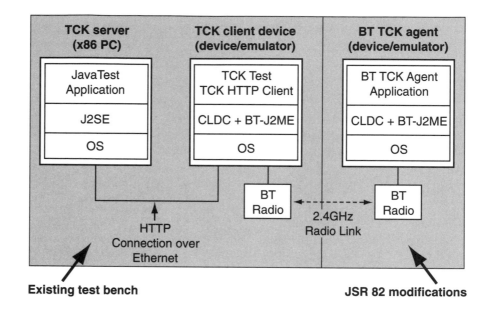

Figure 10.10   JSR-82 TCK setup.

CLDC TCK test setup for use in the JSR-82 TCK test. This TCK agent on the remote device can be one of the following:

- A CLDC (or MIDP) + JABWT application running on a JABWT device
- A native application (non-JABWT) using a native Bluetooth or OBEX implementation

More details on the TCK setup and TCK Agent are available in the documentation that comes with the TCK.

10.5 Summary

This chapter discusses various issues and techniques involved in providing a JABWT implementation for a Bluetooth device. Because the characteristics of the KVM chosen and the Bluetooth stack chosen have a major impact on the details of the JABWT implementation process, it is not possible to list all of the issues that might arise. In addition, the design of JABWT varies between implementations, a factor that gives rise to some unique issues. This chapter discusses the different situations that confront device manufacturers and highlights areas to which an implementer will have to pay close attention.

Depending on the device with which one starts, there would be at most four steps in porting JABWT to that device:

- Add a Java Virtual Machine
- Add a Bluetooth protocol stack
- Implement JABWT including the BCC
- Pass the TCK compliance tests

When going through these steps, an implementer may have the option of choosing components that will ease the integration and implementation of JABWT.

The design for a JABWT implementation needs to address the following potentially challenging issues:

- Managing connections
- Handling events
- Preventing the Java virtual machine from blocking when making time-consuming calls to the Bluetooth stack

The BCC can be implemented as part of the Bluetooth stack, as part of the JABWT implementation, or as a simple set of device settings. The implementation of the `javax.obex` package can be developed totally in the Java programming language, or it can use the native OBEX implementation that comes with some Bluetooth stacks.

Finally the TCK test procedure is discussed. All JABWT implementations have to pass the JSR-82 TCK to claim compliance with the JABWT standard.

11 CHAPTER Closing Remarks

Software standards often are vital to the success of communications technologies. An effective software standard will encourage development of a number of successful applications. Java Specification Request-82, developed by the Java Community Process, standardized the Java APIs for Bluetooth Wireless Technology. JABWT makes it possible to write an application once and then run the application on any Java-enabled device that supports JABWT. Because JABWT was developed with the participation of several companies that develop Bluetooth stacks, we believe it will be possible to implement JABWT in conjunction with a wide variety of Bluetooth stacks. This phenomenon represents a significant change in the way Bluetooth applications will be written and fielded. Because there has been no standard API for Bluetooth stacks, each stack has defined its own API for use by Bluetooth applications. As a consequence, Bluetooth applications have been written to run on a particular Bluetooth stack, and considerable effort has been required to convert that application to run on another Bluetooth stack.

JABWT does not change the fact that Bluetooth stacks all have their own proprietary APIs. JABWT encourages application developers to write their applications to standard JABWT rather than writing them for a particular Bluetooth stack. As device manufacturers adopt JABWT implementations for their Bluetooth devices, JABWT applications will be able to run on those JABWT devices with little or no porting effort on the part of application developers. The different APIs used by the Bluetooth stacks on these devices will be hidden behind the common, standardized API provided by JABWT. The current proliferation of J2ME devices has demonstrated the effectiveness of this strategy and the benefits for J2ME developers. JABWT make it possible for Bluetooth application developers to begin experiencing these same benefits.

One of the goals of JABWT is to allow third-party vendors to write Bluetooth profiles in the Java language on top of JABWT. Companies have already created Bluetooth profiles using JABWT, especially over OBEX.

JABWT was defined with the participation of many individuals from many different companies. Participation of individuals with different backgrounds helped create a robust specification. The members' expertise runs the entire gamut of topics—Bluetooth hardware, Bluetooth protocol stack, J2ME implementation, Java programming language, OBEX, middleware, and mobile devices design. The JSR-82 effort was a true collaboration and unification of two different industries.

The work completed under JSR-197, allows J2SE devices, such as laptops, to incorporate JABWT. J2SE implementations of JABWT will make the API available to a much larger set of users. It makes logical sense to make it possible for J2SE devices to incorporate JABWT, as J2SE devices are all potential Bluetooth devices.

As we move forward, some newer protocols such as BNEP and profiles such as PAN, which could be widely used in Bluetooth devices, could prompt extending JABWT. Voice- and telephony-related topics were not considered in the first version of JABWT, but they can be considered in the next version. As this book goes to press, consumer devices that implement JABWT are just starting to emerge.

Some OEMs manufacturing JABWT devices may want to provide custom application environments for their devices. These manufacturers may want to extend JABWT in a proprietary way and provide additional functionality. This can be accomplished by defining LOCs or LCCs (see Chapter 1). But programs using these classes may not be portable across devices.

This book presents the need for JABWT, explains the overall architecture, and extensively discusses the various facets of JABWT—their use and programming techniques. The book gives insights into the intended use of the APIs. Programming to the APIs is the primary focus of the book, yet the book discusses issues and tricks with implementing JABWT to a device. The book, we believe, gives enough coding examples to help a programmer become proficient at programming with JABWT.

In summary, we believe the basic human desire to stay connected and communicate with computing devices from anywhere and at all times will increase the demand on wireless communications. Standard programming environments for accessing these wireless communications media will help create a myriad of applications. This book presents a simple yet powerful standard API for Bluetooth wireless technology. We hope the power of JABWT will encourage people to write more applications, write Bluetooth profiles with JABWT, and build more JABWT devices.

APPENDIX

A

Complete Code Examples

This appendix contains the complete example code for the service registration MIDlets defined in Chapter 7 and all MIDlets defined in Chapter 8.

A.1 Code Examples from Chapter 7

A.1.1 Classes for Example in Section 7.3.1

DefaultBtsppRecordMIDlet

```
package com.jabwt.book;
import java.lang.*;
import java.io.*;
import java.util.*;
import javax.microedition.io.*;
import javax.microedition.midlet.*;
import javax.microedition.lcdui.*;
import javax.bluetooth.*;

/**
 * The DefaultBtsppRecordMIDlet class illustrates
 * the modification of a service record
 */
public class DefaultBtsppRecordMIDlet extends
  MIDlet implements Runnable, CommandListener {

  StreamConnectionNotifier notifier;

  /**
   * A DefaultBtsppRecordServer instance provides
   * the server capabilities.
   */
  DefaultBtsppRecordServer server;
```

```
/**
 * The form displayed to the user.
 */
private Form output;

/**
 * Creates a DefaultBtsppRecordMIDlet object and
 * starts the server thread.
 */
public DefaultBtsppRecordMIDlet() {
  output = new Form("Default Record");
  output.addCommand(new Command("Exit",
      Command.EXIT, 1));
  output.setCommandListener(this);
  new Thread(this).start();
}

/**
 * Called each time the MIDlet is started. This
 * method sets the current display
 * @exception MIDletStateChangeException never
 * occurs
 */
public void startApp() throws
      MIDletStateChangeException {
  Display currentDisplay =
      Display.getDisplay(this);
  currentDisplay.setCurrent(output);
}

public void pauseApp() {}
public void destroyApp(boolean unconditional) {}

/**
 * The server will wait and accept connections
 * from clients
 */
public void run() {
  LocalDevice theRadio;
  /*
   * Define the serial port service and create the
```

```
    * notifier
    */
    try {
      theRadio = LocalDevice.getLocalDevice();
      server = new DefaultBtsppRecordServer();
      server.askToBeGeneralDiscoverable(theRadio);
      notifier = server.defineDefaultBtsppService();
    } catch (IOException e) {
    output.append("Unable to start server" +
        "(IOException: " +
    e.getMessage() + ")");
    return;
  }

  if (notifier != null) {
    ServiceRecord record =
        theRadio.getRecord(notifier);
    output.append("URL=" + server.getURL(record));
    output.append(server.describeAttributes(record)
        );
  } else {
    output.append("Unable to start server");
    return;
  }

  /*
   * Use the notifier to establish serial port
   * connections
   */
  server.acceptClientConnections(notifier);
}

/**
 * Called each time a command occurs. The only
 * command is the Exit
 * command. This method will destroy the MIDlet.
 */
public void commandAction(Command c,
  Displayable d) {
try {
```

```
                server.shutdown(notifier);
              } catch (Exception e) {
              }
              notifyDestroyed();
          }
      }
```

DefaultBtsppRecordServer

```java
      package com.jabwt.book;
      import java.lang.*;
      import java.io.*;
      import java.util.*;
      import javax.microedition.midlet.*;
      import javax.microedition.io.*;
      import javax.bluetooth.*;

      public class DefaultBtsppRecordServer {

        boolean stop = false;

        public StreamConnectionNotifier
              defineDefaultBtsppService() {
          StreamConnectionNotifier notifier;
          String connString =
              "btspp://localhost:" +
                "68EE141812D211D78EED00B0D0" +
                  "3D76EC;name=SPPEx";
          try {
            notifier = (StreamConnectionNotifier)
              Connector.open(connString);
          } catch (IOException e){
            return null;
          }
          return notifier;
        }

        public void acceptClientConnections(
          StreamConnectionNotifier notifier) {
          if (notifier == null){
```

```
        return;
      }
      try {
        while (!stop){
          StreamConnection clientConn = null;
          /*
           * acceptAndOpen() waits for the next
           * client to
           * connect to this service. The first time
           * through the
           * loop, acceptAndOpen() adds the service
           * record to
           * the SDDB and updates the service class
           * bits of the device.
           */
          try {
          clientConn = (StreamConnection)
            notifier.acceptAndOpen();
          } catch (ServiceRegistrationException
            e1) {
          } catch (IOException e) {
          continue;
          }
        }
      } finally {
        try {
        shutdown(notifier);
        } catch (IOException ignore) {
        }
      }
    }
  }

  void askToBeGeneralDiscoverable(LocalDevice dev) {
    try {
      // Request that the device be made discoverable
      dev.setDiscoverable(DiscoveryAgent.GIAC);
    } catch(BluetoothStateException ignore) {
      // discoverable is not an absolute requirement
      }
    }
```

```java
    public String getURL(ServiceRecord record) {
      String url = record.getConnectionURL(
        ServiceRecord.NOAUTHENTICATE_NOENCRYPT, false);
      if (url != null) {
        return url.substring(0, url.indexOf(";"));
      } else {
        return "getConnectionURL()=null";
      }
    }

      public String describeAttributes(ServiceRecord
          record) {
        int[] attributeIDs = record.getAttributeIDs();
        StringBuffer strBuf = new StringBuffer(100);
        strBuf.append("\n").append(Integer.toString(
          attributeIDs.length));
        strBuf.append(" Attributes: ");
        for (int i = 0; i < attributeIDs.length; i++){
          strBuf.append("<0x");
          strBuf.append(Integer.toHexString(
            attributeIDs[i]));
          strBuf.append(">\n");
        }
        return strBuf.toString();
      }

      public void shutdown(StreamConnectionNotifier
          notifier)
        throws IOException {
        stop = true;
        notifier.close();
      }
    }
```

A.1.2 Classes for Example in Section 7.3.2

ModifyServiceRecordMIDlet

```java
    package com.jabwt.book;
    import java.lang.*;
    import java.io.*;
```

```java
import java.util.*;
import javax.microedition.io.*;
import javax.microedition.midlet.*;
import javax.microedition.lcdui.*;
import javax.bluetooth.*;

/**
 * The ModifyServiceRecordMIDlet class illustrates
 * the modification of a service record
 */
public class ModifyServiceRecordMIDlet extends
  MIDlet implements Runnable, CommandListener {

  StreamConnectionNotifier notifier;

  /**
   * A SerialPortServerExample instance provides
   * the server capabilities.
   */
  RecordModifyingServer server;

  /**
   * The form displayed to the user.
   */
  private Form output;

  /**
   * Creates a ModifyServiceRecordMIDlet object and
   * starts the server thread.
   */
  public ModifyServiceRecordMIDlet() {
    output = new Form("Game Record");
    output.addCommand(new Command("Exit",
        Command.EXIT, 1));
    output.setCommandListener(this);
    new Thread(this).start();
  }

  /**
   * Called each time the MIDlet is started. This
   * method sets the current display
```

```
    * @exception MIDletStateChangeException never
    * occurs
    */
    public void startApp() throws
          MIDletStateChangeException {
      Display currentDisplay =
          Display.getDisplay(this);
      currentDisplay.setCurrent(output);
    }

    public void pauseApp() {}
    public void destroyApp(boolean unconditional) {}

    /**
    * The server will wait and accept connections
    * from clients
    */
    public void run() {
      LocalDevice theRadio;
// Create the server connection object
      try {
        theRadio = LocalDevice.getLocalDevice();
        server = new RecordModifyingServer();
        server.askToBeGeneralDiscoverable();
        notifier = server.defineGameService(theRadio,
              100000L);
      } catch (IOException e) {
        output.append("Unable to start server" +
          "(IOException: " + e.getMessage() + ")");
        return;
      }
      if (notifier != null) {
        ServiceRecord record =
              theRadio.getRecord(notifier);
        output.append("URL=" +
              server.getURL(record));
        output.append(
          server.describeAttributes(record));
```

```
          } else {
          output.append("Unable to start server; " +
            "error in " +
            "SerialPortServerExample.defineService()");
            return;
          }
          server.acceptClientConnections(notifier);
      }

    /**
      * Called each time a command occurs. The
      * only command is the Exit
      * command. This method will destroy the MIDlet.
      */
      public void commandAction(Command c,
        Displayable d) {
        try {
          server.shutdown(notifier);
        } catch (Exception e) {
        }
        notifyDestroyed();
      }
  }
```

RecordModifyingServer

```
package com.jabwt.book;
import java.lang.*;
import java.io.*;
import java.util.*;
import javax.microedition.midlet.*;
import javax.microedition.io.*;
import javax.bluetooth.*;

public class RecordModifyingServer {

  boolean stop = false;

  public StreamConnectionNotifier defineGameService(
    LocalDevice localDev, long highScore) {
```

```
        StreamConnectionNotifier notifier;
        String connString =
          "btspp://localhost:"
            + "0FA1A7AC16A211D7854400B0D03D76EC;" +
          "name=A Bluetooth Game";
        try {
          notifier = (StreamConnectionNotifier)
                Connector.open(connString);
        } catch (IOException e2){
          return null;
        }
        ServiceRecord record =
              localDev.getRecord(notifier);
        // Add optional ServiceDescription attribute;
        // attribute ID 0x0101.
        record.setAttributeValue(0x0101,
          new DataElement(DataElement.STRING,
          "This game is fun! It is for " +
          "two people. You can play it " +
          "on your cell phones."));
        // Add optional DocumentationURL attribute;
        // attribute ID 0x000A.
        record.setAttributeValue(0x000A, new
              DataElement(DataElement.URL,
          "http://www.gameDocsOnSomeWebpage.com"));
        /*
        * Add an application-specific attribute for the
        * highest score achieved by this player to date.
        */
        record.setAttributeValue(0x2222, new
              DataElement(DataElement.U_INT_4,
              highScore));
        return notifier;
    }

    public void acceptClientConnections(
      StreamConnectionNotifier notifier) {
      if (notifier == null) {
```

```java
      return;
    }
    try {
      while (!stop){
        StreamConnection clientConn = null;
        /*
         * acceptAndOpen() waits for the next client
         * to connect to this service. The first time
         * through the
         * loop, acceptAndOpen() adds the service
         * record to
         * the SDDB and updates the service class
         * bits of the device.
         */
        try {
          clientConn = (StreamConnection)
            notifier.acceptAndOpen();
        } catch (ServiceRegistrationException e1) {
        } catch (IOException e) {
          continue;
        }
      }
    } finally {
      try {
        shutdown(notifier);
      } catch (IOException ignore) {
      }
    }
  }

  void askToBeGeneralDiscoverable() {
    try {
      LocalDevice localDev =
          LocalDevice.getLocalDevice();
      /* Request that the device be made
         discoverable */
      localDev.setDiscoverable(DiscoveryAgent.GIAC);
    } catch(BluetoothStateException ignore) {
```

```java
          /* discoverable is not an absolute requirement
          */
      }
  }

  public String getURL(ServiceRecord record) {
    String url = record.getConnectionURL(
      ServiceRecord.NOAUTHENTICATE_NOENCRYPT, false);
    if (url != null) {
      return url.substring(0, url.indexOf(";"));
    } else {
      return "getConnectionURL()=null";
    }
  }

  public String describeAttributes(ServiceRecord
        record) {
      int[] attributeIDs = record.getAttributeIDs();
      StringBuffer strBuf = new StringBuffer(100);
      strBuf.append("\n").append(
        Integer.toString(attributeIDs.length));
      strBuf.append(" Attributes: ");
      for (int i = 0; i < attributeIDs.length; i++){
        strBuf.append("<0x");
        strBuf.append(Integer.toHexString(
          attributeIDs[i]));
        strBuf.append(">\n");
      }
      return strBuf.toString();
  }

  public void shutdown(StreamConnectionNotifier
        notifier) throws IOException {
      stop = true;
      notifier.close();
  }
}
```

A.1.3 Classes for Example in Section 7.3.4

ModifyIntoObjectPushMIDlet

```java
package com.jabwt.book;
import java.lang.*;
import java.io.*;
import java.util.*;
import javax.microedition.io.*;
import javax.microedition.midlet.*;
import javax.microedition.lcdui.*;
import javax.bluetooth.*;
import javax.obex.*;

/**
 * The ModifyIntoObjectPushMIDlet class illustrates
 * the modification of a service record
 */
public class ModifyIntoObjectPushMIDlet extends
    MIDlet implements Runnable, CommandListener {

  // An ObjectPushServerExample instance provides
  // the server capabilities.
  ObjectPushServerExample server;

  // The form displayed to the user.
  private Form output;

  // The local Bluetooth device
  LocalDevice theRadio;

  private SessionNotifier notifier;

  // Creates a ModifyIntoObjectPushMIDlet object
  // and starts the server thread.
  public ModifyIntoObjectPushMIDlet() {
    output = new Form("Object Push Server");
    output.addCommand(new Command("Exit",
        Command.EXIT, 1));
```

```
    output.setCommandListener(this);
    new Thread(this).start();
}

/**
 * Called each time the MIDlet is started. This
 * method sets the current display.
 */
public void startApp() throws
      MIDletStateChangeException {
  Display currentDisplay =
        Display.getDisplay(this);
  currentDisplay.setCurrent(output);
}

public void pauseApp() {}

public void destroyApp(boolean unconditional) {}
// The server will wait and accept connections
// from clients
public void run() {
  try {
    theRadio = LocalDevice.getLocalDevice();
    // The Object Push profile recommends that Push
    // Servers be put in Limited Discoverable Mode
    boolean result = theRadio.setDiscoverable(
      DiscoveryAgent.LIAC);
    if (!result) {
      System.out.println(
        "***setDiscoverable=LIAC failed");
    }
    server = new ObjectPushServerExample();
    notifier = server.defineObjectPushService();
  } catch (IOException e) {
    output.append("Unable to start server" +
        "(IOException: " + e.getMessage() + ")");
    return;
```

```
        }
        if (notifier != null) {
          ServiceRecord record =
                theRadio.getRecord(notifier);
          output.append("Started Server, URL=" +
                server.getURL(notifier));
          output.append(
            server.describeAttributes(record));
          } else {
            output.append("Unable to start server; " +
                "error in " +
              "ObjectPushServerExample." +
              "defineObjectPushService()");
            return;
          }
          server.acceptClientConnections(notifier);
      }

      /**
       * Called each time a command occurs. The only
       * command is the Exit
       * command. This method will destroy the MIDlet.
       */
      public void commandAction(Command c,
        Displayable d) {
        try {
          server.shutdown(notifier);
        } catch (Exception e) {
        }
        notifyDestroyed();
      }
  }
```

ObjectPushServerExample

```
package com.jabwt.book;
import java.lang.*;
import java.io.*;
import java.util.*;
```

```java
import javax.microedition.midlet.*;
import javax.microedition.io.*;
import javax.bluetooth.*;
import javax.obex.*;

public class ObjectPushServerExample {
  int clients = 0;
  int maxClients = 2;
  boolean stop = false;
  LocalDevice localDev;

  /**
   * Create the service record for an OBEX Object
   * Push server as defined
   * by the Bluetooth Object Push profile.
   */
  public SessionNotifier defineObjectPushService() {
    SessionNotifier notifier;
    // The UUID 00001105000... is the long-form
    // UUID for the
    // short form 0x1105 defined for the Object
    // Push service ID by
    // assigned numbers.
    String connString =
      "btgoep://localhost:" +
        "0000110500001000800000805F9B34FB;" +
      "name=OBEX Object Push Server";
    // Connector.open() assigns a RFCOMM server
    // channel
    // and creates a service record using this
    // channel.
    try {
      notifier = (SessionNotifier)
        Connector.open(connString);
    } catch (ServiceRegistrationException e1) {
      // The open method failed because unable to
      // obtain an RFCOMM server channel.
      return null;
    } catch (IOException e2){
```

```
        // The open method failed due to another
        // IOException
        return null;
      }
      try {
        localDev = LocalDevice.getLocalDevice();
      } catch (BluetoothStateException e) {
        return null;
      }
      ServiceRecord record =
          localDev.getRecord(notifier);
      // Add the optional service attribute
      // BluetoothProfileDescriptorList
      ServiceRecordUtilities.setBluetoothProfileList(
        record, 0x1105, 0x0100);
      DataElement objFormatsDE = new
          DataElement(DataElement.DATSEQ);
      // supported format 0x01 = vCard 2.1
      objFormatsDE.addElement(new
          DataElement(DataElement.U_INT_1, 0x01));
      // supported format 0x02 = vCard 3.0
      objFormatsDE.addElement(new
          DataElement(DataElement.U_INT_1, 0x02));
      // Add mandatory Supported Formats List,
      // attribute ID 0x0303
      record.setAttributeValue(0x0303, objFormatsDE);
      // An Object Push Server provides an Object
      // Transfer service.
      // Bit 20 of the Class of Device is for Object
      // Transfer.
      record.setDeviceServiceClasses(0x100000);
      return notifier;
  }

  public void acceptClientConnections(
      SessionNotifier notifier) {
    if (notifier == null) {
      return;
    }
```

```
PushServerRequestHandler requestHandler =
  new PushServerRequestHandler();
try {
  while (!stop){
    Connection clientConn;
    /*
    * acceptAndOpen() waits for the next
    * client to connect to this service. The
    * first time through the
    * loop, acceptAndOpen() adds the service
    * record to
    * the SDDB and updates the service class
    * bits of the device.
    */
    try {
      clientConn = (Connection)
        notifier.acceptAndOpen(requestHandler);
    } catch (ServiceRegistrationException e1) {
      // The acceptAndOpen method failed;
      // possibly
      // because the SDDB is full or violated
      // constraints when modified record.
      return;
    } catch (IOException e) {
      continue;
    }
    // There would be code here to start up a
    // thread
    // to communicate with this client.
  }
} finally {
/*
* Releases the RFCOMM server channel and
* removes the service
* record from the SDDB.
*/
try {
  notifier.close();
} catch (IOException ignore) {
```

```
        }
      }
    }

    public String getURL(SessionNotifier notifier) {
      ServiceRecord record =
            localDev.getRecord(notifier);
      String url = record.getConnectionURL(
        ServiceRecord.NOAUTHENTICATE_NOENCRYPT, false);
      if (url != null) {
        return url.substring(0, url.indexOf(";"));
      } else {
        return "getConnectionURL()=null";
      }
    }

    public String describeAttributes(ServiceRecord
          record) {
      int[] attributeIDs = record.getAttributeIDs();
      StringBuffer strBuf = new StringBuffer(100);
      strBuf.append("\n").append(
        Integer.toString(attributeIDs.length));
      strBuf.append(" Attributes: ");
      for (int i = 0; i < attributeIDs.length; i++){
        strBuf.append("<0x");
        strBuf.append(Integer.toHexString(
          attributeIDs[i]));
        strBuf.append(">\n");
      }
      return strBuf.toString();
    }

    public void shutdown(SessionNotifier notifier) {
      stop = true;
      try {
        notifier.close();
      } catch (IOException ignore) {
      }
    }
  }
```

PushServerRequestHandler

```
package com.jabwt.book;
import java.lang.*;
import java.io.*;
import java.util.*;
import javax.obex.*;

/**
 * The PushServerRequestHandler class handles
 * requests
 * from the OBEX client to store and retrieve
 * electronic business cards.
 */
public class PushServerRequestHandler extends
        ServerRequestHandler {

  // Creates a PushServerRequestHandler object
  public PushServerRequestHandler() {}
}
```

ServiceRecordUtilities

```
package com.jabwt.book;
import java.lang.*;
import java.io.*;
import java.util.*;
import javax.microedition.io.*;
import javax.bluetooth.*;

/*
 * This class provides static methods that are
 * useful for modifying
 * the in-memory versions of service records for
 * JABWT servers.
 */
public class ServiceRecordUtilities {

  public static final int
        ATT_ID_BLUETOOTH_PROFILE_LIST = 0x0009;
```

```java
/**
 * Sets the value of the
 * BluetoothProfileDescriptorList attribute to
 * be the profile represented by a short-form UUID
 * value and version number.
 * @param record The service record to be modified
 * @param profileUuidValue The short-form UUID for
 * the profile from the Bluetooth Assigned Numbers
 * @param version The version of the profile this
 * service conforms to.
 * The format is 0xMMmm where MM is the major version
 * number and mm is the minor version number.
 */
public static void setBluetoothProfileList(
    ServiceRecord record,
    long profileUuidValue, int version) {
        UUID profileUuid = new UUID(profileUuidValue);
        DataElement profileUuidDE = new
            DataElement(DataElement.UUID,
            profileUuid);
        DataElement versionDE = new
            DataElement(DataElement.U_INT_2,
            version);
        DataElement profileVersionPairDE =
            new DataElement(DataElement.DATSEQ);
        DataElement profileDescriptorDE = new
            DataElement(DataElement.DATSEQ);
        // Create a pair with profile UUID and profile
        // version
        profileVersionPairDE.addElement(profileUuidDE);
        profileVersionPairDE.addElement(versionDE);
        // Add the pair to the list of profiles
        profileDescriptorDE.addElement(
          profileVersionPairDE);
        // Set the BluetoothProfileDescriptorList to a
        // DATSEQ data
        // element containing the UUID-version pair
        // for this profile.
        record.setAttributeValue(
          ATT_ID_BLUETOOTH_PROFILE_LIST,
```

```
                profileDescriptorDE);
        }
    }
```

A.2 Code Examples from Chapter 8

A.2.1 Classes for the L2CAP MTU Example

L2capMtuMIDlet

```
package com.jabwt.book;
import java.io.*;
import javax.microedition.midlet.*;
import javax.microedition.lcdui.*;
import javax.bluetooth.*;

public class L2capMtuMIDlet extends MIDlet
        implements CommandListener {
    protected Display display;
    protected Form displayForm;
    protected Command exitCommand = new
            Command("Exit", Command.EXIT, 1);
    protected StringItem displayField = new
            StringItem("", "");
    private final static UUID uuid
        = new UUID("F37995ACFB0B456b8589D1E5FD564825",
              false);
    private LocalDevice device;
    private Form receiveMTUForm = null;
    private Form transmitMTUForm = null;
    private int chosenReceiveMTU;
    private int chosenTransmitMTU;
    private boolean providedReceiveMTU;
    private boolean providedTransmitMTU;
    private boolean isClient = false;
    private Form serverOrClientForm;
    private ChoiceGroup serverOrClient;

    public L2capMtuMIDlet() {
        display = Display.getDisplay(this);
    }
```

```java
public void startApp() {
  serverOrClientForm = new Form("MTU Demo");
  serverOrClientForm.addCommand(exitCommand);
  serverOrClientForm.addCommand(new Command("OK",
      Command.OK, 1));
  serverOrClient = new ChoiceGroup(null,
      ChoiceGroup.EXCLUSIVE);
  serverOrClient.append("Server", null);
  serverOrClient.append("Client", null);
  serverOrClient.setSelectedIndex(0, true);
  serverOrClientForm.append(serverOrClient);
  serverOrClientForm.setCommandListener(this);
  display.setCurrent(serverOrClientForm);
}

public void commandAction(Command c,
  Displayable d) {

  switch (c.getCommandType()) {
  case Command.EXIT:
    notifyDestroyed();
    break;

  case Command.OK:
    if (display.getCurrent() ==
        serverOrClientForm) {
    device = null;
    try {
      device = LocalDevice.getLocalDevice();
    } catch(BluetoothStateException e) {
      displayError("Error",
        "getLocalDevice() got error: " +
        e.toString());
      return;
    }
    if (serverOrClient.isSelected(1)) {
      displayForm = new Form("L2CAP Client");
      displayForm.append(displayField);
      displayForm.setCommandListener(this);
      displayForm.addCommand(exitCommand);
      isClient = true;
```

```
                    getReceiveMTUFromUser(isClient);
                  } else {
                    isClient = false;
                    displayForm = new Form("L2CAP Server");
                    displayForm.append(displayField);
                    displayForm.setCommandListener(this);
                    displayForm.addCommand(exitCommand);
                    getReceiveMTUFromUser(isClient);
                  }
                }
          break;

      case Command.ITEM:
        Form MTUForm = (Form)d;
        if (display.getCurrent() == receiveMTUForm) {
          /*
           * Extract the receiveMTU. If empty, the
           * connection string will not mention receiveMTU.
           */
          TextField receiveMTUField =
                (TextField)MTUForm.get(0);
          String recMTUAsString =
                receiveMTUField.getString();
          if (recMTUAsString.trim().equals("")) {
            providedReceiveMTU = false;
            chosenReceiveMTU = 0; //value will not be used
          } else {
            providedReceiveMTU = true;
            chosenReceiveMTU =
                  Integer.parseInt(recMTUAsString);
          }
          System.out.println("****receiveMTU=" +
                recMTUAsString);
          getTransmitMTUFromUser(isClient);
        } else if (display.getCurrent() ==
              transmitMTUForm) {
            /*
             * Extract the transmitMTU. If empty, the
             * connection
             * string will not mention transmitMTU.
```

```
        */
        TextField transmitMTUField =
                (TextField)MTUForm.get(0);
        String transMTUAsString =
                transmitMTUField.getString();
        if (transMTUAsString.trim().equals("")) {
          providedTransmitMTU = false;
          chosenTransmitMTU = 0; //not used
        } else {
          providedTransmitMTU = true;
          chosenTransmitMTU =
                Integer.parseInt(transMTUAsString);
        }
        System.out.println("****transmitMTU=" +
                transMTUAsString);
        display.setCurrent(displayForm);
        openL2CAPConnection(isClient,
                providedReceiveMTU,
                chosenReceiveMTU, providedTransmitMTU,
                chosenTransmitMTU);
      }
      break;
    }
}

public void destroyApp(boolean unconditionally)
      {}
public void pauseApp() {}

private void getReceiveMTUFromUser(boolean
      isClient) {
  String maxRecMTUPlus1;
  String maxRecMTU = LocalDevice.getProperty(
    "bluetooth.l2cap.receiveMTU.max");
  if (maxRecMTU == null) {
    maxRecMTUPlus1 = "Unknown";
  } else {
    maxRecMTUPlus1
      = (new Integer(Integer.parseInt(maxRecMTU) +
            1)).toString();
  }
```

```
        String initialMTU = Integer.toString(
          L2CAPConnection.DEFAULT_MTU);
        receiveMTUForm = new Form(isClient ?
          "L2CAP Client" : "L2CAP Server");
        String recMtuFieldLabel = "ReceiveMTU \n" +
          (L2CAPConnection.MINIMUM_MTU - 1) + " < x < "
          + maxRecMTUPlus1;
        receiveMTUForm.append(new
              TextField(recMtuFieldLabel, initialMTU, 10,
              TextField.NUMERIC));
        receiveMTUForm.addCommand(new Command("Exit",
              Command.EXIT, 1));
        receiveMTUForm.addCommand(new Command("Next",
              Command.ITEM, 1));
        receiveMTUForm.setCommandListener(this);
        display.setCurrent(receiveMTUForm);
    }

    private void getTransmitMTUFromUser(boolean
            isClient) {
        String initialMTU = Integer.toString(
          L2CAPConnection.DEFAULT_MTU);
        transmitMTUForm = new Form(isClient ?
          "L2CAP Client" :
          "L2CAP Server");
        String fieldLabel = "TransmitMTU \n" +
          (L2CAPConnection.MINIMUM_MTU - 1) + " < x";
        transmitMTUForm.append(new TextField(fieldLabel,
              initialMTU, 10, TextField.NUMERIC));
        transmitMTUForm.addCommand(new Command("Exit",
              Command.EXIT, 1));
        transmitMTUForm.addCommand(new Command("Go",
              Command.ITEM, 1));
        transmitMTUForm.setCommandListener(this);
        display.setCurrent(transmitMTUForm);
    }

    private void openL2CAPConnection(boolean isClient,
      boolean receiveMTUInput, int receiveMTU,
        boolean transmitMTUInput, int transmitMTU) {
```

```
    String url = null;
    String paramString = "";
    if (receiveMTUInput) {
      paramString += ";receiveMTU=" + receiveMTU;
    }
    if (transmitMTUInput) {
      paramString += ";transmitMTU=" + transmitMTU;
    }
    if (isClient) {
      displayField.setText(
        "searching, please wait...");
      DiscoveryAgent agent =
          device.getDiscoveryAgent();
      try {
        url = agent.selectService(uuid,
        ServiceRecord.NOAUTHENTICATE_NOENCRYPT,
            false);
      } catch (BluetoothStateException e) {
        displayError("Error",
          "BluetoothStateException: " +
            e.getMessage());
      }
      if (url == null) {
        displayError("Error",
          "failed to find server!");
        return;
      }
      url += paramString;
      new L2capClient(this).start(url);
    } else {
      url = "btl2cap://localhost:" +
          uuid.toString();
      url += paramString;
      new L2capServer(this).start(url);
    }
  }
  /**
   * Displays an error message to the user.
   *
   * @param title the title of the Alert
```

```
 * @param message the message to display to the
 * user
 */
void displayError(String title, String message) {
  Alert error = new Alert(title, message, null,
       AlertType.ERROR);
  error.setTimeout(Alert.FOREVER);
  display.setCurrent(error);
}
}
```

L2capServer

```
package com.jabwt.book;
import java.io.*;
import javax.bluetooth.*;
import javax.microedition.io.*;
import javax.microedition.lcdui.*;

public class L2capServer extends EchoParticipant
     implements Runnable {

  L2capMtuMIDlet parent;
  private String url;

  public L2capServer(L2capMtuMIDlet parent) {
    this.parent = parent;
    this.out = parent.displayField;
  }

  public void start(String url) {
    this.url = url;
    new Thread(this).start();
  }

  public void run() {
    LocalDevice device = null;
    L2CAPConnectionNotifier notifier = null;
    try {
    device = LocalDevice.getLocalDevice();
```

```
      /* Request that the device be made discover-
        able */
      device.setDiscoverable(DiscoveryAgent.GIAC);
    } catch(BluetoothStateException e) {
      parent.displayError("Error",
      "BluetoothStateException: " + e.toString());
      return;
    }
    try {
      notifier = (L2CAPConnectionNotifier)
        Connector.open(url);
    } catch (IllegalArgumentException e) {
      parent.displayError("Error",
        "IllegalArgumentException in" +
        "Connector.open()");
    } catch (IOException e) {
      parent.displayError("Error",
        "IOException: " + e.getMessage());
    }
    if (notifier == null) {
      return;
    }
    try{
      out.setLabel("["+url+"]");
      for (;;) {
        L2CAPConnection conn =
              notifier.acceptAndOpen();
        echoReceivedL2capPackets(conn);
        conn.close();
      }
    } catch(IOException e) {
      parent.displayError("Error", "IOException: " +
          e.getMessage());
    } catch (IllegalArgumentException e) {
      parent.displayError("Error",
          "IllegalArgumentException: "
          + e.getMessage());
    }
  }
}
```

L2capClient

```
package com.jabwt.book;
import java.io.*;
import java.util.*;
import javax.bluetooth.*;
import javax.microedition.io.*;
import javax.microedition.lcdui.*;

public class L2capClient extends EchoParticipant
      implements Runnable {

  L2capMtuMIDlet parent;
  private String url;

  public L2capClient(L2capMtuMIDlet parent) {
    this.parent = parent;
    this.out = parent.displayField;
  }

  public void start(String url) {
    this.url = url;
    new Thread(this).start();
  }

  public void run() {
    L2CAPConnection conn = null;
    out.setLabel("["+url+"]");
    try {
      conn = (L2CAPConnection)Connector.open(url);
    } catch (IllegalArgumentException e) {
      parent.displayError("Error",
        "IllegalArgumentException in " +
          "Connector.open()\n"
        + e.getMessage());
    } catch (BluetoothConnectionException e) {
      String problem = "";
      if (e.getStatus() ==
    BluetoothConnectionException.UNACCEPTABLE_PARAMS) {
        problem = "unacceptable parameters\n";
      }
```

```
            parent.displayError("Error",
              "BluetoothConnectionException: " +
              problem + "msg=" + e.getMessage() +
              "\nstatus= " + e.getStatus());
        } catch (IOException e) {
          parent.displayError("Error",
            "IOException: " + e.getMessage());
        }
        if (conn == null) {
          return;
        }
        try {
          sendL2capPacketsForEcho(conn);
          conn.close();
        } catch (IOException e) {
          parent.displayError("Error",
            "IOException: " + e.getMessage());
        }
      }
    }
```

EchoParticipant

```
    package com.jabwt.book;
    import java.io.*;
    import java.util.*;
    import javax.bluetooth.*;
    import javax.microedition.io.*;
    import javax.microedition.lcdui.*;

    public class EchoParticipant {

      protected StringItem out;
      private int bytesToSend = 100000;

      void sendL2capPacketsForEcho(L2CAPConnection
          conn) throws IOException {
        byte[] sbuf = new byte[conn.getTransmitMTU()];
        byte[] rbuf = new byte[conn.getReceiveMTU()];
        for (int i=0; i < sbuf.length; i++) {
          sbuf[i] = (byte)i;
```

```
    }
    int count = 0;
    long start = System.currentTimeMillis();
    while (count < bytesToSend) {
      conn.send(sbuf);
      count += sbuf.length;
      count += conn.receive(rbuf);
      /* Display the bytes sent and received so
         far */
      out.setText(Integer.toString(count));
    }
    /* Let the echoer know we are done sending
       bytes */
    conn.send("DONE".getBytes());
    conn.receive(rbuf);
    long end = System.currentTimeMillis();
    out.setText("Done (transferred "+count+
        "bytes)\n"
        + "Elapsed time " +
          (end - start)/1000 + "sec");
}

void echoReceivedL2capPackets(L2CAPConnection
      conn) throws IOException {
  byte[] ibuf = new byte[conn.getReceiveMTU()];
  int transmitMTU = conn.getTransmitMTU();
  int bytesIn;
  int bytesOut;
  int count = 0;
  for (;;) {
    bytesIn = conn.receive(ibuf);
    bytesOut = Math.min(bytesIn, transmitMTU);
    byte[] obuf = new byte[bytesOut];
    System.arraycopy(ibuf, 0, obuf, 0,
        bytesOut);
    conn.send(obuf);
    if ((bytesIn == 4) && (new
        String(obuf)).equals("DONE")) {
      break;
    }
```

```
            count += bytesIn + bytesOut;
            /* Display the bytes received and sent so
               far */
            out.setText(Integer.toString(count));
        }
        out.setText("Done (transferred " + count +
            " bytes)");
    }
}
```

A.2.2 Classes for the Example of Credit-Based Flow Control for L2CAP

L2capFlowControlMIDlet

```
package com.jabwt.book;
import java.io.*;
import javax.microedition.midlet.*;
import javax.microedition.lcdui.*;
import javax.bluetooth.*;

public class L2capFlowControlMIDlet extends MIDlet
    implements CommandListener {

  protected Display display;
  protected Form displayForm;
  protected Command exitCommand = new
        Command("Exit", Command.EXIT, 1);
  protected StringItem displayField = new
        StringItem("", "");
  private final static UUID uuid
    = new UUID("9C68A2AA1EC011D79E6C00B0D03D76EC",
          false);
  private LocalDevice device;
  private Form receiveMTUForm = null;
  private Form transmitMTUForm = null;
  private int chosenReceiveMTU;
  private int chosenTransmitMTU;
  private boolean providedReceiveMTU;
  private boolean providedTransmitMTU;
  private boolean isClient = false;
```

```
private Form serverOrClientForm;
private ChoiceGroup serverOrClient;

public L2capFlowControlMIDlet() {
  display = Display.getDisplay(this);
}

public void startApp() {
  serverOrClientForm = new Form("MTU Demo");
  serverOrClientForm.addCommand(exitCommand);
  serverOrClientForm.addCommand(new Command("OK",
      Command.OK, 1));
  serverOrClient = new ChoiceGroup(null,
      ChoiceGroup.EXCLUSIVE);
  serverOrClient.append("Server", null);
  serverOrClient.append("Client", null);
  serverOrClient.setSelectedIndex(0, true);
  serverOrClientForm.append(serverOrClient);
  serverOrClientForm.setCommandListener(this);
  display.setCurrent(serverOrClientForm);
}

public void commandAction(Command c,
  Displayable d) {
  switch (c.getCommandType()) {
  case Command.EXIT:
    notifyDestroyed();
    break;
  case Command.OK:
    if (display.getCurrent() ==
        serverOrClientForm) {
      device = null;
      try {
        device = LocalDevice.getLocalDevice();
      } catch(BluetoothStateException e) {
        displayError("Error",
        "getLocalDevice() got error: " +
            e.toString());
        return;
      }
      if (serverOrClient.isSelected(1)) {
```

```
                        displayForm = new Form("L2CAP Client");
                        displayForm.append(displayField);
                        displayForm.setCommandListener(this);
                        displayForm.addCommand(exitCommand);
                        isClient = true;
                        getReceiveMTUFromUser(isClient);
                    } else {
                        isClient = false;
                        displayForm = new Form("L2CAP Server");
                        displayForm.append(displayField);
                        displayForm.setCommandListener(this);
                        displayForm.addCommand(exitCommand);
                        getReceiveMTUFromUser(isClient);
                    }
                }
            break;
        case Command.ITEM:
            Form MTUForm = (Form)d;
            if (display.getCurrent() == receiveMTUForm) {
                /*
                 * Extract the receiveMTU. If empty, the
                 * connection string will not mention
                 * receiveMTU.
                 */
                TextField receiveMTUField =
                        (TextField)MTUForm.get(0);
                String recMTUAsString =
                        receiveMTUField.getString();
                if (recMTUAsString.trim().equals("")) {
                    providedReceiveMTU = false;
                    chosenReceiveMTU = 0;
                        //value will not be used
                } else {
                    providedReceiveMTU = true;
                    chosenReceiveMTU =
                            Integer.parseInt(recMTUAsString);
                }
                System.out.println("****receiveMTU=" +
                        recMTUAsString);
                getTransmitMTUFromUser(isClient);
```

```
      } else if (display.getCurrent() ==
          transmitMTUForm) {
        /*
        * Extract the transmitMTU. If empty, the
        * connection string will not mention
        * transmitMTU.
        */
        TextField transmitMTUField =
              (TextField)MTUForm.get(0);
        String transMTUAsString =
              transmitMTUField.getString();
        if (transMTUAsString.trim().equals("")) {
          providedTransmitMTU = false;
          //value will not be used
          chosenTransmitMTU = 0;
        } else {
          providedTransmitMTU = true;
          chosenTransmitMTU =
                Integer.parseInt(transMTUAsString);
        }
        System.out.println("****transmitMTU=" +
              transMTUAsString);
        display.setCurrent(displayForm);
        openL2CAPConnection(isClient,
                          providedReceiveMTU,
                          chosenReceiveMTU,
                          providedTransmitMTU,
                          chosenTransmitMTU);
      }
      break;
      }
  }

  public void destroyApp(boolean unconditionally)
        {}
  public void pauseApp() {}

  private void getReceiveMTUFromUser(boolean
        isClient) {
```

```java
      String maxRecMTUPlus1;
      String maxRecMTU
        = LocalDevice.getProperty(
          "bluetooth.l2cap.receiveMTU.max");
      if (maxRecMTU == null) {
        maxRecMTUPlus1 = "Unknown";
      } else {
        maxRecMTUPlus1 = (new Integer(
          Integer.parseInt(maxRecMTU) +
          1)).toString();
      }
      String initialMTU = Integer.toString(
          L2CAPConnection.DEFAULT_MTU);
      receiveMTUForm = new Form(isClient ?
        "L2CAP Client" : "L2CAP Server");
      String recMtuFieldLabel = "ReceiveMTU \n" +
      (L2CAPConnection.MINIMUM_MTU -1) + " < x < "
          + maxRecMTUPlus1;
      receiveMTUForm.append(new
          TextField(recMtuFieldLabel, initialMTU,
          10, TextField.NUMERIC));
      receiveMTUForm.addCommand(new Command("Exit",
          Command.EXIT, 1));
      receiveMTUForm.addCommand(new Command("Next",
          Command.ITEM, 1));
      receiveMTUForm.setCommandListener(this);
      display.setCurrent(receiveMTUForm);
  }

  private void getTransmitMTUFromUser(boolean
      isClient) {
    String initialMTU = Integer.toString(
      L2CAPConnection.DEFAULT_MTU);
    transmitMTUForm = new Form(isClient ?
      "L2CAP Client" :
        "L2CAP Server");
    String fieldLabel = "TransmitMTU \n" +
      (L2CAPConnection.MINIMUM_MTU - 1) + " < x";
```

```
    transmitMTUForm.append(new TextField(fieldLabel,
        initialMTU, 10, TextField.NUMERIC));
    transmitMTUForm.addCommand(new Command("Exit",
        Command.EXIT, 1));
    transmitMTUForm.addCommand(new Command("Go",
        Command.ITEM, 1));
    transmitMTUForm.setCommandListener(this);
    display.setCurrent(transmitMTUForm);
}

private void openL2CAPConnection(boolean
  isClient, boolean receiveMTUInput,
    int receiveMTU, boolean transmitMTUInput,
      int transmitMTU) {
  String url = null;
  String paramString = "";
  if (receiveMTUInput) {
    paramString += ";receiveMTU=" + receiveMTU;
  }
  if (transmitMTUInput) {
    paramString += ";transmitMTU=" +
        transmitMTU;
  }
  if (isClient) {
    displayField.setText(
      "searching, please wait...");
    DiscoveryAgent agent =
        device.getDiscoveryAgent();
    try {
      url = agent.selectService(uuid,
      ServiceRecord.NOAUTHENTICATE_NOENCRYPT,
          false);
    } catch (BluetoothStateException e) {
      displayError("Error",
      "BluetoothStateException: " +
          e.getMessage());
    }
    if (url == null) {
      displayError("Error",
```

```
                        "failed to find server!");
            return;
          }
        url += paramString;
        new L2capFlowControlClient(this).start(url);
      } else {
        url = "btl2cap://localhost:" +
              uuid.toString();
        url += paramString;
        new L2capFlowControlServer(this).start(url);
      }
    }

    /**
     * Displays an error message to the user.
     * @param title the title of the Alert
     * @param message the message to display to the
     * user
     */
    void displayError(String title,
      String message) {
      Alert error = new Alert(title, message, null,
            AlertType.ERROR);
      error.setTimeout(Alert.FOREVER);
      display.setCurrent(error);
    }
}
```

L2capFlowControlServer

```
package com.jabwt.book;
import java.io.*;
import javax.bluetooth.*;
import javax.microedition.io.*;
import javax.microedition.lcdui.*;

public class L2capFlowControlServer
  extends CreditBased1WayXfer implements Runnable {
  L2capFlowControlMIDlet parent;
```

```
private String url;
CreditIssuer issuer;
L2capBuffers buffers;

public final static int CREDIT_ISSUER_SLEEP =
    100;

public L2capFlowControlServer(L2capFlowControlMIDlet
  parent) {
  this.parent = parent;
  this.out = parent.displayField;
}

public void start(String url) {
  this.url = url;
  new Thread(this).start();
}

public void run() {
  LocalDevice device = null;
  L2CAPConnectionNotifier notifier = null;
  try {
    device = LocalDevice.getLocalDevice();
    /* Request that the device be made
       discoverable */
    device.setDiscoverable(DiscoveryAgent.GIAC);
  } catch(BluetoothStateException e) {
    parent.displayError("Error",
    "BluetoothStateException: " + e.toString());
    return;
  }
  try {
    notifier = (L2CAPConnectionNotifier)
        Connector.open(url);
  } catch (IllegalArgumentException e) {
    parent.displayError("Error",
      "IllegalArgumentException in " +
          "Connector.open()");
    } catch (IOException e) {
      parent.displayError("Error",
        "IOException: " + e.getMessage());
```

```
        }
        if (notifier == null) {
          return;
        }
        try {
          out.setLabel("["+url+"]");
          for (;;) {
            L2CAPConnection conn =
                    notifier.acceptAndOpen();
            buffers = new
                    L2capBuffers(conn.getReceiveMTU());
            issuer = new CreditIssuer(buffers, conn,
                    CREDIT_ISSUER_SLEEP);
            new Thread(issuer).start();
            receiveL2capPackets(conn, buffers,
                    issuer);
            conn.close();
          }
        } catch(IOException e) {
          parent.displayError("Error",
                    "IOException: " + e.getMessage());
        } catch (IllegalArgumentException e) {
          parent.displayError("Error",
                        "IllegalArgumentException: "
                        + e.getMessage());
        }
      }
    }
```

L2capFlowControlClient

```
    package com.jabwt.book;
    import java.io.*;
    import java.util.*;
    import javax.bluetooth.*;
    import javax.microedition.io.*;
    import javax.microedition.lcdui.*;

    public class L2capFlowControlClient extends
        CreditBased1WayXfer implements Runnable {
```

```
L2capFlowControlMIDlet parent;
private String url;

public L2capFlowControlClient(
  L2capFlowControlMIDlet parent) {
  this.parent = parent;
  this.out = parent.displayField;
}

public void start(String url) {
  this.url = url;
  new Thread(this).start();
}

public void run() {
  L2CAPConnection conn = null;
  out.setLabel("["+url+"]");
  try {
    conn = (L2CAPConnection)
      Connector.open(url);
  } catch (IllegalArgumentException e) {
    parent.displayError("Error",
      "IllegalArgumentException in "
          + "Connector.open()\n"
          + e.getMessage());
  } catch (BluetoothConnectionException e) {
    String problem = "";
    if (e.getStatus() ==
BluetoothConnectionException.UNACCEPTABLE_PARAMS) {
      problem = "unacceptable parameters\n";
    }
    parent.displayError("Error",
        "BluetoothConnectionException: " +
    problem + "msg=" + e.getMessage() +
      "\nstatus= " + e.getStatus());
  } catch (IOException e) {
    parent.displayError("Error", "IOException: "
        + e.getMessage());
  }
  if (conn == null) {
    return;
```

```
        }
        try {
          sendL2capPackets(conn);
          conn.close();
        } catch (IOException e) {
          parent.displayError("Error", "IOException: "
                + e.getMessage());
        }
      }
    }
```

CreditBased1WayXfer

```java
package com.jabwt.book;
import java.io.*;
import java.util.*;
import javax.bluetooth.*;
import javax.microedition.io.*;
import javax.microedition.lcdui.*;

public class CreditBased1WayXfer {
  // number of L2CAP packets the receiver has
  // authorized to be sent
  int availableCredits;
  protected StringItem out;
  private int bytesToSend = 50000;

  void sendL2capPackets(L2CAPConnection conn)
        throws IOException {
    boolean sentDone = false;
    byte[] sbuf = new byte[conn.getTransmitMTU()];
    int receiveMTU = conn.getReceiveMTU();
    byte[] rbuf = new byte[receiveMTU];
    for (int i=0; i < sbuf.length; i++) {
      sbuf[i] = (byte)i;
    }
    int count = 0;
    long start = System.currentTimeMillis();
    // listen for credits authorizing sending
    // packets
```

```
        receiveCredits(conn, receiveMTU);
        while (count < bytesToSend) {
          if (availableCredits > 0) {
            conn.send(sbuf);
            availableCredits--;
            count += sbuf.length;
            // Display the number of bytes sent so far
            out.setText(Integer.toString(count));
          }
          maybeReceiveCredits(conn, receiveMTU);
        }
        // Let the receiver know we are done sending
        // bytes
        while (!sentDone) {
          if (availableCredits > 0) {
            conn.send("DONE".getBytes());
            sentDone = true;
          } else {
            maybeReceiveCredits(conn, receiveMTU);
          }
        }
        long end = System.currentTimeMillis();
        out.setText("Done (transferred "+count+
            "bytes)\n"
          + "Elapsed time " + (end - start)/1000 +
              "sec");
    }

    // Read an L2CAP packet. If it has four bytes,
    // then interpret those
    // bytes as new credits for sending L2CAP
    // packets.
    void receiveCredits(L2CAPConnection conn, int
          receiveMTU) {
      int incomingBytes;
      int newCredits;
      byte[] rbuf = new byte[receiveMTU];
      try {
        incomingBytes = conn.receive(rbuf);
      } catch (IOException ignore) {
```

```
      return;
    }
    // assume four bytes are used to encode new
    // credits
    if (incomingBytes != 4) {
      return;
    }
    availableCredits +=
        CreditBased1WayXfer.byteArray2Int(rbuf);
}

// If there is an L2CAP packet waiting to be
// read, then call
// receiveCredits. Otherwise return without
// blocking.
void maybeReceiveCredits(L2CAPConnection conn,
      int receiveMTU) {
  try {
    if (conn.ready()) {
      receiveCredits(conn, receiveMTU);
    }
  } catch (IOException ignore) {
  }
}

void receiveL2capPackets(L2CAPConnection conn,
      L2capBuffers buffers,
  CreditIssuer issuer) throws IOException {
  byte[] ibuf = new byte[conn.getReceiveMTU()];
  L2capPacketBuffer packetBuffer;
  int transmitMTU = conn.getTransmitMTU();
  int bytesIn;
  for (;;) {
    packetBuffer =
        buffers.nextAvailablePacketBuffer();
    if (packetBuffer != null) {
      bytesIn = conn.receive(ibuf);
      packetBuffer.storeBytes(ibuf, bytesIn);
      if ((bytesIn == 4) &&
        (new String(ibuf, 0,
            bytesIn)).equals("DONE")) {
```

```
              break;
          }
        } else {
          if (conn.ready()) {
            System.out.println(
              "Should not get here. No " +
                    "L2capPacketBuffer available " +
                    "to receive incoming packet.");
          }
        }
      }
    issuer.setDoneProcessing();
    out.setText("Done (transferred " +
          issuer.count + " bytes)");
  }

// Convert a four-byte array to an int. The byte
// array is assumed
// to have a big Endian byte order.
public static int byteArray2Int(
    byte[] argBytes) {
    int result = 0;
    // big-endian conversion
    for (int i = 0, j = 0; i < 4; i++, j++) {
      result = result + (((int)argBytes[i] << 24)
            >>> (j * 8));
    }
    return result;
  }
// Convert an int to a four-byte array. The byte
// array will have a big Endian byte order.
public static byte[] int2ByteArray(int argInt) {
    byte[] result = new byte[4];
    // big-endian conversion
    for (int i = 0, j = 3; i < 4; i++, j--) {
      result[i] = (byte)((argInt >>> (j * 8)) &
            (byte)0xFF);
    }
    return result;
```

```
        }
    }
```

CreditIssuer

```java
package com.jabwt.book;
import java.io.*;
import java.util.*;
import javax.bluetooth.*;
import javax.microedition.io.*;
import javax.microedition.lcdui.*;

public class CreditIssuer implements Runnable {
  boolean doneProcessing = false;
  int sleepTime;
  L2capBuffers buffers;
  L2CAPConnection conn;
  int count = 0;

  CreditIssuer(L2capBuffers buffers,
       L2CAPConnection conn, int sleepTime) {
    this.buffers = buffers;
    this.sleepTime = sleepTime;
    this.conn = conn;
  }

  public void run() {
    L2capPacketBuffer packetBuffer;
    int freedBuffers;
    //Issue one credit for each L2capPacketBuffer
    int totalCredits =
         L2capBuffers.NUMBER_OF_PACKET_BUFFERS;
    byte[] issueCreditsPacketPayload =
      CreditBased1WayXfer.int2ByteArray(
        totalCredits);
    try {
      conn.send(issueCreditsPacketPayload);
    } catch (IOException e) {
      System.out.println("IOException when " +
        "issuing initial credits");
```

```
            return;
          }
          while (!doneProcessing) {
            freedBuffers = 0;
            while ((packetBuffer =
                  buffers.nextUsedPacketBuffer()) !=
                  null) {
              count += packetBuffer.getNumBytesStored();
              packetBuffer.eraseStoredBytes();
              freedBuffers++;
            }
            if (freedBuffers > 0) {
              try {
                conn.send(CreditBased1WayXfer.int2ByteArray(
                  freedBuffers));
              } catch (IOException e) {
                System.out.println("IOException " +
                  e.getMessage());
              }
            }
            try {
              Thread.sleep(sleepTime);
            } catch (InterruptedException ignore) {
            }
          }
        }

      void setDoneProcessing() {
        doneProcessing = true;
      }
    }
```

L2capBuffers

```
    package com.jabwt.book;
    import java.io.*;
    import java.util.*;
    import javax.bluetooth.*;
    import javax.microedition.io.*;
```

```java
import javax.microedition.lcdui.*;

  public class L2capBuffers {

  public static final int
    NUMBER_OF_PACKET_BUFFERS = 4;
  L2capPacketBuffer[] packetBuffers;

  L2capBuffers(int receiveMTU) {
    packetBuffers = new L2capPacketBuffer[
      NUMBER_OF_PACKET_BUFFERS];
    for (int i = 0; i < NUMBER_OF_PACKET_BUFFERS;
         i++) {
      packetBuffers[i] = new
        L2capPacketBuffer(receiveMTU);
    }
  }

  public synchronized L2capPacketBuffer
      nextAvailablePacketBuffer() {
    for (int i = 0; i < NUMBER_OF_PACKET_BUFFERS;
         i++) {
      if (packetBuffers[i].available()) {
        return packetBuffers[i];
      }
    }
    return null;
  }

  public synchronized L2capPacketBuffer
      nextUsedPacketBuffer() {
    for (int i = 0; i < NUMBER_OF_PACKET_BUFFERS;
         i++) {
      if (!packetBuffers[i].available()) {
        return packetBuffers[i];
      }
    }
    return null;
  }
}
```

L2capPacketBuffer

```java
package com.jabwt.book;
import java.io.*;
import java.util.*;
import javax.bluetooth.*;
import javax.microedition.io.*;
import javax.microedition.lcdui.*;

public class L2capPacketBuffer {

  int numBytesStored;
  byte[] byteArray;

  L2capPacketBuffer (int receiveMTU){
    byteArray = new byte[receiveMTU];
    numBytesStored = 0;
  }

  public synchronized void storeBytes(byte[] input,
        int length) {
    System.arraycopy(input, 0, byteArray, 0,
          length);
    numBytesStored = length;
  }

  public synchronized int getNumBytesStored() {
    return numBytesStored;
  }

  public synchronized void eraseStoredBytes() {
    numBytesStored = 0;
  }

  public synchronized boolean available() {
    if (numBytesStored == 0) {
      return true;
    }
    return false;
  }
}
```

javax.bluetooth API

This appendix contains a detailed description of each class, method, and field defined by JABWT in the javax.bluetooth package.

javax.bluetooth

BluetoothConnectionException

Declaration

```
public class BluetoothConnectionException extends
        java.io.IOException

    java.lang.Object
      |
     +—java.lang.Throwable
         |
        +—java.lang.Exception
           |
          +—java.io.IOException
             |
            +—javax.bluetooth.Bluetooth-
                  ConnectionException
```

Description

A BluetoothConnectionException is thrown when a Bluetooth connection (L2CAP, RFCOMM, or OBEX over RFCOMM) cannot be established successfully. The fields in this exception class indicate the cause of the exception. For example, an L2CAP connection may fail because of a security problem. This reason is passed on to the application through this class.

Fields

FAILED_NOINFO

```
public static final int FAILED_NOINFO
```

Indicates the connection to the server failed for unknown reasons.

NO_RESOURCES

```
public static final int NO_RESOURCES
```

Indicates the connection failed due to a lack of resources either on the local device or on the remote device.

SECURITY_BLOCK

```
public static final int SECURITY_BLOCK
```

Indicates the connection failed because the security settings on the local device or the remote device were incompatible with the request.

TIMEOUT

```
public static final int TIMEOUT
```

Indicates the connection to the server failed because of a timeout.

UNACCEPTABLE_PARAMS

```
public static final int UNACCEPTABLE_PARAMS
```

Indicates the connection failed because the configuration parameters provided were not acceptable to either the remote device or the local device.

UNKNOWN_PSM

```
public static final int UNKNOWN_PSM
```

Indicates the connection to the server failed because no service for the given PSM was registered.

Constructors

BluetoothConnectionException(int)

```
public BluetoothConnectionException(int error)
```

Creates a new `BluetoothConnectionException` with the error indicator specified.

Parameters

`error`—indicates the exception condition; must be one of the constants described in this class.

Throws

`IllegalArgumentException` if the input value is not one of the constants in this class.

BluetoothConnectionException(int, String)

```
public BluetoothConnectionException(int error,
    java.lang.String msg)
```

Creates a new `BluetoothConnectionException` with the error indicator and message specified.

Parameters

`error`—indicates the exception condition; must be one of the constants described in this class.
`msg`—a description of the exception; may by `null`.

Throws

`IllegalArgumentException` if the input value is not one of the constants in this class.

Methods

getStatus()

```
public int getStatus()
```

Gets the status set in the constructor that will indicate the reason for the exception.

Returns
Cause for the exception; will be one of the constants defined in this class.

javax.bluetooth

BluetoothStateException

Declaration

```
public class BluetoothStateException extends
      java.io.IOException

  java.lang.Object
    |
    +—java.lang.Throwable
      |
      +—java.lang.Exception
        |
        +—java.io.IOException
          |
          +—javax.bluetooth.Bluetooth-
                StateException
```

Description

The BluetoothStateException is thrown when a request is made to the Bluetooth system that the system cannot support in its present state. If, however, the Bluetooth system were not in this state, it could support this operation. For example, some Bluetooth systems do not allow the device to go into inquiry mode if a connection is established. This exception would be thrown if startInquiry() were called.

Constructors

BluetoothStateException()

```
public BluetoothStateException()
```

Creates a new `BluetoothStateException` without a detail message.

BluetoothStateException(String)

```
public BluetoothStateException(java.lang.String
    msg)
```

Creates a `BluetoothStateException` with the specified detail message.

Parameters

`msg`—the reason for the exception

javax.bluetooth

DataElement

Declaration

```
public class DataElement

java.lang.Object
  |
  +-javax.bluetooth.DataElement
```

Description

The `DataElement` class defines the various data types that a Bluetooth service attribute value may have. The following table describes the data types and valid values a `DataElement` object can store.

Data Type	Valid Values
NULL	represents a `null` value
U_INT_1	`long` value range [0, 255]
U_INT_2	`long` value range [0, 2^{16}-1]
U_INT_4	`long` value range [0, 2^{32}-1]
U_INT_8	`byte[]` value range [0, 2^{64}-1]
U_INT_16	`byte[]` value range [0, 2^{128}-1]
INT_1	`long` value range [-128, 127]
INT_2	`long` value range [-2^{15}, 2^{15}-1]
INT_4	`long` value range [-2^{31}, 2^{31}-1]
INT_8	`long` value range [-2^{63}, 2^{63}-1]
INT_16	`byte[]` value range [-2^{127}, 2^{127}-1]
URL	`java.lang.String`
UUID	`javax.bluetooth.UUID`
BOOL	`Boolean`
STRING	`java.lang.String`
DATSEQ	`java.util.Enumeration`
DATALT	`java.util.Enumeration`

Fields

BOOL

```
public static final int BOOL
```

Defines data of type BOOL.

DATALT

```
public static final int DATALT
```

Defines data of type DATALT, which is short for Data Element Alternative. A `DataElement` of type DATALT contains a sequence of other `DataElements` from which one `DataElement` is to be selected. The elements of the sequence can be of any type defined in this class, including DATALT.

DATSEQ

```
public static final int DATSEQ
```

Defines data of type DATSEQ, which is short for Data Element Sequence. A `DataElement` of type DATSEQ contains a sequence of other `DataElements`. The elements of the sequence can be of any type defined in this class, including DATSEQ.

INT_1

```
public static final int INT_1
```

Defines a signed integer of size 1 byte.

INT_16

```
public static final int INT_16
```

Defines a signed integer of size 16 bytes.

INT_2

```
public static final int INT_2
```

Defines a signed integer of size 2 bytes.

INT_4

```
public static final int INT_4
```

Defines a signed integer of size 4 bytes.

INT_8

```
public static final int INT_8
```

Defines a signed integer of size 8 bytes.

NULL

```
public static final int NULL
```

Defines data of type NULL. The value for data type `DataElement.NULL` is implicit; that is, there is no representation of it. Accordingly, there is no method to retrieve it, and attempts to retrieve the value throw an exception.

STRING

```
public static final int STRING
```

Defines data of type STRING.

U_INT_1

```
public static final int U_INT_1
```

Defines an unsigned integer of size 1 byte.

U_INT_16

```
public static final int U_INT_16
```

Defines an unsigned integer of size 16 bytes.

U_INT_2

```
public static final int U_INT_2
```

Defines an unsigned integer of size 2 bytes.

U_INT_4

```
public static final int U_INT_4
```

Defines an unsigned integer of size 4 bytes.

U_INT_8

```
public static final int U_INT_8
```

Defines an unsigned integer of size 8 bytes.

URL

```
public static final int URL
```

Defines data of type URL.

UUID

```
public static final int UUID
```

Defines data of type UUID.

Constructors

DataElement(boolean)

```
public DataElement(boolean bool)
```

Creates a `DataElement` whose data type is `BOOL` and whose value is equal to `bool`.

Parameters

`bool`—the value of the `DataElement` of type BOOL.

DataElement(int)

```
public DataElement(int valueType)
```

Creates a `DataElement` of type `NULL`, `DATALT`, or `DATSEQ`.

Parameters

`valueType`—the type of DataElement to create: `NULL`, `DATALT`, or `DATSEQ`

Throws

`IllegalArgumentException` if `valueType` is not `NULL`, `DATALT`, or `DATSEQ`

DataElement(int, long)

```
public DataElement(int valueType, long value)
```

Creates a `DataElement` that encapsulates an integer value of size `U_INT_1`, `U_INT_2`, `U_INT_4`, `INT_1`, `INT_2`, `INT_4`, or `INT_8`. The legal values for the `valueType` and the corresponding attribute values are as follows:

Value Type	Value Range
U_INT_1	$[0, 2^8-1]$
U_INT_2	$[0, 2^{16}-1]$
U_INT_4	$[0, 2^{32}-1]$
INT_1	$[-2^7, 2^7-1]$
INT_2	$[-2^{15}, 2^{15}-1]$
INT_4	$[-2^{31}, 2^{31}-1]$
INT_8	$[-2^{63}, 2^{63}-1]$

All other pairings are illegal and cause an `IllegalArgument-Exception` to be thrown.

Parameters

`valueType`—the data type of the object that is being created; must be one of the following: `U_INT_1`, `U_INT_2`, `U_INT_4`, `INT_1`, `INT_2`, `INT_4`, or `INT_8`

`value`—the value of the object being created; must be in the range specified for the given `valueType`.

Throws

`IllegalArgumentException` if the `valueType` is not valid or the `value` for the given legal `valueType` is outside the valid range

DataElement(int, Object)

```
public DataElement(int valueType, java.lang.Object
    value)
```

Creates a `DataElement` whose data type is given by `valueType` and whose value is specified by the argument `value`. The legal values for the `valueType` and the corresponding attribute values are as follows:

Value Type	Java Type/Value Range
URL	java.lang.String
UUID	javax.bluetooth.UUID
STRING	java.lang.String
INT_16	$[-2^{127}, 2^{127}-1]$ as a byte array whose length must be 16
U_INT_8	$[0, 2^{64}-1]$ as a byte array whose length must be 8
U_INT_16	$[0, 2^{128}-1]$, as a byte array whose length must be 16

All other pairings are illegal and would cause an `IllegalArgumentException` exception.

Parameters

valueType—the data type of the object that is being created; must be one of the following: URL, UUID, STRING, INT_16, U_INT_8, or U_INT_16.
value—the value for the DataElement being created of type valueType.

Throws

IllegalArgumentException if the value is not of the type valueType or is not in the range specified or is null

Methods

addElement(DataElement)

```
public void addElement(DataElement elem)
```

Adds a DataElement to this DATALT or DATSEQ DataElement object. The elem is added at the end of the list. The elem can be of any DataElement type; that is, URL, NULL, BOOL, UUID, STRING, DATSEQ, DATALT, and the various signed and unsigned integer types. The same object can be added twice. If the object is successfully added, the size of the DataElement is increased by one.

Parameters

elem—the DataElement object to add.

Throws

ClassCastException if the method is invoked on a DataElement whose type is not DATALT or DATSEQ
NullPointerException if elem is null

getBoolean()

```
public boolean getBoolean()
```

Returns the value of the DataElement if it is represented as a boolean.

Returns

The boolean value of this DataElement object.

Throws

ClassCastException—if the data type of this object is not of type BOOL

getDataType()

```
public int getDataType()
```

Returns the data type of the object this DataElement represents.

Returns

The data type of this DataElement object; the legal return values are URL, NULL, BOOL, UUID, STRING, DATSEQ, DATALT, U_INT_1, U_INT_2, U_INT_4, U_INT_8, U_INT_16, INT_1, INT_2, INT_4, INT_8, or INT_16.

getLong()

```
public long getLong()
```

Returns the value of the DataElement if it can be represented as a long. The data type of the object must be U_INT_1, U_INT_2, U_INT_4, INT_1, INT_2, INT_4, or INT_8.

Returns

The value of the DataElement as a long.

Throws

ClassCastException—if the data type of the object is not U_INT_1, U_INT_2, U_INT_4, INT_1, INT_2, INT_4, or INT_8.

getSize()

```
public int getSize()
```

Returns the number of DataElements that are present in this DATALT or DATSEQ object. It is possible that the number of elements is equal to zero.

Returns

The number of elements in this DATALT or DATSEQ.

Throws

ClassCastException—if this object is not of type `DATALT` or `DATSEQ`.

getValue()

```
public java.lang.Object getValue()
```

Returns the value of this `DataElement` as an `Object`. This method returns the appropriate Java object for the following data types: URL, UUID, STRING, DATSEQ, DATALT, U_INT_8, U_INT_16, and INT_16. Modifying the returned `Object` will not change this `DataElement`. The following are the legal pairs of data type and Java object type being returned:

DataElement Data Type	Java Data Type
URL	java.lang.String
UUID	javax.bluetooth.UUID
STRING	java.lang.String
DATSEQ	java.util.Enumeration
DATALT	java.util.Enumeration
U_INT_8	byte[] of length 8
U_INT_16	byte[] of length 16
INT_16	byte[] of length 16

Returns

The value of this object.

Throws

ClassCastException—if the object is not a URL, UUID, STRING, DATSEQ, DATALT, U_INT_8, U_INT_16, or INT_16.

insertElementAt(DataElement, int)

```
public void insertElementAt(DataElement elem, int
        index)
```

Inserts a `DataElement` at the specified location. This method can be invoked only on a `DATALT` or `DATSEQ`. `elem` can be of any `DataElement` type; that is, `URL`, `NULL`, `BOOL`, `UUID`, `STRING`, `DATSEQ`, `DATALT`, and the various signed and unsigned integers. The same object can be added twice. If the object is successfully added, the size is increased by one. Each element with an index greater than or equal to the specified index is shifted upward to have an index one greater than the value it had previously.

The `index` must be greater than or equal to 0 and less than or equal to the current size. Therefore, `DATALT` and `DATSEQ` are zero-based objects.

Parameters

`elem`—the `DataElement` object to add.
`index`—the location at which to add the `DataElement`.

Throws

`ClassCastException`—if the method is invoked on an instance of `DataElement` whose type is not `DATALT` or `DATSEQ`.
`IndexOutOfBoundsException`—if `index` is negative or greater than the size of the `DATALT` or `DATSEQ`.
`NullPointerException`—if `elem` is `null`.

removeElement(DataElement)

```
public boolean removeElement(DataElement elem)
```

Removes the first occurrence of the `DataElement` from this object. `elem` may be of any type; that is, `URL`, `NULL`, `BOOL`, `UUID`, `STRING`, `DATSEQ`, `DATALT`, or the variously sized signed and unsigned integers. Only the first object in the list that is equal to `elem` is removed. Other objects, if present, are not removed. Because this class does not override the `equals()` method of the `Object` class, the remove method compares only the references of objects. If `elem` is successfully removed, the size of this `DataElement` is decreased by one. Each `DataElement` in the `DATALT` or `DATSEQ` with an index greater than the index of `elem` is shifted downward to have an index one smaller than the value it had previously.

Parameters

`elem`—the `DataElement` to be removed.

Returns

true if the input value was found and removed; otherwise false.

Throws

ClassCastException—if this object is not of type DATALT or DATSEQ.
NullPointerException—if elem is null.

javax.bluetooth

DeviceClass

Declaration

```
public class DeviceClass

java.lang.Object
   |
   +—javax.bluetooth.DeviceClass
```

Description

The DeviceClass class represents the CoD record as defined by the Bluetooth specification. This record is defined in the Bluetooth Assigned Numbers document and contains information on the type of the device and the type of services available on the device.

The Bluetooth Assigned Numbers document [30] defines the service class, major device class, and minor device class. The following table provides examples of possible return values and their meaning:

Method	Return Value	Class of Device
getServiceClasses()	0x22000	Networking and Limited Discoverable Major Service Classes
getServiceClasses()	0x100000	Object Transfer Major Service Class
getMajorDeviceClass()	0x00	Miscellaneous Major Device Class
getMajorDeviceClass()	0x200	Phone Major Device Class
getMinorDeviceClass()	0x0C	With a Computer Major Device Class, Laptop Minor Device Class
getMinorDeviceClass()	0x04	With a Phone Major Device Class, Cellular Minor Device Class

Service Discovery

The `DiscoveryAgent` class also encapsulates the functionality provided by the Service Discovery Application Profile. The class provides an interface for an application to search and retrieve attributes for a particular service. There are two ways to search for services. To search for a service on a single device, the `searchServices()` method should be used. On the other hand, if you don't care which device a service is on, the `selectService()` method does a service search on a set of remote devices.

Fields

CACHED

```
public static final int CACHED
```

Used with the `retrieveDevices()` method to return devices found via a previous inquiry. If no inquiries have been started, the method returns `null`.

GIAC

```
public static final int GIAC
```

The inquiry access code for General/Unlimited Inquiry Access Code. This code is used to specify the type of inquiry to complete or respond to. The value of `GIAC` is 0x9E8B33 (10390323). This value is defined in the Bluetooth Assigned Numbers document.

LIAC

```
public static final int LIAC
```

The inquiry access code for Limited Dedicated Inquiry Access Code (LIAC). This code is used to specify the type of inquiry to complete or respond to. The value of `LIAC` is 0x9E8B00 (10390272). This value is defined in the Bluetooth Assigned Numbers document.

NOT_DISCOVERABLE

```
public static final int NOT_DISCOVERABLE
```

A constant indicating a mode where a device does not respond to device inquiries.

PREKNOWN

```
public static final int PREKNOWN
```

Used with the `retrieveDevices()` method to return devices defined to be pre-known devices. Pre-known devices are specified in the BCC. These are devices specified by the user as devices with which the local device will frequently communicate.

Methods

cancelInquiry(DiscoveryListener)

```
public boolean cancelInquiry(DiscoveryListener lis-
          tener)
```

Removes the device from inquiry mode.

An `inquiryCompleted()` event will occur with a type of `INQUIRY_TERMINATED` as a result of calling this method. After this event is received, no further `deviceDiscovered()` events will occur as a result of this inquiry.

This method cancels the inquiry only if the `listener` provided is the listener used when starting the inquiry.

Parameters
`listener`—the listener receiving inquiry events.

Returns
`true` if the inquiry was canceled; otherwise `false` if the inquiry was not canceled or if the inquiry was not started with `listener`.

Throws
`NullPointerException`—if `listener` is `null`.

cancelServiceSearch(int)

```
public boolean cancelServiceSearch(int transID)
```

Cancels the service search transaction that has the specified transaction ID. The ID was assigned to the transaction by the method `searchServices()`. A `serviceSearchCompleted()` event with a discovery type of `SERVICE_SEARCH_TERMINATED` will occur when this method is called. After this event is received, no further `servicesDiscovered()` events will occur as a result of this search.

Parameters
`transID`—the ID of the service search transaction to cancel; returned by `searchServices()`.

Returns
`true` if the service search transaction is terminated, `false` if the `transID` does not represent an active service search transaction.

retrieveDevices(int)

```
    public RemoteDevice[] retrieveDevices(int option)
```

Returns an array of Bluetooth devices that have either been found by the local device during previous inquiry requests or been specified as pre-known devices depending on the argument. The list of previously found devices is maintained by the implementation of this API. (In other words, maintenance of the list of previously found devices is an implementation detail.) A device can be set as a pre-known device in the BCC.

Parameters
`option`—CACHED if previously found devices should be returned; PRE-KNOWN if pre-known devices should be returned.

Returns
An array containing the Bluetooth devices previously found if `option` is CACHED; an array of devices that are pre-known devices if `option` is PREKNOWN; `null` if no devices meet the criteria.

Throws
`IllegalArgumentException` if `option` is not CACHED or PREKNOWN

searchServices(int[], UUID[], RemoteDevice, DiscoveryListener)

```
public int searchServices(int[] attrSet, UUID[]
    uuidSet, RemoteDevice btDev,DiscoveryListener
    discListener) throws BluetoothStateException
```

Searches for services on a remote Bluetooth device that have all the UUIDs specified in `uuidSet`. Once the service is found, the attributes specified in `attrSet` and the default attributes are retrieved. The default attributes are ServiceRecordHandle (0x0000), ServiceClassIDList (0x0001), ServiceRecordState (0x0002), ServiceID (0x0003), and ProtocolDescriptorList (0x0004). If `attrSet` is null, then only the default attributes are retrieved. `attrSet` does not have to be sorted in increasing order, but must only contain values in the range $[0-(2^{16}-1)]$.

Parameters

`attrSet`—indicates the attributes whose values will be retrieved on services that have the UUIDs specified in `uuidSet`.

`uuidSet`—the set of UUIDs being searched for; all services returned will contain all the UUIDs specified here.

`btDev`—the remote Bluetooth device on which to search for services.

`discListener`—the object that will receive events when services are discovered

Returns

The transaction ID of the service search; this number must be positive.

Throws

`BluetoothStateException` if the number of concurrent service search transactions exceeds the limit specified by the `bluetooth.sd.trans.max` property obtained from the class `LocalDevice` or the system is unable to start one because of current conditions.

`IllegalArgumentException` if `attrSet` has an illegal service attribute ID or exceeds the property `bluetooth.sd.attr.-retrievable.max` defined in the class `LocalDevice`; if `attrSet` or `uuidSet` is of length 0; if `attrSet` or `uuidSet` contains duplicates.

`NullPointerException` if `uuidSet`, `btDev`, or `discListener` is null; if an element in `uuidSet` array is null.

selectService(UUID, int, boolean)

```
public java.lang.String selectService(UUID uuid,
        int security, boolean master)
throws BluetoothStateException
```

Attempts to locate a service that contains `uuid` in the ServiceClassIDList of its service record. This method returns a string that may be used in `Connector.open()` to establish a connection to the service. How the service is selected if there are multiple services with `uuid` and which devices to search are implementation dependent.

Parameters

`uuid`—the UUID to search for in the ServiceClassIDList.

`security` specifies the security requirements for a connection to this service; must be one of `ServiceRecord.NOAUTHENTICATE_NOENCRYPT`, `ServiceRecord.AUTHENTICATE_NOENCRYPT`, or `ServiceRecord.AUTHENTICATE_ENCRYPT`.

`master`—determines whether this client must be the master of the connection; `true` if the client must be the master; `false` if the client can be the master or the slave.

Returns

The connection string used to connect to the service with a UUID of `uuid`; or `null` if no service can be found with a UUID of `uuid` in the ServiceClassIDList.

Throws

`BluetoothStateException` if the Bluetooth system cannot start the request because of the current state of the Bluetooth system.

`NullPointerException` if `uuid` is null.

`IllegalArgumentException` if `security` is not one of the following: `ServiceRecord.NOAUTHENTICATE_NOENCRYPT`, `ServiceRecord.AUTHENTICATE_NOENCRYPT`, or `ServiceRecord.AUTHENTICATE_ENCRYPT`.

startInquiry(int, DiscoveryListener)

```
public boolean startInquiry(int accessCode,
    DiscoveryListener listener)
throws BluetoothStateException
```

Places the device into inquiry mode. The length of the inquiry is implementation dependent. This method searches for devices with the specified inquiry access code. Devices that responded to the inquiry are returned to the application via the method `deviceDiscovered()` of the interface `DiscoveryListener`. The `cancelInquiry()` method is called to stop the inquiry.

Parameters

`accessCode`–the type of inquiry to complete.
`listener`—the event listener that will receive device discovery events.

Returns

`true` if the inquiry was started; `false` if the inquiry was not started because the `accessCode` is not supported.

Throws

`IllegalArgumentException` if the access code provided is not `LIAC`, `GIAC`, or in the range 0x9E8B00 to 0x9E8B3F.
`NullPointerException` if `listener` is null.
`BluetoothStateException` if the Bluetooth device does not allow an inquiry to be started because of other operations being performed by the device.

javax.bluetooth

DiscoveryListener

Declaration

```
public interface DiscoveryListener
```

Description

The `DiscoveryListener` interface allows an application to receive device discovery and service discovery events. This interface provides four methods, two for discovering devices and two for discovering services.

Fields

INQUIRY_COMPLETED

```
public static final int INQUIRY_COMPLETED
```

Indicates the normal completion of device discovery. Used with the `inquiryCompleted()` method.

INQUIRY_ERROR

```
public static final int INQUIRY_ERROR
```

Indicates that the inquiry request failed to complete normally but was not canceled.

INQUIRY_TERMINATED

```
public static final int INQUIRY_TERMINATED
```

Indicates device discovery has been canceled by the application and did not complete. Used with the `inquiryCompleted()` method.

SERVICE_SEARCH_COMPLETED

```
public static final int SERVICE_SEARCH_COMPLETED
```

Indicates the normal completion of service discovery. Used with the `serviceSearchCompleted()` method.

SERVICE_SEARCH_DEVICE_NOT_REACHABLE

```
public static final int
        SERVICE_SEARCH_DEVICE_NOT_REACHABLE
```

Indicates the service search could not be completed because the remote device provided to `DiscoveryAgent.searchServices()` could not be reached. Used with the `serviceSearchCompleted()` method.

SERVICE_SEARCH_ERROR

```
public static final int SERVICE_SEARCH_ERROR
```

Indicates the service search terminated with an error. Used with the `serviceSearchCompleted()` method.

SERVICE_SEARCH_NO_RECORDS

```
public static final int SERVICE_SEARCH_NO_RECORDS
```

Indicates the service search has completed with no service records found on the device. Used with the `serviceSearchCompleted()` method.

SERVICE_SEARCH_TERMINATED

```
public static final int SERVICE_SEARCH_TERMINATED
```

Indicates the service search has been canceled by the application and did not complete. Used with the `serviceSearchCompleted()` method.

Methods

deviceDiscovered(RemoteDevice, DeviceClass)

```
public void deviceDiscovered(RemoteDevice btDevice,
    DeviceClass cod)
```

Called when a device is found during an inquiry. An inquiry searches for devices that are discoverable. The same device may be returned multiple times.

Parameters
`btDevice`—the device that was found during the inquiry.
`cod`—the service classes, major device class, and minor device class of the remote device.

inquiryCompleted(int)

```
public void inquiryCompleted(int discType)
```

Called when an inquiry is completed. The `discType` will be `INQUIRY_COMPLETED` if the inquiry ended normally or `INQUIRY_TER-MINATED` if the inquiry was canceled by a call to `cancelInquiry()`. The `discType` is `INQUIRY_ERROR` if an error occurred during processing of the inquiry and causes the inquiry to end abnormally.

Parameters

`discType`—the manner in which the inquiry was completed: `INQUIRY_COMPLETED`, `INQUIRY_TERMINATED`, or `INQUIRY_ERROR`.

servicesDiscovered(int, ServiceRecord[])

```
public void servicesDiscovered(int transID,
        ServiceRecord[] services)
```

Called when service(s) are found during a service search.

Parameters

`transID`—the transaction ID of the service search posting the result.
`services`—a list of services found during the search request.

serviceSearchCompleted(int, int)

```
public void serviceSearchCompleted(int transID, int
        respCode)
```

Called when a service search is completed or was terminated because of an error. Legal status values of the `respCode` argument include `SERVICE_SEARCH_COMPLETED`, `SERVICE_SEARCH_TERMINATED`, `SERVICE_SEARCH_ERROR`, `SERVICE_SEARCH_NO_RECORDS`, and `SERVICE_SEARCH_DEVICE_NOT_REACHABLE`. The following table describes when each `respCode` is used:

respCode	Reason
SERVICE_SEARCH_COMPLETED	If the service search completed normally
SERVICE_SEARCH_TERMINATED	If the service search request was canceled by a call to DiscoveryAgent.cancelServiceSearch()
SERVICE_SEARCH_ERROR	If an error occurred during processing of the request
SERVICE_SEARCH_NO_RECORDS	If no records were found during the service search
SERVICE_SEARCH_DEVICE_NOT_REACHABLE	If the device specified in the search request could not be reached or the local device could not establish a connection to the remote device

Parameters

transID—the transaction ID identifying the request that initiated the service search.

respCode—the response code that indicates the status of the transaction.

javax.bluetooth

L2CAPConnection

Declaration

```
public interface L2CAPConnection extends
        javax.microedition.io.Connection
```

Description

The L2CAPConnection interface represents a connection-oriented L2CAP channel. This interface is to be used as part of the CLDC GCF.

For creating a client connection, the protocol is btl2cap. The target is the combination of the address of the Bluetooth device to which to connect and the PSM of the service. The PSM value is used by the L2CAP to determine which higher-level protocol or application is the recipient of the messages the layer receives.

The parameters defined specific to L2CAP are ReceiveMTU and TransmitMTU. The ReceiveMTU and TransmitMTU parameters are optional. ReceiveMTU specifies the maximum payload size this connection can accept, and TransmitMTU specifies the maximum payload size this connection can send. An example of a valid L2CAP client connection string is as follows:

```
btl2cap://0050CD00321B:1003;ReceiveMTU=512;Transmit
    MTU=512
```

Fields

DEFAULT_MTU

```
public static final int DEFAULT_MTU
```

Default MTU value for connection-oriented channels is 672 bytes.

MINIMUM_MTU

```
public static final int MINIMUM_MTU
```

Minimum MTU value for connection-oriented channels is 48 bytes.

Methods

getReceiveMTU()

```
public int getReceiveMTU() throws IOException
```

Returns the ReceiveMTU that the connection supports. If the connection string does not specify a ReceiveMTU, the value returned is less than or equal to the DEFAULT_MTU. If the connection string did specify an MTU, this value is less than or equal to the value specified in the connection string.

Returns
The maximum number of bytes that can be read in a single call to receive().

Throws
IOException if the connection is closed.

getTransmitMTU()

```
public int getTransmitMTU() throws IOException
```

Returns the MTU that the remote device supports. This value is obtained after the connection has been configured. If the application specifies TransmitMTU in the `Connector.open()` string, this value should be equal to that. If the application does not specify any TransmitMTU, this value should be less than or equal to the ReceiveMTU the remote device advertised during channel configuration.

Returns

The maximum number of bytes that can be sent in a single call to `send()` without losing any data.

Throws

`IOException` if the connection is closed.

ready()

```
public boolean ready() throws IOException
```

Determines whether there is a packet that can be read via a call to `receive()`. If `true`, a call to `receive()` will not block the application.

Returns

`true` if there is data to read; `false` if there is no data to read.

Throws

`IOException` if the connection is closed.

receive(byte[])

```
public int receive(byte[] inBuf) throws IOException
```

Reads a packet of data. The amount of data received in this operation is related to the value of ReceiveMTU. If the size of `inBuf` is greater than or equal to ReceiveMTU, then no data will be lost. Unlike `read()` on a `java.io.InputStream`, if the size of `inBuf` is smaller than

ReceiveMTU, then the portion of the L2CAP payload that will fit into inBuf will be placed in inBuf. The rest will be discarded. If the application is aware of the number of bytes (less than ReceiveMTU) it will receive in any transaction, then the size of inBuf can be less than ReceiveMTU, and no data will be lost. If inBuf is of length 0, all data sent in one packet is lost unless the length of the packet is 0.

Parameters
inBuf—byte array for storing the received data.

Returns
The actual number of bytes read; 0 if a zero-length packet is received; 0 if inBuf length is zero.

Throws
IOException if an I/O error occurs or the connection has been closed.
InterruptedIOException if the request times out.
NullPointerException if inBuf is null.

send(byte[])

```
public void send(byte[] data) throws IOException
```

Requests that data be sent to the remote device. The TransmitMTU determines the amount of data that can be successfully sent in a single send operation. If the size of data is greater than the TransmitMTU, then only the first TransmitMTU bytes of the packet are sent, and the rest are discarded. If data is of length 0, an empty L2CAP packet will be sent.

Parameters
data—data to be sent.

Throws
IOException if data cannot be sent successfully or if the connection is closed.
NullPointerException if data is null.

javax.bluetooth

L2CAPConnectionNotifier

Declaration

```
public interface L2CAPConnectionNotifier extends
        javax.microedition.io.Connection
```

Description

The L2CAPConnectionNotifier interface provides an L2CAP connection notifier.

To create a server connection, the protocol must be bt12cap. The target contains "localhost:" and the UUID of the service. The parameters are ReceiveMTU and TransmitMTU, the same parameters used to define a client connection.

A call to Connector.open() with a valid server connection string will return a javax.bluetooth.L2CAPConnectionNotifier object. An L2CAPConnection object is obtained from the L2CAPConnection-Notifier by calling the method acceptAndOpen().

Methods

acceptAndOpen()

```
public L2CAPConnection acceptAndOpen() throws
        IOException
```

Waits for a client to connect to this L2CAP service. On connection returns an L2CAPConnection that can be used to communicate with this client.

A service record associated with this connection will be added to the SDDB if one does not exist in the SDDB. This method puts the local device in connectable mode so that it responds to connection attempts by clients.

The following checks are done to verify that any modifications made by the application to the service record after it was created by

`Connector.open()` have not created an invalid service record. If any of these checks fails, then a `ServiceRegistrationException` is thrown.

- ServiceClassIDList and ProtocolDescriptorList, the mandatory service attributes for a `btl2cap` service record, must be present in the service record.
- L2CAP must be in the ProtocolDescriptorList.
- The PSM value must not have changed in the service record.

This method does not ensure that the service record created is a completely valid service record. It is the responsibility of the application to ensure that the service record follows all of the applicable syntactic and semantic rules for service record correctness.

Returns
A connection used to communicate with the client.

Throws
`IOException` if the notifier is closed before `acceptAndOpen()` is called

`ServiceRegistrationException` if the structure of the associated service record is invalid or if the service record could not be added successfully to the local SDDB. The structure of service record is invalid if the service record is missing any mandatory service attributes or has changed any of the values described above that are fixed and cannot be changed. Failures to add the record to the SDDB could be due to factors such as insufficient disk space and database locks.

`BluetoothStateException` if the server device could not be placed in connectable mode because the device user has configured the device to be non-connectable.

javax.bluetooth

LocalDevice

Declaration

```
public class LocalDevice

java.lang.Object
   |
   +—javax.bluetooth.LocalDevice
```

Description

The `LocalDevice` class defines the basic functions of the Bluetooth manager. The Bluetooth manager provides the lowest-level interface possible into the Bluetooth stack. It provides access to and control of the local Bluetooth device.

Methods

getBluetoothAddress()

```
public java.lang.String getBluetoothAddress()
```

Retrieves the Bluetooth address of the local device. The Bluetooth address will never be `null`. The Bluetooth address will be 12 characters long. Valid characters are 0-9 and A-F.

Returns

The Bluetooth address of the local device.

getDeviceClass()

```
public DeviceClass getDeviceClass()
```

Retrieves the `DeviceClass` object that represents the service classes, major device class, and minor device class of the local device. This method returns `null` if the service classes, major device class, or minor device class cannot be determined.

Returns

The service classes, major device class, and minor device class of the local device, or `null` if the service classes, major device class, or minor device class cannot be determined.

getDiscoverable()

```
public int getDiscoverable()
```

Retrieves the discoverable mode of the local device. The return value is `DiscoveryAgent.GIAC`, `DiscoveryAgent.LIAC`, `DiscoveryAgent.NOT_DISCOVERABLE`, or a value in the range 0x9E8B00 to 0x9E8B3F.

Returns
The current discoverable mode of the device.

getDiscoveryAgent()

```
public DiscoveryAgent getDiscoveryAgent()
```

Returns the discovery agent for this device. Multiple calls to this method return the same object. This method never returns `null`.

Returns
The discovery agent for the local device.

getFriendlyName()

```
public java.lang.String getFriendlyName()
```

Retrieves the name of the local device. The Bluetooth specification calls this name the *Bluetooth device name* or the *user-friendly name*.

Returns
The name of the local device; `null` if the name cannot be retrieved.

getLocalDevice()

```
public static LocalDevice getLocalDevice() throws
        BluetoothStateException
```

Retrieves the `LocalDevice` object for the local Bluetooth device. Multiple calls to this method will return the same object. This method never returns `null`.

Returns
An object that represents the local Bluetooth device.

Throws

`BluetoothStateException` if the Bluetooth system cannot be initialized.

getProperty(String)

```
public static java.lang.String
        getProperty(java.lang.String property)
```

Retrieves Bluetooth system properties. The following properties must be supported, but additional values are allowed:

Property Name	Description
bluetooth.api.version	The version of JABWT that is supported. For this version it is set to "1.0."
bluetooth.master.switch	Is master/slave switch allowed? Valid value is either "true" or "false."
bluetooth.sd.attr.retrievable.max	Maximum number of service attributes to be retrieved per service record. The string will be in base 10 digits.
bluetooth.connected.devices.max	The maximum number of connected devices supported. This number can be greater than 7 if the implementation handles parked connections. The string will be in base 10 digits.
bluetooth.l2cap.receiveMTU.max	The maximum ReceiveMTU size in bytes supported in L2CAP. The string will be in base 10 digits (e.g., "32.").
bluetooth.sd.trans.max	Maximum number of concurrent service discovery transactions. The string will be in base 10 digits.
bluetooth.connected.inquiry.scan	Is Inquiry scanning allowed during connection? Valid value is either "true" or "false."
bluetooth.connected.page.scan	Can the local device accept a connection from a device if it is already connected to another device? Valid value is either "true" or "false."
bluetooth.connected.inquiry	Is Inquiry allowed during a connection? Valid value is either "true" or "false."
bluetooth.connected.page	Can a connection be established to one device if there is already a connection to another device? Valid value is either "true" or "false."

Parameters

property—the property to retrieve as defined in this class.

Returns

The value of the property specified; null if the property is not defined.

getRecord(Connection)

```
public ServiceRecord
getRecord(javax.microedition.io.Connection notifier)
```

Gets the service record corresponding to a btspp, btl2cap, or btgoep notifier. In the case of a run-before-connect service, the service record returned by getRecord() was created by the same call to Connector.open() that created the notifier.

If a connect-anytime server application does not already have a service record in the SDDB, either because a service record for this service was never added to the SDDB or because the service record was added and then removed, the ServiceRecord returned by getRecord() was created by the same call to Connector.open() that created the notifier.

In the case of a connect-anytime service, there may be a service record in the SDDB corresponding to this service before application startup. In this case, the getRecord() method must return a ServiceRecord whose contents match those of the corresponding service record in the SDDB. If a connect-anytime server application previously made changes to its service record in the SDDB (e.g., during a previous execution of the server), and that service record is still in the SDDB, then those changes must be reflected in the ServiceRecord returned by getRecord().

Two invocations of this method with the same notifier argument return objects that describe the same service attributes, but the return values may be different object references.

Parameters

notifier—a connection that waits for clients to connect to a Bluetooth service.

Returns
The `ServiceRecord` associated with `notifier`.

Throws
`IllegalArgumentException` if `notifier` is closed, or if `notifier` does not implement one of the following interfaces: `javax.microedition.io.StreamConnectionNotifier`, `javax.bluetooth.L2CapConnectionNotifier`, or `javax.obex.SessionNotifier`. This exception also is thrown if `notifier` is not a Bluetooth notifier but is, for example, a `StreamConnectionNotifier` created with a scheme other than `btspp`.
`NullPointerException` if `notifier` is null.

setDiscoverable(int)

```
public boolean setDiscoverable(int mode) throws
    BluetoothStateException
```

Sets the discoverable mode of the device. The `mode` may be any number in the range 0x9E8B00 to 0x9E8B3F as defined by the Bluetooth Assigned Numbers document. When this specification was defined, only GIAC (`DiscoveryAgent.GIAC`) and LIAC (`DiscoveryAgent.LIAC`) were defined, but Bluetooth profiles may add additional access codes in the future. To determine what values may be used, check the Bluetooth Assigned Numbers document [30].

If `DiscoveryAgent.GIAC` or `DiscoveryAgent.LIAC` is provided, then this method will attempt to put the device into general or limited discoverable mode, respectively. To take a device out of discoverable mode, provide the `DiscoveryAgent.NOT_DISCOVERABLE` flag. The BCC decides whether the request will be granted. In addition to the BCC, the Bluetooth system could affect the discoverability of a device.

According to the Bluetooth specification, a device should be limited discoverable (`DiscoveryAgent.LIAC`) for only 1 minute. This mechanism is handled by the implementation of the API. After the minute is up, the device reverts to the previous discoverable mode.

Parameters

mode—the mode the device should be in; valid modes are
DiscoveryAgent.GIAC, DiscoveryAgent.LIAC, Discovery-
Agent.NOT_DISCOVERABLE, and any value in the range 0x9E8B00 to
0x9E8B3F.

Returns

true if the request succeeds; false if the request fails because the BCC
denied the request; false if the Bluetooth system does not support the
access mode specified in mode.

Throws

IllegalArgumentException if the mode is not Discovery-
Agent.GIAC, DiscoveryAgent.LIAC, DiscoveryAgent.NOT_-
DISCOVERABLE, or in the range 0x9E8B00 to 0x9E8B3F.
BluetoothStateException if the Bluetooth system is in a state that
does not allow the discoverable mode to be changed.

updateRecord(ServiceRecord)

```
public void updateRecord(ServiceRecord srvRecord)
throws ServiceRegistrationException
```

Updates the service record in the local SDDB that corresponds to the
srvRecord parameter. Updating is possible only if srvRecord is
obtained with the getRecord() method. The service record in the
SDDB is modified to have the same service attributes with the same contents as srvRecord.

If srvRecord was obtained from the SDDB of a remote device by
the service search methods, updating is not possible, and this method
will throw an IllegalArgumentException.

If the srvRecord parameter is a btspp service record, then before
the SDDB is changed, the following checks are performed. If any of
these checks fails, an IllegalArgumentException is thrown.

- ServiceClassIDList and ProtocolDescriptorList, the mandatory
  service attributes for a btspp service record, must be present in
  srvRecord.

- L2CAP and RFCOMM must be in the ProtocolDescriptorList.

- `srvRecord` must not have changed the RFCOMM server channel number from the channel number currently in the SDDB version of this service record.

If the `srvRecord` parameter is a `btl2cap` service record, then before the SDDB is changed, the following checks are performed. If any of these checks fails, an `IllegalArgumentException` is thrown.

- ServiceClassIDList and ProtocolDescriptorList, the mandatory service attributes for a `btl2cap` service record, must be present in `srvRecord`.

- L2CAP must be in the ProtocolDescriptorList.

- `srvRecord` must not have changed the PSM value from the PSM value currently in the SDDB version of this service record.

If the `srvRecord` parameter is a `btgoep` service record, then before the SDDB is changed the following checks are performed. If any of these checks fail, then an `IllegalArgumentException` is thrown.

- ServiceClassIDList and ProtocolDescriptorList, the mandatory service attributes for a `btgoep` service record, must be present in `srvRecord`.

- L2CAP, RFCOMM, and OBEX must all be in the Protocol-DescriptorList.

- `srvRecord` must not have changed the RFCOMM server channel number from the channel number that is currently in the SDDB version of this service record.

`updateRecord()` is not required to ensure that `srvRecord` is a completely valid service record. It is the responsibility of the application to ensure that `srvRecord` follows all of the applicable syntactic and semantic rules for service record correctness.

If there is currently no SDDB version of the `srvRecord` service record, then this method will do nothing.

Parameters
`srvRecord`—the new contents to use for the service record in the SDDB.

Throws
`NullPointerException` if `srvRecord` is `null`.

IllegalArgumentException if the structure of the srvRecord is missing any mandatory service attributes, or if an attempt has been made to change any of the values described as fixed.
ServiceRegistrationException if the local SDDB could not be updated successfully because of insufficient disk space, database locks, and so on.

javax.bluetooth

RemoteDevice

Declaration

```
public class RemoteDevice

java.lang.Object
   |
   +−javax.bluetooth.RemoteDevice
```

Description

The RemoteDevice class represents a remote Bluetooth device. It provides basic information about a remote device, including the Bluetooth address of the device and its friendly name.

Constructors

RemoteDevice(String)

```
protected RemoteDevice(java.lang.String address)
```

Creates a Bluetooth device on the basis of its address. The Bluetooth address must be 12 hex characters long. Valid characters are 0-9, a-f, and A-F. There is no preceding "0x" in the string. For example, valid Bluetooth addresses include but are not limited to

```
008037144297
00af8300cd0b
014bd91DA8FC
```

Parameters

address—the address of the Bluetooth device as a 12 character hex string.

Throws

NullPointerException if address is null.
IllegalArgumentException if address is the address of the local device or is not a valid Bluetooth address.

Methods

authenticate()

```
public boolean authenticate() throws IOException
```

Attempts to authenticate this RemoteDevice. Authentication is a means of verifying the identity of a remote device. Authentication involves a device-to-device challenge and response scheme that requires a 128-bit common secret link key derived from a PIN code shared by both devices. If either side's PIN code does not match, the authentication process fails, and the method returns false. The method also returns false if authentication is incompatible with the current security settings of the local device established by the BCC, if the stack does not support authentication at all, or if the stack does not support authentication subsequent to connection establishment.

If this RemoteDevice has previously been authenticated, then this method returns true without attempting to re-authenticate this RemoteDevice.

Returns

true if authentication is successful; otherwise false.

Throws

IOException if there are no open connections between the local device and this RemoteDevice.

authorize(Connection)

```
public boolean
        authorize(javax.microedition.io.Connection
        conn) throws IOException
```

Determines whether this `RemoteDevice` should be allowed to continue to access the local service provided by the `Connection`. In Bluetooth, authorization is defined as the process of deciding whether device X is allowed to access service Y. The implementation of the `authorize(Connection conn)` method asks the BCC to decide whether it is acceptable for `RemoteDevice` to continue to access a local service over the connection `conn`. In devices with a user interface, the BCC is expected to consult with the user to obtain approval.

Some Bluetooth systems may allow the user to permanently authorize a remote device for all local services. When a device is authorized in this way, it is known as a *trusted device* (see `isTrustedDevice()`).

The `authorize()` method also checks that the identity of the `RemoteDevice` can be verified through authentication. If this `RemoteDevice` has been authorized for `conn` previously, then this method returns `true` without attempting to reauthorize this `RemoteDevice`.

Parameters

`conn`—the connection that this `RemoteDevice` is using to access a local service.

Returns

`true` if this `RemoteDevice` is successfully authenticated and authorized; otherwise `false` if authentication or authorization fails.

Throws

`IllegalArgumentException` if `conn` is not a connection to this `RemoteDevice`, or if the local device initiated the connection; that is, the local device is the client rather than the server. This exception also is thrown if `conn` is created by `RemoteDevice` using a scheme other than `btspp`, `btl2cap`, or `btgoep`. This exception is thrown if `conn` is a notifier used by a server to wait for a client connection, since the notifier is not a connection to this `RemoteDevice`.

`IOException` if `conn` is closed.

encrypt(Connection, boolean)

```
public boolean
        encrypt(javax.microedition.io.Connection
        conn, boolean on) throws IOException
```

Attempts to turn encryption on or off for an existing connection. In the case in which the parameter `on` is `true`, this method first authenticates this `RemoteDevice` if it has not already been authenticated. Then it attempts to turn on encryption. If the connection is already encrypted. then this method returns `true`. Otherwise, when the parameter `on` is `true`, either

- The method succeeds in turning on encryption for the connection and returns `true`, or

- The method is unsuccessful in turning on encryption and returns `false`. (This can happen because the stack does not support encryption or because encryption conflicts with the user's security settings for the device.)

In the case in which the parameter `on` is `false`, there are again two possible outcomes:

- Encryption is turned off on the connection and `true` is returned, or

- Encryption is left on for the connection and `false` is returned

Encryption might be left on after `encrypt(conn, false)` for a variety of reasons. The user's current security settings for the device may require encryption, or the stack may not have a mechanism to turn off encryption. Also, the BCC may have determined that encryption will be kept on for the physical link to this `RemoteDevice`. The details of the BCC are implementation dependent, but encryption might be left on because other connections to the same device need encryption. (All of the connections over the same physical link must be encrypted if any of them are encrypted.)

Although attempting to turn off encryption may not succeed immediately because other connections need encryption on, there may be a delayed effect. At some point, all of the connections over this physical link needing encryption could be closed or also have had the method `encrypt(conn, false)` invoked for them. In this case, the BCC may turn off encryption for all connections over this physical link. (The policy used by the BCC is implementation dependent.) It is recommended that applications do `encrypt(conn, false)` once they no longer need encryption to allow the BCC to determine whether it can reduce the overhead on connections to this `RemoteDevice`.

The fact that `encrypt(conn, false)` may not succeed in turning off encryption has very few consequences for applications. The stack handles encryption and decryption, so the application does not have to do anything different depending on whether the connection is still encrypted or not.

Parameters

`conn`—the connection whose need for encryption has changed.
`on`—`true` attempts to turn on encryption; `false` attempts to turn off encryption.

Returns

`true` if the change succeeded `false` if it failed.

Throws

`IOException` if `conn` is closed.
`IllegalArgumentException` if `conn` is not a connection to this `RemoteDevice`; if `conn` was created by the client side of the connection using a scheme other than `btspp`, `btl2cap`, or `btgoep` (e.g., this exception will be thrown if `conn` was created with the `file` or `http` scheme); or if `conn` is a notifier used by a server to wait for a client connection, because the notifier is not a connection to this `RemoteDevice`.

equals(Object)

```
public boolean equals(java.lang.Object obj)
```

Determines whether two `RemoteDevices` are equal. Two devices are equal if they have the same Bluetooth device address.

Parameters

`obj`—the object to compare to.

Returns

`true` if both devices have the same Bluetooth address; `false` if both devices do not have the same address; `false` if `obj` is `null`; `false` if `obj` is not a `RemoteDevice`.

getBluetoothAddress()

```
public final java.lang.String getBluetoothAddress()
```

Retrieves the Bluetooth address of this device. The Bluetooth address will be 12 characters long. Valid characters are 0-9 and A-F. This method never returns `null`.

Returns

The Bluetooth address of the remote device.

getFriendlyName(boolean)

```
public java.lang.String getFriendlyName(boolean
    alwaysAsk)
throws IOException
```

Returns the name of this device. The Bluetooth specification calls this name the *Bluetooth device name* or the *user-friendly name*. This method only contacts the remote device if the name is not known or `alwaysAsk` is `true`.

Parameters

`alwaysAsk`—if `true` then the device will be contacted for its name; otherwise, if there exists a known name for this device, the name will be returned without contacting the remote device.

Returns

The name of the device, or `null` if the Bluetooth system does not support this feature; if the local device is able to contact the remote device, the result will never be `null`; if the remote device does not have a name, then an empty string will be returned.

Throws

`IOException` if the remote device can not be contacted or the remote device could not provide its name.

getRemoteDevice(Connection)

```
public static RemoteDevice
        getRemoteDevice(javax.microedition.io.Connect
        ion conn)
    throws IOException
```

Retrieves the Bluetooth device that is at the other end of the Bluetooth SPP connection, L2CAP connection, or OBEX over RFCOMM connection. This method never returns `null`.

Parameters

`conn`—the Bluetooth serial port connection, L2CAP connection, or OBEX over RFCOMM connection whose remote Bluetooth device is needed.

Returns

The remote device involved in the connection.

Throws

`IllegalArgumentException` if `conn` is not a Bluetooth SPP connection, L2CAP connection, or OBEX over RFCOMM connection; if `conn` is a `L2CAPConnectionNotifier`, `StreamConnectionNotifier`, or `SessionNotifier`.
`IOException` if the connection is closed.
`NullPointerException` if `conn` is null.

hashCode()

```
public int hashCode()
```

Computes the hash code for this object. This method returns the same value when it is called multiple times on the same object.

Returns

The hash code for this object.

isAuthenticated()

```
public boolean isAuthenticated()
```

Determines whether this `RemoteDevice` has been authenticated.

A device could have been authenticated by this application or another application. Authentication applies to an ACL link between devices and not on a specific L2CAP, RFCOMM, or OBEX connection. Therefore, if `authenticate()` is performed when an L2CAP connection is made to device A, then `isAuthenticated()` may return `true` when tested as part of making an RFCOMM connection to device A.

Returns

`true` if this `RemoteDevice` has previously been authenticated; `false` if it has not been authenticated or there are no open connections between the local device and this `RemoteDevice`

isAuthorized(Connection)

```
public boolean isAuthorized(javax.microedition.io.-
     Connection conn)
throws IOException
```

Determines whether this `RemoteDevice` has been authorized previously by the BCC of the local device to exchange data related to the service associated with the connection. Both clients and servers can call this method. However, for clients this method returns `false` for all legal values of the `conn` argument.

Parameters

`conn`—a connection that this `RemoteDevice` is using to access a service or provide a service.

Returns

`true` if `conn` is a server-side connection and this `RemoteDevice` has been authorized; `false` if `conn` is a client-side connection or a server-side connection that has not been authorized.

Throws

`IllegalArgumentException` if `conn` is not a connection to this `RemoteDevice`; if `conn` was not created with one of the schemes

`btspp`, `btl2cap`, or `btgoep`; or if `conn` is a notifier used by a server to wait for a client connection, because the notifier is not a connection to this `RemoteDevice`.
`IOException` if `conn` is closed.

isEncrypted()

```
public boolean isEncrypted()
```

Determines whether data exchanges with this `RemoteDevice` are currently being encrypted.

Encryption may have been previously turned on by this or another application. Encryption applies to an ACL link between devices and not to a specific L2CAP, RFCOMM, or OBEX connection. Therefore, if `encrypt()` is performed with the `on` parameter set to `true` when an L2CAP connection is made to device A, then `isEncrypted()` may return `true` when tested as part of making an RFCOMM connection to device A.

Returns

`true` if data exchanges with this `RemoteDevice` are being encrypted; `false` if they are not being encrypted, or there are no open connections between the local device and this `RemoteDevice`.

isTrustedDevice()

```
public boolean isTrustedDevice()
```

Determines whether this is a trusted device according to the BCC.

Returns

`true` if the device is a trusted device, otherwise `false`.

javax.bluetooth

ServiceRecord

Declaration

```
public interface ServiceRecord
```

Description

The `ServiceRecord` interface describes characteristics of a Bluetooth service. A `ServiceRecord` contains a set of service attributes, wherein each service attribute is an (ID, value) pair. A Bluetooth attribute ID is a 16-bit unsigned integer, and an attribute value is a `DataElement`.

The structure and use of service records are specified by the Bluetooth specification in the SDP document. Most of the Bluetooth Profile specifications also describe the structure of the service records used by the Bluetooth services that conform to the profile.

An SDP server maintains an SDDB of service records that describe the services on the local device. Remote SDP clients can use the SDP to query an SDP server for any service records of interest. A service record provides sufficient information to allow an SDP client to connect to the Bluetooth service on the SDP server's device.

`ServiceRecord`s are made available to a client application via an argument of the `servicesDiscovered()` method of the `DiscoveryListener` interface. `ServiceRecord`s are available to server applications via the method `getRecord()` on `LocalDevice`.

There can be many service attributes in a service record, and the SDP protocol makes it possible to specify the subset of the service attributes that an SDP client wants to retrieve from a remote service record. The `ServiceRecord` interface treats certain service attribute IDs as default IDs, and, if present, these service attributes are automatically retrieved during service searches.

The Bluetooth Assigned Numbers document [30] defines a large number of service attribute IDs. The following is a subset of the most common service attribute IDs and their types.

Attribute Name	Attribute ID	Attribute Value Type
ServiceRecordHandle	0x0000	32-bit unsigned integer
ServiceClassIDList	0x0001	DATSEQ of UUIDs
ServiceRecordState	0x0002	32-bit unsigned integer
ServiceID	0x0003	UUID
ProtocolDescriptorList	0x0004	DATSEQ of DATSEQ of UUID and optional parameters
BrowseGroupList	0x0005	DATSEQ of UUIDs
LanguageBaseAttributeIDList	0x0006	DATSEQ of 16-bit unsigned integers
ServiceInfoTimeToLive	0x0007	32-bit unsigned integer
ServiceAvailability	0x0008	8-bit unsigned integer
BluetoothProfileDescriptorList	0x0009	DATSEQ of DATSEQ pairs
DocumentationURL	0x000A	URL
ClientExecutableURL	0x000B	URL
IconURL	0x000C	URL
VersionNumberList	0x0200	DATSEQ of 16-bit unsigned integers
ServiceDatabaseState	0x0201	32-bit unsigned integer

Fields

AUTHENTICATE_ENCRYPT

```
public static final int AUTHENTICATE_ENCRYPT
```

Authentication and encryption are required for connections to this service. Used with the `getConnectionURL()` method.

AUTHENTICATE_NOENCRYPT

```
public static final int AUTHENTICATE_NOENCRYPT
```

Authentication is required for connections to this service, but encryption is not. Encryption can be either on or off for the connection. Used with the `getConnectionURL()` method.

NOAUTHENTICATE_NOENCRYPT

```
public static final int NOAUTHENTICATE_NOENCRYPT
```

Authentication and encryption are not needed on a connection to this service. Used with the `getConnectionURL()` method.

Methods

getAttributeIDs()

```
public int[] getAttributeIDs()
```

Returns the service attribute IDs whose value could be retrieved by a call to `getAttributeValue()`. The list of attributes being returned is not sorted and includes default attributes.

Returns

An array of service attribute IDs that are in this object and have values for them; if there are no attribute IDs that have values, this method returns an array of length zero.

getAttributeValue(int)

```
public DataElement getAttributeValue(int attrID)
```

Returns the value of the service attribute ID provided it is present in the service record, otherwise this method returns `null`.

Parameters

`attrID`—the attribute whose value is to be returned.

Returns

The value of the attribute ID if present in the service record, otherwise `null`.

Throws

`IllegalArgumentException` if `attrID` is negative or greater than or equal to 216.

getConnectionURL(int, boolean)

```
public java.lang.String getConnectionURL(int
        requiredSecurity, boolean mustBeMaster)
```

Returns a String including optional parameters that can be used by a client to connect to the service described by this `ServiceRecord`. The return value can be used as the first argument to `Connector.open()`. In the case of a Serial Port service record, this string might look like "btspp://0050CD00321B:3;authenticate=true;encrypt=false;master=true", where 0050CD00321B is the Bluetooth address of the device that provided this `ServiceRecord`, 3 is the RFCOMM server channel mentioned in this `ServiceRecord`, and there are three optional parameters related to security and master/slave roles.

If this method is called on a `ServiceRecord` returned from `LocalDevice.getRecord()`, it returns the connection string that a remote device will use to connect to this service.

Parameters

`requiredSecurity`—determines whether authentication or encryption is required for a connection.

`mustBeMaster true`—indicates this device must play the role of master in connections to this service; `false` indicates that the local device is willing to be either the master or the slave.

Returns

A string that can be used to connect to the service or `null` if the ProtocolDescriptorList in this ServiceRecord is not formatted according to the Bluetooth specification.

Throws

`IllegalArgumentException` if `requiredSecurity` is not one of the constants `NOAUTHENTICATE_NOENCRYPT`, `AUTHENTICATE_NOEN-CRYPT`, or `AUTHENTICATE_ENCRYPT`

getHostDevice()

```
public RemoteDevice getHostDevice()
```

Returns the remote Bluetooth device that populated the service record with attribute values. It is important to note that the Bluetooth device that provided the value might not be reachable anymore, because it can move, turn off, or change its security mode, denying all further transactions.

Returns

The remote Bluetooth device that populated the service record or `null` if the local device populated this `ServiceRecord`.

populateRecord(int[])

```
public boolean populateRecord(int[] attrIDs) throws
    IOException
```

Retrieves the values by contacting the remote Bluetooth device for a set of service attribute IDs of a service that is available on a Bluetooth device. (This involves going over the air and contacting the remote device for the attribute values.) The system might impose a limit on the number of service attribute ID values one can request at a time. Applications can obtain the value of this limit as a String by calling `LocalDevice.getProperty("bluetooth.sd.attr.retrievable.max")`. The method is blocking and will return when the results of the request are available. Attribute IDs whose values are obtained are added to this service record. If there exist attribute IDs for which values are retrieved, the old values will be overwritten. If the remote device cannot be reached, an `IOException` will be thrown.

Parameters

`attrIDs`—the list of service attributes IDs whose value are to be retrieved; the number of attributes cannot exceed the property `bluetooth.sd.attr.retrievable.max`. The attributes in the request must be legal; that is, their values are in the range of [0, 2^{16}-1]. The input attribute IDs can include attribute IDs from the default attribute set.

Returns

true if the request was successful in retrieving values for some or all of the attribute IDs; false if it was unsuccessful in retrieving any values.

Throws

IOException if the local device is unable to connect to the remote Bluetooth device that was the source of this ServiceRecord; if this ServiceRecord was deleted from the SDDB of the remote device.

IllegalArgumentException if the size of attrIDs exceeds the system specified limit as defined by bluetooth.sd.attr.retrievable.max; if the attrIDs array length is zero; if any of their values are not in the range of $[0, 2^{16}-1]$; if attrIDs has duplicate values.

NullPointerException if attrIDs is null.

RuntimeException if this ServiceRecord describes a service on the local device rather than a service on a remote device.

setAttributeValue(int, DataElement)

```
public boolean setAttributeValue(int attrID,
    DataElement attrValue)
```

Modifies this ServiceRecord to contain the service attribute defined by the attribute-value pair (attrID, attrValue). If the attrID does not exist in the ServiceRecord, this attribute-value pair is added to this ServiceRecord object. If the attrID is already in this ServiceRecord, the value of the attribute is changed to attrValue. If attrValue is null, the attribute with the attribute ID of attrID is removed from this ServiceRecord object. If attrValue is null and attrID does not exist in this object, this method will return false.

This method makes no modifications to a service record in the SDDB. For any changes made by this method to be reflected in the SDDB, a call must be made to the acceptAndOpen() method of the associated notifier to add this ServiceRecord to the SDDB for the first time, or a call must be made to the updateRecord() method of LocalDevice to modify the version of this ServiceRecord that is already in the SDDB.

This method prevents the ServiceRecordHandle from being modified by throwing an IllegalArgumentException.

Parameters

attrID—the service attribute ID.

attrValue—the DataElement that is the value of the service attribute.

Returns

true if the service attribute was successfully added, removed, or modified; false if attrValue is null and attrID is not in this object.

Throws

IllegalArgumentException if attrID does not represent a 16-bit unsigned integer; if attrID is the value of ServiceRecordHandle (0x0000)

RuntimeException if this method is called on a ServiceRecord that was created by a call to DiscoveryAgent.searchServices().

setDeviceServiceClasses(int)

```
public void setDeviceServiceClasses(int classes)
```

Used by a server application to indicate the major service class bits that should be activated in the server's DeviceClass when this ServiceRecord is added to the SDDB. When client devices do device discovery, the server's DeviceClass is provided as one of the arguments of the deviceDiscovered() method of the DiscoveryListener interface. Client devices can consult the DeviceClass of the server device to get a general idea of the kind of device (e.g., phone, PDA, or PC) and the major service classes it offers (e.g., rendering, telephony, or information). A server application should use the setDeviceService-Classes() method to describe its service in terms of the major service classes. This allows clients to obtain a DeviceClass for the server that accurately describes all of the services being offered.

When acceptAndOpen() is invoked for the first time on the notifier associated with this ServiceRecord, the classes argument from the setDeviceServiceClasses() method is OR'ed with the current setting of the major service class bits of the local device. The OR operation potentially activates additional bits. These bits can be retrieved with a call to getDeviceClass() on the LocalDevice object. Likewise, a call to `LocalDevice.updateRecord()` causes the major service class bits to be OR'ed with the current settings and updated.

The documentation for `DeviceClass` gives examples of the integers that describe each of the major service classes and the Bluetooth Assigned Numbers [30] provide a complete list. These integers can be used individually or OR'ed together to describe the appropriate value for `classes`.

Later, when this `ServiceRecord` is removed from the SDDB, the implementation automatically deactivates the device bits activated as a result of the call to `setDeviceServiceClasses()`.

The only exception occurs if another `ServiceRecord` is in the SDDB, and `setDeviceServiceClasses()` has been sent to that other `ServiceRecord` to request that some of the same bits be activated.

Parameters

`classes`—an integer whose binary representation indicates the major service class bits that should be activated.

Throws

`IllegalArgumentException` if `classes` is not an OR of one or more of the major service class integers in the Bluetooth Assigned Numbers document. Although Limited Discoverable Mode is included in this list of major service classes, its bit is activated by placing the device in Limited Discoverable Mode (see the GAP specification), so if bit 13 is set, this exception will be thrown.

`RuntimeException` if the `ServiceRecord` receiving the message was obtained from a remote device.

javax.bluetooth

ServiceRegistrationException

Declaration

```
public class ServiceRegistrationException extends
        java.io.IOException
```

```
java.lang.Object
  |
  +-java.lang.Throwable
     |
     +-java.lang.Exception
        |
        +-java.io.IOException
           |
           +-javax.bluetooth.ServiceRegistration-
           Exception
```

Description

The ServiceRegistrationException is thrown when there is a failure to add a service record to the local SDDB or to modify an existing service record in the SDDB. The failure could occur because the SDDB has no room for new records or because the modification being attempted to a service record violates one of the rules about service record updates. This exception also is thrown if it is not possible to obtain an RFCOMM server channel needed for a btspp service record.

Constructors

ServiceRegistrationException()

```
public ServiceRegistrationException()
```

Creates a ServiceRegistrationException without a detailed message.

ServiceRegistrationException(String)

```
public ServiceRegistrationException(
    java.lang.String msg)
```

Creates a ServiceRegistrationException with a detailed message.

Parameters
msg—the reason for the exception.

javax.bluetooth

UUID

Declaration

```
public class UUID

java.lang.Object
  |
  +—javax.bluetooth.UUID
```

Description

The UUID class defines universally unique identifiers. These 128-bit unsigned integers are intended to be unique across all time and space. Accordingly, an instance of this class is immutable. The Bluetooth specification [1] provides an algorithm describing how a 16-bit or 32-bit UUID can be promoted to a 128-bit UUID. Accordingly, this class provides an interface that assists applications in creating 16-bit, 32-bit, and 128-bit long UUIDs. The methods supported by this class allow equality testing of two UUID objects.

Constructors

UUID(long)

```
public UUID(long uuidValue)
```

Creates a UUID object from long value uuidValue. A UUID is defined as an unsigned integer whose value can range from [0 to 2^{128}-1]. However, this constructor allows only those values that are in the range of [0 to 2^{32} -1]. Negative values and values in the range of [2^{32}, 2^{63} -1] are not allowed and will cause an IllegalArgumentException to be thrown.

Parameters

uuidValue—the 16-bit or 32-bit value of the UUID.

Throws

IllegalArgumentException—if uuidValue is not in the range $[0, 2^{32} -1]$.

UUID(String, boolean)

```
public UUID(java.lang.String uuidValue, boolean
    shortUUID)
```

Creates a UUID object from the string provided. The characters in the string must be from the hexadecimal set [0-9, a-f, A-F]. It is important to note that the prefix "0x" generally used for hex representation of numbers is not allowed. If the string has characters that are not from the hexadecimal set, an exception will be thrown. The string length has to be positive and less than or equal to 32. A string length that exceeds 32 is illegal and will cause an exception. A null input is also considered illegal and causes an exception.

If shortUUID is true, uuidValue represents a 16-bit or 32-bit UUID. If uuidValue is in the range 0x0000 to 0xFFFF, then this constructor will create a 16-bit UUID. If uuidValue is in the range 0x000010000 to 0xFFFFFFFF, then this constructor will create a 32-bit UUID. Therefore, uuidValue may only be 8 characters long.

On the other hand, if shortUUID is false, then uuidValue represents a 128-bit UUID. Therefore, uuidValue may only be 32 character long.

Parameters

uuidValue—the string representation of a 16-bit, 32-bit or 128-bit UUID
shortUUID—indicates the size of the UUID to be constructed; true is used to indicate short UUIDs, that is, either 16-bit or 32-bit; false indicates an 128-bit UUID.

Throws

NumberFormatException if uuidValue has characters that are not defined in the hexadecimal set [0-9, a-f, A-F].

IllegalArgumentException if uuidValue length is zero; if shortUUID is true and length of uuidValue is greater than 8; if shortUUID is false and length of uuidValueis greater than 32. NullPointerException if uuidValue is null.

Methods

equals(Object)

```
public boolean equals(java.lang.Object value)
```

Determines whether two UUIDs are equal. They are equal if their 128-bit values are the same. This method returns false if value is null or is not a UUID object.

Parameters

value—the object to compare to.

Returns

true if the 128-bit values of the two objects are equal; otherwise false.

hashCode()

```
public int hashCode()
```

Computes the hash code for this object. This method retains the same semantic contract as defined in the class java.lang.Object for hashCode() while overriding the implementation.

Returns

The hash code for this object.

toString()

```
public java.lang.String toString()
```

Returns the string representation of the 128-bit UUID object. The string being returned represents a UUID that contains characters from the hexadecimal set, [0-9, A-F]. It does not include the prefix "0x" that is generally used for hex representation of numbers. The return value never is `null`.

Returns

The string representation of the UUID.

APPENDIX

javax.obex API

This appendix contains the OBEX APIs defined by JABWT.

javax.obex

Authenticator

Declaration

```
public interface Authenticator
```

Description

This interface provides a way to respond to authentication challenge and authentication response headers. When an authentication challenge or authentication response header is received, the onAuthenticationChallenge() or onAuthenticationResponse() method is called by the implementation.

For more information on how the authentication procedure works in OBEX, review the IrOBEX specification [29].

Authentication Challenges

When a client or server receives an authentication challenge header, the onAuthenticationChallenge() method is invoked by the OBEX API implementation. The application then returns the user name (if needed) and password via a PasswordAuthentication object. The password in this object is not sent in the authentication response. Instead, the 16-byte challenge received in the authentication challenge is combined with the password returned from the onAuthentication-Challenge() method and passed through the MD5 hash algorithm. The resulting value is sent in the authentication response along with the user name if it has been provided.

Authentication Responses

When a client or server receives an authentication response header, the `onAuthenticationResponse()` method is invoked by the API implementation with the user name received in the authentication response header. (The user name is `null` if no user name is provided in the authentication response header.) The application must determine the correct password. This value should be returned from the `onAuthenticationResponse()` method. If the authentication request should fail, `null` should be returned by the application. (This step is needed for reasons such as not recognizing the user name.) If the returned value is not `null`, the OBEX API implementation combines the password returned from the `onAuthenticationResponse()` method and challenge sent via the authentication challenge, applies the MD5 hash algorithm, and compares the result with the response hash received in the authentication response header. If the values are not equal, an `IOException` is thrown if the client has requested authentication. If the server has requested authentication, the `onAuthenticationFailure()` method is called on the `ServerRequestHandler` that failed authentication. The connection is not closed if authentication fails.

Methods

onAuthenticationChallenge(String, boolean, boolean)

```
public PasswordAuthentication onAuthentication-
    Challenge(java.lang.String
    description, boolean isUserIdRequired,
    boolean isFullAccess)
```

Called when a client or a server receives an authentication challenge header. It should respond to the challenge with a `PasswordAuthentication` that contains the correct user name and password for the challenge.

Parameters

`description`—description of which user name and password should be used; if no description is provided in the authentication challenge or the description is encoded in an encoding scheme that is not supported, an empty string is provided.

isUserIdRequired—`true` if the user ID is required; `false` if the user ID is not required.

isFullAccess—`true` if full access to the server will be granted; `false` if read only access will be granted.

Returns

A `PasswordAuthentication` object containing the user name and password used for authentication

onAuthenticationResponse(byte[])

```
public byte[] onAuthenticationResponse(byte[]
        userName)
```

Called when a client or server receives an authentication response header. This method provides the user name and expects the correct password to be returned.

Parameters

userName—the user name provided in the authentication response; can be `null`.

Returns

The correct password for the user name provided; if `null` is returned, the authentication request has failed.

javax.obex

ClientSession

Declaration

```
public interface ClientSession extends
        javax.microedition.io.Connection
```

Description

The `ClientSession` interface provides methods for OBEX requests. This interface provides a way to define headers for any OBEX operation.

OBEX operations are CONNECT, SETPATH, PUT, GET, and DISCONNECT. For PUTs and GETs, this interface returns a `javax.obex.Operation` object to complete the operations. For CONNECT, DISCONNECT, and SETPATH operations, this interface completes the operation and returns the result in a `HeaderSet` object.

Connection ID and Target Headers

According to the IrOBEX specification, a packet cannot contain both a Connection ID and a Target header. Because the Connection ID header is managed by the implementation, it does not send a Connection ID header if a Connection ID is specified in a packet that has a Target header. In other words, if an application adds a Target header to a `HeaderSet` object used in an OBEX operation and a Connection ID has been specified, no Connection ID is sent in the packet containing the Target header.

CREATE-EMPTY and PUT-DELETE Requests

To perform a CREATE-EMPTY request, the client must call the `put()` method. With the `Operation` object returned, the client must open the output stream by calling `openOutputStream()` and then close the stream by calling `close()` on the `OutputStream` without writing any data. Using the `DataOutputStream` returned from `openData-OutputStream()` works the same way.

There are two ways to perform a PUT-DELETE request. The `delete()` method is one way. The second way to is to call `put()` and never call `openOutputStream()` or `openDataOutputStream()` on the `Operation` object returned from `put()`.

PUT Example

```
void putObjectViaOBEX(ClientSession conn, HeaderSet
       head, byte[] obj) throws IOException {
   // Include the length header
   head.setHeader(HeaderSet.LENGTH, new
                  Long(obj.length));
   // Initiate the PUT request
```

```
        Operation op = conn.put(head);
        // Open the output stream to put the object to it
        OutputStream out = op.openOutputStream();
        // Send the object to the server
        out.write(obj);
        // End the transaction
        out.close();
        op.close();
    }
```

GET Example

```
byte[] getObjectViaOBEX(ClientSession conn,
        HeaderSet head) throws IOException {
    // Send the initial GET request to the server
    Operation op = conn.get(head);
    // Get the object from the input stream
    InputStream in = op.openInputStream();
    ByteArrayOutputStream out = new
            ByteArrayOutputStream();
    int data = in.read();
    while (data != -1) {
      out.write((byte)data);
      data = in.read();
    }
    // End the transaction
    in.close();
    op.close();
    byte[] obj = out.toByteArray();
    out.close();
    return obj;
}
```

Methods

connect(HeaderSet)

```
public HeaderSet connect(HeaderSet headers) throws
        IOException
```

Completes an OBEX CONNECT operation. If the `headers` argument is null, no headers are sent in the request. This method never returns null.

This method must be called and a successful response code of `OBEX_HTTP_OK` must be received before `put()`, `get()`, `setPath()`, `delete()`, or `disconnect()` can be called. Similarly, after a successful call to `disconnect()`, this method must be called before `put()`, `get()`, `setPath()`, `delete()`, or `disconnect()` is called.

Parameters
`headers`—the headers to send in the CONNECT request.

Returns
The headers that were returned from the server.

Throws
`IOException` if an error occurred in the transport layer; if the client is already in an operation; if this method had already been called with a successful response code of `OBEX_HTTP_OK` and calls to `disconnect()` have not returned a response code of `OBEX_HTTP_OK`; if the headers defined in `headers` exceed the maximum packet length.
`IllegalArgumentException` if `headers` was not created by a call to `createHeaderSet()`.

createHeaderSet()

```
public HeaderSet createHeaderSet()
```

Creates a `javax.obex.HeaderSet` object. This object can be used to define header values in a request.

Returns
A new `javax.obex.HeaderSet` object.

delete(HeaderSet)

```
public HeaderSet delete(HeaderSet headers) throws
    IOException
```

Performs an OBEX DELETE operation. This method never returns `null`.

Parameters
`headers`—the header to send in the DELETE request.

Returns
The headers returned by the server.

Throws
`IOException` if an error occurred in the transport layer; if the client is already in an operation; if an OBEX connection does not exist because `connect()` has not been called; if `disconnect()` had been called and a response code of `OBEX_HTTP_OK` has been received; if the headers defined in `headers` exceed the maximum packet length.
`IllegalArgumentException` if `headers` are not created by a call to `createHeaderSet()`.

disconnect(HeaderSet)

```
public HeaderSet disconnect(HeaderSet headers)
    throws IOException
```

Completes an OBEX DISCONNECT operation. If the `headers` argument is `null`, no headers are sent in the request. This method ends the session. A new session can be started by calling `connect()`. This method never returns `null`.

Parameters
`headers`—the header to send in the DISCONNECT request.

Returns
The headers returned by the server.

Throws
`IOException` if an error occurred in the transport layer; if the client is already in an operation; if an OBEX connection does not exist because `connect()` has not been called; if `disconnect()` has been called and

received a response code of `OBEX_HTTP_OK` after the last call to `connect()`; if the headers defined in `headers` exceed the maximum packet length.
`IllegalArgumentException` if `headers` are not created by a call to `createHeaderSet()`.

get(HeaderSet)

```
public Operation get(HeaderSet headers) throws
     IOException
```

Performs an OBEX GET operation. This method sends the OBEX headers provided to the server and returns an `Operation` object to continue with the operation. This method never returns `null`.

Parameters

`headers`—the OBEX headers to send as part of the initial GET request.

Returns

The OBEX operation used to complete the GET request.

Throws

`IOException` if an error occurred in the transport layer; if an OBEX connection does not exist because `connect()` has not been called; if `disconnect()` has been called and a response code of `OBEX_HTTP_OK` is received; if `connect()` has not been called; if the client is already in an operation.
`IllegalArgumentException` if `headers` are not created by a call to `createHeaderSet()`.

getConnectionID()

```
public long getConnectionID()
```

Retrieves the connection ID being used in the present connection. This method returns –1 if no connection ID is being used.

Returns

The connection ID being used or –1 if no connection ID is being used.

put(HeaderSet)

```
public Operation put(HeaderSet headers) throws
    IOException
```

Performs an OBEX PUT operation. This method sends the OBEX headers provided to the server and returns an `Operation` object to continue with the PUT operation. This method never returns `null`.

Parameters

`headers`—the OBEX headers to send in the initial PUT request.

Returns

The operation object used to complete the PUT request.

Throws

`IOException` if an error occurred in the transport layer; if an OBEX connection does not exist because `connect()` has not been called; if `disconnect()` has been called and a response code of `OBEX_HTTP_OK` was received; if `connect()` has not been called; if the client is already in an operation.

`IllegalArgumentException` if `headers` are not created by a call to `createHeaderSet()`.

setAuthenticator(Authenticator)

```
public void setAuthenticator(Authenticator auth)
```

Sets the `Authenticator` to use with this connection. The `Authenticator` allows an application to respond to authentication challenge and authentication response headers. If no `Authenticator` is set, the response to an authentication challenge or authentication response header is implementation dependent.

Parameters

auth—the `Authenticator` to use for this connection.

Throws

`NullPointerException` if auth is `null`.

setConnectionID(long)

```
public void setConnectionID(long id)
```

Sets the connection ID header to include in the request packets. If set, a connection ID is sent in each request to the server except for the CONNECT request. An application needs to set the connection ID only if it is trying to operate with different targets over the same transport layer connection. If a client receives a connection ID from the server, the implementation continues to use that connection ID until the application changes it or until the connection is closed.

Parameters

id—the connection ID to use.

Throws

`IllegalArgumentException` if id is not in the range 0 to 2^{32}-1.

setPath(HeaderSet, boolean, boolean)

```
public HeaderSet setPath(HeaderSet headers, boolean
   backup, boolean create) throws IOException
```

Completes an OBEX SETPATH operation. This method never returns `null`.

Parameters

backup—if `true`, instructs the server to back up one directory before moving to the directory specified in name (similar to cd .. on PCs); if `false`, apply name to the current directory.

create—if `true`, instructs the server to create the directory if it does not exist; if `false`, instructs the server to return an error code if the directory does not exist.

`headers`—the headers to include in the SETPATH request.

Returns

The headers that were returned from the server.

Throws

`IOException`—if an error occurred in the transport layer; if the client is already in an operation; if an OBEX connection does not exist because `connect()` has not been called; if `disconnect()` had been called and a response code of `OBEX_HTTP_OK` was received; if the headers defined in `headers` exceed the maximum packet length.

`IllegalArgumentException` if `headers` are not created by a call to `createHeaderSet()`.

javax.obex

HeaderSet

Declaration

```
public interface HeaderSet
```

Description

The `HeaderSet` interface defines the methods that set and get the values of OBEX headers.

The following table describes how the headers specified in this interface are represented in OBEX and in Java types. The Java types are used with the `setHeader()` and `getHeader()` methods and specify the type of object that must be provided and will be returned from these methods, respectively.

The `APPLICATION_PARAMETER` header requires additional explanation. The byte array provided with the `APPLICATION_PARAMETER` should be of the form Tag-Length-Value according to the OBEX specification, where Tag is 1 byte long, Length is 1 byte long, and Value is up to 255 bytes long. Multiple Tag-Length-Value triples are allowed within a single `APPLICATION_PARAMETER` header. The implementation

Header Values	OBEX Representation	Java Type
COUNT	4-byte unsigned integer	java.lang.Long in the range 0 to 2^{32}-1
NAME	Unicode string	java.lang.String
TYPE	ASCII string	java.lang.String
LENGTH	4-byte unsigned integer	java.lang.Long in the range 0 to 2^{32}-1
TIME_ISO_8601	ASCII string of the form YYYYMMDDTHHMMSS[Z] where [Z] specifies Zulu time	java.util.Calendar
TIME_4_BYTE	4 byte unsigned integer	java.util.Calendar
DESCRIPTION	Unicode string	java.lang.String
TARGET	byte sequence	byte[]
HTTP	byte sequence	byte[]
WHO	byte sequence	byte[]
OBJECT_CLASS	byte sequence	byte[]
APPLICATION_PARAMETER	byte sequence	byte[]

does *not* check this condition. It is mentioned only to allow for interoperability between OBEX implementations.

User Defined Headers

OBEX allows 64 user-defined header values. Depending on the header identifier provided, headers have different types. The table below defines the ranges and their types.

Header Identifier	Decimal Range	OBEX Type	Java Type
0x30 to 0x3F	48 to 63	Unicode String	java.lang.String
0x70 to 0x7F	112 to 127	byte sequence	byte[]
0xB0 to 0xBF	176 to 191	1 byte	java.lang.Byte
0xF0 to 0xFF	240 to 255	4-byte unsigned integer	java.lang.Long in the range 0 to 2^{32}-1

Fields

APPLICATION_PARAMETER

```
public static final int APPLICATION_PARAMETER
```

Represents the OBEX Application Parameter header. This header specifies additional application request and response information.

COUNT

```
public static final int COUNT
```

Represents the OBEX Count header. Allows the connection statement to tell the server how many objects it plans to send or retrieve.

DESCRIPTION

```
public static final int DESCRIPTION
```

Represents the OBEX Description header. A text description of the object.

HTTP

```
public static final int HTTP
```

Represents the OBEX HTTP header. Allows an HTTP 1.X header to be included in a request or reply.

LENGTH

```
public static final int LENGTH
```

Represents the OBEX Length header. Length of the object in bytes.

NAME

```
public static final int NAME
```

Represents the OBEX Name header. Specifies the name of the object.

OBJECT_CLASS

```
public static final int OBJECT_CLASS
```

Represents the OBEX Object Class header. Specifies the OBEX object class of the object.

TARGET

```
public static final int TARGET
```

Represents the OBEX Target header. Name of the service targeted by the operation.

TIME_4_BYTE

```
public static final int TIME_4_BYTE
```

Represents the OBEX Time header by means of a 4-byte representation. Included only for backward compatibility. Represents the number of seconds since January 1, 1970.

TIME_ISO_8601

```
public static final int TIME_ISO_8601
```

Represents the OBEX Time header by means of the ISO 8601 standard. Preferred time header.

TYPE

```
public static final int TYPE
```

Represents the OBEX Type header. Allows a request to specify the type of object (e.g., text, html, binary).

WHO

```
public static final int WHO
```

Represents the OBEX Who header. Identifies the OBEX application to determine whether the two peers are talking to each other.

Methods

createAuthenticationChallenge(String, boolean, boolean)

```
public void createAuthenticationChallenge-
    (java.lang.String realm, boolean
    userID,boolean access)
```

Sets the authentication challenge header. The `realm` is encoded on the basis of the default encoding scheme used by the implementation to encode strings. Therefore the encoding scheme used to encode the `realm` is implementation dependent.

Parameters

`realm`—a short description of the password to use; if `null`, no realm is sent in the authentication challenge header.
`userID`—if `true`, a user ID is required in the reply; if `false`, no user ID is required.
`access`—if `true`, then full access is granted if successful; if `false`, then read-only access is granted if successful.

getHeader(int)

```
public java.lang.Object getHeader(int headerID)
    throws IOException
```

Retrieves the value of the header identifier provided. The type of the `Object` returned is defined in the tables shown previously.

Parameters

`headerID`—the header identifier whose value is to be returned.

Returns

The value of the header provided; `null` if the header identifier specified is not part of this `HeaderSet` object.

Throws

`IllegalArgumentException` if the `headerID` is not one defined in this interface or any of the user-defined headers.
`IOException` if an error occurs in the transport layer during the operation or if the connection has been closed.

getHeaderList()

```
public int[] getHeaderList() throws IOException
```

Retrieves the list of headers that may be retrieved via the `getHeader` method that will not return `null`. In other words, this method returns all the headers available in this object.

Returns

The array of headers set in this object; `null` if no headers are available.

Throws

`IOException` if an error occurs in the transport layer during the operation or the connection has been closed.

getResponseCode()

```
public int getResponseCode() throws IOException
```

Returns the response code received from the server. Response codes are defined in the `ResponseCodes` class.

Returns

The response code retrieved from the server.

Throws

`IOException` if an error occurs in the transport layer during the transaction; if this method is called on a `HeaderSet` object created by calling `createHeaderSet()` in a `ClientSession` object; if an OBEX server created this object.

setHeader(int, Object)

```
public void setHeader(int headerID,
        java.lang.Object headerValue)
```

Sets the value of the header identifier to the value provided. The type of `headerValue` must correspond to the Java type defined in the description of this interface. If `null` is passed as the `headerValue`, the header is removed from the set of headers to be included in the next request.

Parameters

`headerID`—the identifier to include in the message.

`headerValue`—the value of the header identifier.

Throws

`IllegalArgumentException` if the header identifier provided is not one defined in this interface or a user-defined header; if the type of `headerValue` is not the correct Java type as defined in the tables shown previously.

javax.obex

Operation

Declaration

```
public interface Operation extends javax.microedi-
        tion.io.ContentConnection
```

Description

The `Operation` interface provides ways to manipulate a single OBEX PUT or GET operation. The implementation of this interface sends OBEX packets as they are built. If during the operation the peer in the operation ends the operation, an `IOException` is thrown on the next read from the input stream, write to the output stream, or call to `sendHeaders()`.

Definition of Methods Inherited from `ContentConnection`

`getEncoding()` always returns `null`.
`getLength()` returns the length specified by the OBEX Length header or –1 if the OBEX Length header was not included.
`getType()` returns the value specified in the OBEX Type header or `null` if the OBEX Type header is not included.

How Headers Are Handled

As headers are received, they can be retrieved through the `getReceivedHeaders()` method. If new headers are set during the operation, the new headers are sent during the next packet exchange.

PUT Example

```
void putObjectViaOBEX(ClientSession conn, HeaderSet
        head, byte[] obj) throws IOException {
    // Include the length header
    head.setHeader(head.LENGTH, new
            Long(obj.length));
    // Initiate the PUT request
    Operation op = conn.put(head);
    // Open the output stream to put the object to
    // it
    DataOutputStream out = op.openDataOutputStream();

    // Send the object to the server
    out.write(obj);
    // End the transaction
    out.close();
    op.close();
}
```

GET Example

```
byte[] getObjectViaOBEX(ClientSession conn,
        HeaderSet head) throws IOException {
    // Send the initial GET request to the server
    Operation op = conn.get(head);
    // Retrieve the length of the object being sent
    // back
    int length = op.getLength();
    // Create space for the object
    byte[] obj = new byte[length];
    // Get the object from the input stream
    DataInputStream in = trans.openDataInputStream();
    in.read(obj);
```

```
        // End the transaction
        in.close();
        op.close();
        return obj;
    }
```

Client PUT Operation Flow

For PUT operations, a call to `close()` the `OutputStream` returned from `openOutputStream()` or `openDataOutputStream()` signals that the request is done. (In OBEX terms, the END-OF-BODY header should be sent and the final bit in the request is set.) At this point, the reply from the server may begin to be processed. A call to `getResponseCode()` does an implicit close on the `OutputStream` and therefore signals that the request is complete.

Client GET Operation Flow

For GET operation, a call to `openInputStream()` or `openDataInputStream()` signals that the request is complete. (In OBEX terms, the final bit in the request is set.) A call to `getResponseCode()` causes an implicit close on the `InputStream`. No additional data can be read at this point.

Methods

abort()

```
    public void abort() throws IOException
```

Sends an ABORT message to the server. When this method is called, the corresponding input and output streams are closed along with this object. No headers are sent in the abort request. This procedure ends the operation because `close()` is called by this method.

Throws
`IOException` if the transaction has already ended or if an OBEX server calls this method.

getReceivedHeaders()

```
public HeaderSet getReceivedHeaders() throws
    IOException
```

Returns the headers received during the operation. Modifying the object returned has no effect on the headers sent or retrieved.

Returns
The headers received during this `Operation`.

Throws
`IOException` if this `Operation` has been closed.

getResponseCode()

```
public int getResponseCode() throws IOException
```

Returns the response code received from the server. Response codes are defined in the `ResponseCodes` class.

Returns
The response code retrieved from the server.

Throws
`IOException` if an error occurs in the transport layer during the transaction; if this object was created by an OBEX server.

sendHeaders(HeaderSet)

```
public void sendHeaders(HeaderSet headers) throws
    IOException
```

Specifies the headers that should be sent in the next OBEX message sent.

Parameters
`headers`—the headers to send in the next message.

Throws

`IOException` if this `Operation` has been closed or the transaction has ended and no further messages will be exchanged.

`IllegalArgumentException` if `headers` is not created by a call to `ServerRequestHandler.createHeaderSet()` or `ClientSession.-createHeaderSet()`

`NullPointerException` if `headers` is null.

javax.obex

PasswordAuthentication

Declaration

```
public class PasswordAuthentication
java.lang.Object
 |
 +—javax.obex.PasswordAuthentication
```

Description

This class holds a user name and a password.

Constructors

PasswordAuthentication(byte[], byte[])

```
public PasswordAuthentication(byte[] userName,
     byte[] password)
```

Creates a new `PasswordAuthentication` with the user name and password provided.

Parameters

`userName`—the user name to include; this can be null.
`password`—the password to include in the response.

Throws

`NullPointerException` if `password` is null.

Methods

getPassword()

```
public byte[] getPassword()
```

Retrieves the password.

Returns
The password.

getUserName()

```
public byte[] getUserName()
```

Retrieves the user name that was specified in the constructor. The user name can be `null`.

Returns
The user name.

javax.obex
ResponseCodes

Declaration

```
public class ResponseCodes

java.lang.Object
 |
 +-javax.obex.ResponseCodes
```

Description

The `ResponseCodes` class contains the list of valid response codes a server may send to a client.

Important Note

The values of these constants are different from those defined in `javax.microedition.io.HttpConnection`. The values in this class represent the values defined in the IrOBEX specification [29]. The values in `javax.microedition.io.HttpConnection` represent values defined in the HTTP specification.

`OBEX_DATABASE_FULL` and `OBEX_DATABASE_LOCKED` require further description because they are not defined in HTTP. The server sends an `OBEX_DATABASE_FULL` message when the client requests that something be placed into a database but the database is full (cannot take more data).

`OBEX_DATABASE_LOCKED` is returned when the client wants to access a database, database table, or database record that has been locked.

Fields

OBEX_DATABASE_FULL

```
public static final int OBEX_DATABASE_FULL
```

Defines the OBEX DATABASE FULL response code.

OBEX_DATABASE_LOCKED

```
public static final int OBEX_DATABASE_LOCKED
```

Defines the OBEX DATABASE LOCKED response code.

OBEX_HTTP_ACCEPTED

```
public static final int OBEX_HTTP_ACCEPTED
```

Defines the OBEX ACCEPTED response code.

OBEX_HTTP_BAD_GATEWAY

```
public static final int OBEX_HTTP_BAD_GATEWAY
```

Defines the OBEX BAD GATEWAY response code.

OBEX_HTTP_BAD_METHOD

```
public static final int OBEX_HTTP_BAD_METHOD
```

Defines the OBEX METHOD NOT ALLOWED response code.

OBEX_HTTP_BAD_REQUEST

```
public static final int OBEX_HTTP_BAD_REQUEST
```

Defines the OBEX BAD REQUEST response code.

OBEX_HTTP_CONFLICT

```
public static final int OBEX_HTTP_CONFLICT
```

Defines the OBEX METHOD CONFLICT response code.

OBEX_HTTP_CREATED

```
public static final int OBEX_HTTP_CREATED
```

Defines the OBEX CREATED response code.

OBEX_HTTP_ENTITY_TOO_LARGE

```
public static final int OBEX_HTTP_ENTITY_TOO_LARGE
```

Defines the OBEX REQUESTED ENTITY TOO LARGE response code.

OBEX_HTTP_FORBIDDEN

```
public static final int OBEX_HTTP_FORBIDDEN
```

Defines the OBEX FORBIDDEN response code.

OBEX_HTTP_GATEWAY_TIMEOUT

```
public static final int OBEX_HTTP_GATEWAY_TIMEOUT
```

Defines the OBEX GATEWAY TIMEOUT response code.

OBEX_HTTP_GONE

```
public static final int OBEX_HTTP_GONE
```

Defines the OBEX METHOD GONE response code.

OBEX_HTTP_INTERNAL_ERROR

```
public static final int OBEX_HTTP_INTERNAL_ERROR
```

Defines the OBEX INTERNAL SERVER ERROR response code.

OBEX_HTTP_LENGTH_REQUIRED

```
public static final int OBEX_HTTP_LENGTH_REQUIRED
```
Defines the OBEX METHOD LENGTH REQUIRED response code.

OBEX_HTTP_MOVED_PERM

```
public static final int OBEX_HTTP_MOVED_PERM
```
Defines the OBEX MOVED PERMANENTLY response code.

OBEX_HTTP_MOVED_TEMP

```
public static final int OBEX_HTTP_MOVED_TEMP
```
Defines the OBEX MOVED TEMPORARILY response code.

OBEX_HTTP_MULT_CHOICE

```
public static final int OBEX_HTTP_MULT_CHOICE
```
Defines the OBEX MULTIPLE_CHOICES response code.

OBEX_HTTP_NO_CONTENT

```
public static final int OBEX_HTTP_NO_CONTENT
```
Defines the OBEX NO CONTENT response code.

OBEX_HTTP_NOT_ACCEPTABLE

```
public static final int OBEX_HTTP_NOT_ACCEPTABLE
```
Defines the OBEX NOT ACCEPTABLE response code.

OBEX_HTTP_NOT_AUTHORITATIVE

```
public static final int OBEX_HTTP_NOT_AUTHORITATIVE
```
Defines the OBEX NON-AUTHORITATIVE INFORMATION response code.

OBEX_HTTP_NOT_FOUND

```
public static final int OBEX_HTTP_NOT_FOUND
```

Defines the OBEX NOT FOUND response code.

OBEX_HTTP_NOT_IMPLEMENTED

```
public static final int OBEX_HTTP_NOT_IMPLEMENTED
```

Defines the OBEX NOT IMPLEMENTED response code.

OBEX_HTTP_NOT_MODIFIED

```
public static final int OBEX_HTTP_NOT_MODIFIED
```

Defines the OBEX NOT MODIFIED response code.

OBEX_HTTP_OK

```
public static final int OBEX_HTTP_OK
```

Defines the OBEX SUCCESS response code.

OBEX_HTTP_PARTIAL

```
public static final int OBEX_HTTP_PARTIAL
```

Defines the OBEX PARTIAL CONTENT response code.

OBEX_HTTP_PAYMENT_REQUIRED

```
public static final int OBEX_HTTP_PAYMENT_REQUIRED
```

Defines the OBEX PAYMENT REQUIRED response code.

OBEX_HTTP_PRECON_FAILED

```
public static final int OBEX_HTTP_PRECON_FAILED
```

Defines the OBEX PRECONDITION FAILED response code.

OBEX_HTTP_PROXY_AUTH

```
public static final int OBEX_HTTP_PROXY_AUTH
```

Defines the OBEX PROXY AUTHENTICATION REQUIRED response code.

OBEX_HTTP_REQ_TOO_LARGE

```
public static final int OBEX_HTTP_REQ_TOO_LARGE
```

Defines the OBEX REQUESTED URL TOO LARGE response code.

OBEX_HTTP_RESET

```
public static final int OBEX_HTTP_RESET
```

Defines the OBEX RESET CONTENT response code.

OBEX_HTTP_SEE_OTHER

```
public static final int OBEX_HTTP_SEE_OTHER
```

Defines the OBEX SEE OTHER response code.

OBEX_HTTP_TIMEOUT

```
public static final int OBEX_HTTP_TIMEOUT
```

Defines the OBEX REQUEST TIME OUT response code.

OBEX_HTTP_UNAUTHORIZED

```
public static final int OBEX_HTTP_UNAUTHORIZED
```

Defines the OBEX UNAUTHORIZED response code.

OBEX_HTTP_UNAVAILABLE

```
public static final int OBEX_HTTP_UNAVAILABLE
```

Defines the OBEX SERVICE UNAVAILABLE response code.

OBEX_HTTP_UNSUPPORTED_TYPE

```
public static final int OBEX_HTTP_UNSUPPORTED_TYPE
```

Defines the OBEX UNSUPPORTED MEDIA TYPE response code.

OBEX_HTTP_USE_PROXY

```
public static final int OBEX_HTTP_USE_PROXY
```

Defines the OBEX USE PROXY response code.

OBEX_HTTP_VERSION

```
public static final int OBEX_HTTP_VERSION
```

Defines the OBEX HTTP VERSION NOT SUPPORTED response code.

javax.obex

ServerRequestHandler

Declaration

```
public class ServerRequestHandler

java.lang.Object
|
+—javax.obex.ServerRequestHandler
```

Description

The `ServerRequestHandler` class defines an event listener that responds to OBEX requests made to the server.

The `onConnect()`, `onSetPath()`, `onDelete()`, `onGet()`, and `onPut()` methods may return any response code defined in the `ResponseCodes` class. If a value not defined in the `Response-Codes` class is returned, the server implementation sends an `OBEX_HTTP_INTERNAL_ERROR` response to the client.

Connection ID and Target Headers

According to the IrOBEX specification, a packet cannot contain a Connection ID and a Target header. Because it is managed by the implementation, the Connection ID header will not send a Connection ID header, if a Connection ID was specified, in a packet that has a Target header. In other words, if an application adds a Target header to a

`HeaderSet` object used in an OBEX operation and a Connection ID is specified, no Connection ID will be sent in the packet containing the Target header.

CREATE-EMPTY Requests

A CREATE-EMPTY request allows clients to create empty objects on the server. When a CREATE-EMPTY request is received, the `onPut()` method is called by the implementation. To differentiate a normal PUT request and a CREATE-EMPTY request, an application must open the `InputStream` from the `Operation` object passed to the `onPut()` method. For a PUT request, the application is able to read Body data from this `InputStream`. For a CREATE-EMPTY request, there is no Body data to read. Therefore a call to `InputStream.read()` returns –1.

Constructor

ServerRequestHandler()

```
protected ServerRequestHandler()
```

Creates a ServerRequestHandler. Because the constructor is protected, an instance is obtained by defining a subclass.

Methods

createHeaderSet()

```
public final HeaderSet createHeaderSet()
```

Creates a `HeaderSet` object that may be used in PUT and GET operations.

Returns
The `HeaderSet` object to use in PUT and GET operations.

getConnectionID()

```
public long getConnectionID()
```

Retrieves the connection ID used in the present connection. This method returns –1 if no connection ID is being used.

Returns

The connection ID being used or –1 if no connection ID is being used.

onAuthenticationFailure(byte[])

```
public void onAuthenticationFailure(byte[] userName)
```

Called when this object attempts to authenticate a client and the authentication request fails because the response digest in the authentication response header is wrong.

If this method is not implemented by the class that extends this class, this method does nothing.

Parameters

userName—the user name returned in the authentication response; null if no user name is provided in the response.

onConnect(HeaderSet, HeaderSet)

```
public int onConnect(HeaderSet request, HeaderSet
    reply)
```

Called when a CONNECT request is received.

If this method is not implemented by the class that extends this class, onConnect() always returns an OBEX_HTTP_OK response code.

The headers received in the request can be retrieved from the request argument. The headers that should be sent in the reply must be specified in the reply argument.

Parameters

request—contains the headers sent by the client; request never is null.
reply—the headers that should be sent in the reply; reply never is null.

Returns

A response code defined in ResponseCodes that will be returned to the client; if an invalid response code is provided, the OBEX_HTTP_INTER-NAL_ERROR response code is used.

onDelete(HeaderSet, HeaderSet)

```
public int onDelete(HeaderSet request, HeaderSet
    reply)
```

Called when a DELETE request is received.

If this method is not implemented by the class that extends this class, `onDelete()` always returns an `OBEX_HTTP_NOT_IMPLEMENTED` response code.

The headers received in the request can be retrieved from the `request` argument. The headers that should be sent in the reply must be specified in the `reply` argument.

Parameters

`request`—contains the headers sent by the client; `request` never is null

`reply`—the headers that should be sent in the reply; `reply` never is null.

Returns

A response code defined in `ResponseCodes` that will be returned to the client; if an invalid response code is provided, the `OBEX_HTTP_INTERNAL_ERROR` response code is used.

onDisconnect(HeaderSet, HeaderSet)

```
public void onDisconnect(HeaderSet request,
    HeaderSet reply)
```

Called when a DISCONNECT request is received.

The headers received in the request can be retrieved from the `request` argument. The headers that should be sent in the reply must be specified in the `reply` argument.

Parameters

`request`—contains the headers sent by the client; `request` never is null.

`reply`—the headers that should be sent in the reply; `reply` never is null.

onGet(Operation)

```
public int onGet(Operation op)
```

Called when a GET request is received.

If this method is not implemented by the class that extends this class, onGet() returns an OBEX_HTTP_NOT_IMPLEMENTED response code.

If an ABORT request is received during the processing of a GET request, op is closed by the implementation.

Parameters

op—contains the headers sent by the client and allows new headers to be sent in the reply; op never is null.

Returns

A response code defined in ResponseCodes that will be returned to the client; if an invalid response code is provided, the OBEX_HTTP_INTERNAL_ERROR response code is used.

onPut(Operation)

```
public int onPut(Operation op)
```

Called when a PUT request is received.

If this method is not implemented by the class that extends this class, onPut() always returns an OBEX_HTTP_NOT_IMPLEMENTED response code.

If an ABORT request is received during the processing of a PUT request, op is closed by the implementation.

Parameters

op—contains the headers sent by the client and allows new headers to be sent in the reply; op never is null.

Returns

A response code defined in ResponseCodes that will be returned to the client; if an invalid response code is provided, the OBEX_HTTP_INTERNAL_ERROR response code is used.

onSetPath(HeaderSet, HeaderSet, boolean, boolean)

```
public int onSetPath(HeaderSet request, HeaderSet
        reply, boolean backup, boolean create)
```

Called when a SETPATH request is received. If this method is not implemented by the class that extends this class, onSetPath() will always return an OBEX_HTTP_NOT_IMPLEMENTED response code.

The headers received in the request can be retrieved from the request argument. The headers that should be sent in the reply must be specified in the reply argument.

Parameters

request—contains the headers sent by the client; request never is null.

reply—the headers that should be sent in the reply; reply never is null.

backup—true if the client requests that the server back up one directory before changing to the path described by name; false to apply the request to the present path.

create—true if the path should be created if it does not already exist; false if the path should not be created if it does not exist.

Returns

A response code defined in ResponseCodes that will be returned to the client; if an invalid response code is provided, the OBEX_HTTP_INTERNAL_ERROR response code is used.

setConnectionID(long)

```
public void setConnectionID(long id)
```

Sets the connection ID header to include in the reply packets.

Parameters

id—the connection ID to use; −1 if no connection ID should be sent.

Throws

IllegalArgumentException if id is not in the range −1 to 2^{32}−1.

javax.obex

SessionNotifier

Declaration

```
public interface SessionNotifier extends
        javax.microedition.io.Connection
```

Description

The `SessionNotifier` interface defines a connection notifier for server-side OBEX connections. When it is created and calls `acceptAndOpen()`, the `SessionNotifier` begins listening for clients to create a connection at the transport layer. When the transport layer connection is received, the `acceptAndOpen()` method returns a `javax.microedition.io.Connection`, which is the connection to the client. The `acceptAndOpen()` method also takes a `ServerRequestHandler` argument that will process the requests from the client that connects to the server.

Methods

acceptAndOpen(ServerRequestHandler)

```
public javax.microedition.io.Connection
        acceptAndOpen(ServerRequestHandler handler)
        throws IOException
```

Waits for a transport layer connection to be established and specifies the handler to handle the requests from the client. No authenticator is associated with this connection; therefore it is implementation dependent as to how an authentication challenge and authentication response header are received and processed.

Additional Note for OBEX over Bluetooth
If this method is called on a `SessionNotifier` object that does not have a `ServiceRecord` in the SDDB, the `ServiceRecord` for this

object is added to the SDDB. This method requests that the BCC put the local device in connectable mode so that it will respond to connection attempts by clients.

The following checks are done to verify that the service record provided is valid. If any of these checks fails, a `ServiceRegistration-Exception` is thrown.

- ServiceClassIDList and ProtocolDescriptorList, the mandatory service attributes for a `btgoep` service record, must be present in the `ServiceRecord` associated with this notifier.

- L2CAP, RFCOMM, and OBEX all must be in the Protocol-DescriptorList.

- The `ServiceRecord` associated with this notifier must not have changed the RFCOMM server channel number.

This method does not ensure that the `ServiceRecord` associated with this notifier is a completely valid service record. It is the responsibility of the application to ensure that the service record follows all of the applicable syntactic and semantic rules for service record correctness.

Parameters
`handler`—the request handler that will respond to OBEX requests.

Returns
The connection to the client.

Throws
`IOException` if an error occurs in the transport layer.
`NullPointerException` if `handler` is null.
`ServiceRegistrationException` if the structure of the associated service record is invalid or if the service record cannot be added successfully to the local SDDB. The structure of service record is invalid if the service record is missing any mandatory service attributes or has changed any of the values described above, which are fixed and cannot be changed. Failure to add the record to the SDDB can be caused by factors such as insufficient disk space and database locks.

`BluetoothStateException` if the server device cannot be placed in connectable mode because the device user has configured the device to be non-connectable.

acceptAndOpen(ServerRequestHandler, Authenticator)

```
public javax.microedition.io.Connection
      acceptAndOpen(ServerRequestHandler handler,
      Authenticator auth) throws IOException
```

Waits for a transport layer connection to be established and specifies the handler to handle the requests from the client and the `Authenticator` to use to respond to authentication challenge and authentication response headers.

Additional Note for OBEX over Bluetooth

If this method is called on a `SessionNotifier` object that does not have a `ServiceRecord` in the SDDB, the `ServiceRecord` for this object is added to the SDDB. This method requests the BCC to put the local device in connectable mode so that it will respond to connection attempts by clients.

The following checks are done to verify that the service record provided is valid. If any of these checks fails, a `ServiceRegistration-Exception` is thrown.

- ServiceClassIDList and ProtocolDescriptorList, the mandatory service attributes for a `btgoep` service record, must be present in the `ServiceRecord` associated with this notifier.

- L2CAP, RFCOMM, and OBEX must all be in the Protocol-DescriptorList.

- The `ServiceRecord` associated with this notifier must not have changed the RFCOMM server channel number.

This method does not ensure that the `ServiceRecord` associated with this notifier is a completely valid service record. It is the responsibility of the application to ensure that the service record follows all of the applicable syntactic and semantic rules for service record correctness.

Parameters

`handler`—the request handler that responds to OBEX requests.
`auth`—the `Authenticator` to use with this connection; if `null`, then no `Authenticator` is used.

Returns

The connection to the client.

Throws

`IOException` if an error occurs in the transport layer.

`NullPointerException` if `handler` is `null`.

`ServiceRegistrationException` if the structure of the associated service record is invalid or if the service record cannot be added successfully to the local SDDB. The structure of a service record is invalid if the service record is missing any mandatory service attributes or has changed any of the values described above, which are fixed and cannot be changed. Failures to add the record to the SDDB can be caused by factors such as insufficient disk space and database locks.

`BluetoothStateException` if the server device cannot be placed in connectable mode because the device user has configured the device to be non-connectable.

References

1. Bluetooth SIG. Specification of the Bluetooth System, Core, v1.1, www.bluetooth.com, 2000.

2. J. Larmouth. *Understanding OSI*. International Thomson Publishing, www.isi.salford.ac.uk//books/osi/osi.html, 1996.

3. Bluetooth SIG. Specification of the Bluetooth System, Profiles v1.1, www.bluetooth.com, 2000.

4. Miller, B. A. and C. Bisdikian. *Bluetooth Revealed,* 2nd ed. Upper Saddle River: Prentice-Hall, 2001.

5. Bray, J., and C. F. Sturman. *Bluetooth 1.1: Connect without Cables,* 2nd ed. Upper Saddle River: Prentice-Hall, 2001.

6. Bluetooth SIG, Bluetooth Network Encapsulation Protocol (BNEP) Specification, Revision 1.0, 2003.

7. Bluetooth SIG, Hardcopy Cable Replacement Profile Interoperability Specification, Revision 1.0a, 2002.

8. Bluetooth SIG, Audio/Video Control Transport Protocol Specification, Revision 1.0, 2003.

9. Bluetooth SIG, Audio/Video Distribution Transport Protocol Specification, Revision 1.0, 2003.

10. Bluetooth SIG. Bluetooth Qualification Program Website qualweb.opengroup.org.

11. Topley, K. *J2ME in a Nutshell*. Sebastopol: O'Reilly, 2002.

12. Riggs, R., A. Taivalsaari, and M. VandenBrink. *Programming Wireless Devices with the Java™ 2 Platform, Micro Edition*. Boston: Addison-Wesley, 2001.

13. Java Community Process. J2ME Connected, Limited Device Configuration (JSR-30), www.jcp.org/jsr/detail/30.jsp, 2000 .

14. Java Community Process. J2ME Connected Device Configuration (JSR-36), www.jcp.org/jsr/detail/36.jsp, 2001.

15. Lindholm, T., and F. Yellin. *The Java™ Virtual Machine Specification, Second Edition*. Boston: Addison-Wesley, 1999.

16. Java Community Process. Mobile Information Device Profile for the J2ME Platform (JSR-37), www.jcp.org/jsr/detail/37.jsp, 2000.

17. Java Community Process. J2ME Foundation Profile (JSR-46), www.jcp.org/jsr/detail/46.jsp, 2001.

18. Java Community Process. Personal Profile Specification (JSR-62), www.jcp.org/jsr/detail/62.jsp, 2002.

19. Java Community Process. Personal Basis Profile Specification (JSR-129), www.jcp.org/jsr/detail/129.jsp, 2002.

20. Java Community Process. Java APIs for Bluetooth Wireless Technology (JSR-82), www.jcp.org/jsr/detail/82.jsp, 2002.

21. Java Community Process. Generic Connection Framework Optional Package for J2SE (JSR-197), www.jcp.org/jsr/detail/197.jsp, 2003.

22. JINI Networking Technology Home Page, www.sun.com/jini/.

23. Project JXTA Home Page, www.jxta.org.

24. Kumar, C B., and P. Kline. "Bringing the Benefits of Java to Bluetooth." *Embedded Systems, the European Magazine for Embedded Design* 6 (2002) no. 42.

25. Java Community Process., J2ME Connected, Limited Device Configuration 1.1 (JSR-139), www.jcp.org/jsr/detail/139.jsp, 2003.

26. Java Community Process. Mobile Information Device Profile 2.0 (JSR-118), jcp.org/jsr/detail/118.jsp, 2002.

27. Bluetooth SIG, Basic Printing Profile, Revision 0.95a, 2003.

28. Bluetooth SIG, Basic Imaging Profile, Revision 0.95c, 2003.

29. Infrared Data Association®, IrDA® Object Exchange Protocol–OBEX™, version 1.3, 2003.

30. Bluetooth SIG. Bluetooth Assigned Numbers, www.bluetooth.org/foundry/assignnumb/document/assigned_numbers.

31. Fowler, M., and K. Scott. *UML Distilled: A Brief Guide to the Standard Object Modeling Language*, 2nd ed. Boston: Addison-Wesley, 2000.

32. International Organization for Standardization. Code for the presentation of names of languages. ISO 639:1988 (E/F), Geneva, 1988.

33. Internet Assigned Numbers Authority. www.iana.org/assignments/character-sets.

34. The Internet Mail Consortium. vCard – The Electronic Business Card, Version 2.1, 1996. www.imc.org/pdi/vcard-21.txt.

35. The Open Group. DCE 1.1: Remote Procedure Call, Appendix A. Document Number C706, www.opengroup.org/onlinepubs/009629399/apdxa.htm, Reading, UK, 1997.

36. Bluetooth SIG, Personal Area Networking Profile, Revision 1.0, 2003.

37. Bluetooth SIG, Bluetooth Extended Service Discovery Profile (ESDP) for Universal Plug and Play™ (UPnP™). Revision 0.95a, 2003.

38. Bluetooth SIG, Audio/Video Remote Control Profile, Revision 1.0, 2003.

39. Bluetooth SIG, Generic Audio/Video Distribution Profile, Revision 1.0, 2003.

40. Bluetooth SIG, Advanced Audio Distribution Profile, Revision 1.0, 2003.

41. Bluetooth SIG, Hands-Free Profile, Revision 1.0, 2003.

42. Williams, S., and I. Millar. "The IrDA platform," in *Insights into Mobile Multimedia Communication*, ed. D. Bull, C. Canagarajah, and A. Nix. San Francisco: Morgan Kaufmann, 1998. www.irda.org/design/irda_platform.pdf, Infrared Data Association, Walnut Creek, California, 1996.

Index

About the Authors

C Bala Kumar is a Distinguished Member of the Technical Staff at Motorola. He chaired the industry expert group that defined the Java APIs for Bluetooth wireless technology. He currently leads the systems software team for wireless platforms in Motorola's Semiconductor Products Sector. He received his Master's degree in Electrical Engineering from the University of Texas at Austin.

Paul J. Kline is a Distinguished Member of the Technical Staff at Motorola and the maintenance lead for the JABWT specification. He currently works on the System Software Architecture team in Motorola's Semiconductor Products Sector. He received his Ph.D. in Mathematical Psychology from the University of Michigan.

Timothy J. Thompson is a Senior Software Engineer on the System Software Architecture team in Motorola's Semiconductor Products Sector. He was the OBEX architect on the JABWT specification team at Motorola. He received his Master's degree in Computer Science from Texas A&M University.